examination in the preparatory branches, and in all the studies previously pursued by the class they propose to enter.*

Satisfactory testimonials of good moral character and industrious habits will be rigidly exacted.

---

*NOTE. To accommodate those wishing to join the present class at the commencement of the second term, there will be an examination on Thursday, January 28th, 1869. Candidates proposing to enter at that time should confer at once with Professor Fernald, and learn definitely of the course of study pursued by the class during the fall.

This arrangement must not be understood as establishing a precedent for the future.

COURSE OF STUDY---FIRST YEAR.

FIRST TERM.

Algebra—Robinson.
History—Weber.
Physical Geography—Guyot.
Rhetoric—Day.

SECOND TERM.

Algebra—Robinson.
History—Weber (first half term.)
Botany—Gray (second half term.)
Physical Geography—Guyot.
Book-Keeping.
Rhetoric—Day.

THIRD TERM.

Geometry.
Botany (Analysis)—Gray.
Horticulture.
Natural Philosophy.
Rhetoric—Day.

Lectures will be given on Meteorology, Physical Geography, Natural Philosophy, Structural Botany and Practical Agriculture; and English Composition and Declamation will be regular exercises throughout the year.

The First Century

The White Farm, the beginnings of the college.

The campus in 1902.

The campus in the 1970's.

THE FIRST CENTURY
A History of the University of Maine
1865 - 1965

David C. Smith

University of Maine at Orono Press   Orono, Maine 1979

Designed by Arline K. Thomson

Manufactured in the United States of America

First edition

Library of Congress Catalog Card Number: 78–68702

9 8 7 6 5 4 3 2 1

ISNB 0–89101–037–8

This Book Is Dedicated
To
My Colleagues,
My Students,
And
ESPECIALLY
The Class of 1972

Contents

List of Illustrations

Preface

THIS BOOK WAS BEGUN IN 1970. A committee was appointed to investigate the desirability of a scholarly history, after abortive attempts at one in the 1950's. When the author was selected to write the work, he decided to collect data and then to provide a new interpretative study. It might have been possible to simply update Fernald's earlier work (1916), but it seemed obvious that a new and fresh interpretation was needed. Collecting data took nearly three full years, as the files and manuscripts were in a terrible state. Many had been destroyed or lost, and others were simply jumbled into cartons in the vault in Alumni Hall. Still others were in various buildings, cellars, and attics throughout the campus. The work of collection was aided greatly by Florence E. Dinsmore, Winthrop Libby, James MacCampbell, Alice Stewart, Geddes Simpson, Frances Hartgen, Clayton, Sylvia and Katherine Smith.

Edward O. Schriver has been a source of inspiration and a close friend throughout the writing of this and other books. William Baker, Jerome Nadelhaft, C. Stewart Doty, Alice Stewart, Earle Shettlesworth, Geddes Simpson, Matthew McNeary, David Trafford, Charles Virtue, Irwin Douglass, Bruce Poulton, Frank Eggert, Shirley Tardiff, Rita Breton, Arline Thomson, Arthur Johnson, Janet Stratton, Ted Holmes and the late David Tolman have all offered much help and encouragement while the research and writing went on. I am equally sure that there are others whom I have not mentioned.

A special word is necessary dealing with the illustrations and makeup of the book. Arline Thomson deserves the credit for much of that work. The illustration selections and book construction was aided by Al Pelletier, Jack Walas, Muriel Sanford, Terry Kelly, Priscilla Benoit, Hal Borns and Don Stewart. The Bangor Historical

Society was helpful as well. This book reflects the high standard of the University of Maine at Orono Press. Robert Thomson did the essential job of "diabolizing" the book at an early stage. Susan Rocha and Carole Gardner typed the manuscript in their usual inimitable style. To all these my gratitude.

Some years ago in another place I said that college and university histories are written for a variety of audiences. Among them are colleagues, who will read to determine how they would have done the book better; alumni, who are interested in discovering if "their" college is preserved in the book; and new faculty, who hope to determine the taboos and traditions of their jobs. In addition one hopes that some outsiders read the book, especially those persons in Maine who would know more about their state. My mentor, Paul Gates, once advised me not to write this book on the grounds that the work would be dreary and time-consuming, and my audience would be critical of real historical effort. Perhaps he was right, but I owed a duty to a number of people, not least to Gates, to carry on despite his advice.

This book is not another *Tales of Old Siwash*, nor does it recount the adventures of Dink Stover. Neither does it describe the life of a Maine Hobie Baker, if a similar person ever attended Orono. For those who would read such a book, one can only heartily recommend E. E. Chase '13, *Tales of Bolivars Children*, for a work about the "innocent" campus at Orono before 1914. For a slightly greater scale one can also recommend C. H. Patton and W. T. Flood, *Eight O'Clock Chapel*, which deals with campus life at New England private colleges before 1920.

Another university with which I have been associated has three excellent novels of student, academic, and library life: *Halfway Down the Stairs, Been Down So Long It Looks Like Up To*

Me, and *The Case of the Widening Stain.* No such book has yet been written about Maine, or if it has, it is so obscure as to be unknown. Even *Wings of Wax,* a novel about a Maine college president, deals almost entirely with his later life and does not mention Orono. What an opportunity is missed!!

Another thing that this book does not provide is puff journalism, nor is it a book designed to present a view of the "good old days." Perhaps such an item has a place, but it is my feeling that enough such books already exist. Instead perhaps there is room for a work which is scholarly and which treats administrative history and educational change, along with relations with the state's citizens, legislatures and others. It is a sympathetic work, but that is because it also seems to me that the purpose of the state universities was one of the grandest products of the United States Congress, topped only by the implicit promise of the G.I. Bill of Rights. Here was democracy in action, and I can only hope that this history provides some insight into that result.

I could not do my work without the aid and comfort of my wife and family, who provide me with quarters, love, and understanding. In another way, that is true of my colleagues and my students as well, and that accounts for the dedication. For errors I plead the usual guilt; for good work one can begin by thanking the names above.

Bangor, Topsfield, Orono;
September 1, 1978

The First Century

CHAPTER ONE

A Slow Start

THE HISTORY of the University of Maine at Orono is really the history of one state's efforts to provide education for its citizens; education both for life and for the pursuit of happiness. However, the University of Maine, or as it was called for the first thirty years of its life, the Maine State College, did not simply begin full-blown with the Morrill Land Grant College Act, passed by the United States Congress in 1863. A Maine state college had been proposed long before 1863, but its realization was slow and for many years its viability was in doubt. Major questions involved where the school should be located and what it should teach and to whom, all perennial questions which had a continuing impact on the growth and direction of the school. Indeed, their echoes are heard down to the present.

Maine inherited a deep interest in education from her mother commonwealth, Massachusetts. Land in each township was reserved for support of the public schools. Furthermore, Massachusetts enacted legislation giving land to various private academies, as well as to Bowdoin College. Support of education was well-founded when Maine became a state in 1820. One of the first acts of the new legislature was to endow a lyceum at Gardiner to provide agricultural education for local citizens. The school was quite successful, and the state continued to provide a subsidy for a decade. Designed for ordinary people, the school included practical work to temper the learned professions, or so said the founding president.[1]

It was not until the late 1840's that the question of state supported higher education rose again. The Massachusetts Agricultural Society called for the establishment of agricultural education in schools and colleges, and the gov-

ernor of New York followed suit. These demands led a group of Maine farmers to hold two meetings in the chamber of the House of Representatives in which they also called for the establishment of an agricultural school. One newspaper editor greeted the meetings with the comment, "What, then, is waiting except the bill," but interest flagged soon after the adjournment.[2]

When the legislature created a State Board of Agriculture in 1849, many thought it was a prelude to creating an agricultural college. An editorial of the time indicates the strength and depth of their feeling.

> Many ways have been proposed . . ., and among them the establishment of an agricultural school in connection with a stock or pattern farm. If a school would be established where the theory and practice of agriculture could be combined — where the principles of science as they were learned by the study of books and the teachings of competent instructors could be, day by day applied to the operations of the farm, it would in a very great degree elevate the character of our farmers and add to the products of our soil.[3]

Again, during the 1850's, many advocated establishment of an agricultural college. Others wanted an experimental farm, and some wanted the government to subsidize some form of agricultural teaching. All three of these ideas along with establishment of farmers' clubs, purchase of soil chemistry textbooks for farmers, or even high school courses for prospective farmers were put forth as panaceas for Maine's most prevalent problem, "How to Keep the Boys Home."[4] Among the leading figures in this movement, in addition to agricultural editors such as William Drew and Ezekiel Holmes, were Sidney Perham, later to become Speaker of the House and governor;

Anson P. Morrill, to be governor; and Darius Forbes, who edited an influential agricultural page in the Oxford *Democrat*.

Perham began the campaign with a lengthy address before the Oxford County Agricultural Society on October 6, 1853. After rehearsing the problem of out-migration, he called for a program to keep people home, ". . . where they can find a place in which they can be freer from the influence of vice and immorality . . . ." Farmers need education, he said, and they need farmers' colleges where they can perform experiments, run a stock farm, and publish the results. Perham called in this address for the introduction of agricultural studies into the common schools.[5] When he became Speaker in 1855, he could push his beliefs, and Morrill, then governor, reiterated Perham's ideas in his annual address to the legislature.[6]

The York Agricultural Society also lobbied for some sort of formal agricultural education at about this same time. In 1854, Oxford Normal Institute in South Paris began a course of lectures to its students, with night courses for local residents. Apparently the students had a small test garden for experimentation.[7] Although the State Board of Agriculture also discussed this idea and advocated establishing such a school in each county, little more was heard of it.[8]

Perham, Forbes, and others continued their campaign throughout the latter part of the decade. They hailed the gains of other states, as when Michigan founded its agricultural college, and called for Maine to follow with its own school.[9] A more successful idea at that time was the formation of farmers' clubs. Among the first of these, and certainly one of the most significant, was that founded at Bethel, probably in 1853. Other clubs, including a significant one in West Minot, were formed in the Oxford County area in response to the Bethel club and its success.[10] Judging from the reports of its activities, the West Minot group put a great deal of emphasis on education.[11] The State Board of Agriculture noticed the movement and supported it, calling for state expenditure of money for books and documents for the clubs, but all the while suggesting that the results were small compared to all that could be done with a real college for farmers, one to which all could aspire.[12]

Other states and sections had similar experiences, and discussion of the idea of federal support for agricultural colleges began in Congress. Justin Morrill, of Vermont, offered the first of a series of bills in 1857. The Oxford *Democrat* welcomed the bill, or versions of it.[13] The State Board of Agriculture endorsed it. Governor Lot Morrill recommended passage in his annual message in 1860. Over and over again, from 1858 to 1862, various interested groups met and called for passage.[14] A typical comment came from S. L. Goodale of the State Board of Agriculture, who when asked the question, "Shall We Have a Farmers' College in Maine?" produced this strong statement.

> Legislators of Maine! Farmers of Maine! . . . Do We Need a College? Most Certainly we do . . . . Nothing speeds the plow or fattens the crops like brains, and the more they are cultivated before application to the land the better.[15]

The Morrill Act, or the Land Grant College Act, provided for a number of interests then significant in the United States. It was an issue in the Republican national platform of 1860 and had been discussed since the middle 1850's by many as an effort to provide scientific agricultural education outside the older liberal arts colleges. It gave the land-poor eastern states access to the immense amounts of federal land just being surveyed. The act allowed land, or to be more precise land scrip, equal to 30,000 acres for each congressman and senator. The states were mandated by law to sell the land and use the proceeds to establish an endowment to found a college, or colleges, which would teach agriculture and the mechanic arts, as well as instruct in military drill and tactics.

Many eastern states opposed the act because it would form public colleges to compete with private colleges already being aided with government support from the states. However, agricultural interests pointed to the land bank as a source of funds and the distinctive nature of the new curriculum as positive points in favor of establishment. Maine had public lands of its own, so that was not a large issue, but the idea of retaining good Maine youngsters at home through scientific education was appealing enough to obtain Maine support for the bill when it was offered.

The proceeds from the land bank varied from state to state. Maine sold its lands at the fairly low price of under one dollar an acre on the average. An investigation of the low sale price was held later as a way to attack the college, but the results were inconsequential. Other states, especially Rhode Island, dispensed with their scrip at even lower prices. Illinois held on and made much of the funds. New York transferred the lands to Ezra Cornell, who founded Cornell University, and made perhaps the most of the possibilities for its endowment funds. Maine did about as well as could be expected with western lands so plentiful. The alternative, holding the lands for a price rise, took great foresight and nerve.[16]

There were three institutions of higher education in Maine at the time of the act's passage. The earliest of these was Bowdoin, located in Brunswick. Founded at the end of the eighteenth century to act as Maine's Harvard, it played this role fairly well to a small group of students. Bates, located in Lewiston, and Waterville College, soon to be renamed Colby College, were founded under theological auspices. All three of the schools were small, attracted few Maine scholars, and none offered any professional training in the new and rapidly growing fields of engineering, physics, and chemistry.

Farming in Maine had been in a general state of slow decline since the opening of the Erie Canal and the prairie lands of the Middle West. Increasingly, Maine farmers had become subsistence farmers. The main crops, wheat, potatoes, and apples, had all suffered from disease and bad weather from 1840 to 1860. The Aroostook valley was just being opened to new settlers, although the state had promoted a settlement program since the 1820's. Cotton and textile mills had begun to grow fairly rapidly in some Maine cities, but their height was still to come with the immigration of large numbers of Franco-Canadians to operate looms and shuttles.

Maine in the middle 1860's had just begun to think of itself as a distinct social and economic entity, no longer subservient to Massachusetts. This change occurred as the state began to lose a strong position in Congress and the federal government with the entrance of new states and the growing population in the West. A prospective college under the Morrill act must have seemed to many a place to consolidate gains, establish new lines of thought, and arrest the slow decline so clearly perceived by the state's leaders.

The state legislature moved quickly to accept the Morrill grant and set up a college. A bill, which passed the legislature on March 25, 1863, called for establishing an Industrial College of Maine that ". . . should be especially and entirely adopted to supply the educational wants of the 'industrial classes' in the several pursuits and professions of life." However, committee reports on the bill divided on whether a new college or one of the older institutions should be the recipient of the funds.[17]

The State Board of Agriculture took an active role in the discussions of the bill. Its members, especially Ezekiel Holmes, venerable editor of the *Maine Farmer,* were indefatigable in putting forward the idea of a separate college, geared to the "industrial classes." They thought the proposed college should teach military tactics, practical husbandry, general and agricultural chemistry, botany, vegetable physiology and horticulture, zoology, animal physiology, entomology, geology, mineralogy, meteorology, mathematics, surveying, and engineering, as well as "declamation, composition, and debating." To these deliberators, "it [is] equally clear that a scientific education will as effectually

Ezekiel Holmes, a central figure in Maine agriculture in the nineteenth century, strongly supported the idea of a State University.

prepare our young men for practical life, as a classical training would qualify them for literary pursuits, or professional life."[18]

Debate over the proposed school continued throughout 1863, but no action was taken. Geographical rivalries as to where the school should be placed and educational rivalries as to the type of school stymied any progress.

Doubt had been sowed even in the State Board of Agriculture by the time it met early in 1864. Several members raised the difficulty of educating the "industrial classes," bemoaned the lack of sufficient funds, and retailed obligations to the older colleges of the state. This uncertainty led to an appeal to postpone a decision and to ask Congress for a delay past the terminal date of the grant, July 1867. The doubters called for a commission to investigate possibilities. S.L. Goodale then offered an amendment calling for the establishment of the school "at the earliest possible moment." The amendment passed, but the debate indicated the hesitant way in which even the agriculturists faced the considerable expenditure of money involved.[19]

The issue gained urgency, however, with the offer of several farms to the new institution, as well as formal offers to the state from Bowdoin and Waterville College. The governor appointed

Phineas T. Barnes

a three-man commission to discuss the general questions of where and how. Early in April 1864, this group went to work. Debate was fierce. The commissioners analyzed how other states had handled the problem and visited several proposed locations. After discussing the sites, they said funds were inadequate and recommended adoption of the Bowdoin plan to establish at Brunswick a professorship in chemistry as applied to agriculture and the arts. A majority of the House Agriculture Committee accepted the commission report, but a minority called for taking the money and building an entirely new college.[20]

Lobbying began in earnest over these reports. Bowdoin put its case as strongly as possible, but the fact that Waterville, and to some extent Bates, also had claims tended to diminish the force of their arguments. On the side of the independent school were ranged most of the members of the agricultural aristocracy, especially Ezekiel Holmes, S.L. Goodale, and Phineas T. Barnes.

Holmes in particular carried this fight forward and later received credit from contemporary observers for bringing about the transformation in public opinion on the necessity of the new school. Holmes, in their words, "set his face like a flint" against all other ideas. His last weeks were given over entirely to this lobbying; he went from the debate in the statehouse to his deathbed. He coined several homely expressions about the new school that deserve to be remembered. He said, for instance, that it should be "a tub set on its own bottom" and that it should be "as inexpensive to students as possible."[21]

While the legislature debated the reports, the State Board of Agriculture met. Although we do not have the legislative debate, the board's discussion apparently mirrors that debate and discussion in the state. Motions were offered to support an independent school, with an experiment station and model farm, and special lectures for practicing farmers. The group also discussed classical and literary studies. Among the speakers was Samuel Johnson, soon to be the first farm superintendent at the new school. He said the school should have the character of home so that the students and their teachers might form a community by themselves, be near each other always, and work with each other as much as possible. The board adopted the idea of independence unanimously, although debate over Bowdoin's proposals continued even after the vote. Holmes was particularly effective here. After this debate the board accepted the burden of helping a new college, as the legislature was also accepting the duty of beginning it.[22]

The bill that passed on February 24, 1865, and was signed on February 25, was explicit in what the legislature wanted accomplished at the new college. Section fourteen of the bill, after setting out the legal provisions, calling for students to be of good moral character, and mandating that they should engage in actual work, be taught military tactics, and be charged no tuition, instructed that

> . . . it shall be the duty of the Trustees, Directors, and Teachers of the College, to impress on the minds of the students, the principles of morality and justice and a sacred regard to truth; love to their country; humanity and universal benevolence; sobriety, industry and frugality, chastity, moderation and temperance, and all other virtues which are the ornaments of human society; . . .[23]

The newly appointed trustees, sixteen in number representing the counties of the state, issued a notice to the state in the *Kennebec Journal* and met for the first time on April 25, in Augusta, at four o'clock. W.W. Virgin, Norway, was elected the first chairman and S.L. Goodale, Saco, the first clerk. A three-man committee was appointed to investigate the problem of disposing of the land scrip. At a seven o'clock meeting the same day, Hannibal Hamlin, Bangor, was elected president of the board and Phinehas T. Barnes, Portland, treasurer. After inspecting a Togus farm the next day and declaring it "not expedient," the board voted to produce an address to the people of the state "setting forth the aims and needs of the college and soliciting contributions." An executive committee was formed and charged with adopting such measures as would awaken further interest and achieve the objects of the college.[24]

The address to the people was published on May 2, 1865 at Bangor and given wide circulation through the state's newspapers, as well as fliers and broadsides. The address said that some fifty thousand young men were potential

Hannibal Hamlin

students and the more of them that could benefit, the stronger would be the state. The object of the college was to teach the laws of material nature and scientific truths to as large a body as possible. To achieve these results the trustees expected labor to be part of the curriculum. "It is by the union of scientific knowledge with physical industry, that labor becomes most productive, and the laborer gains his worthiest elevation." As the trustees remarked further on in the message,

> It is perfectly well settled, that in our high northern latitudes, no community can exist, with any comfort, unless a very large proportion of its members are actual working men. If the State of Maine is worth living in at all, — and we are more than half a million of souls, who have decided to accept this lot, — we should exalt the condition of our life, by improving all the faculties of the men, who sustain our life by their physical work, and by giving to as many of them as possible, in their early years, the best attainable instruction in those truths of nature, which are the foundation of all our practical arts, and by training them, in well directed habit, to the most perfect manual application of those truths.

The founding legislation mandated that some of the students, if not all, should be domiciled in a household situation in order to provide the restraining and purifying influences of the family. The trustees welcomed this idea and called special attention to these plans in their program. They also noted that military tactics would be a part of the life and the college would be located on a productive farm. In addition, general studies would form an integral part of student life in the new college. After promising no architectural extravagance, the board called for funds and ideas to determine the number and size of buildings; the extent of books, apparatus, and collections; the number of persons to be employed in the college; and the size of the student body.

Before reiterating the need for help, both financial and by way of ideas, and again proclaiming their modest desires, the trustees ended with another statement of the real nature of the college.[25]

The inhabitants of Maine have resolutely sustained very heavy public burdens during the past four years of war. But a good Providence is now restoring to us rest and peace. It will be a noble memorial of this eventful year, if we now devote a generous and grateful endowment to the better education of our working young men. It is they who have won our victories, it is they who are to constitute the life of this state. They have defended our national integrity in perilous war, — let us open to them the highest blessings of peace.

At the end of May, the trustees met in Bangor and Orrington where they looked at an offered farm. No quorum appeared, so a committee simply visited the location. Another committee visited farms in the Topsham area on June 12. In late June, trustees met again and visited another farm in Fairfield. At this meeting they decided to make their decision on location on August 15 and to advertise their intentions in the newspapers of the state. The August meeting, held in the Exhibition Hall of the Sagadahoc County Agricultural Society in Topsham, adjourned without decision to September 13 in Augusta, after the trustees debated the subject and returned to view another Topsham farm. The raising of local funds was apparently the necessary method of getting a favorable decision on the site. The September meeting included discussion of subscription drives for the college underway in Topsham and Bangor, "as well as distinctive features" of the school. The next day, the board rejected the Orrington offer, as only half the $50,000 needed had been raised. Topsham was next considered, and that proposal lost by 5 to 6, although apparently it was held open if enough money were raised in the town.

A committee was appointed to look at other sites, another committee to report on plans and estimates for buildings, and still another to discuss the plan of the school and the courses of study. In late November, a meeting was held in Bangor, again without a quorum; however, a most important meeting began January 23, 1866, in Augusta. Discussion at this meeting centered on two adjacent Orono farms, the White and Goddard farms. Orono, Bangor, and Old Town had raised sufficient funds, or were able to. The final vote in favor of the Orono location was 8 to 7 with Hamlin (Penobscot), Hill (Hancock), Cummings (Aroostook), Moore (Somerset), Farwell (Knox), Day (Lincoln), Woodman (Waldo), and Everett (Piscataquis) in the affirmative. Perley (Cumberland), Dillingham (Kennebec), Goodale (York), Martin (Androscoggin), Perkins (Sagadahoc), Dill (Franklin), and Virgin (Oxford) voted in the negative. Acceptance depended on obtaining a deed and $14,000 within sixty days.[26] Central aspects in the choice of location were the ability of the local community to support the new institution and the nearness of the site to the geographical center of the state. The geographic split in the vote is significant, however.

When the board met at seven o'clock that evening, a motion for unanimity failed. The geographic and regional rivalries were simply too great to break down immediately. A resolution was accepted, however, that "the board of trustees assent to said decision and pledge their faithful endeavour for its advancement and prosperity." Several members who were serving as trustees only until the choice of site was made resigned, including Hannibal Hamlin, who was replaced by Phinehas T. Barnes as the new board chairman. At the next morning's meeting, Goodale, Barnes, and Dillingham were detailed to provide a code of bylaws; Barnes, Perkins, and Dillingham were appointed a new executive committee. It was resolved that the distinctive

The top house, apparently constructed in 1863, is the Frost House, originally a part of the Goddard Farm. It has served as a fraternity house, the University infirmary, and was the original residence of Professor Fernald. It was moved in 1904 to its present location, and as North Hall is now the headquarters of the Alumni Association. The other building, the White Farm, was built in 1833. Farm superintendent Johnson lived here. The building was remodelled as a dormitory for women, and renamed Mount Vernon. The building was destroyed by fire in 1933.

features as set out in the organic act "as compared with the other educational institutions among us" were eminently wise and judicious. A second resolution affirmed that the views and sentiments of the circulated address, mentioned above, especially with regard to plans, buildings, and the general conduct of the college, met with the warm and hearty approval of the board. Both resolutions were unanimous, and with this strong nod to their own work and a turn of the back to those who still wanted Bowdoin, or another site, the board adjourned after a difficult four-day meeting.[27]

Phinehas T. Barnes now became a strong force on the new board. He was born in 1811, graduated from Bowdoin in 1829, and had served as professor of Latin and Greek at Waterville College from 1836-1839. His interests were law, botany, and railroads, and he was, in 1866, editor of the Portland *Advertiser*. While the long discussion about the college was going on, he wrote an important series of articles for the *Maine Farmer* which apparently had a good deal to do with the final decisions. These articles dealt with the German and British agricultural schools, liberal arts schools in the

United States, and the recently founded American scientific schools such as Massachusetts Institute of Technology and Rensselaer Polytechnical Institute. Barnes came to the conclusion that these were all for the wealthy and not what Maine needed. He urged a pragmatic approach in this college, with the main strength to be agriculture, but with mechanical arts and the study of the sea also involved. English grammar and literature and a good library were important. He thought that some other word than college might even be used, since some might want to emulate the older colleges. Endorsing student labor, he felt that students ought to be able to earn their way, rather than having ball teams and boat clubs with their contests and races which fulfilled the need for work without gain. Barnes urged a different length semester from Bowdoin so that students could teach in the public schools during the long vacation from November to May when farmers' work was less arduous. The other six months should be spent in collegiate studies.[28] These articles were duly reprinted and circulated by Goodale in his *Report* of the State Board of Agriculture.

Barnes began to clamor for a new board of trustees, one not organized on county or regional lines. He felt that regionalism was forced on the board by enemies of the college and he continued to oppose regional membership at board and private meetings. When elected president of the board, he protested that his election made it appear that he acquiesced in the county arrangement. (He may even have been absent at the time of the vote.) In hopes that a better arrangement could be found, Barnes resigned from the board.[29]

The board continued to function, but with small numbers of members present and further resignations. In late March they did decide to "erect a good brick building, as soon as practic-

A page from the first catalogue describing the faculty.

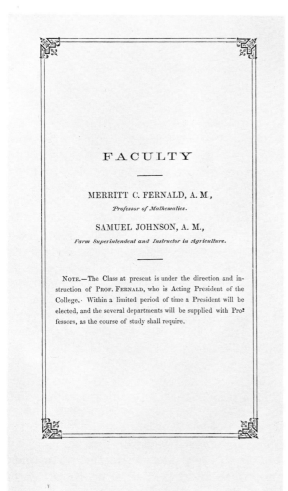

FACULTY

MERRITT C. FERNALD, A. M.,
Professor of Mathematics.

SAMUEL JOHNSON, A. M.,
Farm Superintendent and Instructor in Agriculture.

NOTE.—The Class at present is under the direction and instruction of PROF. FERNALD, who is Acting President of the College. Within a limited period of time a President will be elected, and the several departments will be supplied with Professors, as the course of study shall require.

able" and voted to ask the federal government to help them with the troublesome problem of military tactics. Little else happened, however, and finally a special meeting was called for September 26, 1866, to elect a new board president. When the meeting began only six members had appeared, but telegrams soon brought three more to make a quorum. The group voted to expend $1,000 of the funds raised in Bangor to buy necessary implements for the farm. Then, after several tries, they elected a chairman. The members immediately voted to ask the legislature to reduce the number of trustees and to appoint them without regard to locality, but rather with an eye to their ability and their nearness to the college.[30]

The new governor, Joshua Chamberlain, also was interested in establishing a college that neither mimicked the older schools nor reflected regional prejudices. In his annual address to the legislature in 1866 he had been explicit enough about his desires.

> Such an institution . . . becoming a means of incalculable benefit to the internal prosperity of the state and the glory of her name. Profiting by the experiences of the past but unfettered by its traditions, cramped by no servile imitation of foreign institutions shaped by dissimilar demands, comprehending the best results of the latest scholarship, in full harmony with the living interests of the times, such an institution would afford an education far more valuable than could be obtained by running through the 'curriculum' of our colleges. It would be the chief means of increasing intelligence and enterprise within our borders . . . . We need something in this State which will educate our young men not out of their proper sphere, but into it . . . .[31]

With Barnes' resignation, the governor's call to action, and the failure of the board to organize itself effectively, it was obvious that something had to be done. The remaining members met in late January 1867, and again debated the proper number of trustees. After deciding on a number neither fewer than five, nor more than seven they offered to retire as members and sent a letter to the House Agriculture Committee with their recommendations. A bill proclaiming a new board of seven members became law on February 25, 1867. Resignations came in rapidly over the next month. With the new board, the Maine State College could proceed to hire its

White Hall. The first dormitory and classroom. Fernald and Allen had their offices on the second floor. Destroyed in 1890 by fire, Wingate Hall was built on the site.

College laboratory. Long used as a classroom, it also served as the college bookstore. Now named Fernald Hall, it is still a campus center with a restaurant and several offices.

officers, select its faculty, gather its students, and go about its business of educating the populace of the state.[32] Nearly four years of debate had elapsed with no academic activity, because the questions of locality and curriculum had overwhelmed good intentions.

The new board of trustees faced difficult problems. Many people in the state remained in opposition to the college, objecting both to its plans and its location. The board found itself with two farms, located eight miles north of Bangor outside a small, rough sawmill and manufacturing village, with no transport nearer than the Stillwater terminus of the Veazie railroad. There was opposition in the town. No faculty had yet been secured, no students entered, no curriculum set out — in short, everything was to be done and in an atmosphere that was clouded, if not as Maine people say, "lowery."

The board was a strong one, however. Abner Coburn of Skowhegan, one of the more prominent lumbermen in the state and one of the state's wealthiest men, received a five-year term and at the first meeting was elected chairman (later president) of the board. The other members were also individuals of

strength. S.L. Dike, Bath, was a noted agriculturalist. Lyndon Oak, Garland, a farmer and historian, was to be one of the strongest members in the next twenty-five years. Isaiah Stetson, a lumberman and commission merchant from Bangor, was elected treasurer. William P. Wingate, also of Bangor, had raised the initial $14,000 in the Penobscot area. George P. Sewall of the famous Old Town family and Nathaniel Wilson of Orono completed the board and insured close municipal cooperation, if not aid. Stetson resigned as trustee after his election as treasurer and was replaced by J.F. Perley, another farmer with great interest in the institution's success.

The new board asked J.F. Gilman of Foxcroft to continue to manage the farm and again Barnes was asked to take on the presidency of the new college. Barnes refused, but Gilman agreed to fill out the year. The first board had engaged Frederick Law Olmstead, the famous New York architect, to lay out the college grounds and indicate a plan, and the new board authorized the manufacture of bricks for building.[33]

Soon the board received plans for two new buildings: a chemical laboratory and a student

This old locomotive, The Lion, was exhibited for many years after its retirement in the Crosby Laboratoory. A duplicate sister served the Veazie Railroad and carried M.C. Fernald to Orono to take up his duties.

M.C. Fernald. First faculty member and second president. He set the tone of the University and was a central figure during the first half century.

dormitory. The board asked the legislature for $20,000 to aid in the construction, half of which was provided. The dormitory was White Hall, which served until a fire in the 1890's. The chemical laboratory, then Chemical Hall, is now known as Fernald Hall. In addition, the trustees, in the first real year of operation, built a new ell, a carriage house, and dug a cellar for the Frost house. This building was newly shingled and fitted with blinds, chimney, and new furnace. The Frost house, renamed North Hall, was later moved to its present location where it has served many students first as the infirmary and more recently as a center for alumni activites. The other farmhouse on the campus, the White homestead, was given a new cistern and furnace. It, too, served the campus for a long time, eventually being completely remodeled and renamed Mount Vernon near the turn of the century. It served as a women's dormitory for a time, later as a residence for bachelor faculty, and was finally destroyed by fire in June 1933.[34]

Most of the bricks for Chemical Hall were manufactured on the college grounds, 264,000 the first year. In addition tiles and pipe were manufactured for draining the college fields, a project begun in 1869.[35]

The board also began to gather the college faculty. First to be hired was Merritt C. Fernald, who was paid $1,200 a year to come from his post at Foxcroft Academy to be professor of mathematics. Samuel Johnson was hired as farm superintendent at $900. He was to provide his own furniture; his wife was to be "matron" and to run the dairy. Fernald and Johnson began their duties July 15, 1868. Together they started to arrange the course of instruction at the college, the requirements for admission, the hours of labor, "the regulations for the governance of students," and "make all necessary arrangements for the opening and successful working of the institution."[36]

Fernald and Johnson were appointed a committee to purchase necessary college apparatus, and Fernald was directed to make and record meteorological observations. Johnson purchased the necessary beds, mattresses, tables, chairs, and sinks for the dormitory rooms for the new students. Finally, the trustees sent a notice of the opening to Bangor, Portland, Lewiston, and Boston papers as well as the *Maine Farmer*. The notice was also circulated as a broadside.[37]

When Fernald and Johnson and their families arrived they found a farm with quite good soil already in a productive state thanks to the work of Gilman, the first superintendent. The Fernalds moved into the Frost house, while Johnson and his family lived in the White homestead.

The students arrived to take entrance examinations on September 17, 1868. They were tested in geography, arithmetic, English grammar, and algebra as far as quadratic equations. Satisfactory testimonials of good moral character and industrious habits were also required. Half a dozen appeared for examination; four were accepted. They settled in to classes Monday, September 21. Later the class grew to a dozen who attended at least part of the first four years. Six of them graduated, and at the fiftieth anniversary celebration, five of these were able to attend.[38]

The farm itself was in operation before the opening of the school which meant that the college looked, if not prosperous, at least not bleak to these early pioneers. In 1867, for instance, the fields produced 100 tons of hay, 10 tons of straw, 8 bushels of beans, 350 bushels of barley (14 acres), and 600 bushels of potatoes (6 acres). In addition, 50 apple trees produced 20 bushels, and there were 5,000 trees in the nursery. Workmen had set out 500 maple, elm, and evergreens, although the evergreens were not very successful. A nursery of pear trees had produced 400 transplants, of which 300 had survived. The farm stock included 3 horses, 7 cows (2 newly purchased), 2 three-year-old steers, 2 two-year-old steers, 3 yearlings, 2 heifers, 22 sheep, 14 lambs, and 1 Southdown buck. The sheep had been sheared of 90 pounds of washed wool; the farm produced 22 lambs, which were sold. The farm also had a Durham bull given by Coburn and 2 Durham heifers with calf (one of the heifers died in October after breaking her leg in her stall). Two Suffolk pigs and 2 part Chesters completed the livestock. The farm produced 1,500 pounds of pork that year.[39]

The next year the farm was run by Johnson. He got less hay (90 tons), but more potatoes (1,100 bushels). The farm raised less barley (85 bushels), but added 3 acres of buckwheat, which was plowed under. The apple and pear nurseries thrived that year, as did the livestock which increased to 26 cattle (including 4 calves), 5 horses (one was used only for the carriage), 5 pigs, and 40 sheep and lambs. The students dug 700 bushels of the potatoes and thus reduced their board from $3 to $2 per week. One interesting facet is that these two early superintendents had already begun to experiment with different fertilizers to determine results for interested observers.[40] Research began at the university before there was an operating college.

Instruction in the early days of the school was fairly rudimentary. Johnson and Fernald were earnest, however, and at the first break in November, they went for a visit to Amherst to look at the new Massachusetts College of Agriculture. President Clark of Massachusetts agreed to help them find an instructor in botany and horticulture. The visitors received encouragement from Professor Agassiz, who urged them to provide a plant house and botanical garden for experimental purposes. Later Fernald went alone to examine both Cornell and Michigan Agricultural Colleges. These early visits were of considerable importance in setting the early tone of the school. The first colleges under the Morrill Act tended to keep close tabs on each other and adopted successful ideas and experiments from sister institutions.

It was also these early visits that emboldened the trustees to ask for the first substantial funds for the new school.[41] As Fernald said when reporting on the early work of the students and on his and Johnson's efforts, "What is asked by the Trustees is really a *moderate sum* when we consider the *actual needs* of the college now just commencing its career, providing its various departments are to be in any manner respectably supplied." Fernald realized that there would be opposition, but, as he said, other schools, especially Michigan, had moved their legislatures from opposition to support.[42]

While the students began their work, the farm produced, and the two professors attempted to organize and plan, the board of trustees continued its routine business. For instance, in these early days, it accepted gifts (of silverware, plans for a privy, and books), invested its funds, paid out for work on building construction, printed the first catalogs (and sent copies to the legislature), and obtained guns for

Charles F. Allen, first president.

An early view of the campus from across the Stillwater River. Buildings include Brick Hall (later Oak), White Hall, and Chemical Hall. The boat in the foreground was used by lumbermen and river drivers and was called a bateau.

drill purposes from the keeper of the Bangor arsenal. "The boys inquire daily with much anxiety in regard to the appropriations," was reported to the board, and one suspects the board itself also inquired. The Bangor Commercial College supplied an instructor of bookkeeping. The board supported Fernald in his opposition to the hazing which began as soon as the second class arrived in August 1869.

More items were purchased as they were needed. Invariably the board let Professor Fernald buy "such as he thought was necessary." Professor S.F. Peckham, a new faculty person, appeared on campus to superintend the equipping of the laboratory, and bills were authorized to pay for lecture tables, pneumatic troughs, stoves, "and such other fixtures as the engineers of the Institution immediately demand." The library began to subscribe to scientific periodicials. The board made Fernald acting president, raised his salary to $1,800, and hired his wife to teach modern languages.

In 1870 the board attended hearings in the legislature and testified for the college requests. When the money was appropriated they authorized completion of the laboratory, using

student labor to dig cellars and drains as well as to make bricks. More college lands were graded and underdrained, and the trustees debated what sort of dormitory rooms they should provide.

More bills were contracted: seaweed collections, $75; tools, $350, and a shed to cover them; philosophical apparatus (as scientific equipment was then called), $250; and chemicals for the new laboratory, $150. During the winter of 1871, the college let one or two of its teams to local loggers. By that spring a boarding house, intended to be self-sufficient, was in operation. The college seal was adopted. The Library grew. The faculty also began to increase in size as more and more students entered each fall, and even many during the year as funds became available for them. (The college allowed people to enter almost at will in these earliest years, if they passed the appropriate examinations.)

Early in 1871 the presidency was offered to Governor Chamberlain, who refused it. A new superintendent, Joseph Farrington, replaced Johnson. The trustees nominated a farm committee, one of the more important board committees for the next thirty or so years, to arrange for his duties and advise him on management. In May of 1871, Fernald was authorized to hire a teacher of civil and mechanical engineering. As the young college ended its third year, the faculty included professors of chemistry, civil engineering, natural history (Charles H. Fernald), as well as M.C. Fernald. The first president had been hired, Charles F. Allen. The board now agreed to borrow $10,000 to complete the buildings then under construction, and when the new president appeared at the college he found a school well under way, with buildings, faculty, a course of instruction, a flock of students, and a working farm. Much remained to be done, however, by way of education of the tax-paying population and this would be Allen's job, whether he realized it or not.[43]

Allen was not a person unknown to the board when he was approached about the presidency. He had served on the examining committee for students since the end of 1869. Since his graduation from Bowdoin in 1839, he had been both a successful teacher and preacher. At the time of his inauguration he was a fifty-five-

year-old Methodist clergyman. His inauguration was the first major public ceremonial function of the institution and was, as a result, well covered by the newspapers of the state. Portland papers, for instance, sent special correspondents.

The Congregational Church in Orono was the inaugural site. After music and a short prayer, former governor Coburn delivered an address recapitulating the history of the college. Allen's inaugural address touched on most of the themes he would pursue over the next few years. He discussed the need for intelligent labor to make the country great. He stressed democratic education and called the older classical colleges to account for their failure to provide it.

> Here is an institution entirely new, with no distinction between classical and scientific courses, where manual labor and study are combined, devoid of the inducements to extravagance found elsewhere, needing no gymnasiums and boat-clubs, but utilizing the muscular training of its students, and tied down to no compliance with antique formulas.

He closed his remarks with comments on the necessity to attend to the morals and manners as well as the mind. After further prayers and music, the new president offered a benediction. The board of trustees and others then repaired to inspect the grounds and buildings of Allen's new charge.[44]

Allen apparently viewed his job as essentially one of continuation of Fernald's work on the campus, constructing and equipping the necessary buildings, but he had a strong feeling that away from the campus he should create the highest opinion of the college in the minds of the citizens. He pursued this policy with intensity before both the legislature and the college's natural ally, the State Board of Agriculture, as well as with the state's farmers.

The decade of the 70's was taken up basically with these duties. The college grew steadily, if slowly. In 1871 the students made 500,000 more bricks, of which 114,000 were sold. Ten more acres were tiled and drained. The farm by this time supplied all the college's milk, butter, cheese, eggs (with a surplus for sale), beef, pork, and vegetables. Raspberries, blackberries, strawberries, asparagus, and grapes were grown. The farm fields produced in addition to the crops of before, some wheat, peas, corn, and a fairly large amount of rutabagas (300 bushels), English turnips (30 bushels), and mangelwurzels (75 bushels).[45]

The buildings and grounds improved also. In 1874 a magnificent, and controversial, new barn was erected. Storm windows and shutters were purchased for the buildings at about this time as the trustees agreed that "the discomfort of conducting recitations in the chapel and mathematics lecture room in cold weather would be largely obviated. . . ." A forge shop was built and in 1882, when a new one was constructed for mechanical engineering, the old shop became the first gymnasium. The grounds of the college were all graded, seeded to clover, and new paths laid out in 1876. By 1881, nine wooden and two brick buildings adorned the campus.[46]

The members of the legislature's agricultural committee now customarily came to the campus to view the results of their appropriations. In 1872 the committee members were very pleasantly surprised and described the institution in detail for their colleagues. However, they realized that the college would cost money

and ended their report with an interesting discussion.

> After a candid consideration of the subject your Committee have come to the conclusion that the State should either abandon the enterprise altogether, as unprofitable; or they should treat it as worth their countenance and patronage and give it such pecuniary support as will enable it to thrive, and finally attain a flourishing condition . . . .It may be doubtful if it will not always be a source of contention and complaint . . . . Is it not now too late to wake the affections? Does not the good faith and dignity of the State demand the fulfillment of the contract? Is not the child already adopted and a large amount of money advanced for its support? Can we honorably abandon it?[47]

This committee said that two new buildings were needed, one a president's home, since he was then living in Bangor. The funds were provided, some to reimburse those advanced by members of the board. In 1873 the legislature allowed another $24,000 to be used for new buildings, tools, grading and other improvements, and for the college debt, but with the provision that no further debts be contracted.[48]

The next three years were difficult as the legislature became increasingly recalcitrant. In 1874, when the legislative committee appeared, Allen sent teams to the depot to insure that the members received good treatment. They attended regularly held classes in the morning and inspected the buildings, student rooms, and new barn after lunch. Finally, after a two o'clock chapel service, committee members retired to the president's house for a "small collation," before leaving for the depot.[49]

When the Agricultural Committee held its hearing, Allen did most of the testifying, since only one trustee was there. The committee recommended $12,500, which the legislature approved, but only after a long debate. Allen thought the hearing fair but difficult, when he reported to Lyndon Oak, "I did what I could to influence the leading men to deal liberally with us, but the present legislature are disposed to scan very narrowly all appropriations for any beneficial object." As he went on in discussing the visit to the campus by the committee, "Our visitors at the College expressed themselves in favor of a practical education but intimated very strongly that it must be done without much cost." The House was the more difficult body,

COMMENCEMENT

CONCERT!

MAINE STATE COLLEGE, ORONO,

CLASS OF 1872.

The Mendelssohn Quintette Club,

Assisted by the distinguished Vocalist,

MRS. J. W. WESTON,

Will give a CONCERT at the METHODIST CHURCH, Orono, on

Wednesday Eve'g, Aug. 7th.

Tickets, 75 Cents,

To be had at the Stores of D. Bugbee & Co., Bangor, S. Libby, Orono, and E. A. Pond, Oldtown.

Doors open at 7.30 ; - - - Concert to commence at 8 o'clock.

A Special Train will be run from Bangor, leaving the Depot at the foot of Exchange Street at 7 P. M.; returning after the Concert.

Announcement of College event in 1872.

"for there are quite a number that would kill us and be glad to administer the estate. Some are vexed that their schemes are frustrated and in revenge strike at anything that is brought forward."[50] Of course the depression and long slump of the 70's were simply making their impact on the young college.

The new governor, Nelson Dingley, was apparently friendly though not very aggressive. When the legislature met in 1875, he praised the school but indicated that he thought the funds ought to come primarily from private donations. The House apparently agreed with him and cut the funds from the requested $27,000 to $10,000. Allen was discouraged as he did not know where to trim and feared that both students and faculty might go elsewhere. He was determined to succeed but felt it hard to "practice the lessons of economy forced upon us by the 'powers that be.'"[51]

The next two legislative sessions, in 1876 and 1877, were very important to the young college in Orono. Substantial attempts were made in both legislatures to cut back the appropriations to nothing, to set the school adrift, and free the state from further responsibility.

In 1876 the trustees entertained the committee, on a strikingly cold day, and sent them away with answers to questions then circulating the state as to the cost of the new barn. Apparently satisfied with the progress, the committee accepted the trustee recommendations for $23,500 and asked the legislature for the entire amount, needed to erect another house, a building for a chapel and meeting place, as well as lecture rooms. In addition, the trustees needed $3,500 to pay outstanding bills. The governor supported the claims of the college, but not with such strength as to give any special joy.[52]

A major attack on the bill was levied in the Senate, and the amount of the appropriation cut back to $8,000. An attempt in the House to further cut back the amount ot $5,000 brought forth a long and impassioned address on the part of John Wyman Phillips of Orrington. Phillips rang the changes on the college's hopes and ideas and the fact that the legislature had been niggardly in helping the trustees do their work. After calling attention to the number of graduates already successful, he was able to hold the cut to $8,000. The next year another at-

Benjamin F. Gould

George E. Hammond

Edwin J. Haskell

Heddle Hilliard

George O. Weston

Eber D. Thomas

Members of the first graduating class, 1872. Four were in civil engineering, one in agriculture (Weston) and one in the elective course (Haskell).

tempt was made in the Senate to cut back the $15,218 appropriation to $8,000; it was barely defeated by a vote of 13 to 10. The final appropriation passed by 17 to 7, but both these votes were indications of how strong opposition was to the school. To a great extent it came from the western half of the state. Prominent in these attacks were Bowdoin graduates still feeling the slight that college had received in 1864-65.[53]

Difficulties continued with the legislature in 1878 when a resolution passed indicating that the governor and council might, if they chose, accept "proposals from denominations, associations, or organizations, to take the State College" and sustain it. Apparently no one came forward to relieve the legislature of its burden. The next year the legislature mandated the payment of tuition in an effort to defray the increasingly rising costs to the taxpayers. The tuition funds cut down the requests of the trustees, and in 1880 the governor commended the institution to the legislature as meriting "favorable consideration," especially as it now demanded "but little for its support."[54]

The college attempted to meet the demands of the legislature. In 1876 the trustees moved that "there shall be no abridgment in the amount of instruction afforded students in any of the Departments of the College." In 1878 the faculty held a special meeting to consider the condition of the college. A considerable discussion of the courses of study and of the future took place, at the end of which the secretary noted the general feeling that they "should do well to confine [themselves] more closely to agriculture and the mechanic arts." After the trustees also held a general discussion the next month, they sent a committee to confer with the faculty on salaries. The faculty was allowed to sell surplus dormitory furniture, and "on account of the present financial condition of the college it was expedient to terminate the engagement with Professor Francis L. Hills. . . ." Hills agreed to stay until December 1 to help out. Salaries were lowered somewhat for those who remained, although even those funds were finally raised by borrowing against bonds of the city of Bangor. After this series of events, President Allen resigned. An earlier attempt at resignation had failed as the board had prevailed upon him to remain, but he now wished to return to preaching, "without loss of interest in the welfare of the noble enterprise of giving the best education to those who are to engage in productive industry. . . ."[55]

The activities of the 1879 legislature marked the turning point in the early affairs of the school. With the imposition of tuition fees the requests of the college were lessened, and the trustees implicitly agreed by accepting tuition not to be so importunate, at least for some time.

Faculty and trustees feared the legislature and were relieved when the college was not dismantled. The farm superintendent was somewhat buoyed by the visit of the committee, and ex-governor Coburn felt that they had a good hearing in Augusta. Apparently the final result on the levying of tuition came after an excellent speech by J.P. Madigan of the board. The trustees agreed to print 2,000 copies of the speech for distribution to the state. They also began to canvass for a new president at this Augusta meeting. A letter of Coburn's reporting on their deliberations deserves quotation in detail.

> In relation to the Presidency I am sorry you [Lyndon Oak] were not there. I think if you had been we should have elected Prof. Fernald on the spot. Madigan and I advocated it and Dike and Boardman were for shoving it off . . . . Wingate and Hinks talked both ways so that neither of us dared to test it by vote.
>
> The Harrison man [illegible] wasn't there. Do you know what his notions are? It may be well to sound him before our next meeting. So we shoved everything off till our next meeting at the call of the clerk, say about the middle of Feb'y. I shall resign to take effect soon after that meeting.[56]

In March, the board, by unanimous vote, tendered the presidency to M.C. Fernald, who accepted. Fernald, who had worked hard before the last legislature, was none too sanguine of support from that quarter, and, after saying to Lyndon Oak that another faculty person was needed, proposed establishment of an endowment fund. He said Coburn might give $200,000 and brought up the possibility of changing the name of the school to Coburn College to "put it on an essentially independent basis." With tuition charges, a new president, and some prospects from Coburn, the crisis was passed.

One of the main reasons for the passing of the crisis was the considerable educational effort undertaken by Allen and others, but especially Allen, before every audience they could find in the state and particularly before the college's natural constituency at that time: farmers and the State Board of Agriculture. Once, when dealing with the needs of the college, Allen told a trustee who had apparently queried him on the profitability of the farm and the utility of student labor that profit and utility were not the only reason for existence. He went on to describe his work:

In public addresses, articles in the papers, and private interviews, I have placed the institution before the people; but now when the Legislature has such a fit of 'economy on the brain', members admitting the value and character of the institution will haggle about the details of expenditure.[57]

Allen unselfishly promoted the interests of the college, an early activity which probably saved the school during the later attacks of the decade.

The college began its efforts at education of the State Board of Agriculture in 1868 when S.F. Dike, of the board, addressed his fellows on "The Relationship of the Industrial College to the Common Schools." The agricultural board felt that they should have been appointed as the trustees, and finally, in response to this criticism, the legislature put a faculty member on the State Board of Agriculture in 1869 and ordered one meeting a year held near the Maine State College.[58]

The first such meeting was held on the campus on October 19, 1869. Class recitations were heard; the board examined the buildings, the farm, and the stock. Both the agricultural board and the trustees addressed the students and faculty. Professor G.E. Hamlin, then a professor at Colby, was very complimentary. As usual most of the discussion involved the merits of student labor. When the board continued with their regular meeting in Bangor the next day, the work of the college was the main topic as farm experimentation was discussed and several students gave demonstrations of their prowess in physical geography. The evening meeting included a general discussion of the philosophical role of the college and its students in the improvement of life. Among the speakers was Theophilus Copen Abbott, a Maine native who was president of the Michigan Agricultural College. His views supporting Maine State College and its labor system were given great credence. More students appeared on the last day, showing their knowledge in the area of "natural philosophy as applied to agriculture," and the board ended its meetings with a half day on potato culture.[59]

In 1871 Allen and other faculty attended many meetings. Among them was one of the Penobscot County Agricultural Society, where Allen described the interests of the college and the farmer as being indentical. Most of the student body and faculty attended the society's fall session in Lincoln. Allen chaired one meeting where he descanted again on the virtues of the school. The State Society's 1872 annual meeting was held in Paris. The first speaker was Governor Perham who discussed "How to Keep the Boys Home" and mentioned the work of the college in this regard. The indefatigable Allen then followed with a major address on the "Aims and Methods of the Maine State College . . . ." insisting that farming took brains. He again used his illustration of farmers' colleges not needing gymnasia and boat clubs to make a better person. "True, there may be a lack of fashionable foppery and elegance, but young men trained up under the combined influence of physical and intellectual culture are manly in their deportment." Fernald was also present and remarked in response to a question about student behavior, "Their primary object in going there is to obtain an education. Nothing should be permitted to interfere with that."[60]

In Skowhegan later that year, the junior class gave a demonstration of their work in agriculture. Allen spoke again at the fall meeting

The president's house when first built. Fire, rebuilding and remodelling make it somewhat different and more ornate today. Coburn Hall can be seen to the left and Holmes Hall to the right of the residence.

of the State Society, in 1873, in Houlton, this time on the effort of the college to eliminate outmigration. Once more the junior class appeared for a demonstration. Later in the convention both Fernald and Allen gave prepared addresses.[61]

The campus entertained the convention of 1874. The traditional attendance at recitations and visits to the buildings were arranged. Professors Aubert in chemistry, Fernald in mathematics, Pike in engineering (tensile strength), and C.H. Fernald in comparative anatomy and elementary agriculture (uses of manure) offered lessons. After dining with the students, the men watched the cadets at drill. That evening the farm superintendent reported on experiments in wheat drilling and swine feeding. Allen discussed the newly formed scientific society.[62] Several of the speakers asked for patience in expecting results.

Allen and Fernald continued their work with the State Society in 1875. Allen spoke at the spring meeting on "Agricultural Education," giving his now familiar remarks as to the benefits of his work, and at the fall meeting where he discussed "Practical Education." In this speech he elaborated somewhat on his previous remarks.

> The industrial college is to be no mere professional school to fit students exclusively for any one department of business, where the art of farming alone, or any other art, engrosses the entire thought. But it is to be a college with ample facilities to lay the deep foundation of liberal culture, especially adapted to the utilities of life . . . To teach to do, as well as teach to know, will engage the efforts of the instructor. Education in the field and in the laboratory are necessary to fit one for success in life.[63]

Fernald discussed similar themes and urged support of the college "to hasten the time which shall be recognized as the golden age of American civilization."[64]

In the centennial year students traveled to Fryeburg to display their uniforms, drilling ability, and classroom skills. Much of the emphasis was on engineering, which disturbed farmers, who did not want to hear too many essays on "The Value of Chemistry to Farmers," "The Use of Mechanics to Farmers," and "Bookkeeping." Other topics, entomology and market gardening, were better received.[65]

At its annual meeting at Newport in 1877, the State Board of Agriculture formed a committee to investigate what was needed to enlarge, increase, and promote the agricultural department of the state. The committee members said they wanted to hear students on "purely agricultural pursuits" only. Both the Fernalds spoke, but so did a professor Carmichael from Bowdoin who, in the process of discussing "What Science May do for Farming," took a few gratuitous swings at the Maine State College for not producing enough farmers. After listening to reports on student experimentation on fertilizers, sugar beets, and sweet corn, Allen again took the stage to talk on "The Education of Farmers and Mechanics." He defended the work in technology as well as that in agriculture and called for an experiment station to do what Carmichael proposed.[66]

The issue was fairly joined again. Those who had wanted the school at the beginning had been mostly farmers, who viewed it as a possible way to keep Maine's young people at home and to promote agricultural interests. The founders, however, although perfectly willing to follow these laudable aims, recognized reality and began with a much more realistic view of their college. The school was to broaden and deepen its offerings almost from the first day of operation, but nearly always with the opposition of those who feared these new changes.

Notes

1. Clarence Day, *A History of Maine Agriculture*, Orono, 1963, deals with the school. The speech is used by B. Walker McKeen, speech at the Chicago Worlds Fair in 1893, *Agriculture of Maine*, 1894, 67-8. *Christian Intelligencer*, (Gardiner) March 25, April 15, September 16, 1831.

2. Norway *Advertiser*, May 4, 1849. On meetings in H.R., see *Advertiser*, June 22, and the *Maine Farmer* in June, 1849.

3. Norway *Advertiser*, August 17, 1849.

4. *Farmer and Artizan*, (Portland) September, 1852, article "Legislative Aid to Agriculture." See my "Maine Resources and the State — Toward a Theory of Maine History," in Arthur Johnson, ed., *Sesquicentennial Papers: Miscellaneous*, Orono, 1971, 45-64 for a statement of the proposition that "keeping the boys home" has been a central theme of Maine history.

5. Oxford *Democrat*, November 4, 1853 prints the speech.

6. Oxford *Democrat*, January 12, 1855 for a comment on Morrill's speech. See his *Annual Message*, 1855.

7. *Transactions* of the Agriculture Societies of the State of Maine for 1850, 1851, and 1852. Augusta, 1853, Part I, 97-114, "Agricultural Education". Oxford *Democrat*, February 3, March 3, 17, April 14, 28, 1854 on the Oxford Normal experiment. February 24, 1854, letter from S.P., on State Board of Agriculture. The best description of knowledge at this period is Henry S. Olcott, *Outlines of the First Course of Yale Agricultural Lectures*, C.M. Saxton and Barker, New York, 1860. For another useful description see Solon Robinson, *Facts for Farmers and the Family Circle . . ,*New York, 1867, chapter 12.

8. *Drew's Rural Intelligencer*, August 25, 1855; December 27, 1856; Oxford *Democrat*, February 16, 23, March 2, 1855.

9. Oxford *Democrat,October 26, 1855; March 6, June 5, 1857; Drew's Rural Intelligencer*, January 27 (speech by Sidney Perham at Kennebec County Agricultural Society, at Wayne), April 14, 1855. Some of this agitation aided in the establishment of normal schools, see *Sixth Annual Report of Superintendent of Common Schools*, Augusta, 1859, 19-24. *Transactions* of State Agricultural Societies, Part I, Drew's Address October 3, 1850 at South Berwick, "What Can Be Done Adequately to Promote the Agricultural Interests of Maine?", 7-21, esp. 12, 14, 20; *Drew's Rural Intelligencer*, January 13, March 23, 1855; Oxford *Democrat*, January 26, February 9, 1855, all these were brought on by Morrill's annual message in which he called for a model or experimental farm. See House Documents, 1853-54, in *Public Documents*, No. 17, calling for agricultural textbooks, and No. 27, for an experimental farm. On the textbook issue see Oxford *Democrat*, January 18, February 8, 29, 1856, and throughout, the *Maine Farmer* on these issues as well.

10. Oxford *Democrat*, October 13, 1854, reprinting Forbes' address to Oxford County Agricultural Society, October 5, 1854, and a series of reports from the Bethel Club, the brainchild of N.T. True, then the head of Gould Academy, for example, February 8, 1856 on "Kitchen Gardens and Vegetables". The West Minot and Hebron club made its appearance in a notable letter from L., in the same issue.

11. Oxford *Democrat*, February 8, 1856, November 20, 1857, speech of N.T.T. before West Oxford Agricultural Society, at Fryeburg, October 22, 1857; and November 13, 1857 speech of A.L. Burbank before Bethel Farmer's Club, October 14, 1857. This club maintained a lending library for members.

12. Oxford *Democrat*, March 6, 1857, report of a committee on farmers' clubs, headed by S.L. Goodale. How many farmers' clubs there were at this time is unknown, but they are noticed over most of the settled part of the state, with some of them being quite active. It is easy to see why the Grange made such an early foothold in Maine with this beginning.

13. Oxford *Democrat*, January 1, January 29, February 5, 12, 19, 26, 1858 reporting action of societies, including a big meeting in Bangor on January 25, 1858. Also Aroostook *Pioneer*, quoted in *Democrat* of March 12, and a further *Democrat* editorial of August 6, 1858.

14. Annual *Report* Superintendent of Common Schools, 1859, 19-24; Address of Lot M. Morrill, to Joint Session, January 6, 1860; Sen. Doc., No. 22, 39th Legislature, 1860; Board of Agriculture, *Report*, 1859, S.L. Goodale, "Agricultural Education" 249-264; *Report*, 1861, 17-19; 8th Annual *Report*, Superintendent of Common Schools, 1861, 68-9.

15. 7th Annual *Report* of Board of Agriculture, Augusta, 1863, Annual meeting, January 15, 1862, 146-153 for Goodale's address.

16. This story can be seen in Earle Ross, *Democracy's College*, 1942. For land disposal generally, Cornell's success, and agriculture in this period, see Paul W. Gates, *The Wisconsin Pine Lands of Cornell University*, 1941; *History of the Public Land Law Development*, 1970, and *The Farmer's Age 1818-1860*, 1962.

17. Message of Abner Coburn, January 8, 1863; *Report* of Superintendent of Common Schools, 1862, Augusta, 1863, 106-107. Forty-second Legislature, Senate Doc. No. 12 (majority report), No. 10 (minority).

18. 8th Annual *Report,* Board of Agriculture, 1863, Augusta, 1864. The debate occurs at 42-56, with the quote at 44, and 56. See also 267-271, "Proposed Agricultural College", as well as The School Superintendent's *Report,* 1863, "Action in Regard to the Agricultural College," 30-34. Annual Address of Governor Samuel Cony, January 7, 1864, 16-18. He had no preference.

19. Ninth Annual *Report* Secretary of Board of Agriculture, 1864, Augusta, 1865, 74-76.

20. 43rd Legislature, House Doc., No. 6 (F.O.J. Smith to Samuel Cony, February 2, 1864, offering his farm). Cony's *Address* January 5, 1865 (he now favored one of the established colleges). Report of the Commissioners, signed December 19, 1864, in Ninth Annual *Report,* Board of Agriculture, 177-204 (and Goodale's remarks refuting this on 205-7); 44th Legislature, House Doc. No. 8, Majority accepting report, and No. 39, calling for new college.

21. E. Holmes, "The Lessons of the Hour," speech before Kennebec County Agricultural Society at Readfield, October 20, 1864, in Abstracts of Historical Societies, in Secretary's *Report,* 1864, 111-112. "Death of Ezekiel Holmes, M.D.", by Stephen L. Goodale, in *Agriculture of Maine,* 1865, 205-7, as well as sketch of Holmes' life by D.T. True, 207-226. Two biographies of Holmes exist, and both leave something to be desired with regard to his place in his contemporary life.

22. Secretary's *Report* of Board of Agriculture, 1865 (Augusta, 1865), Annual Meeting called on January 18, 1865. Debate extends from 15-72. *Journal of H.R.,* 44th Leg., 80, 81, 109, 186, 191, 204, 207, 240, 241. *Senate Journal,* 253, 271.

23. Chapter 532, *Laws of Maine,* 1865, 529-532, Section 14 is at 532.

24. Trustees Minutes, April 25, 1865 (Augusta). Hereafter, where the place is not indicated it is Orono; April 26, 1865 (Augusta, Togus). Kennebec *Journal,* April 16, 1865.

25. Broadside dated May 2, 1865, Bangor, and signed by Hannibal Hamlin and the other members of the Board, "State College of Agriculture and the Mechanic Arts (For the State of Maine)". This is reprinted in a number of places, and perhaps as conveniently as any in *Report* of the Secretary of the State Board of Agriculture, 1865, S.L. Goodale, "The State Agricultural College," 227-232.

26. Trustees Minutes, May 30, (Bangor); letter B.F. Nourse to Board May 15, 1865; June 27-8, (Waterville), August 15 (Topsham) 16, (Topsham), September 13 (Augusta), September 14, 1865 (Augusta), January 22, (Bangor), January 23-5 (Augusta), 1866.

27. Trustees meetings (Augusta), January 23-26, 1866.

28. *Maine Farmer,* February 22, March 3, 19, April 23, December 6, 1866. In *Agriculture of Maine,* 1866, "The Colleges for the Industrial Classes, Con-

templated by the Act of Congress of 1862," 199-235. And on Goodale's proposal, annual meeting January 17, 1866, 348.

29. Phineas Barnes to Goodale, February 3, 1866 in minutes of Board.

30. Trustees minutes, March 28 (Bangor), March 29 (Bangor), Executive Committee April 16 (Bangor), 1866; September 26, 1866 (Augusta).

31. Annual Message, Governor Joshua Chamberlain, 1867.

32. Trustee Meetings, January 29, 1867, and resignations in minutes following. Especially see letter Samuel F. Perley (Naples) to Goodale, April 4, 1866 refusing to serve on the board and citing Barnes' letter and reasons of before. One of the last acts of the old board was to offer the presidency to Phineas Barnes, but no answer was recorded, and one doubts if he was even notified. The Orono town meetings that raised the money and obtained the proper deeds occurred February 26, 1866 and March 11, 1867. (Copies of minutes of meetings dated March 9, 1869 in Lyndon Oak folder.) William P. Wingate raised $14,000 of the money needed in Bangor, and the town of Orono then purchased the farms. The 1867 appropriation appeared only after the town agreed to sell the farms to the state. The 1866 meeting rejected the offer, apparently until they were sure they would get the college, but the 1867 meeting approved the sale. See *Cadet,* March, 1890, and letter April, 1890, Nathaniel Wilson to the editor, setting the record straight. For a sister's greeting see *The Maine Normal,* Farmington, Vol. 1, [February, 1867].

33. Olmstead's plans are dealt with in Laura Roper, *F.L.O. A Biography of Frederick Law Olmstead,* Baltimore, 1973, 36-40, 54, 87-9, although there are errors in her account; see Trustees Minutes April 24, May 15 (Bangor), June 12, June 20, 1867. Portland *Transcript,* February 2, 1867; Bangor *Whig and Courier,* June 22, 1867. Olmstead came to Orono December 21, 1866. 46th Leg. H. Doc. 57. *Plan of a Village Adapted to the Requirements of the INDUSTRIAL COLLEGE OF THE STATE OF MAINE,* New York, 1867.

34. Trustees minutes, June 21 (Bangor), (this meeting also accepted a prize Durham bull from Coburn, and two pigs from another source). August 1, December 4, 1867; January 28, February 4, 1868 (last two Augusta). Chapter 274, *Laws of Maine,* 1868; Chamberlain's Address, 224-5.

35. Oxford *Democrat,* July 19, 1867; Bangor *Whig* June 25, 1867; Portland *Daily Press,* August 30, 1867; Trustees Minutes, March 11, April 8, 21, 1868; Annual Report Trustees, 47th Leg., Sen. Doc. No. 3.

36. 47th Legislature, Sen. Doc. No. 3, Report of Trustees, dated December 1, 1867; Treasurer's Report (same document); Trustees Minutes, March

11, June 30, July 1, August 4, 5, 1868. The July 1 meeting was held in Bangor. Gov. Joshua Chamberlain to Oak, March 3, 1868 (more money needed and will recommend).

37. Trustees minutes, August 4, 5, 1868. The report of the opening was very widely circulated, as I have seen copies in papers as obscure as the Presque Isle *Sunrise,* September 18, 1868. Discussion of the requirements will appear in a later chapter. The early memories of Mary L. Fernald, the wife of the President, occur in *The Maine Spring,* Vol. II, No. 4 (June, 1922), 12-16.

38. Broadside, "The State College of Agriculture and the Mechanic Arts," undated, but sometime in summer, 1868; reminiscences in *Maine Campus,* 1922; Letter, M.C. Fernald to George O. Weston, '72, September 17, 1868 accepting him for entrance (in class of '72 folder).

39. 47th Leg., Sen. Doc. No. 3.

40. Samuel Johnson to Lyndon Oak, November 9, 1868, in Oak folder. Early monthly accounts of the farm survive in detail from January, 1869 to April, 1871, for November, 1874, April to November, 1875, and in detail for May, 1875. The 1869 accounts summarize as follows with receipts first, and expenditures second. Jan. $99.29 — $1,114.63; Feb. $345.44 — $240.32; March, $9.83 — $380.37; April, $866.86 — $470.32; May $179.33 — $158.15; June, $165.31 — $509.95; July, $54.23 — $388.40; August, $252.56 — $149.07; September, $34.60 — $100.17; October, $30.30 — $222.86; November, $1,330.23 — $912.93; December, $430.81 — $504.85. These early superintendents often loaned money to the farm to keep it running.

41. M.C. Fernald to Lyndon Oak, December 21, 1868; Samuel Johnson to Oak, December 14, 1868 on Amherst visit; Fernald to Oak January 11, 1869. The Ithaca and East Lansing visits are discussed in this letter.

42. Fernald to Oak, January 11, 1869.

43. Trustees minutes, October 22, December 3, 1868; December 15, (Augusta), April 7, June 25, August 5, October 19, November 25, December 16, 1869; February 9, (Augusta), April 26, April 28, May 18, June 2 (Orono, and in evening in Bangor), July 28, July 30 (Bangor), November 22 (Orono, Bangor), 1870; January 12 (Augusta), January 13 (Augusta), January 25 (Augusta), 26 (Augusta), May 17, June 6, August 1, 2, 31, 1871; M.C. Fernald to Oak, January 29, 1869; February 23, 1869; February 16, 1869; March 6, 1869; Chamberlain's Annual *Address,* 1870, 15-6. Some early bills and letters also survive; J.F. Luhave and Co. to S.F. Peckham, January 31, 1870; bills James Tiffany (Providence) November 30, 1869; H.M. Raynor (NYC) December 15, 1869; Boston Belting Co. December 31, 1869; S.L. Libbery to S.F. Peckham (paid July 25, 1871); Wood Bishop Co., May 19, 1871. These bills were nearly all to equip Chemical Hall, over which Peckham had cognizance. Early instructors, most of whom gave only a set of

lectures, included Calvin Cutter (anatomy, physiology, hygiene), Corydin B. Lakin (bookkeeping), X.A. Willard (dairy farming), A.S. Packard (useful and injurious insects), James J.H. Gregory, (market farming and gardening), E.S. Morse (comparative anatomy and zoology), Henry E. Sellers (military), John Swift (botany and horticulture), and Mary L. Fernald (French and German), from 1871 *Catalogue of Maine State College.*

44. The best account of the event appeared in an article by Lemont, Portland *Advertiser,* September 2, 1871. The inaugural occurred on Thursday, August 31. Lemont took the occasion to describe the buildings and grounds in some detail. Allen took over an institution with 21 Freshmen just entering, and 17 students in the other classes. Lemont thought the biggest needs to be books for the library and items for its cabinet, but otherwise prospects were good. Allen's first appointment occurs in Trustee Minutes, November 25, 1869.

45. On Chemical and Brick Halls, see long undated report to Trustees from Fernald (late 1868?); Samuel F. Dike to Oak, June 24, 1867; Portland *Transcript,* August 6, December 3, 1870; Trustees Annual Report, 1870, 1871. Waterville *Mail,* November 25, 1870. Events, from a student point of view, may be followed in Diary of James Walter Weeks, '77.

46. Faculty minutes, February 16, 1874; Fernald to Oak, January 22, 1876, and undated '75, (the quote); *Reporter,* July, 1876; *Transit,* 1884, *Pendulum,* 1881 and 1882.

47. 51st Leg., Sen. Doc. 52, dated February 15, 1872.

48. *Annual Report* Trustees, 1872; Governor Perham's Address, 7-8; Chapter 56, *Laws of Maine,* 1872; Chapter 183, *Laws of Maine,* 1873.

49. C.F. Allen to Oak, February 13, 1874.

50. Allen to Oak, February 20, 1874; Samuel F. Dike to Oak, September 1, 1874; *Reporter,* Vol. 1, No. 9.

51. Allen to Oak, February 25, 1875; Isaiah Stetson to Oak, March 20, 1875; Dingley's *Address,* 62. *Report of the Evidence and Conclusions of the Committee to Investigate the Sale of the Agricultural College Scrip Made to the 55th Legislature,* Sprague, Owen and Nash, Augusta, 1876. 55th Legislature, Sen. Doc. 15, listed amounts appropriated for MSC from 1867 to 1875.

52. Seldon Connor's Address, 1876, 158-160; Trustees Minutes, (Augusta), January 28, 1875; Letter Lyndon Oak to Trustees, November 6, 1875 "The exigencies of the College are such as to demand a full attendance of the board." The Barn appears in plan and cut in *Agriculture of Maine,* 1874.

53. Holograph of Phillips speech (25 pps.) loaned to me by his grandson, William Phillips, '72. *Journal of Senate of Maine,* 1877; 164, 184, 197, 202, 346, 361. It is more difficult to document the Bowdoin re-

mark, but it was so widely said in the 1870-1890 period as to be totally believable, even though Bowdoin also supplied much help, and some of the early faculty. Phillips was a Bowdoin man, of course. Phillips, incidentally, was in the 1877 Legislature as a Senator where he continued to be a strong advocate of the college.

54. Chapter 258, *Laws of Maine,* 1877; Connors' *Address,* 1877; 1878; Chapter 57, *Laws of Maine,* 1878; (the resolve asking for others to come forward); Chapter 90, *Laws of Maine,* 1878; Chapter 173, *Laws of Maine,* 1879 (tuition); Chapter 197, *Laws of Maine,* 1880; Davis's *Address,* 1880. *Leg. Doc.,* 1878, H.R. No. 11, to divide up the University with other colleges; Sen. Doc. 58 (new proposals); H.R. 130, 155 (appropriations); *Leg. Doc.,* 1879, H.R. No. 51, 119.

55. Trustees minutes, April 5, 1876; January 17, 24, 1877 (visits of comm. to college); September 19, Exec. Comm. September 20, 1877; January 23, (Augusta), 1878; Special Faculty Meeting, March 28, 1878; Trustees, April 24 (Bangor); 25; June 24 (Bangor), 25, 26 (Allen's resignation). August 1, 1876 (first resignation).

56. J.R. Farrington to Oak, February 4, 1879. Farrington had lent the school $4,000 since 1875. Trustees Minutes, January 17, 1879 (Augusta); Coburn to Oak, January 18, 1879.

57. Trustees Minutes (Bangor), March 19; November 18, 1879; Sixtieth Leg., (1881) Sen. Doc., No. 65 on trip to Orono; Fernald to Oak, December 27, 1878; February 22, 1879. C.F. Allen to Oak, February 13, 1874. Allen also related in this letter his work on the chimney draft in the new buildings. He was able to fix the laboratory but not Brick Hall; which continued to smoke.

58. *Agriculture of Maine,* 1867, Johnson's address, 30-8; 1868; Dike's address 63-87 with the commentary, further comment appears at 241-4; 1869, Geo. B. Loring, "The Connection of the State Board of Agriculture with the Agricultural College," 221-236. The new act was approved March 1, 1869 as a result of this comment.

59. *Agriculture of Maine,* 1869, detailed discussion of meeting from 309 on. On Abbott, who spoke on "Agricultural Education and Agricultural Colleges," 383-392, see *Kennebec Journal,* November 16, 1892; *New York Tribune,* March 6, 1893.

60. *Agriculture of Maine,* 1871, *Agriculture of Maine,* 1872, 19-37 for Allen's address.

61. *Agriculture of Maine,* 1872, (Allen spoke at the meeting of the East Oxford Agricultural Society at Dixfield in September as well that year); *Agriculture of Maine,* 1873, 97-9; 331-351; 413-4.

62. *Agriculture of Maine,* 1874, 359-368.

63. *Agriculture of Maine,* 1875, Charles F. Allen, "Agricultural Education," 94-105; "Practical Education — and the Aims and Methods of the Maine State College," 195-202.

64. *Agriculture of Maine,* 1875, M.C. Fernald, "The Influence of Education Upon Labor," 72-83.

65. *Agriculture of Maine,* 1876, Fernald 48-69; Aubert, 166-178 (on M.S.C. experiments 177-8); also see Samuel F. Boardman, "Historical Sketch of the State College, Its Aims and Methods," 208-220. Weeks Diary, November 4, 1876. He was one of the speakers.

66. *Agriculture of Maine,* 1877, on what they wanted to hear, 236ff; on speeches, C.H. Fernald, 56-77; M.C. Fernald, 114-131; on Carmichael, 257-272, his attack on M.S.C. is at 271; Student exercises appear at 236-256 and Allen's address at 221-235.

CHAPTER TWO

The Fernald Presidency

MERRITT C. FERNALD, Allen's successor, was to remain president of the institution from 1879 until 1893. During that time funding to the college from the legislature did not increase in any appreciable amount, but federal funds and private gifts helped somewhat. Perhaps the greatest achievement of Fernald's tenure was the establishment of courses of study with substantial merit, especially courses outside the field of agriculture. Admission standards rose steadily, and although the school did not graduate large numbers, many of those graduated had distinguished careers. The faculty reached a stability during these years that also raised the standards of the school.

Funding remained a problem. After the imposition of tuition in 1879, the student body decreased by a fifth, and the number of persons who began college and were unable to finish, often because of lack of funds, increased. Governors of the state, as well as individual members of the legislature, were sometimes very sympathetic to the college, but the appropriations did not increase substantially and when they did increase at all the added funds were often to be used for specific programs. Federal funds from the Hatch Act, establishing experiment stations, and the Second Morrill Act, providing direct funding to the agricultural and mechanic arts colleges started in the sixties, did aid the growth of the institution to an important degree, as did private gifts, of which the greatest was $100,000 from the estate of Abner Coburn.

Perhaps the low point of the period was reached in early 1880, when a committee of the House of Representatives heard but rejected a bill that would have limited the course of study to a maximum of three years and would have restricted income to investment, gifts, and tuition. The legislature did raise $6,500 to pay for instruction, farm experiments, apparatus, library books, and repairs of buildings. The next year, when the legislature began biennial sessions, the amounts provided were $3,500 annually. The governors in this period were friendly, both Harris M. Plaisted and Frederick Robie being farmers. Robie was prominent as longtime master of the state Grange and was known politically as "Farmer" Robie. As a result of these agriculturally minded governors, in 1883, the biennial amounts rose to $6,500 each year for the college.[1]

Robie asked, in 1883, for the establishment of a state experimental station, and it was provided in 1885. The biennial appropriation was $12,400, of which part was earmarked for specific subjects. Robie continued to champion the college in his requests to the legislature, and, with the strong support of the Grange and other farmers' spokesmen, the college began to get more recognition from that body. In his 1885 speech to the legislature, Robie compared what had been done for Michigan and its agricultural college with the provisions for Maine, a comparison in which Maine suffered. After his comments, he closed his request to the legislature with the following:

This is a college for the people, and should receive a popular support, and I would urge that the State give the Institution a liberal appropriation. It is gaining in public confidence, represents an important place in our system of popular education, and should be strong and progressive in all its points.[2]

Funds increased from a number of sources in 1887. The next governor, Joseph R. Bodwell, was not as explicit as Robie, but the

The first mechanical engineering shop. These photos, both exterior and interior, date from about 1885. The building stood where Alumni Hall now stands and it later served as a storage building for agricultural machinery in the area behind the Maples.

Oak Hall and White Hall in the mid-1890's. Oak, formerly Brick Hall, was named for trustee Lyndon Oak.

groundwork was well laid. The legislature appropriated $34,600 for the biennium: $25,000 to erect a building for natural science and agriculture (Coburn Hall), $2,500 for apparatus, $1,000 for sewer and a water supply, and $1,000 for repairs. This bill carried an interesting rider providing compulsory punishment for students who assaulted other students, which tells us something of student life at the time, a subject to be treated later. The $100,000 was received from the Coburn bequest and quickly deposited in 4% bonds of the state. In the same year the federal experiment stations were created and brought more funds and another building (Holmes Hall) to the campus. Although these funds were not for instruction, they did release other monies for that purpose. The state college herd unfortunately suffered a disastrous loss from tuberculosis about this time, so some of the joy at the increased resources was tempered by the necessity to replace the herd and by the criticism in the agricultural press.[3]

Two years later, when the legislature convened, the situation continued much as before with the new governor, Edwin C. Burleigh, generally supporting the institution. The legislature allowed $30,000 for the biennium: $6,000 to replace the herd, $2,950 for fitting Coburn, $1,000 for the library, $2,900 for the various departments, $2,000 for greenhouses, $3,000 for a water supply from the Stillwater, and funds for sidewalks, heating plants, forges, drawing tables, rebuilding some of Chemical Hall, lathes, planes, and a foundry. Of this money, $20,000 was to be expended in 1889, and that year marks the date that the campus began to assume the shape that is well-known today.

When the second Morrill Act passed in 1891, the legislature responded by suspending tuition charges for a brief period. It appropriated $24,500 for the college for the biennium, but $16,000 of this was to rebuild Wingate Hall (formerly White) which had been destroyed by fire. In addition a foundry, display cases in Coburn, a dairy building, a tool shed, a standpipe for fire protection ($3,600), and a hose cart in case of further fire disasters were all provided for in the total amount. The federal Morrill Act funds were welcome. They came to $15,000 for the year 1890 with an increase of $1,000 for each year, until in 1900 the amount was $25,000. This total was in addition to the funds for the experiment station which were $15,000 annually.

During Fernald's last year as president, the legislature continued to provide funds at the same standard with an appropriation of $12,000 to furnish Wingate, improve the landscaping on the campus, build a potting shed and silo, and buy a fair amount of apparatus for the mechanical and civil engineering departments. This appropriation raised the entire amount allotted by the state in the first quarter century, 1868-1893, to $293,718. It was perhaps not a huge amount, but it did provide a start to the college, and with it the board of trustees and the faculty had provided a place where good education was available to at least some of the citizens of the state.

When Fernald left the presidency, the school again faced a sort of crossroads. It could continue to serve the limited clientele it had thus far, or it could branch out and become a true university. Whichever road it chose, controversy was sure to develop, for no institution could receive funds in the above amounts and not have close scrutiny from the taxpayers as to how those funds were being utilized, particularly in a state beginning to suffer declining population and a slowing economy.[4]

One of the reasons the legislature had been willing to give most of the funds requested was that it was generally happy with the college. Fernald lobbied well, making a strong attempt to set up an endowment fund, although this attempt did not succeed except for the Coburn bequest. Allen had acted as a publicity agent during his presidency, while Fernald had maintained the school on the campus. After Fernald's appointment as president, he continued to expend his energies in raising the standards of the school, searching for endowment possibilities, doing some scholarly work, and lobbying for the college and for the other Morrill schools. An effective lobbyist, he attended conferences in Washington in 1872, 1881, 1884, and in 1887 was elected vice-president of the new Convention of Agriculture College Presidents and Experiment Station Directors. Fernald was a strong factor in the movement that led to the independence of the stations, while some presidents had pushed for complete subordination to the colleges.[5]

Holmes Hall. The wings were added to the original building in 1899 and 1904. This photo is from the latter year.

He found time to do some research, keeping the meteorological records meticulously until his retirement and publishing articles on Mount Katahdin, the history of the school, and other matters. In 1885, in response to an attack in the *Lewiston Journal* saying that the Maine State College was not practical and that too many graduates left the state thus not giving taxpayers any real value, he wrote an article that indicated clearly his philosophy of education.

Educational Institutions were not established for immediate benefit of those who are in middle age, or in advanced life, however much indirectly such persons may be benefited by them; but rather for the young that they may be better equipped and prepared for the work of life than were their fathers before them. Such institutions can only be properly judged by what they do for the rising generation . . . .[6]

Fernald was remembered by one as "dignified, *venerable, courteous, methodical,*" and as having a sense of humor, though being routine-prone. In his classroom he determined a recitation order and followed it for the semester; students also followed it, preparing well when their turn was coming, and enjoying themselves at other times. Precise in all his work, Fernald prepared a complete budget for the European tour given him by the faculty in 1908 and boasted that he had overspent his budget by only five cents. When he retired, the Alumni Association passed a resolution expressing appreciation of his "patient

An early view of the campus. From left to right, the buildings are Oak, White, Fernald, the QTV House, Coburn, Maples, the college farm, and in the foreground the President's house. The picture was taken between 1887 and 1889. The early tree planting has mellowed the ruder scenes of the early days.

perserverance and indomitable energy.'' One famous alumni remarked some years later in a letter, ''. . . remember me to Prof. M.C. bless the dear old man. I owe him more than I ever hope to repay. I remember him as everyone else does, as one of finest teachers, and best of men.'' The choice of such a person as early president meant that the school was led clearly, honestly, directly, and methodically on a way that still survives.[7]

The trustees also were very interested in the college and dealt much more minutely with college affairs than is the case today. Their regular business included supervision of building construction, ''extending the sewer drains from Brick Hall to the river,'' choosing the boarding house steward (often a problem as the students were unhappy with the food), and worrying about the course in military instruction, first as to what uniforms should be worn and later the preservation of the course as the War Department began to cut back its expenditures.[8] In April 1881, they ruled ''that it is the judgement of the trustees the best interests of the institution require the residence of the members of the Faculty upon the college premises, and that said members be required to occupy the college buildings for rent or board so far as accommodations will allow. . . .'' The next year they ruled that all students not living at home also had to live at the college unless especially excused.[9] In 1884 the board decided that the grounds bounded by the highway to Stillwater

and the driveway from the farmhouse and the president's house were to be kept as a permanent lawn or park, as it still is.

The farm was not profitable, and the farm superintendent was unhappy and wanted more money. Also, the endowment fund was not succeeding. So Fernald was perhaps justified in 1884 in feeling strain as when he wrote a letter suggesting that the farm superintendent's salary was sufficient from ''the careful study which it has seemed necessary for me to give to the finances of the institution and the very anxious and trying time which I have not been able to avoid at each legislative session in acting to keep the finances intact. . . . At his present salary, I regard him the best paid officer in the college grounds, putting the President's salary out of consideration . . . .''[10]

Salaries at the school were not large. Senior officials received $1,500 to $1,800 annually, new faculty not much more than $600 or $800. Faculty were relieved of janitorial duties in the 1880's, however, and janitors hired. Their duties were very detailed. They were listed in 1876 as: sweeping, dusting, keeping in order all of the college halls and recitation rooms, tending the furnace, making gas (for illumination, as the college had its own facilities), ringing the bell, keeping doors and windows closed at night during storms and cold weather, and helping the farm superintendents and faculty if necessary. In 1884 the students petitioned to raise the janitor's salary to $40 per month, and in 1886 to

This photo dates from 1902-3. The buildings, on a more heavily wooded campus, are Oak, Wingate, (with the tower), Fernald, the shops, Alumni Hall, Coburn, the standpipe, and Holmes Hall. This is a fall photograph taken after the leaves fell to reveal the new construction.

$50. The actual pay was $45 per month until into the 1890's.[11] At first professors housed the janitors and their families in their homes, but in 1885 the college began to consider building tenements for its janitorial and farm labor force.

Another financial problem for Fernald and the board near the end of the decade concerned a part of their small endowment funds invested in construction bonds issued on a Hallowell school. The college held a mortgage on the building of the school and its land, a bad investment which the board continued although Fernald advised against it. Finally, after forcing a change in administration of the school, the college withdrew what it could. The owners, the State Conference of Congregational Churches, had to be informed that they had a moral obligation to pay their debts. Some money was returned, and the college reinvested the funds in western mortgages which were thought to be a better risk.[12]

The planning and construction of Coburn Hall, the first major building addition since the earliest days, gives insight into the workings of the college. Funds for the building were requested in 1885, but were denied as the legislature was more interested in the establishment of the experiment station. However, an implicit promise was made to fund the building in 1887.[13]

The new building was discussed by the trustees as early as November 1884. It was to be located on the site of the Q.T.V. Society, a

The QTV house, the earliest fraternity. Members lounging in front are brothers of N.E. Wilson, '88, who saved this photograph. The fraternity, founded in 1870, was housed in several locations before its eventual removal to the fraternity row area.

local fraternity that had a small building on the campus. The fraternity, founded in 1870 and the first at the college, was to be relocated on the street passing the farmhouse, thus beginning fraternity row. President Fernald and trustee Lyndon Oak were to locate the new building site; a committee was charged with providing plans for the building, to be called Coburn Hall. The board decided to provide Brick, White, and Chemical halls with water supply and urinals also, as well as sewer connections to empty into the Stillwater. The sewer dumping place was to "be a sufficient distance so that the water supply shall not be contaminated." The Maine Experiment Station whose building was being constructed nearby at this time also, provided some of the funds to help with the water supply costs, although the station was rationed in its usage to 200 gallons of water a day maximum. The wells for the new water supply were witched, or dowsed, for the trustees. As Fernald said to Lyndon Oak, "A Mr. Trask of Bangor who bores wells and who is *skilled in the art of the witch hazel branch for finding water* has decided upon a location for the wells." In early 1887 an architect was chosen and the building begun, its site picked in reference to Holmes Hall, the experiment station building. The trustees agreed to assume the cost of a major ceremony when Coburn Hall was to be dedicated.[14]

The table indicates what made up the expenditures for the building.

COBURN HALL — EXPENDITURES

Common Expenses	303.21
Architect (F.E. Kidder)	822.65
Supt. Construction (G.H. Hamlin)	300.00
Contractors (J & J Philbrook)	19,987.00
Steam Heat (Getchell and Co.)	2,159.00
Fixtures, furniture (W.O. White)	2,422.50
Grading, sundries, toilets	549.44
Totals	26,543.80
(Legislature provided	25,000.00)

The dedication held June 26, 1888, was, like Allen's inaugural, an event used to show off the college to the state. Fernald welcomed the audience and Allen, returned for this occasion, offered a prayer. The highlight of the program was a full-dress history of the college by Lyndon Oak. The building committee chairman and the president of the State Senate both spoke briefly, while Fernald and Professors Harvey

and Balentine, who accepted the building for the faculty, responded. Music, addresses from local legislators, and a speech by Horace Estabrooke ('76) for the alumni followed. The program finished with an ode and benediction. The proceedings of the affair were published by the college, and the account was widely circulated by the school and its friends. The sturdy building still stands. In recent years it is increasingly useful, aalthough no longer the focus of the community that it was in the first thirty-five years of its existence.[15]

Two major developments changed and modified the college fairly substantially in the late 1880's. One was the establishment of the experiment station. The other was the destruction of the college herd from tuberculosis. Both deserve separate treatment.

Governor Robie had asked for the state to establish an experiment station as early as 1883. In 1885, $5,000 was allocated for the first year of operation. The station's primary purpose, as stated by the law, was to aid in fertilizer control; the act establishing the station set fertilizer marking and manufacturing standards, and the station was to inspect to insure quality. Agricultural forces in the state were overjoyed with their victory in achieving something they had wanted since the 1850's.[16]

Then, in 1887, the Congress passed the Hatch Act establishing experiment stations in each state. The Maine station went out of business, being absorbed by the new federal station. The annual appropriations of approximately $6,000 for the new station made possible a new building to house the staff, at that point located in a back room of the laboratory. A new plan of organization was set up; a station council was to be composed of the president, the director, the professors of agriculture, natural history, horticulture and veterinary science. Trustees were added and a budget adopted. An unfinished barn was transferred to the station for completion. Members were sought for the council from the State Board of Agriculture, the Grange, and the State Pomological Society. By 1889-90 the station budget was over $15,000. In that year the major amounts allocated were: salaries, $8,450; water supply, $2,000; construction, $750; printing, $1,500; experiments, $1,000; chemical lab, $600; travel, $300; horticulture and fruit work, $250; veterinary work, $300. Station experiments began in

Coburn Hall, on a spring day soon after construction. The velocipede at the steps helps set the scene.

earnest in 1890 (although college farm experiments had been conducted and the results published even in the 1870's) with authorization of experiments in potato, mixed grains, wheat, barley, poultry marketing, potato rust, fungi, insecticides (especially for use against the cabbage worm), Paris Green, and fodder digestion. In that year the Station Council discussed seed distribution, growth in horticultural and pomological work, and the possibility of a substation in Aroostook County.[17]

The station will be treated in more detail later, but this account will give an indication of the immediate role the station and its personnel took in the college. That they did so was just as well, because the farmers of the state witnessed a disaster at the college that would do as much damage to the school's hopes as the establishment of the experiment station did to raise them.

An epizootic broke out in the college barns in March 1886. The State Veterinary Surgeon, Dr. Bailey, and another surgeon, from Washington, came to inspect. They diagnosed tuberculosis

and ordered some of the herd destroyed. The visitors did find "the buildings among the best and most commodious [we] had ever visited, and that every provision for the maintainence of perfect health among its occupants had been fully and amply secured."

Doctor Bailey did a postmortem on a cadaver and afterward isolated even more of the cattle, eventually slaughtering two, both of whom were diseased. On April 6, the governor and the Executive Council inspected the barns and asked for more advice from Washington on the disease. It was finally decided to kill the entire herd. Postmortems were performed on the animals with the governor, physicians, stockowners, reporters, and others present; all cattle were found to be diseased. Many citizens were convinced that "book-learning" or the feeding of cottonseed meal had created the situation. The veterinary, injured by these "foolish remarks," conducted a detailed investigation and found that the disease may have been present on the grounds as early as 1876, as a tuberculin cow had been sold to a local milk

*J.R. Farrington, an early farm superinten-
dent.*

dealer in that year. The animal had been killed
in 1879 when the disease appeared in a virulent
form. Others had died in 1881, but the deaths
had not been reported; pressure for profits had
caused the farm to be secretive about its
problems. When Joseph Farrington came as
farm superintendent in 1881, he spent much
time in building up the herd, but the disease had
lingered on.

After the slaughter, the buildings were all dis-
infected, the floor boards in the barns replaced,
and finally all the bulls in the state which had
been associated with the herd (14) were ordered
killed, stirring great controversy among their
owners. The State Legislature held a hearing on
the case. Many who appeared were testy and
short with the committee, either because they
were involved personally, such as Z.A. Gilbert,
or because they wished the college damage.
Eventually the Commissioners of Cattle Disease
(both Gilbert and the surgeon were members)
held a lively Portland meeting in which arguments over the propriety of individual actions,
especially with regard to the slaughter, were
loud and harsh.

In the testimony before the legislative committee Z.A. Gilbert was the star witness. His reputation as secretary of the Board of
Agriculture, member of the college trustees and
that body's farm committee, as well as Cattle
Commissioner was as stake. Although he appeared with counsel he did not handle the situation well. It came out in the testimony that prior
to the Portland meeting he had attempted to
hold a rump meeting with an acquiescent commissioner, who ordinarily never attended meetings, in order to prevent Bailey from securing
the order to kill the animals. The hitherto silent
commissioner sided with Bailey, however.
(There was a comic-opera chase by Bailey of
Gilbert through Portland streets to find the location of the meeting.) Eventually Bailey resigned
in order not to cause more difficulty for the college, although he was obviously in the right.

Although the college replaced the herd in the
next two years, mostly with funds from the
Coburn legacy, the reputation of the school had
suffered considerable damage. Farmers could
not believe that a school charged with teaching
scientific farming would allow this sort of thing
to occur, and the rather odd activities of Z.A.
Gilbert, as well as the actions of the early farm
superintendents in selling animals even though
disease was known or suspected, did severe
harm. In a crucial area the college had been
tried and found wanting. The disease might
have occurred anyway, as an epizootic was
prevalent in the United States during this
period; the difficulty in Orono was the method
in which it was handled by responsible officers.
The ensuing coolness between Gilbert and the
rest of the board was to be a factor in the next
big fight at the institution, as Gilbert did not
support the university as strongly as he might
have.[18]

Despite the serious problem of the tuberculin
herd, Fernald, while writing to Oak about
another matter in May 1887, remarked,
"College affairs are running quietly. Never
more so. I hope they may so continue."[19] In
fact, with the additional funds from the second
Morrill Act available, the college was in its best
shape, and most of the rest of Fernald's term
ran quite smoothly. After the Morrill bill passed
and the money was appropriated, the trustees
met for two full days to determine the direction
of the college with its new funds. At the first of

The college farm about 1895.

the meetings, at the Penobscot Exchange Hotel in Bangor on the evening of November 5, 1890, the entire time was spent "in discussing the question of expenditure of funds to be received . . . and particularly concerning the course in Agriculture and Horticulture." Speeches were made to the trustees by Z.A. Gilbert, who besides being prominent on the State Board of Agriculture was sometime editor of the *Maine Farmer,* as well as by the head of the state Grange. Gilbert presented a detailed plan for a two-year agriculture course. Discussion continued the next morning, and it was voted to have a final formal plan for a two-year course presented for trustee approval at the annual meeting, to be held in June for the first time.

From a financial point of view, this November board meeting marks the beginning of the modern college administration. It was decided that at the June meeting the president, with the advice of the faculty, was to propose a budget. The board would modify and approve, and the treasurer would then pay the bills without further authorization. Increase or diversion of funds would be only by special trustee vote. Bills would be approved by a special auditing officer, and separate accounts were to be kept of all income, departmental expenditures, and other matters connected with the new course. The board also authorized special officers, clerical aid, and definite office hours for the college treasurer.[20]

Other matters taken up at this meeting included approval of the employment of pro-fessors of horticulture, English literature, physics, and electrical engineering; the bestowing of more power in the area of hygiene and sanitation on the college veterinary as a result of the tuberculosis disaster; and the authorization of employment of assistants in civil engineering and chemistry. The board voted to ask the next legislature for buildings for dairy husbandry and for civil and mechanical engineering. They authorized the first telephones for the college. Finally, they raised salaries; Fernald's to $3,000, the full professors to $1,800, and others in proportion. When they were through with their reallocations, the budget looked as follows:

Budget (1890-1891) Maine State College[21]

Agriculture and Dairy	3,000
Chemistry	1,200
Physics	1,000
Civil Engineering	1,500
Mechanical Engineering	1,500
Natural History	2,000
Library	3,000
Improve Farm	1,000
Oil Coburn Walks	100
Farm Furnace	150
Cement Cellar — Pres. (House)	150
Walks and Roads	300
Print, Bind Met Reports	50
Chairs — Recitation Room	100
Adv. *Industrial Journal*	10
Prof. Webb to Cornell	200
Heat Mech. Shop	245
Safe	250

This view was taken from atop the standpipe. It shows an excellent view of the farm fields and greenhouses. Note the two men working in the field. The president's house, with the familiar aspect of the cupola after the renovation, Holmes Hall and Coburn are also prominent in this photograph. The date of picture is apparently September, 1896.

By the next spring even more money was available; so the trustees moved to improve the grounds and the water supply, the latter by building a standpipe (on the present observatory site). The new mechanical engineering and civil engineering building plans were accepted; the dairy building authorized. By the end of Fernald's term the annual budgets had risen to nearly $110,000, with faculty salaries of $22,000. In 1891 the legislature refused a request for a new gymnasium for students; a building was converted to that use. In 1893 the board authorized expenditure of $2,500 to finish laying out the grounds according to a plan of the teacher of horticulture, Professor Munson. After the rebuilding of the president's house in 1893, following a June 11 fire, the older section of the campus must have looked much as it looks today.[22]

As the college grew physically, its curriculum and faculty underwent substantial changes. The various courses of study will be discussed later in this chapter, but this is an appropriate time to mention those faculty members who entered the service of the college in the period and remained to make a substantial mark on the school. In 1873 George H. Hamlin came to

teach engineering courses and remained until retirement in 1898. Alfred Aubert moved from Cornell in 1874 to teach chemistry until 1909. Allen Rogers, hired in 1879 to teach modern languages, was a campus fixture until 1908. Walter Balentine, the first professor of agriculture, taught until his unexpected death in the early 1890's. His wife, Elizabeth Abbott Balentine, for whom Balentine Hall is named, was to be extremely important in the next era of the college. After graduating in 1882, Walter "Jim" Flint became a part-time instructor, moving to full-time when he received an advanced degree in 1885. He remained on the faculty nearly to World War I, teaching mechanical engineering. C.H. Fernald was the first professor of natural history, until his departure in the late 1880's. His research, especially in entomology, set a high standard, both in that discipline and for the college as a whole. In 1887 the college hired James N. Hart, '85, whose career continued until World War II. He served as the college's first dean and as acting president. Hart lived into his mid-nineties and attended the dedication of Hart Hall in 1956. His talk at that dedication helped inspire this work. In 1891 Welton Munson was hired with the

Morrill land grant funds, as was Horace M. Estabrooke, '76. Others who made major contributions, particularly in agriculture, in this period, were the farm superintendent, Joseph Farrington, and Professors Lucius Merrill, 1887 to 1930; Fremont Russell, 1889 to 1932; and Winthrop Jordan '72 (1887-1896) at the experiment station. James Bartlett served the station as chemist from 1885 to 1926.

A letter authorizing the hiring of James N. Hart shows how faculty was assigned at this time.[23] Modern administrators may well envy the easy assignment of work loads as well as the salary demands.

> Mr. Hart should be engaged for two years $600 for first, $800 the second. Mr. Hart will have more to do than Mr. Goodridge (another new instr.) Will have to teach Alg., Geom., Trig., Anal. Geom., and calculus. Rhetoric for Professor Rogers and in the afternoon attend to drawing and field work as there shall be need.

The courses offered at the college, particularly during the first quarter century or so of its existence, often reflected both internal and external forces. When the school opened its doors in 1868, most of the students were presumed to be agricultural specialists. It soon became obvious from the demand for another course that this was not so. Almost immediately an elective course, generally known until the nineties as science and literature, was created. When Allen became president in 1871, changes were made and four courses were to be offered: agriculture, civil engineering, mechanical engineering, and the elective course. Unhappiness over these changes caused the resignations of Professors Peckham and Swift, as well as Johnson, the farm superintendent. When Aubert took Peckham's place in 1874 it was but a short time before a fifth course was added, chemistry. These courses remained essentially the same until 1893.

Admission requirements were modified soon after the opening of the school. As early as 1873, one professor wanted to change the condition of admission, "so as to bring up the standard," and thus allow the professional students the "opportunity to get some general culture." After a committee deliberated the question, more geometry was set as a requirement for admission. Rhetoric was added to the freshman year in place of rhetorical praxis, one

George Hamlin

Alfred Aubert

Allan Rogers

Walter Balentine

Walter 'Jim' Flint

C.H. Fernald

James N. Hart

James M. Bartlett

apparently the philosophic study, the other oration. Trigonometry became a sophomore subject, and two courses in English literature were added, one required and the other a senior elective.[24] By 1876 the admission examinations to be passed included arithmetic, grammar, geography, history, algebra, and geometry. In 1886 logarithms, bookkeeping, and physical geography were added. The sites of the examinations were increased to nine in 1883, ranging from Presque Isle and Pembroke to Biddeford. The age of earliest admission was raised from fifteen to sixteen in 1890.

In 1894 the college took the unusual step of granting admission without examination to graduates of selected secondary schools on the strength of the schools' curriculum. A circular was prepared laying out the college requirements and sent to all the state's high schools with the approval of the state superintendent of schools. A faculty committee visited the schools and inspected them closely; if the administration of the school changed, the school was forced to reapply. Students so admitted were on a semester trial and, if unsatisfactory, the privilege of admission without examination could be withdrawn from the school. This admission method, along with possible conditional admission in one or two subjects for those not scoring high enough in high school, remained the primary method for selection for a quarter of a century or more.[25]

When the college was young, the curriculum was simple and the hours of recitation were fixed and routine. The schedule indicates how the class day looked in the early 1870's.(Table 1)

Although the two semester system did not really begin until 1876, there was a change in the late spring (college went until mid-August in those days). (Table 2)

Table 1

Hour	Frosh	Soph	Junior	Senior
8:00	Algebra	French	Rhetoric	Mineralogy
9:00	Bookkeeping	Trig	Dis. Geom. or German	Mineralogy
10:00	Botany	Chemistry	Zoo. or Civil Eng.	Mental Phil. or Civil Eng.
11:00	Physics	Chemistry	Calculus	U.S. Constitution
1:30-3:30		Freehand or Mech. Drawing	Zoo. or Mech Drawing	Mech Drawing

Table 2

Hour	Frosh	Soph	Junior	Senior
8:00	Geom.	Surveying	Logic/Germ. Lit	
9:00	Botany	French	Calc. or Astronomy	Engineering/ Moral Philosophy
10:00		Eng. Lit./ Chem. Lab	Eng. Lit., Entom., Desc. Geom.	Geology
11:00	Physics	Chem. Lab	Mechanics	Political Economy
1:00-4:00	Labor	Draw/Surv.	Draw/Field Work	Drawing/Field Work

Courses were occasionally short, and where two are indicated in the same time period, the class would change in mid-semester to the other discipline. The third period of study began in July and it follows to complete the year's work for all classes.[26]

Table 3

Hour	Frosh	Soph	Junior	Senior
8:00	Rhetoric	Botany	Anal. Geom.	German/ Engineering
9:00		Geom.	French	Stereotyping
10:00	Algebra	Chem.	Physiology	Anal. Physiology/ Eng. Lit.
11:00	Phys. Geog.	Chem.	Engineering	Hist. of Civilization Eng./Astronomy

Students in the Physics laboratory in Wingate Hall. Photograph dates from the mid-90's. This may be an examination scene.

In 1876 the new course in chemistry was added. The first two years remained the same, but human anatomy and analytical chemistry (with recitation) were added for the first term in both the last two years of the course, along with a heavy emphasis on German in those years and some form of chemistry in each of the other two semesters.

Shopwork, added to the curriculum in 1876, was a feature taken from a Russian system of labor in education shown at the Centennial Exhibition and used both at Maine and M.I.T. No funds were provided for the shop, however, and in 1878 the mechanical engineering students let it be known that they would leave if the situation continued. Faculty and students started a fund. Governor Coburn gave $250, and a modest beginning was made with a room in the laboratory. Several pieces of student work were exhibited at the Portland State Fair where they won medals, and as a result of these successes a building was constructed in 1880.

The balance room where precise measurements were performed.

The life of students in courses was tightly organized, as a perusal of the rules governing the laboratory will indicate. It was open from 8:00 a.m. to midnight each day, under supervision, with a stiff schedule of fines for such matters as leaving gas unattended, water running, emptying acid into the sinks, failure to weigh properly, or to clean adequately. Those who did not stow their hats and coats were to be fined, and fines were made for visiting other tables overmuch, and finally "loud talking, singing, whistling, loitering, before, after or during exercises, and sitting on tables, are strictly forbidden."[27]

The two courses in civil and mechanical engineering were split in 1880, and a new professor was hired to develop the two engineering courses in a separate and distinct way.[28] Before, although technically different courses, they had been taught similarly and usually by the same people. Both courses stressed problem solving. After the move to two semesters in 1876, the trustees ended the undergraduate Civil Engineer and Mechanical Engineer (C.E. and M.E.) degrees, but ruled that after three years of practice in the field, with a thesis, the C.E. or M.E. degrees could be granted to holders of the B.C.E. or B.M.E. The C.E. and M.E. degrees were rough equivalents of graduate and professional degrees.[29]

The first electrical engineering shop.

A Master of Agriculture was also authorized, but no one ever received it. Other degree

Professor G.H. Hamlin's office, Wingate Hall. Dean Paul Cloke was a later occupant. The furniture was comfortable and the fireplace must have been welcome. A classroom appears through the open door.

holders could earn their advanced degrees with appropriate theses and professional work, after this period. General graduation requirements included a thesis, and the college faculty spent some time considering odd subjects but usually accepted them. These included phrenology and refutation of attacks on the college. Most subjects submitted were traditional, of course.[30]

Some indication of the way the college viewed itself and its courses is shown by the division of the appropriations by discipline. In 1877 chemistry received $500; mechanical engineering, $450; drawing, $100; physics, $350; natural history, $350; and agriculture, $250.[31]

Relatively few student materials from this era survive, but we can see a bit of what the school must have been like from the point of view of the undergraduate student from the effects of Edmund Abbott, B.S. Chemistry '76. He saved an autograph album; a notebook of natural science sketches, mostly watercolor; a notebook for geology; a detailed personal account book; chemistry notebooks with details of experiments; and a biology notebook with miscellaneous notes on reading, elocution, and pedagogy. On elocution, taught by a Mr. Hofman, he took only half a page of notes and then remarked, "Remainder of them were not taken and 'it was well.' " At the end of this notebook was included a "cure for drunkenness" which had had a "good recommendation in England." It called for five grams of sulphate of iron, one peppermint, eleven drachms of water, and one drachm of spirits of nutmeg. This draught was to be taken twice a day. To complete Abbott's profile, his junior thesis was on "Insanity," and his graduation thesis was entitled, "The East or the West."[32]

One of the forces that affected the curriculum of the college was the admission of women by provision of the legislature in 1872. The trustees immediately set up a committee "to prescribe such rules and regulations as they may deem necessary to secure the largest benefit to *them* consistent with the *general* interests of the col-lege."[33] By 1874 enough women had appeared so that the board ruled that no omission of regular studies could take place unless an equivalent course was substituted.

Between the entrance of the first woman to Maine in 1872 and the end of the century, only fifty-nine women attended the school. Of this group, twenty-nine graduated (three in science, one in chemistry, one with an LL.B., and the rest in the elective course), five received two-year certificates in library economy, and twenty-five did not graduate. The table indicates when these pioneers were at the university.[34]

Louise H. Ramsdell, '74
First Woman Student

WOMEN AT THE UNIVERSITY OF MAINE
1872-1900

Year of Graduation	Degrees (#'s)	Others Attending	Remarks
1872			
1873			
1874	1		
1875			
1876	1		
1877	2		
1878	1	1	Percia A. Vinal, M.S., '82 (first woman grad. degree)
1879	3		
1880	2		
1881	5	3	
1882			
1883	1		Jane C. Michaels, M.S., '94
1884	2	3	Harriet C. Fernald, M.S., '88
1885			
1886			
1887	1		Alice A. Hicks, M.S., '91
1888		2	
1889	2	1	One died while student
1890	1		
1891			
1892			
1893		1	
1894			
1895		6	2 libr. certs.
1896		1	libr. cert.
1897		2	libr. certs.
1898	3		2 sci.; 1 chemistry
1899	2	7	1 sci.
1900	2	3	1 LL.B. from Law School
Totals	29	30	

In addition to these degrees, in 1896 an honorary Master of Philosophy was granted to the noted Bangor educator, Mary Sophia Snow. She was the only woman to receive an honorary degree until the presidency of Clarence Cook Little, an advocate of women's rights. In 1924 Hilda Ives received an M.A.(H), in 1925 Ada Comstock an LL.D.(H), and in 1926 Kate Estabrooke an M.A.(H).

In the first years of women's attendance at the school the problem of course substitution was dealt with by the college in a very tentative way. The first woman, Louise Hammond Ramsdell, '74, was a friend of the Fernalds and transferred to Maine, living with the Fernalds as she had done at their earlier home. She received her degree with high marks and made little impact on the campus. The next woman, Florence Cowan, graduated with the class of 1876. With her, problems began. In 1873 the faculty ruled that she had to take the course on elements of agriculture, although Ramsdell had apparently not had to take the principles of anatomy, another requirement. In 1874 the faculty relented and excused Cowan from the course in surveying. In that same year, when the women (five were in attendance) began to question the usefulness of such courses as mechanical drawing and principles of agriculture, the faculty voted to turn to the trustees for a ruling. No action resulted, so the faculty decided to excuse Cowan from certain anatomy classes and later ruled that mechanical drawing was optional, but freehand drawing must be the substitute. By 1877, women of the class of 1880 were allowed to present general history in place of mechanical drawing, although the next year the option was freehand drawing and tinting. At first, history of England was allowed in lieu of agriculture, but that was soon withdrawn. In 1881 women were excused from taking cattle feeding on the grounds that it was useless for them and disagreeable to them; later a young woman was allowed to substitute French for farm drainage. Apparently very little other discrimination occurred, or at least none of the women remembered much. Most of them were coddled, living with faculty or at home, and their college experience did not really happen outside the classroom.[35]

As has been noted several times, the agricultural course remained controversial throughout this period. The college had been

Florence Cowan, '76   *Alicia Emery, '77*

Emma Brown, '78   *Annie Mae Gould, '79*

Nellie Holt, '79   *Percia Vinal, '79,*
M.S., '82

With one exception, these are the earliest women graduates after Ramsdell. The photographs are their graduation portraits.

founded in great part through the efforts of the farming interests, of whom many were upset when a large number of students chose not to take the farming programs. By 1878, when Winthrop H. Jordan was appointed instructor in agriculture, he found himself offering more of his time in "literary instruction" than in his specialty. Because of this he proposed a change in curriculum which was substantially granted by the trustees. Farm labor remained integral for these students, and new courses were offered: Qualitative Chemistry, Principles of Plant Feeding, Experimental Farming, Agricultural Engineering, and Farm Drainage.

In 1881 a dispute broke out in the agricultural press over the courses offered, and the faculty wrote letters to the *Maine Farmer* defending their position. The State Board of Agriculture took notice of the argument with remarks in the annual report such as, "The agricultural college is an outgrowth of the pressing need for liberally educated farmers. . . ." and "The future prosperity of agriculture demands that farmers provide the best possible educational advantage for their children." In the nineties this problem intensified, as some thought the college had not done enough, and others wanted to offer it encouragement to do more in agriculture. The

trustees asked the faculty to provide a general agricultural course for all students in the college. The final result was the establishment of a two-year course and various short courses in dairy husbandry, sheep husbandry, and other areas in an effort to change the student wishes. But the agriculture course, no matter how it was changed, remained the course least sought by undergraduates throughout the first quarter century of the college's existence.[36]

COURSES OF GRADUATES
UNIVERSITY OF MAINE 1872-1892

Year	Chem.	BCE	BME	Ag.	BSL	M.S.	C.E.	M.E.
1872		1		1	1		3	
1873					3		4	
1874					5		1	
1875				2	3		10	3
1876	4			2	14		7	7
1877	1	5	4		5			
1878	3	5	2		3			
1879	3	7	5	1	6			
1880	3	3		3	6			
1881	3	9	3	2	7	1		1
1882	2	5	4	5	5	2	2	
1883	4	5	1	1	3	2	2	1
1884	1	5	1	3	2	1	2	
1885	3	5	4	3	1	2	3	2
1886	3	10	3			1	1	
1887	2	10	4	1	1	1		1
1888	5	6	6	4	1	4	1	2
1889	3	4	2	2	3	1	4	3
1890	5	13	15	4	1	1	5	1
1891	5	8	6	2	2	2	1	
1892	1	9	7			5	1	
1893	2	7	4	3	1	4	4	1
1894	2	7	7		1	1	2	3
1895	1	12	5		1	1	2	3
1896	1	14	10	1		1	1	
Totals	57	150	93	40	75	30	56	28

In 1895 and 1896 one person graduated with a B.Sc. degree. Through 1876 the degrees of C.E. and M.E. were undergraduate degrees, and if those are added to the undergraduate total, the first twenty-five graduating classes chose their careers in the following way:

175	Bach. of Civil Engineering (BCE)
103	Bach. of Mechanical Engineering (BME)
75	Bach. of Science & Literature (BSL)
57	Bach. of Chemistry (BCh.)
40	Bach. of Agriculture (BAg)
450	

Marcia Davis, '80

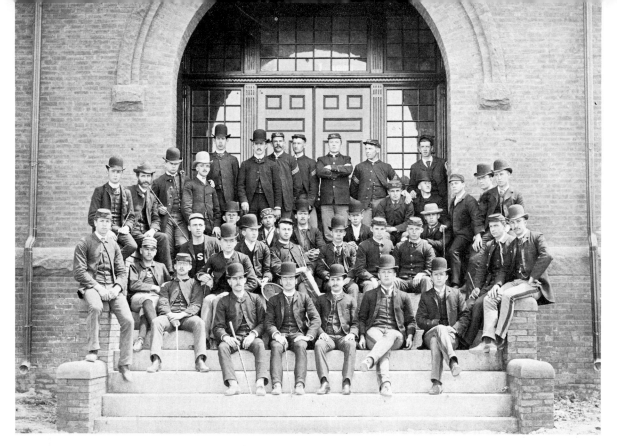

The class of 1890. Student clothing, here as always, has the appearance of a prescribed formula. Some appear in their cadet uniforms.

The elective course, the alternative to agriculture, also created difficulties almost as soon as it was instituted. In 1874, for instance, several students wished to modify it and substitute history for quantitative analysis. The faculty sent the president to talk with them, and the matter was tabled for a time. At the end of the year the faculty also discussed the elective course. One professor (Pike) thought it much too loose and undefined, giving students too much liberty and causing them to choose their courses unwisely and without system. He proposed a definite course in science and literature and a course in chemistry. M.C. Fernald defended the course, but the other faculty were divided. The chemical course was soon established, and in the next year the elective course students were required to register their choice of subjects with the faculty secretary before the term began. When the courses were modified greatly in 1876, the students presented a petition requesting retention of the science and literature option as they "objected to being obliged to take an agricultural course when they did not intend to become farmers." The petition was granted.[37]

Still controversy hung on, and in 1878 the faculty tentatively eliminated the science and literature and the chemistry courses, both principally attended by women. Changes proposed by the faculty included substitution of history of England for surveying, for women, and astronomy and agricultural chemistry for astronomy and mechanics in the junior year. Astronomy was the women's elective. In the last year they wanted dairy farming, stock breeding, and cultivation of cereals for one course, with women allowed to substitute logic. Men were no longer to be taught logic, but were to take applied mechanics and agricultural engineering instead. Also, in the senior year, were added landscape gardening, sheep husbandry, and care and feeding of domestic animals as a new course. Rural architecture, along with lectures in veterinary science, horticulture, and arboriculture were to replace mental and moral science. These changes were discussed for over a year, but the trustees would not provide the necessary faculty so the original courses remained with only cosmetic changes. Eventually the science and literature students were allowed to replace plant feeding with English history, some other agricultural studies with inductive logic, and agricultural chemistry with descriptive astronomy. Agriculture and civil engineering students were encouraged to add forge work to their courses at about the same time. [38] After this, the curriculum remained the same until the mid-nineties.

Other subjects also were areas for experiment. In 1880 the trustees allowed "a lady from the Provinces" to provide a class in shorthand "providing it do not interfere with the student's regular work." Other special courses were offered in reading and photography. Eventually such courses were to lead to the university's extension program, although that was primarily agricultural in nature. [39]

As the college grew in size, the library became more and more important to students and faculty. At first it consisted of a few gift books and the Fernalds' personal library, but in 1872 the college purchased the library of Ezekiel Holmes and in 1876 it was given the library of the Bangor Mechanics Association on condition that volumes be retained unless duplicates were received. Abner Coburn gave funds at various times: $500 in 1873 to be split

President's office, Coburn Hall basement. The painting is of President Allen.

one half for general literature, $100 for *Appleton's Encyclopedia,* $100 for natural history, and the rest for general books. Others donated $100 for physics and civil engineering volumes.

In the early days library circulation was limited, but M.C. Fernald, C.H. Fernald, and Farrington, the farm superintendent, were steady borrowers. A small room located in one of the recital halls, the library was open only two hours a day until the nineties. Professors Aubert and Hamlin did not use the library much, if at all. The first librarian, C.H. Fernald, asked to be relieved in 1873, and in the next years the faculty passed the responsibility around. In the middle eighties Allen Rogers was sent out to solicit contributions of books and money and was successful enough in his work that in 1887 M.C. Fernald, Hamlin, and an assistant spent some time cataloging holdings. In that year the college spent $600 on new books, about what it would spend annually throughout the Fernald administration. In 1890 Harriet C. Fernald, daughter of the president, was appointed librarian and served for some years in that position. Later, Ralph Kneeland Jones, '86, was to serve as the college librarian for a long period. [40]

The Maine State College became famous, along with Cornell, for its student labor system inaugurated when the college opened. Designed to cut the cost of education as well as to train young people in the general idea of work, this system lasted in some form until the raising of tuition in 1881. It deserves a close look as an effort to make the college more democratic and more responsive to the needs of the type of people coming to the college for training. Labor was a college obligation and grades were given for it as for any subject. At first, the college labor course was organized into three departments: Agricultural, under the farm superintendent; horticultural, under the instructor in botany, horticulture, and landscape gardening; and the special department, under "competent student control." The special department made compost, conducted experiments, carried mail, arranged exhibits, tended fires, and so on. Entomological specimen collection was also included here. [41] Veterans of the student workers in the 1930's and 1960's will recognize the germs of their programs.

The library, Coburn Hall, about 1895. Those in this obviously posed photograph are, left to right, Prof. Horace Estabrooke, '76, M.S., '84, Frank Damon, '95; Prof. Allen Rogers, and Harriet C. Fernald, '84; M.S., '88. The painting of President Allen appears on the wall in this photograph.

Soon it became necessary to outline the rules of labor closely. A committee of trustees wrote a set of regulations and published them for students. All were to be ready to perform three hours of labor for each of the five work days of the week. A warning bell was struck at 12:45 p.m. and a work bell at 1:00 p.m. each day. Three hours later a quitting bell rang. Labor was to cease then, not before. Student captains in the special departments were in charge of the labor to be performed. Each student was responsible for his own reports and care of

tools. During work hours students were to refrain from ''unnecessary, continued or boisterous conversation, or noise of any kind, and from every act . . . calculated . . . to disturb or interfere with the successful progress of any student's work.'' Play, sport, and horseplay, especially about the buildings, gardens, and lawns, was forbidden. Demerits were handed out for transgressions. The special department was something of a plum for upper-classmen and for those who were particularly well behaved. Students did receive compensation, at a rate determined by the faculty and based upon their grades, with a maximum of ten cents per hour. At their conclusion the rules read,

> It is expected that both officers and students will faithfully endeavor to promote the moral as well as the mental and physical well being of all connected with the College, and cultivate a feeling of interest in and responsibility for the advancement and prosperity of the Institution.[42]

There was much work to be done at the college. In the fall of 1871 students worked about 150 hours for the farm superintendent. Jobs included taking up a carpet in the farmhouse, picking stones from the lawn, plowing fields, and scraping to level the college lawn. The next spring they stoned the cellar of the president's house and graded the lawn there, as well as laying turf and plowing. The following fall they put sawdust banking around the dormitories and the president's house as part of their stint.[43]

As the number of students increased, work was not available for all. In 1874 upperclassmen did only surveying and lab work. Pay by this time was based upon "fidelity and efficiency," but grades were based only on fidelity. By 1875 the labor requirement had to be reinforced as off-campus students were not participating. Finally, when tuition was raised in 1881, the faculty ruled that labor was to be continued only insofar as it was of an instructional nature.[44]

With this ruling the labor experience ended. It was not a failure, but it simply could not be applied on such a large scale. It seemed to have worked very well when the college was young and so much needed to be done to make it look presentable.

Another program which seemed at first to be outliving its usefulness was military drill. The school had been founded in a wartime atmosphere, but when that disappeared, as it had by 1880, the necessity of the drill program was questioned. One or two of the instructors were very unpopular, but also the small size of the school made the War Department hesitate to send officers to such a detachment. Initially the students were taught by local volunteers, and many times no drill was performed at all in the 1870's. By the 1880's the trustees were more desirous of complying with the law and petitioned the War Department to supply them with of-

ficers. In fact, a special diploma was authorized for extra study and proficiency in such matters as the makeup of European armies, the U.S. Army regulations, field fortifications, field service and operations of war, as well as campaigns and modern weapons.

Eventually those officers posted to the campus were more popular, and in the nineties the trustees even sent one of them, perhaps the best liked, Mark Hersey, to Harvard to take a course in physical culture. On returning he acted as general faculty manager of athletics, and supervised the new gymnasium.[45]

This college that we have been describing was very much the creation of President M.C. Fernald. He was discouraged at some points in his tenure. The failure to raise a larger endowment was a problem for him, although the Coburn bequest certainly was a major achievement. On at least one occasion he nearly gave up hope for the school, as when he told Lyndon Oak, "I was too much worn and in need of rest to attempt anything active in the vacation beyond what I was obliged to do. Any time I could work was fully taken."[46] However, when offered another presidency in the West a few years later, he said, "I have concluded to still share the fortunes (I trust that they may not be misfortunes) of this college and have written to Iowa to this effect."[47] His educational philosophy, his research, and his work for the schools founded under the Morrill act all made him a strong leader for the young school. However, the college changed so greatly that by the early nineties pressure built up for Fernald to resign. The issue was brought to a boil when the Western Maine alumni held two meetings, in February and May of 1892. A resolution was adopted calling for a special meeting of the board of trustees to discuss the decreasing enrollment and the prejudicial statements "widely circulating" about the college. The alumni believed that a crisis was at hand. The special board meeting was held at Waterville where an alumni committee presented its views and called for Fernald's resignation. The president heard of the meeting and offered his resignation to the board at that time. It was accepted, effective July 1, 1893, at the board's next meeting, in Orono, three weeks later.

Throughout the fall meetings were held, and at one time a vote was called asking Fernald to

This charming print appeared originally in a history of Penobscot County in 1882. From a different vantage point than is usual, the college buildings, Brick Hall, White Hall, Fernald Hall, the shops, and the farm buildings may all be located in the background. The cadet troop drilling in the foreground would have reassured readers, most of whom would remember the Civil War. The inset of the college farm features the commodious and controversial barn.

withdraw his resignation. The motion failed and the search for a new president went on. The position was offered to Seldon Connors of Portland, with Fernald to become professor of mathematics and astronomy. Connors refused, others were canvassed, and further lengthy discussion followed, but contrary to rumor "no vote whatever" was taken. Eventually Abram Winegardner Harris took the job.

Fernald spent a year in Dover, returned, and served out a long career as professor of philosophy and mathematics.[48] When he retired in 1908, the university gave him an honorary LL.D. and made him an emeritus professor. He continued to teach occasionally. After seeing the first history of the institution through the press, his life came to an end in 1916.

The issue at hand in Fernald's resignation was the future of the school. Fernald did not see it as clearly or as widely as some of the alumni and trustees. The new president, Harris, did, and his term of office and that of his successor were to be taken up in seeking the broadening of the institution that these groups wanted. At the end of a quarter of a century the college had come of age.

Notes

1. *Legislative Documents, 1880,* H.D., 95; H.D. 110; *1881,* S.D., 65; *1883,* S.D. 22; 30; *1885,* S.D. 36; *Laws of Maine,* 1881, Ch. 13, Ch. 60, *1883,* Ch. 89, Ch. 96, Ch. 130, Ch. 196 (adding an alumni member to the board of trustees); *Public Documents of Maine,* 1881, Harris Plaisted's *address* to the legislature, 1883, Frederick Robie's *address,* 186-7, 199-200.

2. *Laws of Maine,* 1885, Ch. 196; Robie's *address,* 301-2; *Leg. Doc.,* S.D. 36.

3. *Laws of Maine,* 1887, Ch. 54; 105; 119; *Address* of Governor Bodwell, 79-81; *Leg. Docs.,* Senate Doc., 18, S.D. 52.

4. H. Docs., *1889,* 299; Sen. Docs., *1889,* 80, 102; Sen. Docs., *1891,* 59; *Laws of Maine, 1889,* Ch. 226, 229; Burleigh's *Address, 1889,* 142-3; *Laws of Maine, 1891,* Ch. 23, 284, also 43, Burleigh's *Address,* 1891, 137-8; *Laws of Maine, 1893,* Ch. 178; Leg. Docs., *1893,* H.D. No. 198 gives an account of all appropriations from 1868 to 1892 year by year. On the fire, Faculty Minutes, February 10, August 10, 1890. The fire escapes were knotted ropes, students were the hose company members. See R.K.J. (Ralph Kneeland Jones) '86 to editors, *Cadet,* May 1889 on recent legislative activity.

5. Trustee Minutes, Augusta, January 31, 1872; November 24, 1885; Faculty Minutes, September 12, 1881; *Cadet,* November 4, 1887 for report on Fernald's trip and election; *Agriculture of Maine,* 1872, his report on first convention held.

6. *Agriculture of Maine,* 1872, M.C. Fernald, "Protection from Lightning"; *College Reporter,* Vol. 1, No. II, November 14, 1874, "Scientific Observations on Mount Katahdin;" U.S. Bureau of Education, Circular No. 3, 1903 *Contr. to Amer. Educ. Hist.* No. 36, E.W. Hall, *History of Higher Education in Maine,* Fernald wrote Chapter VII on UMO. Also see article in *New England Magazine,* April-May, 1887. The exchange in *Lewiston Journal* began July 17, 1885, and was finished in the *Cadet,* August 28, 1885, from where the quotation is taken.

7. Recollections of James Gannett, delivered in a speech in 1922; *Cadet,* October, 1892, for their solution; letter, Abram Harris' file, Oliver Crosby, St. Paul, Minnesota, to E.A. Balentine, December 11, 1901.

8. Trustees Minutes, June 27, November 28, 1882; April 24, June 6, September 4 (Special, Bangor), November 27, 1883.

9. Trustees Minutes, November 23, 1880; April 7, November 22, (Bangor), 1881; June 27, 1882. It was not until the 1930's that faculty were freely allowed to live outside Orono, in fact, although campus residency was removed as the size of the faculty grew.

10. Trustees, June 23, 1884; Letter Fernald to Oak, December 4, 1884.

11. Faculty Minutes, August 28, September 4, 11, 1876; April 14, 1884, petition from students, November 15, 1886, another student petition on janitorial salaries. Letter Fernald to Oak, March 21, 1885.

12. Mortgages on Hallowell Classical Academy, January 1, 1882; Fernald to Oak, February 26, 1882; Joshua Nye to Oak, February 10, 1882; A.M. Robinson to Oak, February 17, 1882; W.P. Hubbard to Wingate, February 9, 1882; Fernald to Oak, February 28, 1885; Chase to ? (illegible), May 25, 1888; Memorial to Congr. Churches, June, 1888; Trustees Minutes, March 31, 1887; June 26, 1888. They received 50% on the bonds, see minutes, March 22, 1889.

13. Fernald to Oak, February 28, 1885.

14. Trustees, November 25, 1884; June 23, 1885; March 31, 1887; June 26, 1888; Fernald to Oak, September 18, 1885 (quote on wells), April 17, 1888.

15. *Dedication of Coburn Hall,* Orono, 1888. *Maine Farmer,* June 28, 1888. Oak died on February 17, 1902 and the *Maine Campus* March 1, 1902 has an informative obituary with a comment from M.C. Fernald.

16. Maine *Leg. Docs.,* 1883, Sen. No. 15; *Laws of Maine, 1885,* Ch. 294; *Agriculture of Maine,* 1885, 254-6; 329-332; *Agriculture of Maine,* 1887, M.C. Fernald, "The Experiment Station and its Work," 20-25; Trustees Minutes, June 28, 1887.

17. Trustees Minutes, Bangor, February 16, 1888; March 23, 1889; June 25, 1889; Experiment Station Report Annual Meeting, March 5, 1890; *Agriculture of Maine,* 1888, Annual Report, Station, 1888; with sketches, 1889, D.H. Knowlton, 108-115; 1891, 24-31 (good photos).

18. This is covered in detail in Report of the *Special Committee to Investigate the Course of the Outbreak of Disease Among the Cattle at the State College Farm, the Loss and Disposal of Cattle Therefrom and the Doings and Correspondence of the Commissioners on Contagious Diseases Among Cattle in Relation to the Same, Together, With the Testimony Taken Before the Committee,* Sprague, and Nash, Augusta, 1887. Also see "Majority Report of the Commissioners for Maine on Contagious Diseases of Animals," 63rd Leg., Sen. Doc., No. 26, 1887 (66 pps), and detailed correspondence reprinted in there from which this story has been taken largely. Trustees Minutes, June 28, November 22, 1887; November 27, 1888; March 23, 1889. Later, in 1897 another tubercular cow was discovered, and although she caused anxious moments, the case was isolated

and did not figure in the earlier difficulties. C.D. Woods to A.W. Harris, November 26, 1897 (in Trustees letter November 27, 1897).

19.   Fernald to Oak, May 24, 1887.

20.   Trustees, November 5 (Bangor), November 6, 1890.

21.   Trustees Minutes, November 6, 1890.

22.   Trustees Minutes, April 10, April 22 (Bangor), November 24, 1891, June 28, November 9, (Bangor), 1892; March 21, May 11, February 21 (Bangor), 1893.

23.   Fernald to Oak, December 27, 1886. One might add that Hart would also help mold the college into the University of our time before he was finished.

24.   Faculty Minutes, March 3, 10, 1873.

25.   Faculty Minutes, June 26, 1876; June 14, 1880; March 5, 1883; April 2, 1894; Trustees Minutes, November 23, 1886; November 6, 1890.

26.   Faculty Minutes, February 5, April 21, July 12, 1873.

27.   Rules of the Laboratory of the Maine State College . . ., S.F Peckham, January 16, 1871.

28.   *Dedication of Coburn Hall,* Lyndon Oak's history, 8-29; Fernald to Oak, August 4, 14, 1880; Trustees Minutes, April 25, 1878; November 18, 1879; November 23, 1880.

29.   Faculty Minutes, July 13, 1874; Trustees (Orono Town Hall), August 5, 1874; August 1, 1876; November 22, 1876; *Maine State College, Course on Elementary Mechanical Drawing,* Tolman and White, Boston, 1875, standard problems, followed by such items as roof truss, v-threaded screws, and square-threaded screws.

30.   Faculty Minutes, July 27, 1874; April 10, 1876; March 12, 1877.

31.   Faculty Minutes, February 12, 13, 1877.

32.   His manuscripts are in the Class of 1876 materials, Fogler Library, Special Collections Room. Another good source is the J.W. Weeks '77 Diary.

33.   Trustees Minutes, March 13, 1872; *Laws of Maine,* 1872.

34.   *Alumni Directory, University of Maine,* Orono, 1952. The best accounts of the first women at Maine occur in a lecture by Ava Chadbourne "Maine Co-Eds of the 1870's and 1880's," undated, but after 1952, and an extension of this article into two, "Pioneering Co-Eds", and "Maine Co-Eds Few and Far Between in 80's, 90's", *Portland Sunday Telegram,* July 1956; September 16, 1956, (Clippings in my possession). Photos of the first 16 illustrate these articles which deal mostly with their later lives.

35.   Trustees Minutes, November 18, 1874; Faculty Minutes, September 14, 1873; April 20, October 5, November 17, 1874; July 26, 1875; February 7, 1876; February 6, 1877; February 18, 1877 (November 19, 1877 on Hy of Eng.); February 7, August 22, 1881.

36.   Report of Jordan to President, 1878; New Agricultural Curriculum, 1879; 1881; 1890; 1893-4; Faculty Minutes, March 28, 1881 for letter writing to *Farmer* in response to articles throughout March, April, 1881; *Agriculture of Maine,* 1882, p. 80, 87-8 for quotes; *Agriculture of Maine,* 1890, I.O. Winslow, "Education for Farmers," 55-65; 1891, 120-152 on Dairyman's meetings, and especially 151, 152. A.M. Robinson to Lyndon Oak, February 21, 25, 1884; Trustees Minutes, Bangor, November 9, 1892.

37.   Faculty Minutes, February 16, 1874.

38.   Faculty Minutes, June 15, 22, July 13, 1874; July 26, 1875; November 20, 1876; April 18, 22, May 20, 1878; October 30, November 17, 1879; March 14, 1881; April 17, May 1, November 20, 1882. See the daily calendars in Chapter V. For a student view of the changes *College Review,* Vol. 1-No. 1-4 [April 1876-1877].

39.   Faculty Minutes, November 8, 1880, on shorthand; Faculty Minutes, December 19, 1892 for a proposed outline of extension; Trustees Minutes, November 24, 1891 for reading and photography.

40.   Trustees Minutes, March 13, 1872; August 1, November 22, 1876; November 25, 1884; November 22, 1887; November 6, 1890; Faculty Minutes, February 17, March 24, April 7, 1873, October 26, 1885, March 5, 1888; *Cadet,* March 1891; A notebook showing library circulation beginning August 27, 1870.

41.   Broadside, "Organization of Labor," approximately 1868, but undated. This document also lays out responsibility of the faculty members involved, as to annual reports and so on. The farm superintendent was charged with "requir[ing] of the students propriety of deportment," while the head of the Horticulture department was charged "to strive to cultivate, in the students, a love and taste for the beautiful and the ornamental."

42.   Broadside, "Labor Regulations of the Maine State College of Agriculture and the Mechanic Arts," approximately 1870, signed by Lyndon Oak, S.L. Goodale, and S.F. Perley.

43.   Ledger sheets, "Statement of A/C Between Farm and the Other Departments, Jan. 1, 1873."

44.   President's annual report, 1874; Faculty Minutes, July 28, 1873; August 27, September 6, 1875; March 28, April 4, 1881.

45.   Trustees Minutes, April 24, 1878; June 27, 1882; November 27, 1883; May 11, 1893 — Military will appear in another connection soon.

46.   Fernald to Oak, April 15, 1879; May 24, June 4, August 4, 14, 1880 (the last quote).

47.   Fernald to Oak, December 19, 1884.

48.   Trustees Minutes, June 7, 1892; Fernald's resignation was dated May 13, 1892; June 26, 29, December 9, 1892 (Waterville); February 21, 1893 (Bangor). On Fernald's new duties see Fernald to A.W. Harris August 8, 14, 22, 1896; Harris to Fernald August 11, September 9, 1896. When Fernald left he apparently took his papers with him, for none survive. Those used occur in other places, especially in Lyndon Oak's file. Fernald reported at length on his European tour, *The Maine Campus,* December 21, 1909, 133-136. When Fernald died in 1916, the faculty reviewed his career and passed a resolution saying, "His energy, courage, patience, persistence, careful economy, and tact in dealing with people were vital factors during years of misunderstanding, hostility and meager resources." Fernald attended every commencement from 1872-1915. Faculty Minutes, March 13, 1916.

CHAPTER THREE

Making a University

IN THE FIRST QUARTER CENTURY of the college's existence, emphasis was on the establishment of a stable school, with a modest curriculum, good faculty, and the necessary buildings. The following years sought to extend the college in new directions, to establish, in fact, a university. By the early 1890's, additional funds provided by the federal government and an increasingly strong and vocal alumni group supported a campaign to create a university in place of the college. The new president, Abram W. Harris, former director of the Office of Experiment Stations in Washington, apparently took the task as his charge. The campaign, a difficult one and one that created many enemies, was successful by 1897.

The opposition to change was immediate, although subdued at first. It soon surfaced with a full-fledged assault led by President Hyde of Bowdoin and some legislators in Augusta. The ensuing battle was very hard fought, but the university won through, and although some attacks were to continue at least through the 1920's, the opponents were never again in a position to put the complete quietus on the school. No sooner was the battle for a university won than a controversy between the president, faculty, and student body led to a major crisis, followed by a student strike.

When the student conflict was finally resolved, the university, under President Harris' successor, could look toward a future with few of the major irritants that plagued its first half century of life. It had achieved its modern situation and could look forward to sustained growth — growth only diminished by the exigencies of national and international economic and political affairs.

Upon his arrival at Maine, direct from the experiment station position in Washington, President Harris found what one press observer, Wallace R. Farrington, called "general apathy" toward the college. Farrington, later a distinguished governor of Hawaii, asked for a student to be named as local reporter for his journal in an effort to drum up newspaper interest in the school. He said, "Most of the papers don't care whether the boys remain dormant or not . . . . The whole institution might dry up and blow away for all the newspapers of this section [Rockland and the coast] might learn."[1] Harris began to remedy the situation almost immediately. To still opposition, if there were any there, he spoke before the State Board of Agriculture, mentioning the idea of changing the college to a university. He began speaking of this idea elsewhere also. The agricultural interests in the state, frightened of losing control and perhaps of having the agricultural course diminished, descended on Harris personally and by letter.

Z.A. Gilbert, now editing the *Maine Farmer,* wrote a six-page letter to put forth his point of view. In it he rehearsed the struggle for the independence of the school, pointing out that liberal appropriations had come from farming interests. Gilbert felt that the time was ripe for extraordinary efforts in the cause of agricultural education, and "if there must be retrenchment let [it] *now* fall elsewhere." Gilbert went on to call attention to the *Farmer's* role in mobilizing public sentiment and remarked that he had been assured that Harris would agree with his view once he had observed the record more closely.[2] Others urged Harris to make his statements on agriculture "more direct and emphatic" if he wished success with the legislature.[3]

Alumni, not as interested in agriculture, exulted over the growth that seemed on the horizon. When one of them wrote asking Harris to attend a big alumni meeting in New York during April

1895, he closed his invitation with the words, "We want to hear about the 'boom' that our college is enjoying, from someone who has been on the campus during the past year."[4]

And a boom was underway. A bill was offered in the House that would have granted the college the proceeds of a special and permanent tax of one-tenth mill on each dollar of property valuation in the state. The bill did not pass, as it came as something of a surprise, but it indicated future strengths. The governor, Henry B. Cleaves, noted the tremendous growth of the school with double the number of students, as well as new courses in electrical engineering and pharmacy, but the legislature was not yet prepared to go the route of a mill tax. Instead $20,000 was provided for each year of the biennium, most of the funds being allotted for new construction. While the legislature debated these bills and the future of the college, the battle foreseen in the previous year's correspondence broke out in full force. When the Board of Agriculture met in Augusta just as the

Abram W. Harris

legislature was convening, the first item of debate was membership on the experiment station council. The secretary of the board, B. Walker McKeen, who served on the council, called for someone else to serve. This was endorsed by a second speaker, who said McKeen was the best choice, but "the college has lacked for sympathy in some parts of the State, and would it not be better to take a man from some other part of the State?" The other part of the state would be Cumberland County. McKeen was returned by vote; but the discussion of the issue pointed up the controversy. After the meeting the group, along with the legislative committees on the college, on agriculture, and on education, chartered a special train to go to Orono and inspect the college.[5]

When the committees returned to Augusta they reported the mill tax out of committee with an "ought to pass" recommendation. William Haines, '76, who had taken his B.S. in the elective course, acted as floor manager in the House for the college. He made the first speech, comparing the amounts given MSC with those received by colleges in other states. The bill was tabled, however, and a substitute offered to provide $25,000 annually for ten years. It was amended to $10,000 for two years with strong opposition speeches given by members from southern Maine who dwelt on the cost of the college in relation to the cost of normal schools. These spokesmen raised the question of the college's purpose, and asked why the school should not stick to its original goals. Haines then spoke again and offered an amendment to raise the figure to $15,000 for one year and $10,000 for the next. The bill passed by a vote of 77 to 48 and was sent to the Senate.

In the Senate there was very strong opposition. Senator Wiggin of Aroostook County offered the strongest defense of the college. Several votes were taken; the Senate turned down $15,000 for each year and, by a vote of 13-8, also defeated $25,000 for two years. Finally $40,000 for the biennium was generally agreed to, and the bill was tabled. Later a corridor agreement was apparently made to raise the figure to $25,000 annually again, and this passed 20-7. When the latest amount came back to the House, it was tabled for a week. During this time debate was shrill outside the legislature. The bill finally was passed, but was then recalled, and when discussed was tabled

President's office, Coburn basement, with Harris at work at his desk. The furnishings, especially the oriental rugs, are more opulent than in Fernald's time. Fernald wrote his own letters. Harris had a secretary, also seen, and most letters were typed.

pending the budget hearings. Finally, on March 9, the bill passed providing $20,000 for each year of the biennium.[6]

The failure to achieve more in the legislature led to recriminations. Z.A. Gilbert was convinced that Haines had let the university forces down in order to preserve his own political ends. As the editor said, "So he has given away ten thousand dollars, imposed upon the Committee by treating us as a [surrenitity?] and by this course inferentially carrying us around in his pocket to do his bidding when he wanted anything but to be ignored where his ends to be served."[7] This may or may not be true; there is no evidence to support Gilbert's position. Although many contemporaries felt the amount achieved was the maximum possible, they also felt the debate had been damaging and began to look for another method of financing the school, one which would avoid an unpleasant argument every other spring.

In July there was a long discussion as to how the legislative dispute might be bypassed, an attempt to provide a plan "that shall relieve you

of the *humiliating duty. . .* of the biennial legislative mangle." Harris unwisely had no plan, other than the mill tax, although he did not give up completely.[8] In fact, he continued to put out his gospel about the purposes of the college primarily to the audience most difficult to reach, the farmers. As he said on one such occasion, "The first mission of the State of Maine, its agriculture, and its State College, is not the upbuilding of the material interests we call Maine . . . but rather to start in the right way our boys and girls. . . ." This sort of comment did lead to some increase in scholarship funds but not much else.[9]

It was obvious that the next, 1897, session of the legislature would be very important. In the summer of 1896 Harris took a long vacation to prepare himself for the ordeal. The college remained in the capable hands of Elizabeth Balentine, faculty secretary, but Harris would be the key upon his return. The legislature sponsored a special committee to make a major visit in order to deal with the problem of support. The committee members were to arrive on the campus in

October 1896, and were to stay two or three days. Harris attempted to get trustees to join him in the meeting. Haines, however, thought that trustees were not important, since he regarded the visit as an insult, and for his part he would "risk you with the crowd." Harris, in the event, did a good job, supplying information to the committee and sending them follow-up letters after their visit.[10]

He also began to put together a campaign with the goal of promoting acceptance of his idea of a university. Dynamic speakers such as W.R. Pattangall, '84, went on the stump in Washington County, along with Samuel Libbey of Orono. Libbey said in a letter to Harris, "Now I want some more data for use at Corinna Sat. next when the College is to be attacked, vigorously, *because* it does not 'turn out' more farmers and because the Experiment Station is run by the U.S. govt. and is not part of the College!" Others, such as F.O. Beal, mayor of Bangor, joined the campaign. Apparently Harris held a banquet at the college for his local supporters in late November 1896. Both Pattangall and Beal were invited, and Pattangall thought the atmosphere there good.[11]

Outside the college Harris also brought up his big guns. He wrote to presidents of other schools. Thomas F. Hunt, Ohio State, W.A. Henry, Wisconsin, and I.P. Roberts, Cornell, were among those who responded immediately. Henry, for instance, said, "I do not think farmers should grow up to be a distinct class from our other citizens either in dress, habits of thought, expression, wants, or otherwise, and an agricultural college that truely does its work will help break down all tendencies toward exclusiveness or separation."[12]

Harris was so cheered by Henry's comments that he wrote a long letter detailing his problems. Claiming that when the term "agricultural college was heard one could be sure that an enemy had announced himself," Harris thought his Station Council was working behind his back to sabotage his efforts. As he said, when this occurred he thought of Henry, and a thing Henry "said at the Knoxville convention. . . . In describing your work you said that almost every man who came to look over your dairy would ask how much it cost to make a pound of butter. You said, 'I believe in knocking that kind of man down at the first blow and I will tell him it costs $5.00 a pound, and then

we come down to business.' " Harris went on to say that he was determined to "knock them down" in Maine and that he was "determined to assert our rights to that field or any other field, if the good of the State demands it."[13]

Harris spared no attempts to support his side, and he scored one early coup when he was able to get Senator Justin Morrill, father of the act that established the agricultural colleges, to comment. Morrill, in a letter to A.C. True of the United States Department of Agriculture which was sent to Harris, said that the first act was designed to provide for education in all ways, and then went on with words that Harris was to use again and again all spring.

> I would hope that no farmer or mechanic would be so illiberal as to wish to have the monopoly of education in any of those Land Grant Colleges. It will do the professional students good to be educated side by side with those who expect to obtain a living by labor.[14]

When the legislature met in January 1897, the sides were set and ready for battle. Bills were filed calling for a mill tax and for changing the name from Maine State College to University of Maine. One bill called for giving graduates of the state college the same rights and professional privileges as the graduates of other schools in the state; what these rights and privileges are no one seems to know now, nor did they then. The governor was guarded but optimistic in his speech, although he did not advocate the change of name. Early reports were pessimistic, but Harris, who took up station in the Augusta House, wrote to Elizabeth Balentine, "Do not be frightened by the report. We are going to make a grand fight. The Committee is with us to a man and the report is calling out our friends. I begin to enjoy things."[15]

After these opening feints the committee again went to Orono to visit. All was prepared for their arrival. Isaiah Stetson of the trustees wrote that between ninety and one hundred members of the House were coming. He hoped the university had all details covered as he said:

> We will [?] you from Waterville. Do not forget to have some cigars for the boys at the lunch and at the banquet. They will pay better attention to what you say if they have a good cigar.

The governor's council had been critical of some aspects of the proposed changes, so Harris addressed himself primarily to these

Wingate Hall in its original form. The tower was a casualty of a fire in 1946.

criticisms in his speech at the banquet. Fortified by their cigars, the legislators heard Harris open deceptively with comments on state lands, the fact of the experiment station being a separate entity, and a warning to legislators not to make comparisons with Massachusetts. He then shifted to discuss science and engineering, pointing out the great growth in manufacturing in the United States. He said the college still held to its original designs, but that programs like medicine and pharmacy were necessary. Laboratories cost money, but duty to students overrode the cost. He went on, saying that even though many thought the school expensive, it had, in fact, spent less money from 1867 to 1896 than reform schools in Maine, normal schools in Maine, or the Massachusetts Agricultural College. Then Harris moved on to discuss the real meat of his address. Permanent appropriations were necessary, along with free, or nearly free, tuition; it was up to the legislators to allow the poor to go to college. Saying Maine had not progressed and making a comparison with the South, he remarked, ". . . we are forced to the

conclusion that so far as higher education is concerned, Maine is almost the worst state in the Union for a white boy to be born in." Moving from this to a discussion of other state universities, he said that Maine men graduating from college would be more useful to society, and that they would be no competition to other colleges, and especially Bowdoin, in the state. Finally he touched chords these men must have recognized. For him, the message in the books of Elijah Kellogg, the great Maine juvenile author, were among the reasons he had gone to college, and he wanted that opportunity for everyone. Kellogg had advocated education as the best device to make society good for all persons. We are, said Harris, in a *new* emergency (a reference to the founding during the Civil War), and it must be faced, and by those who heard his voice.[16] The speech was widely printed and received very powerful and favorable comment in the press and elsewhere.[17]

With this speech the chances of Harris' success became good. He now master-minded a campaign which featured articles in newspapers, petitions and letters from students, along with motions of support, especially from Grange groups.[18] Not all farm organizations supported him, however, and chief among the opponents was Z.A. Gilbert. Gilbert used the past to attempt to refute Harris, claiming that the people in the state did not want or need the change and that the school now was moving in opposition to the founders' wishes. He claimed that when they beat Bowdoin and Waterville in the founding struggle in the sixties, the founders had promised to do nothing like this, and he closed with a remark that "these fights, these disruptions and the feelings they arouse among the people hurt the cause of industrial education among us."[19] Now it was up to the legislature.

The first of the hearings was held on February 26, and dealt with appropriations for the next decade. Harris spoke and then Haines, who closed his remarks with, "The College should not be blamed because so few farmer's boys adopted the agricultural course. This was an institution which gave boys from the farm the opportunity to get a practical education at a low cost, and leave their country environments." Haines thought the opposition came from the jealousy of older schools, as well as discontent with the work of the experiment station on commercial feed and seed materials. Gilbert's brother, a lumberman and farmer from Canton, opposed the appropriation.[20]

The House began discussion of the bill on March 9. An amendment was offered calling for a mill tax, and then an amendment for $25,000 each year for a decade. After debate, the second amendment passed the House 72-46. It was tabled and referred to committee again by a vote of 74-33. A motion to adjourn failed 63-38, and the bill was recalled and passed 70-33. The Senate tabled the bill the next day and set debate for March 16.[21]

In that debate many amendments were proposed cutting the amounts and the periods for which they would be provided. All the old arguments were rehearsed again and again. The final touch came from another Aroostook senator, Stearns, who said that the state had an obligation to educate to the highest capacity. It was noon and the body adjourned for lunch with predictions of a vote of 17 or 18 to 13. In the afternoon, after a brief continuation of debate, an amendment providing $20,000 passed 18-13.

Reimposition of tuition also passed, 17-13, and an amendment cutting the ten years to two was defeated 18-13. When it came time to deal with the name change the House barely debated the subject and passed the measure 67-49. In the Senate the debate was long and stormy, but the change passed 23-3.[22]

When the news reached Orono, a giant celebration took place with firing of guns and cannon, ringing of bells, and the cutting of classes. The band paraded, and the students immediately adjourned to the Opera House in Bangor where they gave the performance on the boards a "grand hoorahing." Other events included a musical recital in Old Town and special military drills. When Harris arrived back from Augusta, the student body marched to the electric cars, rode to Bangor, presented a special drill at the railroad station, cheered Harris, and formed a parade downtown with the Bangor High School cadets. More bells were rung and whistles blown for this great triumph. Harris then held an informal reception at his home with several of the members of the legislature present to take the plaudits of the crowd.[23]

The trustees held a special meeting at which they accepted the new name and agreed to give graduates of the former college new diplomas if they requested them. The faculty met and offered their advice, mostly dealing with tuition ($30 yearly) and the imposition of a registration fee ($5) and an incidental fee ($10) each term. Needy students were allowed to offer notes in place of payment. This same faculty meeting changed the name of the Department of Agriculture to College of Agriculture and set up a committee to investigate establishing a law school.[24]

All in all a gala time was had by everyone. The congratulations to Harris rolled in from over the country. Perhaps George W. Atherton, president of Pennsylvania State College, can stand for them all.

> Your victory is a most notable one, and must have important results for the future, not alone in Maine but as part of the general movement (National movement) for the better education of the people.[25]

Harris remained at the university for four more years. During that time the attacks on the school, although present, remained muted. In

An early photo (mid-1880's) of the Cadet Corps band, predecessor of the marching band.

1899, when the legislature next met, there were attempts to repeal the ten-year appropriation, and the governor called for a return to biennial appropriations in his address. The Bowdoin *Orient,* a student newspaper, commented from time to time in opposition to the university, and others kept up their campaign as well. One such opposition spokesman was discussed frankly in a series of letters to Harris.

> He (Blanchard, Franklin County Senator) is out-spoken in his opposition at the present time, and I find there are other graduates of the different colleges in the State, who, while they are dis-crete nevertheless, hostile to its interest and disposed to do whatever they can against it secretly. In my judgment, it is men like those that you have the greatest cause to fear.

Harris took the tried and true course of speaking as often as possible on the university situation and kept close contact with Haines as to the personnel on the important committees. The Speaker of the House, I.K. Stetson, had served on the board of trustees so the situation

there was substantially easier, and the attacks soon diminshed. There was some reason for worry about the opposition because, although the agricultural group had supported the general university position under pressure in 1897, these persons were more closely attached to C.D. Woods of the experiment station than to Harris. This situation was complicated because Woods made enemies elsewhere and some might op-pose the university to punish Woods, or so it was thought. Haines was constantly worried that Harris would do the wrong thing, say the wrong thing or, worse still, support the Democrats, with whom he had strong interests and affinities. Harris went to lobby the legislature near the end of the session and the university survived unscathed.

At this point Harris left Maine to take the directorship of the Jacob Tome Institute in Baltimore. In 1906 he assumed the presidency of Northwestern University, and after retiring from there served as Corresponding Secretary of the Methodist Board of Education until 1924. He finally retired to a new home in Manset,

Mount Vernon, after rebuilding and renovation for use as the first women's dormitory.

Maine, from which he observed the university with interest.[26] When Harris left, there were, as usual, rumors that he was asked to resign. It was true that some students were unhappy, most notably the editors of the 1900 *Prism,* a student yearbook, and some alumni as well, but Harris did not leave for these reasons. Perhaps it was time to seek greener fields. In any case, he had accomplished his goal of making a real university.[27]

Some of those who were disgruntled were alumni of the old college who felt that the change was a bad one. Elizabeth Balentine, so well known among the alumni, generally dealt with these. One of her answers deserves quotation.[28]

> I am also anxious to have you see how rapidly this institution is growing and to prove to you that it will soon, if it does not already deserve the name of 'University.' You are not the only alumnus who has objected to having the name changed.
> It is not at all strange that one becomes attached to a name, in fact I have known more than one young lady to declare that she would never be willing to give up her name, yet she has found that circumstances altered the case entirely. You cannot know what disagreeable blows the college

has had from every side. Certain classes have sneered at us because they thought we were only an agricultural college while the other side threw stones at us because we did not turn out more farmers . . . . Our regular begging trips to Augusta have been robbed of half their sting.
> I think no one can have a greater love for the old 'Maine State College' than I have, but I have been right here all of these years and realize the need of the change of name. Every step upward has had to be fought but the struggle is easier each time.[28]

This letter stated the case for the change clearly. Harris' successor would have some difficulties as the attacks on the institution began once the ten-year period ended, but they would be beaten back from the foundation already set by Harris. Harris pursued the change to university with all his energies. He had time to do little else while at Maine, although he did remodel (from his own plans apparently) the old White farmhouse into the first women's dormitory, Mount Vernon, supervise the building of the new gymnasium and drill hall, and oversee the planting of some twenty-five hundred trees and shrubs. The university grew rapidly with two new departments, law and pharmacy. In addition, John F. Hill, the new governor, supported a request for a new civil and mechanical engineering building and in 1903 it was granted.

From the outside the situation seemed very calm. Newspapers commented that "old prejudices" had given way to friendliness. When the new president, George Fellows, arrived, William DeWitt Hyde, the Bowdoin president, was magnanimous in his greeting.

> This is a large state and there is abundant room for all the work we all can do. I congratulate you and the University on the bright prospects before you there and can assure you of the most hearty cooperation in your efforts to build up a University worthy of Maine.

Fellows attended the 1902 Bowdoin commencement and stayed with Hyde in his home. This was to be the high point of their relationship.[29]

Fellows, who had received his Ph.D. from the University of Berne and had taught history at Indiana and Chicago before coming to Maine, did attempt to repair some of the fences on the agricultural side, but nothing other than a return to the past would satisfy the sectarian interest.[30] And then, in 1903, in the debate over granting funds for the mechanical engineering machine shops and laboratory, a heavy blow was struck at the foundations of the new university. When the fund resolve was introduced, an amendment followed granting the funds only if the university would discontinue its courses in Latin and Greek. This amendment was introduced by Barrett Potter of Brunswick, a Bowdoin graduate apparently very close to President Hyde. Since Latin and Greek were requirements for the B.A. degree, eliminating them would endanger that degree and the school's status as a university.

Potter remarked quite explicitly that the reason for the attack was to support the other, private, colleges, and he also made it plain that the funds used for these courses should go to those colleges. It was a crucial speech, one on which the future of the university hung. The response was given by Representative Thompson, '91, of Orono, who referred to the difficulties of the 70's and 80's on the same score. The legislature did not pass the Potter amendment, but it seemed a near thing, and the battle, once thought won, was now renewed. The next year or two would be occupied with

George E. Fellows.

The president's house, after remodelling in 1893. The trees now hide the Victorian excesses here seen in all their controlled variety. Another fire offered the architects their opportunity.

choosing sides and fighting.[31] At the very next meeting of the legislature, in 1905, less was heard of the issue, although there was some discussion of the amount of money the institution had cost since its beginning. The university prepared the case for its requests clearly, and when the legislature adjourned it had granted $12,000, a small increase, for both 1905 and 1906. The Education Committee, however, decided to investigate the situation raised by the continuing controversy, setting the stage for a great confrontation in Portland in the spring of 1906.[32]

The students were much exercised over these events, especially so when the legislature invaded the campus for a look. One student's letters preserve something of how they thought of the situation at the time.

> What a stir! What a 'hurly-burly', what a change of schedule, what hunger and all because the Maine legislature chose to visit our college last Friday. With their wives and friends two hundred strong, they invaded our little kingdom, monopolized our rooms and ate our little dinner. Legislators to the right, legislators behind, asking impossible questions, and like the farmers, which many are, saying and doing comical things. But since mankind is undeniably selfish, we put our best foot forward . . . . [33]

The legislative committee met in Portland on May 22 and 23, 1906, to discuss the university's future. Fellows spoke, as did Hyde, Presidents Chase of Bates, White of Colby, and Gibbs of New Hampshire. Other speakers were Henry Lord, president of the board of trustees of the university, A.J. Durgin and S.L. Boardman from the board, and J.M. Brockie of the class of 1906. Fellows went well prepared, including being armed with an exchange of letters with Potter and Russell W. Eaton, '73, who lived in Brunswick. The exchange had occurred in 1902 or 1903, and, along with letters to Eaton from President Hyde, seemed to prove Potter's dependence on Hyde for his thoughts. The question before the committee was whether the state was doing too much for the university according to the directives of the original charter. Potter chaired the committee and Thompson, his earlier opponent, was its secretary. The meeting, held in Portland City Hall, had a heavy attendance.

Fellows and the others from Orono simply dealt with the past, while stressing the students'

need for an education that was inexpensive but included both practical and cultural aspects of life. Hyde's speech was a piece of invective; he stated that if the university would only give up the B.A. degree, go back to 1896, and allow an intercollegiate commission to rule the state's higher education, all would be well, otherwise, opposition to the university would never end. White called for an intercollegiate commission for the state, with each college limited in its curriculum. The hearing adjourned, although the debate continued in the newspapers for some time. The speeches were reprinted widely, so the state had an opportunity to discuss the role of the university prior to the meeting of the 1907 legislature where its role would be debated again and perhaps decided once and for all.[34]

Support for Orono's position flooded into the president's office. Alumni from far and near wrote pledging assistance and congratulating Fellows on his work so far. Fellows himself continued on the road, speaking in the fall before the state teachers' convention. At least one person even wrote to Potter, stressing Fellows' recent strong work in behalf of agriculture. Toward the end of the year, as the legislature was about to convene, Fellows sent a letter to alumni asking their specific and general support of the university's position. This document, dated December 22, 1906, and circulated in flyer form, said that the university appropriation was about to expire and made the case for an increased appropriation in the legislature. Fellows defended the liberal arts courses, called them necessary, and pointed out that when the funds were first provided the student body was only just over 200, while in 1906-7 there were 687 students in attendance. Fellows said that a dormitory, an agricultural building, a heating plant, a physics building, and better quarters for chemistry were imperative. He asked alumni to lobby legislators in behalf of their old school and requested comments on their positions so that he could plan his strategy.[35]

When the legislature met, the joint special committee gave its reports. The majority report said that although the university did have a just obligation to students in attendance, the committee was opposed to duplication of liberal arts courses because of the expense, competition with other schools, and "because it retards the progress of the University itself." The minority report disagreed and called such an attitude "unwise" and proposed an annual appropriation for the school.[36]

Many university advocates apparently hoped for institution of a mill tax to meet annual needs, although some others counseled acceptance of nearly anything if only the B.A. degree could be retained. A major lobbying effort was organized. Fellows set up his headquarters in Augusta, with ex-representative Thompson as the university's spokesman. Ralph Kneeland Jones, the librarian, coordinated efforts on the campus, obtaining petitions (especially strong ones were issued by both the technical and agricultural faculties) and providing Fellows with information with which to counter the attacks. Petitions from students were circulated to members of the legislature from their counties. Local agencies such as the Old Town Board of Trade and others joined the effort. The Old Town group sent a committee of five to lobby along with Fellows. Both sides circulated printed materials. The university's was a card covered with print on both sides. It dealt, in italic type, with such queries as *"Are Maine Boys less valuable than those of their nearest neighbor?"* Bowdoin alumni also followed the petition route, and they issued their position in a broadside, "Hon. Barrett Potter of Brunswick, Replies to the Bangor *Commercial.*" Potter's final sentence was, "It [the issue of whether the university teaches the courses well or not] is as well as anything else to distract attention from the major issue, which is whether the State of Maine needs the duplication." Fellows answered this blast with one of his own to the Lewiston *Journal,* where Potter had first printed his remarks.

People on the campus answered individual letters, and newspapers in the state were urged to come out in favor. Many, such as the Waterville *Sentinel,* Belfast *Republican Journal,* and the Bangor *Commercial,* did. The *Maine Farmer* and the Lewiston papers, as well as others, supported the Bowdoin position. The Lewiston *Journal* was the strongest supporter of Potter while the Bangor *Commercial* played the same role for the university. The *Commercial,* for instance, printed letters saying that if Potter won, university athletic teams would have to undergo the leech (meaning to be bled and presumably weakened physically)

before playing Bowdoin. One writer said that in 1888, although Bowdoin called them "potato diggers," Maine had won all the same.[37]

At the height of the struggle Fellows and Jones arranged for a shower of telegrams to appear in Augusta, and when Fellows made speeches he was fond of quoting such telegrams. The *Maine Campus,* the university's student newspaper, issued several extras, the first reprinting Hyde's attacks at the Portland meeting.

The real confrontation occurred when Fellows delivered a major speech to the Education Committee on February 7. In this speech, twelve close-packed pages when it was reprinted, Fellows discussed the history and the relation of agricultural colleges to the older institutions, told of the desirability of not spending time lobbying, and asked for the mill tax as the only funding method that was fair and would take the university out of politics. His peroration deserves quotation.

> It is no small work to build up a perfect educational scheme. It means the richest brain and blood of experts; of men trained in this particular calling; of men who unselfishly lavish their best strength upon it and with hope of very small financial gain. These men are working for a principle, for a cause, for educational progress in its highest sense. Gentlemen, if they cannot work uninterruptedly in Maine they will be driven to some other place where they can so work. Our best men are not unsought . . . .
> Do you choose to have a sturdy, healthy, typical-of-your state educational representative, or will you have a cripple? We are giving her to you perfect in health and as near perfectly coordinated as our limited means have permitted. The choice of what she shall be from now on is yours.[38]

On February 25, the committee offered its recommendation: the university should be granted $45,000 each year for the biennium, to be used to build a central heating plant and an agricultural building, and to have $80,000 for other expenses during that time. A minority called for imposition of a mill tax.

A lengthy debate on the findings and on the university ensued in the House on March 5. Retention of the B.A. degree went through by a vote of 123-12, since no one other than the extreme opponents wished to return to the past. On other issues the split was less clear. On a vote to provide $55,000 per year, plus the buildings, the university lost 76-48. A vote appropriating $65,000 annually for a decade lost 72-55. Adjournment also lost, 62-42. Finally the House authorized $65,000 for two years by 79-34. On the next day, the Senate overturned this by a vote of 16-14 to accept the appropriation only if the B.A. degree were abolished.

This vote was a disheartening blow. The lobbying forces again began to speak and work at great length. Some of this lobbying was so strong that senators found themselves spending the better part of one day debating the ethical position of students, some of whom apparently threatened reprisals for negative votes. Finally, on March 26, after another lengthy debate on the issue, the Senate reversed itself, unanimously, and accepted the House bill. Again the university had won out over those forces hoping to limit its activites to agriculture and technology.

The issue played itself out in the papers of the state and the Northeast, with a sort of coda occurring when the *Nation* supported the university in an article in its May 23 issue, in answer to positions taken in letters on May 2 from a Bowdoin representative. The last of the discussion occurred in June when the *Yale Alumni Weekly* also defended Bowdoin and attacked the university. A Yale alumnus who was a member of the committee minority supporting the university answered this with a letter stating the institution's position.

Fellows sent a letter to presidents of land-grant colleges in other states summarizing the affair, which was, for a time, a *cause celebre* in higher education circles. The state head of the Knights of Pythias said it all best, however, when he congratulated Fellows and indicated that it would all be up to "the boys" to produce for those who had supported them in Augusta.[39]

In 1909 the issue reopened briefly. Many were still unhappy, and when the appropriation was passed the bill called for the university to establish no more departments. Haines thought this was "a dirty stab in the back," but more important was the fact that the amount received rose to $100,000 each year for 1909 through 1912. At first the governor vetoed this bill because it was too large, but a meeting with the governor and his council along with board members caused the veto to be withdrawn. Haines and the others had attempted to protect the university from attacks, but the amounts appropriated were certainly large enough to sweeten the curtailment blow.[40] Bowdoin and the other enemies of the school had fought a strong fight, but in the end they had lost and the university had withstood the strongest onslaught to date. In retrospect, the attack on the B.A. degree was obscured by the demand for more money, and although the mill tax was lost, the appropriations were increased substantially, and the B.A degree, with all that it meant philosophically and emotionally, was retained. That was the real issue, for if it had been lost, the university would have reverted to collegiate status.

President Fellows certainly had won a great victory. He was, as the *Campus* said, the toast of the university and deserving of the thanks of every person associated with the school. For that reason it is all the more ironic that at the height of his popularity, he should be engaged in a problem that would cause his downfall and precipitate a confrontation on the campus even greater, perhaps, than the one in Augusta.

There had been a long history of student and faculty discontent and mutual distrust on campus. Student hazing and the social mores of the students precipitated conflict. The next chapter will discuss these problems, which plagued the school from its founding, in the context of campus life. For now, it is sufficient to say the hazing, the harassment of underclassmen, was forbidden, and in 1896, after a number of expulsions and much discussion, a treaty with the faculty was signed which allowed the expelled students to return, forbade hazing, and provided a pledge of no-hazing to be signed by every entering student. This tactic had been attempted many times before, but this time it seemed to work fairly well.[41]

However, by 1904, the situation had deteriorated again. During that winter the paddling of underclassmen became frequent, and several malefactors were suspended. By 1907 the razoo (running the gauntlet of paddles on hands and knees) had returned to college life. At the same time, problems of social conduct became acute. President Fellows prohibited visits to upstairs bedrooms at Mount Vernon, the women's dormitory, where he said "some acts of impropriety" had been observed. Women were prohibited from entering fraternities. Evening walks without chaperones were also forbidden, as apparently a pregnancy or two had resulted on these walks, and finally, as the crowning touch, the traditional cots and "cozy corners" at the spring dances were forbidden by the president, with faculty agreement. During the period of the 1909 legislature meeting the faculty had allowed the rules to be broken, apparently in fear of student riots at a crucial time of the debate. Hoping to prevent trouble, the faculty deliberately did not attend the dance in question where the cots and "cozy corners" reappeared. "An undercurrent of irritation spread against the president," fanned by town and gown difficulties, and reinforced particularly by an outbreak of hazing at Orono High School. This irritation was an "inevitable result of rapid growth," said Fellows, but the difficulty had reached a point of no return by the spring of 1909.[42]

Unhappiness was great on both sides. A University Council had been formed to deal with discipline in 1904, but students on it were in a distinct minority position. In 1906 one student group, "The Old Guard of 1906," defied the faculty and openly practiced hazing. The faculty censured them, suspended the leaders for a year, but then withdrew the suspension after a public apology by the students. At this time outside interests, especially athletics and music, had so overtaken student time that a number of faculty meetings were held to attempt control of these activities and especially the concomitant outside soliciting of funds for them during chapel. From these meetings came the position of a faculty manager of athletics; less chapel; and rules on how many organizations a student might belong to, on freshman competition, on the purposes of chapel, and on conduct in the laboratories.

In 1907, when a serious cheating scandal created more of a gulf between faculty and students, a special faculty committee was appointed to investigate the morals of the university. The investigation resulted in a new discipline committee "to deal with student dishonesty, immorality, and other like offenses . . . ." Unfortunately, the president was in sole charge of this new group. By the spring of 1909, the editor of the campus newspaper found it necessary to write several editorials on the deterioration of student-faculty relations. Faculty held another long meeting on these problems in May of 1909, soon after the difficulty with the dance. A dis-

turbance in chapel by the senior class followed. More meetings resulted, calling for censorship of the *Prism* (in those days primarily an insult book). At a June meeting, the faculty, after proposing more physical training for the students, passed a resolution that set out their case.

> The spirit of lawlessness that has been steadily growing among the students during the past few years would seem to indicate the presence of some disturbing influence that needs to be remedied.

The trustees also discussed the issue, approved the president's strong measures, authorized a renewal of the freshman no-hazing pledge, set a limit of one-half of any fraternity to be freshmen, and called for an audit of fraternity books. A disaster seemed imminent after these events.[43]

The new gymnasium, Alumni Hall, erected in 1901, quickly became a headquarters for student social affairs. Here it is shown decorated for a dance. The most prominent feature is the famous "cozy corners." Social mores in the process of change made such areas contentious. The photograph may provide modern viewers with a slightly different idea of the Victorian period.

During the summer a letter was sent to all returning students calling their attention to the trustee rules. When college opened, a series of class gatherings requested a meeting which class representatives held with Fellows and a number of the trustees. A definition of improper hazing was arrived at at this meeting eliminating the night razoo, heavy paddling, and river dunking. Students signed no-hazing pledge cards and classes began. Almost immediately a controversy arose over what now constituted legal hazing. Sophomores, unhappy that their traditional roles were diminished, became very restless. They posted several proclamations, which were removed at presidential order. Three times this happened. Fellows also made a chapel appearance calling for the end of hazing. The sophomore class met and voted to defy the orders and to strike if necessary in order to be allowed to haze the freshmen.

On October 6 an all-night hazing, without the razoo, took place. During the next week the faculty held a series of meetings, and the discipline committee interviewed nearly all students and eventually suspended those found most guilty; forty others were censured. The punishment was announced at the close of chapel, October 13. A mass meeting immediately took place in front of Alumni Hall. Classes held meetings in which they were addressed by the Senior Skulls, an organization begun in 1906 to promote cooperation within the school, who had met with the faculty. Petitions asking for reinstatement were circulated, with the sophomores and juniors supporting a strike if reinstatement was denied, while the other two classes voted to wait and see. At noon on the fourteenth, the two middle classes went on strike. The faculty decided in meeting (which was always chaired and dominated by the president in these times) not to grant the petition. The other two classes then joined the strike, and during the afternoon students held a series of meetings on the football field. Everyone but the football team now was on strike, the students voting to exempt the team as they had a chance at the state championship. That night the president sent letters to all parents calling attention to the chain of events and pointing out that students were leaving college in support of the illegal events noted in the earlier letters to homes.

The strike continued, and the students also sent a letter to parents, proclaiming the fact that difficulties were occurring. A rump (always termed this by faculty groups) meeting of the Penobscot Valley Alumni met and drew up a statement calling for the president and faculty to withdraw their suspensions. Over the weekend the situation deteriorated somewhat, with many students leaving and others moving to tents pitched overlooking the campus. At noon each day, those remaining held a parade around the football field, singing songs and shouting defiance. On the eighteenth the Penobscot Valley group met again, and a substantially larger attendance made the meeting seem more legitimate. By this time other alumni meetings had been held.

The alumni supported the students, but the faculty insisted on dealing with each case separately upon the student's return. The faculty and alumni held several more meetings, as the strike continued. By the Wednesday of the next week the faculty were apparently willing to take back all but the original eight suspended. An alumni meeting was also held with the trustees. By this time it was apparent that even if the strike came to an end, Fellows would probably have to go. Finally, on the twenty-second, the strike ended. The faculty held a special meeting to deal with the eight suspended students. All faculty members, including the experiment station staff, attended, and each case was dealt with in front of advocates present from the student body. Seven of the students were found guilty by votes ranging from 36-6, 34-6, to 28-12, while one was found not guilty, 33-5. By the end of November the situation eased considerably as the faculty agreed to allow the seven suspended to return at the end of the semester and the sophomores agreed to end the hazing in all forms. The alumni groups, by this time terribly disturbed over the adverse publicity, acted as mediators. The final votes and petitions were agreed to on November 15. Although we do not have detailed reports of the alumni, trustee, and student discussions in the last week, apparently the students insisted on a new president in return for their agreement to end their strike. All unofficial accounts of the affair have suggested such a quid pro quo, although it cannot now be verified. At any rate, Fellows found another position during spring semester, and when college opened in the fall of 1910, was replaced as president by Robert J. Aley. In addition, some other faculty were hired, including, significantly, an athletic director, Edgar Wingard.[44]

By early spring, however, Fellows thought he had weathered the storm, apparently, as he sent the trustees a copy of the *Campus* as an example of the "chastened and improved student mind." However, when he began to call for a fund drive for a student union, one alumnus was quite blunt about where Fellows stood after the affair was over.

> You know as well as I that a large number of the alumni do not feel very kindly toward you. They would not enter into anything proposed by you; if it was a good thing for the University, because they would think it would reflect credit upon you, and that is what they do not wish at this time.[45]

The student strike and its consequences is one of those events that greatly plague the historian. There seems to be little real reason why this situation should have been carried so far. Fellows did not adopt extreme regulations, for that time, and his faculty backed him strongly. However, it is significant that the alumni backed the student insurgents so strongly. One assumes that the impact of Fellows' regulations on social mores (especially the elimination of the "cozy corners" at the dances) must have been more cutting than it now appears. Student social affairs often served to expend excess student energy. To curtail them when student-faculty hostility was still present, though latent, may have been more than the strained relations could bear. When one considers that the school had been under heavy attack for a number of years by the legislature, attack culminating in the great hearing in Portland, the student eruption may have been a heretofore hidden time bomb. The alumni must have retained their feelings for the student body more strongly than is common, to take its side so fiercely. Perhaps President Fellows became a surrogate sacrifice for the general university problems. In any case, he seems to have been a victim of the unrest. Fellows went on to university posts in Illinois and then to a professorship of history at the University of Utah. His successor, Robert J. Aley, who had been chairman of the state

This scene, taken from a postal card dated October 28, 1909, shows students demonstrating during the great strike. The legend on the back says, "This is another picture taken during the strike. The students marching around the football field. Have got to go to class now but will write between four-thirty and six."

board of education in Indiana, was to make work with the alumni one of his highest priorities.

It is instructive to notice that one of Aley's first appearances was before the Penobscot Valley Alumni group. He indicated his view of the university to them.

> A state university exists primarily to serve the state. It is not founded to further the cause of any sect, party, or class. It exists for the whole people. It must serve the people and their interests in a direct way; it must help the agriculture, the horticulture and the animal industries of the State. It must help solve the engineering problems necessary in the further development of the State. It must lead the way in the discovering and exploitation of new resources. It must contribute its part in the production of a higher culture. A state University, more than any other, must keep in mind its relation to the state. Unless it can justify its existence by its ability to serve the state in many ways, it has but little excuse for existing.[46]

He went on to say that the university existed for the purpose of "making men"; its business was public business, and it was in a position to lead and form public opinion. These were exemplary remarks, but had a hidden meaning for those who had known the previous twenty, and especially the past three, years.

During the period under discussion, while Harris and Fellows served as presidents, the Maine State College became the University of Maine, both in legal fact and in the eyes of most of the state's citizens. On the campus, rules were made under which life would be lived. The nature of the curriculum was established. Here the college experience of the twentieth century took firm shape. Courses were rewritten; new professors were hired, some of whom became famous figures on the campus. New buildings, most notably Lord, Alumni, and Carnegie halls, were constructed. All in all a visitor to the campus in 1913 would have found substantial change from 1893, although some of the change had taken place very subtly and over the entire period.

Admission procedure was handled in a routine way, although a very close watch was kept on the high schools of the state, and from time to time adjustments in requirements were made. By 1908 the admissions examinations assumed that the applicant would pass two-hour

examinations in both algebra and advanced algebra and other shorter examinations in chemistry, English (where he would discuss Macaulay's *Essay on Milton*, Milton's *L'Allegro, Il Penseroso,* and *Comus,* and Shakespeare's *Julius Caesar),* French, German, plane geometry, American history, solid geometry, Latin, English and Roman history, physiography, physics, and physiology. Not all needed to be passed, but conditional admission followed in the two or three failures permitted.

While attending the university, students were required to write twelve themes during their last three years and make seven declamations, although debate work did count toward this requirement. The 120 hour rule for graduation was adopted in 1902 with four years of English, four years of mathematics, two of language, two of science, as well as three years of work in one's major subject being necessary to receive the degree. Courses were five hours in length, rather than three. Physical culture was required after 1902 for the first two years, with no credit, and later it was even added for juniors and seniors, except those in military drill or athletics. Excused absences, rules for athletic and musical absence, and the twenty-four hour double-cut rule on the eve and return of holidays had all made their appearance by 1907.

In that year the differences between the B.A. and the B.S. degrees were clarified, with Maine continuing to demand either Latin or Greek for the B.A. (although the courses in Latin and Greek in translation or in Latin and Greek history remained options). Other schools were dropping the classical requirements, but "Maine will still insist," said the faculty. In 1911 the B.A. degree was discussed again and the attainment of a C average installed as a graduation requirement in the Arts College, established in 1906. In 1915 a course in required reading, essentially a great books course, was proposed but did not pass. Undergraduate theses were made optional in agriculture that year, but remained requirements elsewhere.[47]

New rules were instituted for faculty governance in 1898 and later modified in 1911. These rules mostly determined who could vote on what, but in this time the president's word remained law. Some committees were begun in order to spread the work load. Monthly meetings of the faculty were mandatory with the faculty having by the close of this period

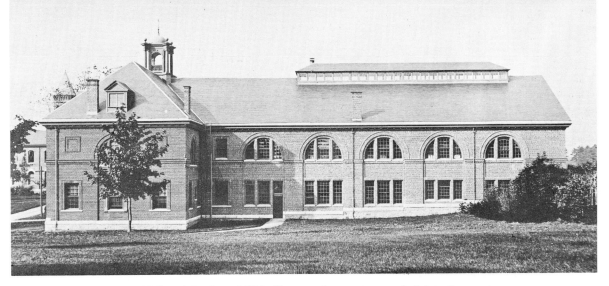

Alumni Hall, originally a drill hall/gymnasium, now an administrative center.

jurisdiction in matters of discipline and, subject to the trustees, educational policy.

The real factor in faculty happiness, of course, was sufficient salary to keep good people. As the president of Missouri said to Fellows, when answering a letter on faculty salaries, "Give as liberal as you can possibly afford to your good men whether you are in immediate danger of losing them or not. If you have a good horse it pays to keep him well."[48]

Some changes were made in the curriculum. Summer school was instituted in 1895 and grew steadily. By 1909, forty-eight courses were offered, mostly to teachers, with special lectures at night and a recreation program; 101 students were in attendance, of whom 36 were women.[49]

The colleges began to take clear shape as well. The arts college was the weakest and remained so for some time, with technology clearly the strongest. Major efforts were made to raise the level of both arts and agriculture with new courses and new faculty. The trustees debated whether or not to hire women, especially in biology, which gave staffing trouble in 1906, and occasionally they struggled with a department, as when they voted in 1914 to authorize the president to inform the English department, "that the continuance of their services in the University depended upon their attitudes of cooperation and helpfulness."[50] Some courses were very strong, such as civil engineering and forestry; the last grew rapidly after its beginnings in 1903. In engineering there were powerful attempts to associate the university with a growing effort toward a technology ex-

periment station. Electrical engineering broke off and became a separate discipline. New faculty were also added in the college of technology. When G.H. Hamlin retired, after teaching one-half of the first quarter century's graduates, he was replaced by the soon-to-be famous "Scissors" Weston. That curriculum was modernized substantially in content in 1907.[51]

A new department of education was instituted in 1906. Fellows and Aley were both very interested in pedagogy and the state's public schools, and their ties with Payson Smith of the State Board of Education were close.[52] Agriculture was placed under the experiment station in 1897, but it was separated again in 1902, with the appointment of W.D. Hurd as professor. In 1904-5 a considerable student increase was noted, due in part to curriculum reorganization and to new courses in poultry husbandry, and in home economics, which became quite active by 1915. These subjects tied in with the very important work in the state with boys' and girls' clubs, which acted as a feeder system for the university.[53]

By the end of this time there was some evidence of even more change in the university, with more substantial professional degrees being discussed in pulp and paper, and the arts college providing required survey courses, especially in the sciences, to its undergraduates.[54]

Some important new buildings were constructed during the latter half of this period. First was Alumni Hall with its gymnasium and drill hall, later converted to a women's gymnasium and little theater, and finally to become the major administration building for the entire campus. This building, given through alumni donations, was first discussed in 1898 and, in the height of fever over the Spanish-American War, the money came in fairly quickly. It was built and dedicated in 1901. Physical education became a reality and, soon after a requirement, which in 1906 the trustees thought important enough to warrant a new instructor, with part of his duties to "care for the morals of the students."[55] Lord Hall, housing the mechanical and electrical engineering departments, was constructed and dedicated in a major public ceremony in 1904. This building was authorized by the legislature in 1903 and marked an effort

to provide each major division of the college with a building. The library, Carnegie Hall, came from a personal gift of $50,000 by Andrew Carnegie. President Fellows worked for nearly five years on this project, as Carnegie did not usually give buildings to colleges, but the reports of the meeting and defeat of Bowdoin in Portland in 1906 apparently caused the philanthropist to change his mind. Later the Carnegie people were very pleased to say that the building, unlike many built through their gifts, was constructed within the budget allotted by the university in the gift request. Another major dedication was held upon its completion.[56]

At the end of the era, a new chemistry and physics building was authorized, Aubert Hall, as was part of the funds for a new women's

An interesting photo of the gymnasium interior. The apparatus then in use for physical training and gymnastics are clearly visible as are the roof support beams. Here the dances were held as well.

A very early view of Carnegie Hall, built as a new library in 1903. The barn still looms in the background. Today the building houses the art department and galleries. The landscaping of today allows the building to blend with the campus.

A view of Alumni Hall soon after construction, perhaps at the dedication, or more probably at a graduation ceremony. Dress styles are pre-1910 and there are still a few parasols to be seen.

Lord Hall, named for an early trustee, originally constructed for engineering classes, now houses music, journalism and the offices of the Maine Campus. The Lion just appears at the right.

Aubert Hall, named for the first professor of chemistry, soon after its construction. New wings and additions change the building substantially today.

dormitory. The latter, Balentine Hall, would not be constructed until after World War I.[57]

In order to staff these new courses and utilize the new buildings, a number of new faculty made their appearance. Not all made a major contribution, but several deserve mention. In addition to ''Scissors'' Weston, others of importance were Edith Patch, in entomology, one of the most intellectually distinguished persons and prolific publishers ever to be at Orono; Caroline Colvin, in history, first woman to be head of a major university department in the country; and John P. ''Paddy'' Huddilston, who began his distinguished and well-known career in classics in 1898. These persons were to be fixtures on the university scene until well into the 1930's.

Laura Comstock, in home economics, and Ralph McKee in pulp and paper chemistry, made their appearances in this period and made substantial contributions, although not giving their entire lifetimes to the school. There were losses, as when Walter Balentine died suddenly in 1894. These persons, and many others who were at Maine for brief times or who were less widely known during their time at Maine, were the strength of the university and made it possible for Harris, Fellows, and Aley to ac-

complish their work with the legislature and
with the citizens of the state.[58]

The one other person who deserves special
mention is Elizabeth Balentine. When her
husband died so suddenly, the university gave
her a temporary job as a clerk. She soon progressed to being treasurer of the college briefly,
secretary to the faculty for a long time and
finally registrar in 1912. Her tenure with the
university dated from the earliest days as she
was the niece of President Allen. During the
twenty years she served the faculty and the president she may well have been the most
powerful, and at the same time, the best liked
person on the campus. When she died the campus went into mourning, as did most of the
alumni. It was said of her that she could call by
their first names every student at the university
from the mid-1880's to her death. Her
friendship was often the major factor in stilling
potential alumni quarrels with the progress of
the university in later years. Two comments
suffice, one from the faculty and one from a
contemporary student. When she died in 1913
the faculty held a special meeting, and passed a
resolution.

> No one knew the university better nor served it
> more faithfully than Elizabeth Abbott Balentine.
> . . . Her industry will be our inspiration, her
> courage our cheer, and her unselfish life will
> compel our admiration while her memory en-
> dures.[59]

Somewhat earlier, a student, in writing to his
fiancee, made similar judgements.

> One of our receiving committee was Mrs. Balen-
> tine, our college secretary for 20 years, and I
> was very proud to escort her to and from the
> dance. She is so pleasant, wise and helpful that
> any of the boys will tell you they had rather
> work a day for her than turn over their hand for
> Prexy.[60]

Mrs. Balentine's death marked the end of an
era. A half century was over, and the school
would never fight the same battles for recognition again. Routines were established, traditions
fixed in place, and attitudes made firm. In the
half century to come, events outside the campus were often to be the ruling factors on campus, but those situations would be faced with
standards set by the past and would be easier to
handle for that reason.

*Prof. Charles P. "Scissors" Weston,
'96, in the classroom*

Elizabeth Abbott Balentine

Notes

1. Wallace R. Farrington to Harris, June 5, 1894.

2. *Agriculture of Maine, 1893*, for Fernald on the subject, p. 228, and Harris, 131 ff.; Z.A. Gilbert to Harris, June 9, 1894.

3. G.M. Twitchell (Secretary of Maine Board of Agriculture) to Harris, June 8, 1894.

4. L.W. Riggs '85 (C.C.N.Y.) to Harris, March 13, 1895.

5. *Agriculture of Maine, 1894-5*, Report of Annual Meeting; *Leg. Docs.*, 1895; House Doc. 16; House Doc. 34; Sen. Doc. 102; Cleave's Annual Address, 1895; *Laws of Maine*, 1895, Ch. 82.

6. The best available account today is in *The Cadet*, April, 1895, "The College Bill," and Oxford *Democrat*, January 29, February 26, March 5, 1895.

7. Z.A. Gilbert to Harris, March 9, 1895.

8. Harrison Hume (State Senate) to Harris July 1, 1895; Harris to Hume, July 6, 1895.

9. *Agriculture of Maine, 1896*, 233; E.P. May to Harris, July 1895; August 3, November 1, 1895; May to Henry Lord, May 16, 1895. *Turf, Farm and Home* Circular announcing competition. May was the editor of the paper.

10. E.A Balentine to Harris, May 20, 1896; May 26, 1896; Harris to Russell B. Shepherd, October 2, 1896; William Haines to Harris, October 6, 1896. Other letters have been destroyed.

11. W.R. Pattangall to Harris, August 18, 1896; February 6, 1897; Samuel Libbey to Harris, November 9, 1896; F.O. Beal to Harris, November 23, 1896; Edwin J. Haskell '72 to Harris, February 15, 1897; Harris to Haskell, February 20, 1897.

12. Hunt to Harris, February 13; Henry to Harris, February 15, Roberts to Harris, February 10, 1897.

13. *Agriculture of Maine, 1897*, "Education for the Farmer," by Harris; Harris to Henry, February 20, 1897. W.H. Jordan gave a series of speeches to Farmer's Institutes in 1894-5 entitled "Industrial Education in Maine", *Agriculture of Maine, 1894-5*, 99-112, in which he discussed the relationship of engineering and agriculture fairly and lucidly.

14. Justin H. Morrill to A.C. True, February 10, 1897; Harris to True, February 20, 1897.

15. *Leg. Docs., 1897*, S.D., 6, 85; H.D., 179, 336, 347; Powers *Address*, 1897, Harris to E. Balentine, January 20, 1897.

16. *Cadet*, February, 1897, a special issue; Bangor *Whig*, February 5, 1897. Harris also gave much the same speech to a farmers' meeting on February 11 in Augusta. The cigars letter is Stetson to Harris, February 3, 1897.

17. F.B. David (Bangor Theo. Seminary) to Harris, February 5, 1897.

18. Harris to Balentine, February 16, 1897; February 17 (both twice); Bangor *Commercial*, February 22, Somerset Pomona Grange, February 9, Sagadahoc County Grange, February 24, B.D. Farnham to Harris, February 27; *Commercial*, March 2 (on debate at Phippsburg meeting of Sagadahoc) Penobscot Pomona approved, see *Cadet*, March, 1897.

19. Piscataquis Grange opposed, see Harris to them March 22; Gilbert to Harris, March 1, 1897.

20. Bangor *Commercial*, February 26, 1897. Legislative Record, 1897, 260-9.

21. *Cadet*, March 1897.

22. *Cadet*, April, 1897. Some still were unhappy, see *Maine Farmer*, April 6, 1897, "The Act is Done." Legislative Record, 1897, 316-20; 329-332; 420. Bangor Daily *Commercial*, March 10, 12, 1897.

23. *Cadet*, April, 1897, Oxford *Democrat*, January 26, March 2, April 13, 1897.

24. Trustees Minutes, April 28, 1897; *Laws of Maine*, 1897, Ch. 547; 551; *Resolves*, Ch. 215.

25. W.H. Jordan to Harris, March 21, 28, 1897; Ralph K. Jones to Harris (undated notes); Harris to Jones, undated note; E. Fenno Heath to Harris, August 30, Harris to Heath, September 1; N.H. Morton '76 to Harris, March 30, 1897 and return April 1, 1897; Atherton to Harris, June 14, 1897.

26. Trustees Minutes, March 21 (Bangor); June 12, 13 (Waterville); June 27, 1893; *Bangor Daily News*, February 25, 1935.

27. *Leg. Docs.*, 1899; H.R. 111, 361; S.D. 68; Power's *Address*, 1899, 79; Hill's *Address*, 133-4; Haines to Harris, October 12, November 24, 1900; January 17, 1899; December 14, 1898; November 12, 1900; Return letters, December 13, 1898; March 10, 1899; October 15, 1900; Harris to J.W. Mitchell, October 26, 1898; Mitchell to Harris, October 27, 1898 (quoted); Harris to L.C. Southard, September 14, 1901; Southard to Harris, September 12, 1901; I.K. Stetson to Harris, December 15, Harris to Stetson, December 16, 1898; *Agriculture of Maine* 1898, Harris, "The Farmer and Education," "The Relation of Agriculture to Higher Education," 1899, James S. Stevens, "The Democracy of Education," 219-233; 1900, W.H. Jordan, "The Next Step in the Education of the Farmer," 75-94; Harris, "The Debt of Agriculture to Education," 159-171; Bowdoin *Orient*, March 2, 1898; Portland *Press*, April 25, 1900; Lewiston *Journal Weekly*, September 8-13, 1900; Maine *Campus*, reporting on work of Harris with magic lantern in Oxford County, November 14, 1899; May 1, 1900, on resignation rumors; Hill's *Address*, 1903, 78; *Laws of Maine*, 1903, Resolves, Ch. 90.

28. A.M. Goodale '75 to Balentine, January 24, 1900; her return is February 16, 1900.

29. Bangor *Commercial,* December 1, 1902; Hyde to Fellows, April 24, June 15, 1902.

30. Z.A. Gilbert to Fellows, September 13, 1902 (A Bangor conference was held); November 27, 1904; Mayo to Fellows, February 27, 1903; Fellows to Mayo, February 28, 1903.

31. *The Maine Campus,* April 1, 1903, verbatim accounts of the speeches. Harris to Fellows, February 27, March 25, 30, 1903 (Harris came and spoke to Penobscot Valley Alumni in crisis period.)

32. Maine *Campus,* October 15, 1904; Haines' son chose Bowdoin over UMO, see Haines to Fellows, January 6, 1904; *Leg. Docs.,* 1903, H.R. 149, 182, 349, 520, 521; *Laws of Maine,* 1905, Resolves, Ch. 67. *Leg. Docs.,* 1905; H.R. 28, 191, 198; Hart to Fellows, December 29, 1905 (using students to lobby); William D. Hurd to Fellows, December 29, 1905 (attempting to get a larger share for agriculture) in Trustees materials for March 24, 1906; Faculty Minutes, October 23, November 6, 1905, changing College of Liberal Arts to College of Arts and Sciences, and giving A & S the right to award both B.A. and B.S. degrees. Haines' letter about his son is worth quoting in part. "This is quite a disappointment to me — but I did not like saying *shall* and *shant* in this matter of going to college with only one boy."

33. Merton R. Lovett, '06 to Margaret, copies in my possession.

34. Trustees, 1906 folder, with a 101 page typed, nearly verbatim description of hearings and speeches, *Maine Campus,* June 12, 1906; *Kennebec Journal,* May 27, 1906; *Lewiston Journal,* May 24, 1906; J.A. Roberts to Fellows, May 25, 1906; W.E. Walz to Louis Southard, May 12, return May 22, 1906; *Bangor Commercial,* for an address by Walz, May 11, 1906; series of letters to Horace M. Estabrooke in June, 1906 who had apparently written to most of his former students, and the file Hyde to Eaton, January 8, 1902, Eaton to Fellows, May 18, 1906; Eaton to Potter March 22, 1902.

35. G.E. Thompson to Fellows, October 9, 1906; L.W. Riggs '85 to Fellows August 17, 1906 (Riggs was professor of chemistry at Cornell by this time) Payson Smith to Fellows, October 27, 1906; L.O. Southard to Fellows, undated. Trustees Minutes, November 3, 1906; A.W. Gilman to Barrett Potter, December 14, 1906.

36. Fellows to Alumni, December 22, 1906; *Leg. Docs.,* 1907 Sen. 20 (majority); Sen. 152, (minority), House, 303, 304. The reports were reprinted in *Campus,* January 29, 1907. S.L. Boardman to Fellows, February 20, 1907; E.A. Balentine to Fellows, February 14, March 13, 1907; E.H. Gleason to Fellows February 12, 1907.

37. Evidence for all this comes from a folder entitled "B.S. Degree". C.C. Garland to Fellows, January 31 (Old Town), J.M. Brockie, January 24, Lewiston *Journal,* February 21, Fellows to *Journal,* February 13, J.R. Talbot '04 to Fellows, March 17 (on Bowdoin petitions) Waterville *Sentinel,* February 23, Belfast *Republican Journal,* January 31, W.D. Hurd to W.B. Kendall, March 13, *Maine Farmer,* February 7; *Bangor Daily Commercial,* January 27, letter from D; February 3 letter from Wallace Farrington, edit February 16, letter from H, same issue, February 23 edit; February 25, letter H again; February 26 letter from grange, also edit; February 27, edit; March letters from law student, "An American" and entire issue of March 5, all these 1907.

38. *Campus,* January 28, March 5, 12, 1907. Fellows' speech before the Education Committee was reprinted by the *Campus* and circulated. *Bangor Daily Commercial,* March 5, 1907: They were choleric when the Senate overturned the vote, saying, "The People's University will sooner or later prevail. The common folks of Maine, not the aristocrats, are with this institution to the last."

39. *Laws of Maine,* 1907, Resolve, Ch. 176; *Kennebec Journal,* March 23, 1906 (for the bribery debate); *Maine Campus,* March 19, April 16, June 4, 1907; *Nation,* May 2, 23, 1907; *Yale Alumni Weekly,* June 5, 12, 1907, letter E.H. Gleason to Fellows, June 11, with enclosed letters to Yale, L.C. Southard to Fellows, April 4, March 28, 1907, detailing his work with Boston *Transcript* in holding up information. Willis B. Hall to Fellows, April 2, 1907; *Agriculture of Maine,* 1907, 110-3.

40. *Laws of Maine,* 1909, Resolves, Ch. 24, 269; *Leg. Doc.,* 1909, H.R. 5; Haines to Fellows, March 6, 1909; Trustees Minutes, December 1, 1908. Fellows to Haines, March 15, 1909; Fellows to Sumner P. Mills, March 27, 1909; Bangor *Daily Commercial,* March 25; *Bangor Daily News, Kennebec Journal,* March 26, 1909.

41. "Hazing" Folder, report September 2, 1896; Treaty November 29, 1899; Hart to Fred L. Eastman, November 2, 1909.

42. Fellows to Trustees, November 22, 1909.

43. Faculty Minutes, June 9, September 18, 24, October 22, November 5, 19, 26, December 17, 1906; February 4, May 9, June 13, 1907; May 3, 17, 18, 20, 21, June 1, 5 (quote), 1909. Trustees meetings, March 19, June 8, 10, 1908; June 8, 11, 1909, letter "To the Friends of the University of Maine," from Fellows, explaining policy and circulated to parents, *Campus,* March 9, 1909. Also the letters from Hart and Fellows in Notes 41, 42 that give history of the case.

44. At this distance in time it is difficult to recreate the situation exactly, and although I have discussed the matter with several participants, most of them were Sophomores, or Freshmen, and did not participate in any of the affair negotiations. In addition the event has grown in size during alumni gather-

ings since that time. The events of the time can be reconstructed from *Maine Campus,* October 19, September 28 (also edit); October 26 (also edit), November 2 (also edit), November 9, November 23, 1909, October 4, 1910 (Aley's coming). For the documents see Faculty Minutes, October 14, 15, 18, November 1, 15, 16, 29, 1909; Trustees Minutes, November 22, 1909; letter Fellows to Trustees, November 22, 1909; Hart to Eastman, November 2, 1909; letter class officers to faculty, November 12, 1909; E. A. Balentine to students, November 16, 1909; Fellows to L.C. Southard, October 20; October 23; A.C. Gilman to Fellows, October 18; E.D. Winslow (Pres. of Board) to Fellows October 23, (Winslow attended a Portland meeting with students), Fellows to Winslow October 25; Fellows to Haines, January 21, 1910; *Bangor Daily News,* January 21, 1910.

45. Fellows to Winslow, March 17, 1910; E.J. Haskell, '76 to Fellows, April 14, 1910.

46. *Maine Campus,* December 6, 1910. By 1913 the faculty were again deploring "the present objectionable dances" at the recent Junior Prom, although no "cozy corners" were reported. Faculty Minutes, May 12, 1913. Faculty attempted to deny degrees to those involved in 1909, but failed June 4 (twice), 6, 1910.

47. Faculty Minutes, October 2, November 23, December 13, 20, 27, 1899; April 28, May 5, 12, 19, October 6, 1902; November 18, 1907; November 30, 1908; A & S Faculty, December 3, 1912; May 6, November 4, December 21, 1912; November 1, December 6; 1915; Trustees, November 23, 1896; Ag. Faculty, May 24, 1915; *University of Maine Regulations* (rev. to June, 1908); *Admission Exam,* September, 1908; Harris letters on admissions 1893-1901. Another account of these years appears in Karl Pomeroy Harrington, *An Autobiography of a Versatile and Vigorous Professor,* Boston, 1975, esp. 117-121; 133-139. Harrington worked on the admissions policy and was close to Harris.

48. Faculty, September 20, 26, 1898; January 10, 24, 1910; May 25, June 5, 10, September 19, 1911; Trustees, June 23, 1898; June 13, 1911; R.H. Jesse to Fellows, February 18, 1903.

49. Trustees, May 3, 1895; June 13, 1911; Summer School 1909 *Maine Bulletin,* XI, No. 4.

50. Folder "classics," George D. Chase to Hauck, August 31, 1940; Trustees, March 24, 1906; June 9, 1914.

51. *Maine Campus,* November 15, 1901; January 15, 1903; April 3, 1906; J.L. Stevens to Trustees, November 3, 1896; Harris to Haines, February 17, 1896, and whole folder on "Tech. Exp. Station;" Al

Rohner to Fellows December 22, 1906; Faculty, April 8, 15, 22, May 6, 1907. Forestry began in technology and was not moved until 1908 and it was also located partially in Augusta as well. Trustees, April 14, 1903; June 7, 1904; June 12, 1906; April 27, 28, 1909.

52. Trustees, May 1, 1906; letters Haines to W.W. Stetson; GEF to Payson Smith, April 14, 24, 1909; RJA to Smith, December 2, 1910; Aley's presidential address to N.E.A., San Francisco, July, 1911.

53. Trustees, (Bangor) March 16, 1898; June 12, 1900, June 10, November 25, 1902; April 14, November 23, April 25, 1905; letter college of agriculture to Trustees, June 7, 1904; March 19, 1908; June 8, 1908; June 9, 1909; Lewiston *Journal,* February 17, 1906, "How They Teach Farming at the University of Maine."

54. A & S, March 4, 12; February 3, May 5, 1913; Ralph McKee to Boardman, May 2, 1913 (in Tech. meeting, May 26, 1913); Tech. meetings, June 8, 1912; Trustees, June 13, 1911; *Maine Bulletin,* XIII, No. 8.

55. Trustees, December 12, 1899; March 2, 1900; June 10, 1902; June 12, 1906; Haines to Harris, January 9, 1900.

56. *Maine Campus,* December 1, 1904; February 15, 1905; November 6, 1906; *American Architect and Building News,* June 24, 1905; Trustees, March 24, 1905; Carnegie Library File, esp. Fellows to Carnegie, February 9, 1905; *Bangor Commercial,* February 11, 1905; Memo, "Library Appropriations, 1899-1900."

57. *Maine Campus,* March 18, 1913; *Laws of Maine,* Resolves, Ch. 99, 126, 128.

58. On Walter Balentine, See *Cadet,* May, 1894; For others mentioned, see Trustees, September 14, 1897; November 26, 1897 (Huddilston's authorization); June 10, 1902; June 9, 1903; June 12, 1906 (Miss Colvin) to give her equal pay, Fellows to Trustees, June 12, 1906; January 29, 1942, for a memorial to Fellows.

59. Trustees, July 17, November 27, 1894; June 14, 1895; *Maine Campus,* February 11, 1913, for the eulogies and letters on her life. Any reading of the correspondence of the University in those years would agree with her significant role, although she never held a faculty or major administration appointment until just before her death. The quote is from the faculty minutes, January 22, 1913.

60. Merton Lovett to Margaret (in my possession) February 22, 1904. For another student perception which agrees with this see Joseph H. Bodwell, "I Recall 'College Days' at the University of Maine," *Maine Life,* January, 1971.

CHAPTER FOUR

Life at Maine

FOR MANY, if not most, students, leaving home to go to the university, or going "away to school," was the beginning of an irrevocable break with their families. The university was placed in the uncomfortable role of transitional parent, a role often disliked by both students and faculty. In the period before 1914 most college campuses in the United States were the scenes of long-smouldering battles between faculty and students caused by the schools' parental role and also by student questioning of the content and usefulness of courses. Maine, from its beginning to the first World War, was no different from other schools in seeing many campus events directly related to that friction. There were also, of course, many good times, and much of life consisted simply of routine learning. Both aspects need investigation, not least to demonstrate how the youths of the past are really very like the youths of the present.

In the early days, arrival on the campus was not a simple matter. Until the electric cars came through from Bangor in the nineties, the choices were the train from Bangor to Stillwater or the stage from Bangor to Orono. A campus figure for most of these years, "Uncle Ben" Mosher met the trains and stages with his express wagon. He would announce to the new students his views on many of the things that they should and should not do and was always available for a confidential chat. Uncle Ben would drop the students before their dormitories, where they would find in their rooms a double or two single beds, husk mattresses, a table, a washstand, and two chairs, all often in fairly poor shape from the previous users' care. Frequently students provided their own furniture.[1]

Board averaged about three dollars a week in the early days, with laundry and fuel at about fifty cents per week extra. Students were required to make their beds, sweep their rooms, and to post a bond or provide their own furniture for their rooms, which were free along with tuition. Even with these small costs, collection of payment was difficult from the very earliest times.

Students were generally dissatisfied with the amount and type of food. The simple institutional meals varied from fair to bad, although students usually thought them the latter, and attacking food often became a method of getting relief from other frustrations. As early as 1870 or 1871 a "tea riot" broke out, with crockery smashed and much noise in the dining room when the steward refused to provide tea at dinner. The faculty was not sympathetic to the students; thus, when another disturbance broke a few months later they passed a resolution praising the *"almost parental interest"* in the student welfare exhibited by the steward and his wife, who should expect and get the "same propriety of deportment" as if they ran a private boarding house. That fall the trustees adopted new rules of payment and dealt with irregular attendance and with cost. "Students cannot graduate in debt to the college," was their solution to the lack of payment. As late as 1877, however, the trustees were still adjusting board problems with the steward and students.[2]

The next real disturbance occurred in the 1880's. By this time the boarding house was well established, with the steward buying in bulk and operating from a little annex room next to the dining hall. Board had dropped to $2.60 a week, and to $2.50 if fifty students were in attendance.[3] But by 1884 the steward had fallen behind in his payments to local merchants and to the college for funds advanced. Trustee committees were appointed to "regulate affairs" but were not very successful. In early spring 1885 petitions circulated about the quality of the food. In May, after further petitions, the students went on strike, walking en masse to Orono after refusing to eat the prepared food. After a series of meetings the faculty voted to allow them to eat at the downtown hotel, although one meal a day had to be taken at the boarding house. The situation worsened, and eventually the students, mostly seniors, were threatened with not graduating unless they returned to the boarding house. The students then petitioned the trustees concerning the situation, with limited results, but finally a new steward, who was declared to be "quite, quite satisfactory" was brought in.[4]

Similar situations continued to recur throughout the period. Their intensity varied, as often complaints about the food were simply an indication of other, more serious student complaints. However, for students earning their own money, as most did, simple food at low cost was sufficient.

A few term bills survive so we can judge what it cost to go to M.S.C. in those years. For instance, C.M. Brainard, '76, paid $41.51, $37.77, $45.36, and $45.46 for his last four semesters in college. Board was the largest bill, averaging about $30.00 per semester.[5] In 1887 a semester bill amounted to $85.82 with nineteen weeks of board at $2.60 the largest item. Room rent, now charged, was $5.00 and fuel $9.73. This student also paid $.25 for repairs and $1.29 for washing and ironing.[6] Ten years later the bills were only slightly higher.[7]

Student Expenditures 1891-95

G.G. Atwood '95

Travel	$ 77.00
Clothing	75.00
Incidentals	22.00
Board	255.00
Room Furnish	14.00
Fuel	55.00
Military etc.	18.00
Books	90.00
Stationery/Draw.	11.00
Laundry/Mend	33.00
Other	28.00
Totals	$678.00
Vacation Exp.	175.00
	853.00

C.A. Frost '95

Travel	$ 44.65
Books	47.05
Drawing Inst.	27.30
Clothing	83.75
Athletics	14.75
Incidentals	55.19
Board/Washing	335.33
Rent/Fuel/Repairs	263.40
Class Expenses	21.50
Fall Freshman Year (not itemized)	70.00
Total	$962.92

This photograph and the one on the facing page show the trolley cars of the Bangor, Orono, and Old Town Railroad. The cars travelled on a regular schedule between these towns, and students used (and misused) them regularly. When they left the trolley, entrance to the campus was along this road. The president's house, Coburn Hall, and the engineering shops can be seen through the trees. Buses would make their regular stops here later. Both of these photos date from the 1890's.

There were irritants other than bills and food, and chapel was a major one. Chapel had been compulsory since the opening of the school but by the nineties many questioned its value. The first to stop attending services were the faculty; in 1890 the student newspaper remarked, "The chapel seems to have no attraction whatever for

These two photographs show the first two college chapel rooms. To the right is Professor Aubert lecturing on chemistry in Fernald Hall. The lower photo shows the chapel room in Coburn Hall set up for services. The change came in 1888, and the Aubert photograph is taken afterward. Later, chapel was held in Alumni Hall after its construction.

Henry L. Lander, Steward, 1877-1884.

the members of the faculty.''[8] A variety of changes were tried in order to retain chapel: making it shorter, making it partially voluntary, and including other than religious exercises. Eight-five students presented a petition in 1893 asking that they be excused, and, although it was denied, discussion continued and compulsory chapel dropped (but reinstated within a month!). By 1894 chapel included declamations and oratory from students, as well as religious services. In 1899, when church attendance on Sunday in Orono churches was made voluntary, chapel began to be less important. By 1916 its primary purpose was to provide talks creating a professional spirit among the students; but as long as M.C. Fernald lived some aspects of the religious service remained, and he often led the Friday service even after his retirement in 1908.[9] Chapel would disappear for good by the 1920's.

As will be remembered, in the first decade the college year included three terms and lasted from sometime in September to early August. At the time of the curriculum changes in 1876, the terms were decreased to two, the first running from August first to Thanksgiving, followed by an eleven-week vacation. Most students taught in rural elementary schools during this vacation. The second term ran from February to the Wednesday before the Fourth of July. This allowed students to participate in the haying season, where their labor was much needed. In 1885 the student newspaper ran a poll to determine preference. Of those voting, seventeen favored continuation of the system, sixteen wanted two equal terms with an eight-week vacation, and eight wanted something different. It was 1896 before the faculty adopted the two-term system in roughly the same time period as now, although it did not go into operation until 1898.[10]

When the college moved into the two-term system, there was a wholesale review and analysis of the curriculum. This discussion began over the efficacy of teaching Latin and Greek. After several meetings a new curriculum was adopted, and although it was slightly modified in 1879, these were the routines that students followed at the college until the turn of the century, when the addition of courses and faculty made wide variation possible.[11] All students had an identical freshman and sophomore year as follows:

Freshman

First Term	Second Term
9 Phys. Geog.	Farm Drainage and Botany
10 Algebra	Algebra and Geometry
11 Rhetoric	French
P.M. Labor	Bookkeeping and Labor

Sophomore

8 French & Farm Equipment	6 Surveying (Women-Hy of England)
9 Trigonometry	8 Mech. Cultivation of the Soil
10 General Chemistry	9 Anal. Geom. and Calculus
11 Botany	9-10 Qual. Chemistry
P.M. F.H. Murrays Chemistry	11 English Lit. and Physics
(A standard text)	P.M. Mech. Drawing and Field Work

The last two years follow for the major courses of study.

AGRICULTURE
Junior

First Term	Second Term
8 Physiology	8 Astronomy & Pecks Mechanics
9 Ag. Chemistry	9 German
(Ladies — English Literature)	10 Zoology and
10 German	&
11 Physics	11 Entomology
P.M. Chemistry (Ladies —	P.M. Chemistry and Exp. Farming
Analysis of English Authors)	(Ladies — Analysis of American Authors)

Senior

8 Hist. of Civilization	8 Mineralogy and Geology
9 Logic	9 Mental & Moral Philosophy
10 Comparative Anatomy	10 U.S. Const. & Pol. Economy
11 Dairy Farming & Stock Breeding	11 Cereals, Landscape Gardening,
P.M. Exp. Farming & Agric.	Rural Architecture & Sheep Husbandry
Botany (Ladies — Hist. Readings	
& Analysis)	

MECH. ENGINEERING

Junior Year

First Term	Second Term
8 Calculus	8 Astronomy
9 Machinery and Mill Work	9 German
10 German	10 Machinery and Mill Work
11 Physics	11 Desc. Geometry
P.M. Machine Drawing & Shading	P.M. Geometric and Cabinet Proj. and Perspective

Senior Year

8 Physiology with Juniors	8 Mineralogy & Geology
9 Logic	9 Steam Engine Desc. & Spec.
10 Steam Engine	10 U.S. Const. & Pol. Economy
P.M. Machine Drawing	P.M. Machine Drawing and Designing
Applied Desc. Geometry	

CIVIL ENGINEERING

Junior Year

First Term	Second Term
8 Calculus	8 Astronomy
9 Hencks Field Book	9 German
10 German	10 First Part Rankine's C.E. & Mechanics
11 Physics	11 Desc. Geometry
P.M. Field Work & Shading	P.M. Geometric and Cabinet Projects & Perspective

Senior Year

8 Physiology With Juniors	8 Mineralogy and Geology
9 Logic	9
10	10 U.S. Const. & Pol. Economy
11 2nd Part Rankine's C.E.	11 3rd Part Rankine's C.E. & Special Designs
P.M. Stereotomy [mapmaking?] Topography and R.R. Work	P.M. Machine Drawing & Designing

CHEMISTRY

Junior Year

First Term	Second Term
8 Physiology	8 Chemistry
9 Chemistry	9 German
10 German	10 Zoology
11 Physics	&
P.M. Laboratory Work	11 Entomology
	P.M. Laboratory Work

Senior Year

8 Hist. of Civilization	8 Mineralogy & Geology
9 Logic	9
10 Comp. Anatomy	10 U.S. Const. & Pol. Economy
11 Chemistry	11 Chemistry
P.M. Laboratory Work	P.M. Laboratory Work

A class of prospective engineers meeting in Wingate Hall perhaps at the turn of the century. The experiment in place suggests some study in electricity is in progress.

After the 1879 changes, freshmen found themselves taking physiology rather than rhetoric in the first term and farm drainage was dropped. In the second year, farm equipment and mechanical cultivation were also dropped, and mechanical drawing and forge work became electives. The other courses remained essentially the same for the last two years, except that civil engineers worked less with the dreaded Rankine. Rankine was the author of a famous and very difficult text widely used in engineering colleges.

In addition to class work these students, like any students, were interested in other matters. Hazing occupied a remarkable amount of time, as did a certain amount of high jinks. Both were part of that continuous war between the faculty and students that was the custom in those days. Who would rule the campus was a question to which answers were neither always forthcoming, nor always the same.

In the early 1870's, as an example, there were no modern plumbing facilities on the campus. Privies were provided, but in a central location (approximately where the cannons are now), and on cold winter days students from White or Oak found the walk too arduous. For that reason they used the basement of their dormitories as makeshift privies and emptied

their slops outside their windows. The faculty found these practices intolerable and held many meetings to discuss how to get the students to mend their evil ways. At one meeting, after "much faculty talk on the subject," it was decided to speak "plainly and openly" with the students. Although drains were dug and eventually sewers built, the practices continued. Students were caught, the president "admonished" them, but still the lazy and unclean continued their behavior.[12]

In the mid-1800's the sanitation problem coincided with another long-term difficulty. There had been instances of disorder in the dormitories and a weekly inspection by the president and a faculty person was instituted in an effort to ease the situation. Occasionally some students would not unlock their doors, but by and large the inspection did eliminate much of the disorder. Soon, however, the president nominated others to do the inspecting and in the early 1880's the job fell to a West Point graduate assigned to the campus. (There were still some vestiges of Civil War era military discipline at the school).[13]

The young military officer given the inspection job, Lt. Edgar Howe, was not much liked by the students for he did his inspections with white gloves (he even insisted on the proper

Professor W.A. Pike,
an early faculty member

A postal photograph of a famous hazing incident. The
"Old Guard of 1906" are drilling their victims. The
cannon has just been fired. Alumni Hall surveys the
event.

placement of toothbrushes on washbowls) and in his classrooms insisted on a West Point atmosphere. In the fall of 1883, sophomores petitioned that he be removed from his trigonometry class because they could not understand him. Following a number of meetings between faculty and students, the students were made to apologize. It was obvious that this was a crisis for student-faculty relations. Howe took over the room inspection in the spring, and after one or two difficult scenes, the students all met in one room and would not rise when he and Fernald entered. The faculty ruled that the students were in insurrection, further ruled that inspection was a part of drill, and passed out demerits for all who refused to allow Howe to enter. The situation smouldered until March, when students first stole all the guns from the armory, then captured Howe and locked him in a basement still being used as the substitute privy. After a day and a half there, Howe asked for a transfer, which was granted, and although demerits were again awarded, the students, as a contemporary remarked, "for once won a partial victory."[14]

Other minor matters of control included the small incident concerning a student, F.B. Mallett, ex'77. Mallett put cow-itch in the bed of Professor Pike, who complained, and the faculty suspended Mallett. He simply moved into another dormitory, while his class asked for another hearing. Eventually Mallett's father appeared, demanded a second hearing, asked for an apology, and threatened suit for false arrest. The faculty collogued, retained legal advice, asked Mallett's father to bring his evidence of false arrest, and voted 5-3 to resist him if he came. The father did not produce the evidence and the boy left the college, so faculty power was retained, if only by default.[15]

More serious were the almost continuous cases of hazing. Faculty hated the practice, but the students thought it a sign of their manhood and of their independence from outside control. The faculty waged a battle throughout this period to end it. However, in its most rigorous forms hazing lasted until the strike of 1909 and was not finally abolished until the 1930's. Oftentimes these battles ended with serious confrontations between students and faculty.

Hazing usually involved having freshmen obey certain rules, such as marching properly, not wearing certain clothing, carrying matches

The mounted display animals from the museum frequently left their homes. Some climbed buildings. Others went for strolls. This one, eyeing the camera with trepidation was often harnessed for the edification of parents and friends.

for upperclassmen and always addressing them as "sir," and never speaking to women on the campus. Those who transgressed these rules were visited at night by masked men, often armed with swords or guns, who made the recalcitrant drill. Occasionally paddling or being tossed in the river were the punishments.[16]

One of the first acts of the trustees in the second year of student attendance at the college, 1869, was to decry hazing and to support the faculty in its suppression of it. The student council discussed it in 1873 and asked for and received a resignation from college from the worst offender. Hazing continued, and in 1874 a student sought and received permission to resist entrance into his room. One hazer was demasked when he met with opposition, was suspended for a year, and given twenty-four hours to absent himself from the town.[17]

At their annual meeting in 1877 the trustees adverted to hazing, called with "deep regret" for the shielding of students from the practice, and announced, again, that they would back any suppression methods. An especially bad hazing season in 1878 resulted in four students being dismissed outright and a fifth suspended for a

year. A student petition for reinstatement was denied. In 1879 the faculty made the signing of an anti-hazing pledge a condition of entrance, and the trustees gladly accepted the condition. The pledge follows:

> So long as I remain a student in the Maine State College of Agriculture and the Mechanic Arts, I regard myself in honor-bound to abstain from lawless conduct — and all those acts of annoyance towards others, denominated 'hazing' and I hereby not only pledge myself to abstain from such acts, but to discontenance them in others.[18]

The situation seemed somewhat better, although there were scattered incidents, as in 1882, when one student lost his derby and another retained his "only by show of pistol." All sophomores received four demerits for this escapade (ten was cause for dismissal).[19] In 1885 another confrontation resulted in student petitions for reinstatement of those dismissed and finally probation for the guilty students after they agreed to again take the oath.[20]

The next year matters got worse when a hazing incident was stopped and five students were suspended. Coincidentally, the faculty was at-

This remarkable photograph (from the first decade of the college) shows students ostensibly studying together. The clay pipes indicate nonchalance, while the books demonstrate diligence. The kerosene lamp threw a good deal of light.

tempting to enforce the compulsory chapel rule then being honored in the breach by many. When no students had appeared after fifteen minutes at the next chapel, the faculty voted to ask individuals where they stood and if they supported the rules or not; if not, they were to be suspended and given twenty-four hours to leave the campus. In addition, the faculty agreed not to meet with any more student committees. Freshmen agreed to obey the rules, but thirty-six upperclassmen were suspended. Another chapel was then held and some students left while the suspensions were being discussed. As a result seven more were suspended. A letter was sent home to parents declaring that the students were "in open rebellion" because of the faculty's role in the suppression of hazing. If students would promise obedience to the regulations they would be allowed to return after ten days, otherwise, they would be dis-

missed. Several students refused to leave the premises and were offered the alternative of dismissal or signature of the anti-hazing pledge. Within five days college routines were restored, since students were unwilling to test the strength of the rules any further. The student newspaper sided with the faculty, indicating that most students did not want hazing, and for that reason it disappeared, or at least was diminished for a while.[21]

The hazing pledge was revised in 1890, but in 1893 another minor insurrection took place after severe hazing of a disliked student, who left. Suspensions were made and a class strike, of one day's duration, followed. In 1895 another similar event occurred, but the suspensions were lightened after petition. Students had pointed out to the faculty in their petitions that no one had been injured, as there had been in 1878. More hazing occurred in 1896 and 1899,

The Cadet *editorial board, 1887-1888. Fifth from the left is the editor, D.E. Campbell, '88. The straw on the floor is mystifying. The cabalistic signs on the cheeks were added later and indicate their fraternity memberships. Heads are held in photographers' vices here.*

followed by suspensions, meetings, discussions, and a new pledge, which in 1899 was given to all students by the president himself. After administration of the pledge, the suspensions were lifted, which seemed to be the routine way of handling this type of incident until 1909 when the famous student strike occurred, with its hazing overtones, although much else was at stake there. The pledge continued, and hazing decreased.[22]

There was also a fair amount of drinking and intoxication, even in as straitlaced a school as M.S.C. In 1873 drinking in student rooms was followed by an incident in Houlton while students were on a trip to perform before the State Board of Agriculture, and then another incident in Orono. Considerable discussion followed as to whether suspension would bring the leading student back to the fold or not. The result of the matter was a public repentance at chapel,

nine demerits, and assurance that this was simply a freak occurrence. In 1880, following an election bet, there was another scene in the college rooms, but the procurer of the "lager beer" was simply suspended. Election time was always a problem as well, and in both 1880 and 1888 banners were flown and torn down by the opposition before rules as to who could fly, where, and for how long were instituted.[23]

In that era, faculty and trustees also spent a good deal of time and effort preventing smoking. It was banned both in front of and in the college buildings. Prohibition was futile, though, and finally tobacco was simply not sold in the college store. But smoking continued for men at least. Later, smoking by women was an issue throughout the 1920's.[24]

Even playing ball was forbidden near the college buildings for a long time. Of course, organized sports soon took the place of casual playing and fields were provided. Once organized athletics began, the scene shifted from hazing of freshmen to hazing of the opponents and their supporters, and later to wild celebrations of famous victories. A major confrontation apparently took place between Bowdoin and Maine supporters at a Bath rally for W.J. Bryan in 1896. An arrest followed the melee, and, as President Hyde said to President Harris, ". . . I think there will be no more trouble." Later, in 1902, Maine had a strong baseball team, losing only to the New York Giants on a southern trip. The first game of that trip was won by Maine over Wesleyan, 4-3, after Wesleyan scored two runs in the ninth inning. News of this win was telegraphed back, and the students reacted by holding a giant rally, burning one of the electric car waiting rooms. The next year a victory over Bowdoin also produced what one faculty member called a "drunken carousal," but no buildings burned, only a huge bonfire.

In 1905 members of the football team, in celebration of their good season, attempted to steal the G.A.R. cannons from Mount Hope cemetery in Bangor and were only just thwarted, but perhaps the worst of these acts occurred

The baseball nine of the class of 1877, in front of White Hall. This was the first organized sport on the campus. Teams played other classes. It would be a few years before the schedules extended beyond the campus. Equipment was rudimentary.

after the winning of the state track meet in 1913. A special train returned from Bowdoin with supporters of the school, and when it stopped for water in Waterville, a quick raid was made on Colby buildings. The scene on the train grew wilder and drunker. Upon arrival at Orono, a great melee culminated in the burning of another waiting room building. Faculty deplored this destruction and the riots, but could do little about them because they were so widely attended by the student body. It was an era when great happenings were often accompanied by property destruction, especially on college campuses. Maine was no exception to that rule.

The appearance of Dockstadter's Minstrels or some other major touring vaudeville group became the occasion for most of the student body to attend the Bangor Opera House. If the groups were well prepared, opening with the M.S.C. songs and pointing their jokes at the faculty, the audience was appreciative; if they were not well prepared, the audience became increasingly boisterous, throwing items at the performers, shouting, singing, and sometimes stopping the show. Performers in this period knew how to react, and did. Only tyros did not prepare for these audiences and have material for them. In fact some performers worked only the college town circuit with special materials for the students.

The return from the Bangor performances was also apt to be a wild and sometimes drunken scene, especially on the last car on Saturday night. Either the car might be damaged severely or it might be pulled off the tracks or the students might refuse to pay. The worst of these affairs occurred in October 1903, and the car company threatened to end its service, but of course the service continued. On the campus, there were always skeletons to put on the gable in Coburn or on the roof at Winslow, or calves to be placed in equally difficult and strange locations. Professors often found the wheels on their buggies changed or cannon in their classrooms. These were the events that made college life the unique experience it was for men of these generations.[25] As observed before, women for the most part lived sheltered lives away from campus.

Students stole fruit from the college orchard, hens and turkeys from the poultry houses, or honey from the hives, and had forbidden feasts on the hill away from the campus or occasionally in their rooms. No matter how the faculty hoped for student self-discipline, or how often they said that the stolen items were the material of farm experimentation, the depredations went on. Suspensions were the rule for those caught. Sometimes there was embarrassment as in 1892 when Louis C. Southard's son was caught in the coop with three chickens. The president said to his leading alumnus, "I presume you agree that the same sentence [rustication] will be necessary." Southard could only accept the dictates of his alma mater.[26]

The sophomores' indiscriminate bullying of the freshmen gradually declined in favor of more organized activities. The faculty was willing to accept these sorts of activities as being a part of student life and to ignore the fact that it was still the same old hazing, although now transferred to a different location. A number of soon-to-be traditional events began. By 1900 it was customary for the sophomores to parade the freshmen in their night shirts through the campus. In the 1920's the route was around Balentine Hall, the first women's dormitory. Before this time the new class always attempted to paint its class numbers on the standpipe while the older group tried to prevent it. The scene was sometimes quite physical in tone. Class athletic teams were always part of the milieu, and it was traditional for the freshman-sophomore football game to be fought over a large bag of peanuts. This custom degenerated into the peanut scrap of the later period.

Other trials of strength were the flag scrap, over control of the football field after the first home game, and the Frogpond scrap, over control of the land near the power house. A large mud pond was located there and winners and losers alike were usually mud covered. Another place of contention was the steam plant itself. Classes usually held class banquets whose site and menu was kept secret because the opposition class traditionally captured the president after the banquet, carried him away (a favorite destination was Macwahoc), and left him to make his way home. Such were the days, as hazing itself disappeared somewhat or made its home in fraternity initiations free from the spying eyes of the faculty and president.[27]

Not all the events were as free and easy; sometimes students shot off guns and pistols in their rooms or sometimes students suffering un-

SOPHOMORE PROCLAMATIONS

The annual sophomore proclamations to the freshmen appeared last Tuesday night, and are surely good enough to bear repeating.

FRESHMEN!

Give heed to these RULES laid down by your ELDERS and BETTERS, the

CLASS OF 1907

to assist you in casting aside your robes of verdancy, and in your aping the ways of college men, to prevent you from becoming too deeply involved in the labyrinthine circumplications and multiflexuous aufractuosities thereof.

FIRST—Under no circumstances whatever will Freshmen be permitted to smoke on the College Campus.

SECOND—Freshmen must not carry canes or smoke pipes.

THIRD—Freshmen must not wear a derby hat or display kid gloves.

FOURTH—Freshmen must always show their respect and give precedence to Ladies, Faculty and Upper Classmen.

FIFTH—Freshmen must not accompany Ladies.

SIXTH—Freshmen must not wear anything but college emblems on Clothing.

FURTHERMORE

We do advise Freshmen to keep off the grass, as the similarity of appearance would render them inconspicuous. For the prevention of colic, croup, measles, whooping-cough and sore gums among the Freshmen Class, we advise them to have their milk bottles sterilized at least once a week.

1907

Hazing rules were often phrased in this fashion, taken from the Maine *Campus in 1905, in order to emphasize the difference between freshman and upper classmen.*

Photo of the Cadets encamped at Searsport, Maine, 1894. The students honored their new president by naming their bivouac, Camp A.W. Harris.

This stiff formal portrait shows the commissioned officers of the Cadet Corps in 1902. The swords are still an important part of the uniform, while the caps, jackets and trousers, although somewhat different, are reminiscent of Civil War uniforms. These cadets would have been the first officers to lead drill in the new gymnasium, built soon after the Spanish-American War.

requited love were unable to deal with the world away from home. Cheating was also a problem, and finally, after an especially bad two or three years of it and repeated attempts to form honor codes, the faculty announced a clear list of penalties in 1907.[28] Frequently the faculty attempted to mobilize student allies to help police the college of these transgressions; therefore some form of student government was often present. It usually held little power and soon fell into disuse. In this period, the faculty and the president controlled the campus, made the rules, and determined punishments. Students usually were aligned on the other side. Although it may be too much to say that campus life was a continuous battle between students and faculty, that battle lurked under the surface and often came to light.[29]

Another major part of college life, for the men at least, was the compulsory drill and military exercises. The local drill group, the Coburn Cadets, occasionally won prizes for their expertise, but more often drill was a cause of discontent. Many students did not want to participate; the drill master was sometimes disliked, as when Lieutenant Howe was at the school; even the style of uniforms was complained of and was changed from time to time by the War Department.[30] Athletic and musical organizations were all exempt from drill in this period, and the student newspaper remarked, ". . . no one would greatly miss the military department if it remained dormant for all time."[31] By the end of the 1880's attendance was low and only the annual encampment seemed to interest students.

The cadets went away for an encampment every year during the 1890's, usually to Lewiston, but also to Castine and Searsport. At camp they drilled, stood guard, participated in war games, and generally, from the accounts, had a good time sparking the young women of the area. Eventually the encampments were stopped because some students disliked the tent life, but they were continued as long as they were useful publicity for the college. The Spanish-American War seems to mark the end of these trips.[32]

When that war came students, who were not so rattled as the press, watched with much interest. They debated the question of the *Maine's* sinking, suggesting that an international board of arbiters should decide on the cause.

Gradually public opinion was whipped up and some forty students from the Coburn Cadets enlisted and were feted in a mass meeting. Few of them fought, but five died of disease (four were students, one an alumnus). The governor lauded the enlistees for their efforts, but this first venture into real military life apparently soured many on the campus, for there was a falling off of drill and finally a period, through most of 1900 and 1901, when no drill at all was held. After this the military did remain part of campus life, but it had a much less central role than before. Even in its more popular time uniforms, drilling, and encampment were the extent of involvement for most students; getting excused was the rule for many.[33]

Fraternities were also a part of student life, although less so in the period before 1900 than at many other colleges. Their heyday came in the immediate prewar period and the 1920's, although one feels that they were still of relatively less importance at Maine than at some

A.C. Lyon, '02, in his den at the Phi Gamma Delta House. He is the central figure in the front row on the opposite page as well.

Spearen Inn, a local boarding house. It became a fraternity house in the 1920's, housing Sigma Phi Sigma (disbanded in 1936) at first and later Tau Kappa Epsilon. The building was used as a student dormitory after 1903 on a leased basis and as needed until its purchase in 1921.

Kappa Sigma house when first built.

other places, as substantial numbers of students were not members and even student organizations were less of a province of fraternity politics than elsewhere. The first of the fraternities, the QTV society, was begun in 1870 but did not attract much attention during its first two or three years. Eventually it obtained a chapter house, which became a great trial for the trustees as the order found itself constantly in debt. There are many mentions of fraternities in the records but mostly in requests for loans from the trustees. Trustees were caught in a bind because the fraternities increasingly provided housing for students, and thus were a useful adjunct to a college oftentimes strapped for funds.[34]

During scarlet fever epidemics in 1895 and 1899 fraternity houses were used as pest houses by the college, which disturbed some of the members but apparently cut the spread of the disease. As the fraternities grew and affiliated with national organizations, irritations mounted among them so the Senior Skull organization was formed in 1906 to aid in college unity and promote kindlier feelings among the fraternities.

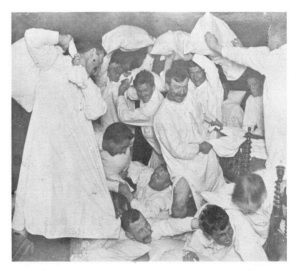

Irving Harry "Ike" Drew, '99, and Wilkie Collins "Skog" Clark, '00, in their room in the original Phi Gamma Delta House. The amount of memorabilia is wonderful to behold both in this and Lyon's room, p. 87.

The Beta Theta Pi brothers in a pillow fight in 1892. North Hall housed this fraternity. The freshman are on the floor. "Scissors" Weston is in the bottom group, second from the right.

By 1910 many of the fraternities were still in bad financial condition. When freshman initiation was dropped for one year, faculty members were worried enough to write the board. James N. Hart put it well.

> I understand, of course, that the Trustees naturally look at the filling of the new dormitory as a business proposition but in view of the rather unsatisfactory financial condition of many of the fraternities, it is possible that their prospects should be considered also.[35]

There were, of course, many other student organizations. From 1874 to the present there has been some sort of student publication. The *College Reporter* appeared monthly from 1874 to 1878, and the *College Review* through 1876-77. In the 1880's there was a series of fraternity type yearly publications, the *Pendulum,* from 1881 to 1884, and the *Transit,* for 1884. The class histories in these volumes yield a good deal of detail of hazing and other minor events in those years. In August 1885, a monthly entitled the *Cadet* appeared and was published until 1899 when the *Maine Campus*

A nice shot of part of fraternity row. Phi Gamma Delta is the house beyond Mount Vernon. Orono is in the distance.

THE PROGRAM

PERSONNEL

THE GLEE CLUB

Geo. P. Goodwin, - - Leader

First Tenors	*Second Tenors*
W. H. Burke	R. R. Drummond
R. S. Coffin	E. D. Blaisdell
R. M. Foster	G. H. Hill
Geo. P. Goodwin	A. Plummer
B. A. Young	

First Bass	*Second Bass*
C. Boyle	J. T. Bates
R. Fellows	T. F. Bye
F. W. Files	C. W. Reynolds
E. O. Sweetser	S. M. Bird
E. J. Wilson	

Accompanist, - - T. F. Bye

THE BANJO ORCHESTRA

S. M. Bird, - - Leader

First Banjos	*Second Banjos*
S. M. Bird	C. P. Fagen
F. D. Southard	W. J. St. Onge
L. D. Barrows	C. W. Reynolds

First Mandolins	*Second Mandolins*
R. R. Drummond	W. B. Alexander
R. W. Haskell	E. D. Blaisdell
F. F. Smith	E. R. Richards
	H. C. Stetson

Guitars	
T. F. Bye	B. T. Harvey
A. J. Pennell	F. H. Harlow

Mandola	*Violoncello*
R. H. Alton	A. W. Sprague

PART FIRST

I Ein fideles Marschlied. *Juettner*

GLEE AND MANDOLIN CLUBS

II Devil's Patrol . . . .

MANDOLIN CLUB

III Bandolero, Vocal Solo . . *Stuart*

MR. SWEETSER

IV B' Gosh . . . . *Jennings*

BANJO ORCHESTRA

V Reading . . . . *Selected*

MR. GOODRICH

VI "Comic" Medley . . . *Shattuck*

GLEE CLUB

PART SECOND

I Zeono Waltzes . . . .

MANDOLIN CLUB

II To the Evening Star . *Wagner*

Solo for Violoncello

MR. SPRAGUE

III Carry Me Back to Old
Virginny . . . . *Bland*

GLEE CLUB

Tenor Solo by MR. GOODWIN

IV Silver Crown Schottische . .
. . . . *Jennings*

BANJO SEXTET

V Maine Campus Song . . . .
. . . . . . *Arr. by O. F. Lewis*

GLEE AND MANDOLIN CLUBS

PERSONNEL

THE MANDOLIN CLUB

R. R. Drummond, Leader

First Mandolins

R. R. Drummond

R. W. Haskell

F. D. Southard

F. F. Smith

Second Mandolins

W. B. Alexander

E. D. Blaisdell

E. R. Richards

H. C. Stetson

Guitars

B. T. Harvey   A. J. Pennell

F. H. Harlow

Mandola	*Violoncello*
R. H. Alton	A. W. Sprague

Violin

R. R. Drummond

READER

J. K. Goodrich

The program for the spring concert of the various musical clubs in 1905. The pieces played as well as the instrumentation tells us much of the period.

Professor J.P. "Paddy" Huddilston.

replaced it, first as a bi-monthly, later as a weekly, and more recently as a bi-weekly. the *Campus* was described by its first editors as "a live newsy college journal, one which will be of interest to the student body and the alumni" and "free from many of the objectionable features so often noticed in many college periodicals." Readers since that day will be able to determine for themselves how well the journal has met its early goals.

Perhaps the first of the college societies with a cultural or intellectual bent was the Scientific Society of 1870. Later the college boasted such groups as the Deutscher Verein, Press Club, Mathematical and Physical Society, Philosophical Club, and the Literati.[36] The establishment of university courses in 1897 resulted in the establishment of honorary fraternities, first Alpha Sigma Eta (to be renamed Phi Kappa Phi almost immediately), and then the Maine Chapter of Sigma Xi.[37] Maine's

"As You Like It," the cast shown here, was the first significant public dramatic performance, May 22, 1907, Wednesday of Junior Week. This is an all-male cast.

chapter of Phi Kappa Phi was the founding chapter, and the national society dates from this beginning. Other campus organizations included the YMCA (1881), Bicycle Club (1884), the Gymnasium Association (1884?), and the Baseball Association (1882?), a form of intramural society.

It was not really until the twentieth century that the fine arts — music, art, and theatre — were to make much impact at Maine. In all three areas the growth was due to singular faculty members who devoted large amounts of time to the effort. In music the prime mover was a Bangor musician who served as a professor of music for many years, Adelbert Sprague. It was he who began the university orchestra, glee clubs (which had been organized on a class basis before), and eventually the marching band. Sprague was a showman himself and was able to create interest in music wherever he or one of his organizations went.

Theatre was very much a personal production of Windsor P. Daggett, who arrived in 1906 to teach speech with an emphasis on drama. The Maine Masque, first known as the Dramatic Club, began that winter, and in May the group put on *As You Like It* in an all-male production. It proved to be a smash hit. Daggett remained until the war and led the Masque and drama at Maine successfully after this strong beginning.

In art the central person was John Homer "Paddy" Huddilston. A character on the campus, he had written on Greek vase art for his dissertation and used Greek and Roman art objects and photographs to illustrate his famous classics courses. When the new gymnasium was built Huddilston asked for the old one (the converted shop then used as a gymnasium) for an art museum, and it was granted to him. To support the museum Huddilston founded the art guild "to further the cultural life of Maine." From 1900 to 1904 monthly lectures were given to a membership that was always wider than the campus. The members obtained many reproductions and began the now-famous university collection. The collection was housed in Carnegie for a time, then on the top floor of Stevens when that building was constructed, before being returned to its present location in Carnegie.[38]

There were always school connected songs sung by Maine undergraduates and alumni. In the earliest days one popular campus song was an attack on the hated Rankine, torturer of civil engineers. It went like this:

Lincoln Colcord, '05, author of "The Stein Song."

> Come all ye close students, and listen and hear
> I will sing of a man and a bold engineer
> Who wrote large red volumes of many a ream
> And went by the memorable name of Rankine.
> Chorus:
> Singing fulcrum and lever, connections and points
> Resultants and motions with dead working joints.[39]

Other early songs were "Way Down on the Maine State Farm," and "Sing a Song of Maine, Boys!" Soon there was a college hymn, written by Horace Estabrooke, '76, that began "Dear College Home: With Thee Peace and Prosperity Ever Remain." None of these efforts was completely satisfactory as a representative college song; therefore, in 1898 the student newspaper sponsored a contest for a song that would have "that rollicking, swinging quality that it makes the blood thrill to listen to it." Several were written, but none given the prize, although they were printed in the *Campus.* The search continued, and in 1900 a song, called the "Maine Campus Song," was being sung. It was also called the "Stein Song" because the verses could be sung as a drinking song. The chorus sometimes went:

> For it's *always* fair weather
> When good fellows get together
> And life's in its springtime
> On the campus of old Maine.

Professor Adelbert Sprague, '05, composer of "The Stein Song" and later chairman of the music department.

This song was very similar to a Harvard song, however, and the hunt for something distinct continued. In the summer of 1902 Adelbert Sprague was playing an engagement at Bar Harbor when he heard the march "Opie." He rewrote part of it and gave the music to Lincoln Colcord, '05, who wrote the words. The glee club performed the new song, "The Stein

The first football team, 1892. Lore Rogers, '96, a famous alumnus, for whom Rogers Hall was named, is at the left of the next to last row. These uniforms are "moleskins" and canvas. Those with the canvas shirts are linemen.

Song," although many were disturbed by the anti-prohibition nature of the tune. By 1907, when Sprague returned from graduate study, the song was the college song that had been hunted for and it soon drove all the rest into oblivion.[40]

The one occasion when all these songs would be sung was the famous Maine Night, a fixture in college life from 1902 to the first World War. Usually on the eve of the Bowdoin (or very occasionally Colby) football game, it was held in the chapel with songs, speeches, cheers, and much attention to alumni, the more famous of whom would be introduced and give speeches of short duration cheering the football team on to great efforts. After the festivities a giant bon-

fire would be lit for the edification of the students. By 1915 Maine Night was an occasion for alumni gatherings everywhere. These events began when the alumni association was becoming strong following the first efforts in 1895 to change the college to a university. In those days Portland and Boston groups were especially active. The Parker House in Boston was reserved for a special day and the Maine alumni journeyed to the event. From this it was an easy transition to the Maine Night on the campus as the focus of alumni spirit.[41]

Sports, including football, were important extracurricular activities at the college. Baseball came first with class teams in 1877, followed by a few games with local town teams. The first

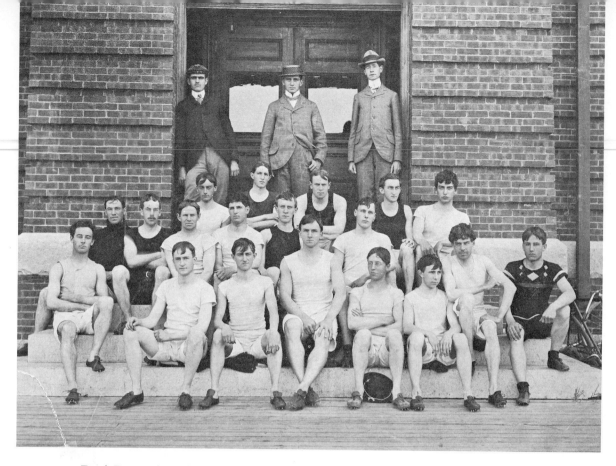

Track Team, 1899. The spiked shoes and uniforms would not change for forty years. The managers, in the back here, would dress differently however.

college game was lost to Colby in the spring of 1880, by 6-1. The next year the team was successful over Bates and Bowdoin. The time allotted for practice as well as the hoped-for trips away became a problem for the faculty. In 1885 a state league was formed, playing a nine-game schedule, a league which Maine was in and out of for a few years. In 1887 a tour was taken to New Brunswick, but not Nova Scotia, as that was deemed to be too far. By this time baseball was a major campus sport.[42] The class teams continued to be fielded, fall and spring.

A sort of rugby was played on the campus in the early 1880's with the first game lasting for two hours before one team scored. Some say a game was played with Tufts in 1887, but the first real attempts actually began later with club teams in 1889 and a freshman and varsity team in 1892. By 1895 a local athletic association supervised football as to whether or not bills were paid. Although this was a period of many "ringers" and paid athletes, Maine did not have that problem. However, after professional coaches began to be used at the school (the first

was Edgar R. Wingard, football coach and athletic director from 1910 to 1916), two or three small incidents did occur with money for equipment being used to supplement athlete incomes. Football soon became very important. Perhaps 1912 and 1913 were the high points in this period with the 1912 team going undefeated except for a 7-0 loss to Harvard in Cambridge, a game in which the Boston papers thought Maine had tied 0-0, as the clock seemed not to run until Harvard had scored at the end of the game.

In 1913, although losing badly to Harvard, Maine was undefeated in the state, and tied Yale 0-0. The 1903 team was also undefeated in the state, but lost to Harvard 6-0 and Holy Cross 5-0. When the forward pass was legalized in 1906, Maine pioneered in its use and was very successful with it from 1906 to 1908 under the restrictive rules of that time. In 1913, when the football team had its success and the cross country team were New England champions, a special train brought the teams from Portland to Bangor to a parade with bands and fireworks, preceding a special performance at the Bijou

Theatre where the vaudevillians keyed their show to Maine using the Maine cheerleaders and ending with the Maine school songs.[43]

Basketball, after 1901, and track were also very important, especially competition for the State Championship in track. In fact, sports and music were such attractions at this time that a set of rules as to participation, absences, subscription drives, and other matters had to be devised by a faculty-student committee which worked for nearly two years. This committee effectively dealt with the issues, and sports and music did not dominate student life, although they remained prominent on the Maine campus.[44]

Gradually the faculty and the students had come to an understanding about the purposes of the college and of those who were part of it. Regulations, although still often negative in tone, were not as harsh as they had been, and the establishment of routine, tradition, and outside interests as an integral and not dominant part of life had cut down the sources of irritation for both faculty and students. The demerit system disappeared sometime in the late 1880's or early 1890's, but there was still a system of arrearage examinations [standard examinations given for those who missed finals], and excuses had to be presented for absence from any college exercise. The standard rubric, "Each student is expected to be present at every college exercise for which he is registered" had made its appearance, and enforcement was always possible. The only real changes came when Mount Vernon was opened in 1901 for young women with the promulgation of new rules for chaperones, attendance by young men, and so on. By the end of this period most persons on the campus knew quite clearly what the boundaries of conduct were, and as a result life moved smoothly for most students.[45]

According to his diary, one student's life looked like this for a few days in 1898 and was quite typical.

March 9 . . . In PM worked in drawing room plotting campus. Went out and measured buildings with Boardman and Lombard.

March 10 Had recitations all the AM. college meeting after chapel 'Bounc' scrap had PM off Plugged up studies some went to debate in evening . . . .

March 12 raining wrote out chapel report handed them in to Mrs. Balentine plugged calculus in PM . . . wrote theme in PM . . . .

March 14 . . . Preliminary in Physics. calculus finished plotting campus commenced training plugged all evening on calculus. . . .[46]

Commencement week was a major occasion, at least by the 1880's. The student bade good-bye to the place that had replaced his real home and also bade good-bye to his associates in this transition period, both on the faculty and among the other students. It tended to be an emotional experience. In the 1870's major concerts were given for the audience before the students gave their graduation addresses. The assembled then listened to an orator from another locality, although in some years the orator was not used as too much time was taken with other things.[47] In the 1880's the proceedings were much more stylized, with orations, histories, poems, prophecies, valedictories, the singing of class odes, and for quite a time, the smoking of a pipe of peace.

By 1885 the commencement events took nearly a week. On Saturday declamations by the sophomores and music by the college orchestra began the week. On Sunday a baccalaureate sermon was preached. On Monday the juniors had their exhibition, with a Bangor orchestra the star attraction at the performances. On Tuesday the cadets drilled; in the evening the president gave a reception while the fraternities held open house for their alumni. On Wednesday the actual exercise occurred with a grand commencement dinner, and in the evening, in 1885 at least, the Philomea Quartette of Boston with Signor Buitrago, lead violinist, gave a concert. Thursday was the class day with poems, prophecies, and the pipe of peace. Friday the campus was quiet as students began to leave. All students and faculty participated in these events and many alumni returned as well.[48]

By the nineties an Ivy Day or Arbor Day celebration was added to these festivities. Coburn Hall was the scene, as the plants and plaques still attest. Other events included a farmers' field day and a grand banquet for alumni. In 1894 caps and gowns were worn for the first time. By 1909 some of these events were moved back to Junior Week to coincide with the Promenade, and in 1911 the time was cut back even further when commencement

Louis W. Riggs, '85

Lore A. Rogers, '96

Ballard F. Keith, '08

Frank Lamson-Scribner, '73

seemed as though it might last all month. These numerous activities were symbolic of the difficulty of leaving this place that had become so much a home.[49]

This is a history of the college and not its graduates, but some mention must be made of those who had distinguished careers once away from the school. Leaving aside those graduates who came back to their alma mater to teach, there are several from this period who deserve some attention. Foremost, perhaps, would be Frank Lamson-Scribner, '73, author of a dozen books (including *Weeds of Maine,* which went to press while he was a freshman) and a distinguished botanist who was chiefly responsible for modernizing the University of the Philippines and the Philippines Department of Agriculture. He rose to be one of the highest civil employees in the United States Department of Agriculture and supervised most of the U.S. exhibits at world's fairs after 1910.

Another graduate was Dana T. Merrill, '98, who became a brigadier general with a distinguished army career. C.A. Morse, '79, was an outstanding railroad builder and engineer. Other famous engineers were Frank E. Weymouth, '96, who built the Colorado Aqueduct and rose to be chief engineer in the U.S. Bureau of Engineers; Frank A. Banks, '06, built the Grand Coulee; and Frank Crowe, '05, the Boulder Dam. J.V. Cilley, '83, became the head man in the Argentinian railway system. R.B. Manson, '96, and C.H. Farnham, '97,

Francis Crowe, '05, left and Frank A. Banks, '06, right, great dam builders from the Civil Engineering course.

helped build much of the Chinese railway system. Others of importance were Whitman H. Jordan, '75, who became head of the New York State Agriculture Experiment Station and turned down the presidency of his alma mater in 1901; Ballard Keith, '08, the first Rhodes Scholar; Louis Warner Riggs, '85, a professor of chemistry at Cornell; George Perkins Merrill, '79, head geologist at the Smithsonian; and Wallace R. Farrington, '91, a noted newspaper man who rose to be governor of Hawaii and governor-general of the Philippines. Later, he was head of the department of education and founder of the university in Hawaii.

William T. Haines, '76, was governor of the state, and William Robinson Pattangall, '84, became the leading Democrat in his day. Lore Rogers, '96, was an eminent scientist and, later, historian. Although others might search the alumni directory and find different persons who deserve mention, this list will indicate that some Maine graduates did have distinguished careers. The two areas of importance, as one would expect, were agriculture, especially botany and entomology, and engineering, especially civil and railroad engineering.[50]

Where did these young students come from? Mostly from Maine, of course, but by 1930 all the states and most of the territories had contributed some students. The leading states, after Maine, were Massachusetts, New York, New Jersey, Connecticut, Pennsylvania, New Hampshire, and California. In Maine the leading counties were Penobscot, Cumberland, Kennebec, and Aroostook. Hancock, Oxford, Piscataquis, Somerset, Washington, and York all produced more than one hundred students in the first sixty years. Some sixty-three students appeared in Orono from Canada during this period, with Quebec producing thirty-one and Ontario thirteen of these. One came from Alberta, ten from New Brunswick, and seven from Nova Scotia as well as another one from Newfoundland. Latin America provided twenty-eight students, including Cuba, nine; Brazil, six; Argentina, five; and Panama, five. Twenty-four came from other parts of the world, with Turkey, four, and China, eight, the only countries with major contributions.

When the college was begun in the sixties, high hopes were held that it would begin to reverse the drain of Maine's bright young men, but in this the college, even if it slowed that drain somewhat, was not successful. What it had done was to provide an opportunity for some of Maine's young people to be educated at home, for a relatively small sum. When they graduated they had more to offer; not least of this was the attitude of mind and the character that had distinguished Maine people before and now combined with the education received on the Orono campus. Campus life in those days, whether in the classroom or out of it, was responsible for these young people and, on balance, one has to regard the products of this campus life with interest and respect.

Notes

1. Reminiscences of J. Hart, '85; E.J. Haskell, '72 in *Campus*, May 3, 1922; "Reminiscences" of 1874-5 in *Cadet*, July, October, 1894; on Uncle Ben, see *Prism*, 1895; *Cadet*, January, 1897; Class of 1875 Book, typed copy c. 1910; Not all arrivals were pleasant. In 1898 a terrible blizzard came as the train arrived for the second semester. A wreck occurred, and four students were severely injured. *Cadet*, March 1898.

2. Trustees, May 1, August 5, 1873; March 21, 1877; Faculty, June 16, 1873; *Catalogue* of the Maine State College, 1874; *Cadet*, December, 1894. Oak folder, petition of 1874 with 73 signatures, including some faculty. E.M. Blanding, '76 was the leader of the dissidents, who were hoping for less "salt fish and musty white bread."

3. Trustees, June 29, 1880; June 27, 1882.

4. Trustees Minutes, June 23, November 25, 1884; June 23, 1885; June 29, 1886, Faculty Minutes, March 9, May 29, June 1, 2, 1885; May 10, 1886. There were other bad times, as in 1904 when a near insurrection occurred over the food. See president's letter to trustees, June 7, 1904.

5. Term Bills in Class of 1876 folder.

6. Harris file, "Odds and Ends." The student identification is incorrect on the bill.

7. Harris Correspondence, his letter to seniors of May 29, 1895 brought these out.

8. *Cadet*, May, 1890.

9. Trustees Minutes, February 21, 1893; November 27, 1894; December 12, 1899; Faculty Minutes, September 5, October 18, 1894, November 4, 25, 1895; Harris to E.A. Balentine, December 13, 1899; Tech Faculty meetings, February 28, 1916. Weeks Diary, February 15, 1875. James Stacy Stevens, Karl Pomeroy Harrington, Abram Winegardner Harris, *The Chapel Service Book for Schools and Colleges*, New York, Concinnati, 1920.

10. Trustees, June 6, 1871; Faculty July 17, 24, 1876; November 16, 23, 1896; *Cadet*, September 28, October 28, 1885.

11. Faculty, September 11, 26, 29, November 6, 1876; November 10, 1879; Trustees, November 18, 1879. Weeks Diary, April 6, 1876.

12. Faculty meetings, March 30, May 18, June 1, 1874; April 12, 1875; March 27, 1876; April 17, 1882; Trustees Minutes, April 22, 1874.

13. Faculty, February 5, 17, 24, March 3, 7, April 7, 14, 1873.

14. Faculty, October 24, 25, 1883; August 11, 1884; March 2, 1885; *Cadet*, January, 1895, an article by Ralph Kneeland Jones, '85 who participated.

15. Faculty meetings, March 29, 30, April 5, July 7, 12, 19, 20, 1875. Weeks Diary, April 4, 1875.

16. Faculty, September 18, 1882.

17. Trustees, August 5, 1869; Faculty, October 6, 1873; August 31, September 7, 17, 1874.

18. Faculty, August 19, 20, 22, 23, 26, 1878; February 17, 1879; Trustees, June 24, 26, 1879; College *Reporter*, Vol. 5, No. 1 (1878).

19. Faculty, September 18, 1882.

20. Faculty, August 24, 27, 31, 1885.

21. Faculty Minutes, October 13 (two meetings), 15, 18, 1896. *Cadet*, October 29, 1886, November 4, 1887, May-June, 1896 F.P.B., "A College Insurrection."

22. Faculty, November 21, 1893; September 9, 1896; November 28, December 4, 1899; June 8, 1901; Trustees, November 6, 1890; *Cadet*, December, 1893; September 28, 1895; *Campus*, December 15, 1899; February 16, 1903, this issue editorialized, "judicious hazing, well applied, is one of the greatest civilizing agents known to the scientific world of today." On the hazing aspect of the great strike see J.N. Hart (Acting Pres.) to E.B. Winslow, September 13, 1910 (in Winslow's folder).

23. Faculty, October 20, 28, 1873; Fall, 1880; September 27, 1880; *The Cadet*, December, 1894, on the 1888 campaign.

24. Faculty, May 26, June 2, 9, August 6, 1873; July 26, 1875; Trustees, May 18, June 8, 1909.

25. William Dewitt Hyde to Harris, October 1, 1896; Nathaniel Butler to Harris, June 6, 1899 (no trouble with Colby); *Cadet*, May, July 1891 (skeleton perambulations); *Campus*, March 15, 1902; May 20, 1913 (building burnings); J.P. Huddilston to Fellows, April 25, 1903 in folder "Drinking (Alcoholic Beverages)"; Trustees of Mount Hope Cemetery to Fellows, November 6, 1905. Bangor, Hampden and Winterport Railway to Fellows, October 6, 1903; enc. copies of conductors' reports of October 6, and other supporting letters. See for vaudeville, John Dimeglio, *Vaudeville, USA*, Popular Press, 1973 and for the atmosphere in other colleges in New England, *Eight O'Clock Chapel*, New York, 1924.

26. Faculty, September 1, 8, 1873; March 9, 10, 13, 27, 1876; November 22, 1897; *Campus*, December 15, 1902; Fellows to L.C. Southard, December 2, 1902; (Southard was a founder of the Alumni organization.) Faculty, December 8, 10, 1902.

27. The best account of Maine college life in the 1880's is in the reminiscences of James N. Hart, '85. A good book that discusses life in the class of 1913 is E.E. Chase, *Tales of Bolivar's Children*, Waterville, 1914. Bolivar was a large tin elephant that served as

the University's mascot for a time before World War I. Also see Joseph H. Bodwell's, '15, memoirs in *Maine Life*, January, February, 1971. Contemporary accounts of scraps are in *Campus*, January 4, 1902; May 31, September 23, 1913; *Cadet*, October, 1892. The *Campus*, March 15, 1974 has a recent recounting. There are a number of descriptions of events in the Merton Lovett letters, in my possession, see October 29, 1902 to Margaret; also September 18, 27; November 5, December 6, 11 (also Fellows to Lovett December 11, 1903 he was suspended); April 1, 1904 and others in 1905.

28. On guns, Faculty, April 11, 1881; on love April 8, 9, 12, 1878; and *Campus*, June 13, 1911; on cheating, Faculty, May 9, 1907.

29. Trustees, January 13, 1871; Faculty, February 5, 17, 24, March 3, 1873; September 6, 1875; April 1, 3, 1878; April 13, 1896; December 8, 10, 1902; *The Transit*, 1884, 23.

30. Fernald to Oak, February 16, 1869; *Cadet*, October, 1894 on military in 1874; *Pendulum*, 1883; Faculty, August 31, 1874; Trustees, August 3, 1875; June 26, 1877; January 23, 1878 (Augusta); November 28, 1882; November 27, 1883; November 22, 1887.

31. Faculty, September 16, 23, 1889; February 24, 1890; March 10; September 9, 1896; March 23, 1897; March 29, 1897; September 21, 1898; Trustees, November 28, 1893; *Cadet*, September, 1890 edt. attacking continuous drilling; *Campus*, November 1, 1899 (quote); June 1, 15, 1901; Reginald L. Fernald to Harris, August 30, 1897.

32. *Cadet*, November, 1892 on Castine; Searsport *Weekly News*, October 10, 1893; Faculty, September 3, 6, 1897; March 7, 14, 22, April 11, 18, May 2, 1898; April 10, 1899.

33. From a student point of view the entries in Clinton Cole diary, 1898 are interesting. Also see *Cadet*, May, 1898; October 1898; Faculty, May 10, April 9, 25, June 4, September 26, 1898; Trustees, June 23, 1898; June 12, 1900; Llewellyn Powers, *Address*, 1899, p. 1873. Faculty, April 23, 1900; June 8, September 20, December 16, 1901; January 6, 13, February 3, 24, May 12, 1902; October 12, 1903; March 15, 1904. The cadets were used in a martial law way at the Bangor fire of 1911, see *Campus*, May 9, 1911; Harris to Trustees, October 28, 1898.

34. Faculty, April 6, 13, 1874; February 7, 14, 1876; Trustees, November 22, 1876; November 24, 1885; November 23, 1886; March 31, 1887; June 25, 1889; June 23, 1891; May 3, 1895; August 6, 1896; December 4, 1895; April 28, June 22, 1897; March 2, 1900; June 10, 1901; February 16, 1911, the president and treasurer are directed to require and enforce "a prompt and material reduction" in fraternity accounts owed.

35. Faculty, February 18, 19, 1895; June 13, 15, 16, 17, 22, 29, 1899; Trustees, June 13, 1899; *Campus*, May 31, 1913; Hart to S.W. Gould, July 20, 1910. Sororities made their appearance in 1903. See

Campus March 10, 1914 for an early history. QTV became Phi Gamma Delta and the history of their earliest years appears in *The "Omega Nu*," Phi Gamma Delta, Orono, 1901. See also the various publications, *The Transit*, and *The Pendulum* in the 1880's. An inter-fraternity council was created to handle fraternity government in this period. For an attack by a contemporary see *Campus* November 1, 1904.

36. Hart Correspondence, Hart to Charles F. Emerson, November 4, 1915; a folder "Scientific Society" with some corres., c. 1916 in regard to its history. Among materials still extant are minute books from the Deutscher Verein, Press, Mathematical, and Philosophical Clubs in the period 1900 to 1910. *Campus*, May 24, 1908 for the Literati.

37. Faculty, February 15, 18, March 8, 15, June 19, 21, September 6, 13, November 22, 1897, and Edward O. Schriver *In Pursuit of Excellence: A History of Phi Kappa Phi*, Orono, 1971 on these fraternities.

38. *The Maine Alumnus*, May, 1956, special on Masque, and Sprague's obituary. *Campus*, May 2, 1904 the musical clubs had 63 members, 44 of whom entertained on trips, (19 major concerts were given). Trustees, June 10, 1901; Huddilston to Harris, June 24, 1901; Art Guild Minute book 1900-04; Huddilston's recollections of September 1, 1954, and the Art Guild constitution.

39. *College Reporter*, June, 1878; *Cadet*, May, 1893; Five verses followed, all to the tune of *Villikens and His Dinah*.

40. *Cadet*, March, November, 1898; *Maine Alumnus*, January, 1930. Sprague's comments, p. 69. The first singing was noticed in *Campus* February 15, 1905.

41. Letters to alumni, R.K. Jones, January 16, February 20, 1897; *Campus*, March 1, 1900, Harris at Boston alumni meeting; December 1, 1902 on second Maine night; *Maine Bulletin*, Vol. XVIII, special, October, 1915.

42. Faculty, May 2, 9, 31, 1881; May 26, 1884; March 16, 30, 1885; June 26, August 23, September 6, 20, 1886; March 5, 12, 22, 1887.

43. Faculty, October 24, November 14, 1892; March 25, April 1, 1895; *Cadet*, November, 1889; *Campus*, November 21, 1913; December 18, 1947; Wingard's file, especially R.J. Aley to Wingard April 3, 1917.

44. Faculty June 9, September 18, 24, October 22, November 5, 19, 26, December 17, 1906; February 4, 1907. The minutes of the committee are in the file "Special Committee on Outside Interests (c. 1906-1907)."

45. *General Regulations*, Maine State College (1887-1888?); *Information for the Guidance of Students*, Revised to June, 1916; *Campus*, April 30, 1907.

46.   Diary entries are from Clinton Cole, 1899 diary.

47.   Posters for several of these concerts are in the special collections at Maine; See Bangor *Whig and Courier,* August 8, 1872; August 5, 1875 for accounts; Faculty, April 20, 1877. Weeks Diary, July 29, 1876; May 23, July 15, 1877.

48.   *Cadet,* August 28, 1885; Class Day Program, 1882 in my possession. *Cadet,* July, 1892; July, 1894; Faculty, May 15, 1893, Arbor Day program; Mary S.

Snow to Harris, June 11, 1897, agreeing to speak at commencement dinner, Commencement Program, June 28, 1893 in my possession. Many of the early class histories are preserved in their folders, and are very useful.

49.   Faculty, March 23, 1909 on junior week; *Campus* May 13, 1913.

50.   Jordan's file, Jordan to Harris, February 17, 1896; September 14, 1901; E. Balentine to Harris, August 28, 1901 and Jordan to Balentine, August 28, 1901

CHAPTER FIVE

The War, the SATC,
and President Aley

MOST PEOPLE in 1914 perceived the future to be a tranquil one in which moderate growth and progress seemed likely. Unfortunately, greed, cupidity, and economics intervened, and that tranquil world was destroyed almost at the high summer of its civilization. To the world came death, disruption of life, and destruction; to the University of Maine came some death, disruption of life through introduction of military discipline, and destruction of the smooth flowing campus serenity through inflation, suspicion, and animosity. Some, if not all, of the hard won gains of the previous twenty years were on a way to be wiped out, almost as a tangential by-blow of World War I.

The university operated on a budget of about a quarter million dollars in 1914. The allocation of this money is shown by the table.[1]

University of Maine: Budget 1914-15

Item		Amount
Agriculture		27,000
Arts and Science		5,000
(Library	2,420	
Biol.	1,200	
Physics	1,200	
Law (Janitor/interest)		3,500
Technology		9,000
Travel/office expense		6,000
Care/repair buildings		12,000
Heat/Lights/Water		20,000
Salaries		163,300
Admin.	15,000	
Agr.	31,000	
A & S	68,000	
Law	7,500	
Tech.	41,000	
Total		245,800

Roughly half of this money came from state appropriation. Another $50,000 was raised by tuition charges, $50,000 was provided by the federal government, $10,000 came from endowment funds, and the rest from rents or the sale of various items. Unfortunately, the amount of expenditures rose fairly steadily, in fact to $254,000 by 1917 (with another $20,000 placed in a sinking fund). As the war costs increased, and inflation with them, the budgeted amounts did not meet the bills as they had before the war. Adding to the deficit the diminished amounts from tuition in the wartime period, the university found itself in a precarious financial situation by 1919.

In addition, salaries remained fairly low, with the president receiving only $6,000 per year, deans, $3,000, professors $2,300 (up from $1,700), and others in proportion so that the demand for more money increased with the inflation.

Biennial needs in 1916 had been set at $597,061 and $175,000 more for new construction. The 1917 legislature provided about $100,000 for the new construction and mandated another rise in tuition, but even these new funds came nowhere near the budget demands. In 1919, in the first legislature after the war, $180,000 was appropriated for each year of the biennium; however, this was $20,000 a year less than what was projected in trustee budget requests. Soon there would have to be a day of reckoning, and when that day came the university hoped to have sympathetic governors and legislators.[2]

The situation on the campus was little better. The university governance was described by one observer as follows:

Our institution is working under an 'unwritten constitution', and in the main, as we have no bylaws. Our method of administration has become a growth, the various officers and faculties have been granted powers from time to time by the Trustees on suggestions made by the faculty.[3]

No real organization meant no real control of expenditures or savings. Reaction to problems was weak. Too, the salary situation loomed as a potential troublemaker. As the president wrote: "The salaries of our professors are absurdly low. It is the best, however, we can do with the present income. . . ."[4] Thus the University of Maine faced the war period. Most of these problems became acute only after the war; during the emergency new issues arose on the campus, such as the importation of army troops to replace students and difficulties concerning the law school.

When the war broke out in Europe in 1914, most Maine students did not pay much attention at first, thinking it to be just another of the little skirmishes that had plagued the Balkans for forty years. As the war widened, interest in it grew, but few thought the United States would participate. The university somewhat grudgingly sent fifty students to a five-day encampment in Augusta held by the Maine National Guard in June 1915 to provide instruction for an increasing group of potential soldiers. In 1916 the mood on campus changed. The student newspaper thought the state of preparedness (the use of that word indicates some shift in sentiment) poor. The editors called for voluntary drill, saying, "We owe to the Nation, the State, the University, and to ourselves to put our best efforts into this work." A chapel exercise was devoted to Rupert Brooke and his sacrifice, and the next week a "Wilson Club" was formed, receiving the endorsement of the *Campus*. At the Democratic convention in Bangor the club formed a marching escort for the various speakers.[5]

Later in the year President Robert J. Aley agreed to serve as an official with the League to Enforce the Peace, a predecessor of the League of Nations organizations; an evening course was begun to provide military training for local business and professional men; and funds were raised to aid in work in prison camps in Europe.[6]

After President Wilson was reelected and the prospects of war seemed suddenly nearer, extreme patriotism seized many. Alumni wrote militaristic letters to their old college. One wanted to know, "What plans are being put into action in the way of making the under-graduate body of the University of Maine prepared for the best service to our country should war be declared?" Another, after announcing that he was too old to fight, and saying that if he were younger he would return to Orono to raise a regiment, went further. "My object in writing you at this time is to learn what steps, if any, are being taken to close the University and send all the boys or as 'Teddy' would say, all who have 'red blood in their veins,' to the front." He closed his letter with "Three Cheers for the Red, White, and Blue." Not all were as eager as this sanguinary correspondent, but many, including most prominently President Aley, wanted the university to become deeply involved.[7]

A mass meeting of students voted unanimously to extend to Wilson their "sincere and loyal support," and Aley immediately wrote him to that effect. A parade in Bangor in mid-March turned out seven thousand persons, one thousand from the campus, and another in Portland three days later was even larger, with the corps of cadets and the university band as leaders. A mass assembly on the campus preceded the Portland parade. These parades and rallies occurred before war was declared and were orchestrated by Aley, who informed all faculty and students of their expected attendance. At these parades he spoke of the danger facing the country, and recited an oath, written by himself, entitled, "My Creed." Toward the end of March Aley suggested to the faculty that they march in a group in another parade planned for Bangor. This second Bangor parade, sponsored by the Bangor Committee of Public Safety, was received well by the military and others who wanted the U.S. to enter the war.[8]

There was at the same time a good deal of opposition in the state and on the campus (as well as elsewhere in the country) to America's entrance into the war, but it was suppressed in the atmosphere of militarism generated by the various committees of public safety. Patriotic fervor swept the state. The Bangor Chamber of Commerce, organizing the parade on April 4, headed its letter, *"GET IN LINE FOR BANGOR'S PATRIOTIC DAY DEMONSTRATION"* and closed it with "The Chamber of Commerce requests and expects the cooperation of all the organizations and citizens." Aley, as college president, was in an especially good position to whip up sentiment, and he did so.

On the campus the atmosphere was described by the student newspaper as "bordering on nothing short of panic;" and one student wrote to his mother "nobody studying now, only military. Everything is war here." The paper listed the names of those congressmen brave enough to vote against entrance into the war and urged people to write them in opposition to their stands. It also urged the university to grant credit for wartime service and called for the establishment of volunteer companies among the juniors and seniors. Half the coeds had enlisted in a Red Cross program. To contest frightening rumors that flooded the campus, an official bulletin board was established once war was declared. The military department announced extension of its regular courses and the start of new voluntary courses in first aid and map reading. Senator Hale, who had spoken at the great rally in Bangor, was regarded on the campus as sufficient authority for the necessary war, and the *Campus* reprinted his words.

> I maintain that in the future, when England, and France, and America decide that there shall be no further wars, there *will* be no further wars. That way, and through no International Peace Alliance, I believe lies the future freedom of the world from all wars.[9]

The faculty changed the hours of classes to suit the military (for instance, chapel now was held only on Wednesday), and the president wrote one alumnus,

> The disposition of everyone at the institution is to be of the greatest service possible. So far as I know, there is no disposition on the part of any individual connected with the institution to shirk any responsiblity.[10]

There were relatively few voices of moderation in this hullaballoo. One was James Hart, who, although wrong in his predictions, did urge using one's head about the war. He counseled students to remain in school, except those who had something special to offer, such as coast patrol, signal service, or instructors. As he said to one applicant for advice,

> The news from abroad gives promise that the war will be over before our men are called to go abroad, and we are hoping that all or nearly all of our men will be back in the fall.[11]

However, on the campus the atmosphere of anxiety seemed to affect not only the faculty and students, but also the president and the board of trustees. The standard committee on

Robert G. Aley, president during the difficult World War I years.

administration was enlarged to deal with questions arising from the war. Recommending opening classes a few weeks later in the fall, which the board accepted, the committee also called for a single week's vacation at Christmas, no Easter vacation, and only a three-day weekend commencement for at least the wartime period.[12]

The trustees created a special research committee of five faculty, five alumni (three of whom had taught at Maine), and three trustees to deal with the situation. At the first meeting with this group in April 1917, the president presented plans to reduce the overall salary payroll of teaching faculty, while raising salaries of those teachers who remained. The reduction would be made through consolidation of classes, elimination of courses, and requirement of more work from faculty. To save money, two faculty appointments were terminated im-

During the S.A.T.C. era, the chapel, in Alumni Hall, was fitted as a Y.M.C.A. canteen and reading room for the troops. Many of these men came from Ohio, and the banner indicates their origin. This room was later used as the campus theatre and now houses television studios. The photograph comes from the scrapbook of Nelson F. Mank, '17, The doorway to Alumni Hall, not shown here, featured a large sign, ARMY YMCA.

mediately and all except administration telephones were discontinued.

The research committee reported at the next trustee meeting that peace and prosperity rested "fundamentally upon the advancement of knowledge by scientific research," and called for an extension of this aspect of the university. They recommended the appointment of researchers to be the equivalent of professors in the university.[13] At this same meeting Aley reported that registration was down to 700 students and that the great increase in costs of upkeep and maintenance would mean a $60,000 deficit. Due to the soaring costs of food, the trustees raised board charges to $5 a week, and they raised room rents also, up $1 a week.

In accordance with his plan to reduce the faculty payroll, the president recommended the release of all instructors and the leaving of other vacancies unfilled. To replace the two men let go in April, the president acted as head of the education department and the dean became acting head of the English department. Work in journalism was suspended and the journalism instructor put on leave without pay. The technology extension division was virtually suspended. Teaching hours were increased and instructors were sent to teach in allied departments. If enrollment did go up, but only if it did, the president was authorized to employ absolutely needed instructors. In August there was an attempt to abolish Huddilston's classics department; that failing, its course format was changed somewhat. Two trustees voted against paying his salary, apparently on the grounds that Greek civilization had little to offer the world of 1917.[14]

When college opened in the fall, Aley announced that 100 Maine men were already in training. He urged students to "conserve, construct, and economize." At the annual faculty reception, illumination came from lamps and candles, and after "old American songs" were sung, the professor of home economics addressed the group on food conservation. The campus featured a large banner with the legend, "You must choose between lending now or becoming slaves of the Hun." Under this warning students were exhorted to open savings accounts and buy Liberty Bonds. A rally for bonds, held in the Orono town hall, was attended by many students. Aley also undertook a massive speaking tour in Illinois, Pennsylvania, and California on the subject of food conservation. One result of this tour was the discovery of a song, "Canning the Kaiser," which was printed and sent along with Christmas parcels to Maine people in France serving in either the American Expeditionary Forces or in Red Cross units.[15]

On the campus, summer courses in first aid, Red Cross work, dietetics, home gardening, and military drill were instituted, paid for with $700 provided by the governor and council. The courses were open to all, and prominent persons in the state aided in the lecturing. Students in the College of Agriculture who did farm work were allowed to substitute this time for regular college work. The college forest was made available to faculty for home fuel wood at a dollar a cord. Dean Hart cut a cord for his home during Christmas and told a friend in a letter, "Quite a number of the faculty have already cut a cord or more wood."[16]

Through the spring of 1918 attention centered on the war. The first alumni deaths brought reality home to the campus. Attendance was still off, by a quarter. Those who left for military or farm labor were given credit in the courses being taken at the time of their departure. The Maine cadets marched in Bangor to stir up enthusiasm on the anniversary of the great patriotic observance of 1917. During this time Aley got involved in an issue that was to have a long-range effect on a part of the curriculum. As sentiments rose over German, or pro-German, textbooks, the president lent himself to an anti-German campaign which resulted in the elimination of German language courses.

One difficulty on campus lay in obtaining enough fuel for the buildings. Eventually student help was used to unload the railroad coal cars within the time alloted for delivery. The university planned to plant its fields to meet the food emergency: 14 acres to corn, 9 to millett, 29 to oats, 12.5 to oats and peas, and 118 to hay. A special military curriculum was planned for fall which included personal sanitation, map reading, military history, military sketching, topography, psychology of war, military French, international law and relations, and much physical training.[17]

The reason for these additions to the curriculum was that the university campus, like others throughout the country, was about to be

President Aley at a tree planting ceremony in 1918, near Coburn Hall. SATC troops formed the audience, off the scene shown here.

The cadet band in the World War I period. There is a wider variety of instruments than the earlier illustration. Notice the puttees worn by these men.

taken over by the military. Designed "to develop as a military asset the large body of young men in the colleges" and "to prevent unnecessary and wasteful depletion of the colleges through indiscriminate volunteering," the policy called for students to be organized in a Students' Army Training Corps (SATC). The committees of public safety agreed to take on the job of publicity for the program in the state. All males over eighteen were encouraged to enlist; they were put into military uniforms, given military training, put on call if needed and paid thirty dollars a month for their service. The college became a military barrack. Fraternity activities were suspended, fraternity houses commandeered, and nonmilitary residents became subject to military discipline if they remained in them. At Orono the men now came under the discipline of army officers and regular campus rules no longer applied to these students.[18]

The military regulation of daily campus life provided a sharp contrast to prewar days. The detail of life was unbelievable, with the curriculum and all other aspects laid down from Washington. After Aley found that young women appeared to be everywhere, and at all times, and that they demonstrated "unseemly behavior," they were allowed on the campus, with strict chaperonage, only in evening and on Sunday. The note to the military officer on this subject was simply one of hundreds that went back and forth as the campus did not adjust well to the presence of the army. Perhaps the final indignities came when the army began to call the campus a post, removed doors from the dormitories to make the buildings more like a barrack, prevented smoking in the corridors on the threat of a two-week confinement, and sent "persistent malefactors" to Camp Devens. The particular memo discussing these orders closed with the following:

> The class punch ball contest is authorized. Fighting, rowdyism, or other disorder, will be severely punished. Men should be carefully warned.[19]

Of course there were still many civilians on the campus, and memos like this emanating from the former Reserve Officers' Training Corps office and interfering in the routine of college life were more than President Aley and his colleagues could stand. Aley also found, to his dismay, that little studying went on and class absence was tremendous. Four different class schedules in the first two months made life even more difficult for the civilian leaders.

Fall registrations in 1917 amounted to 913. In 1918 these fell to 211, but 726 SATC men were on the campus: 212 infantry, 31 aviation, 54 ordnance, 203 engineers, 23 signals, 31 chemical, 69 motor transport, 10 medical, and 93 in the naval section. Along with the invasion by the military came influenza and quarantine, and right behind that came orders from Washington that each SATC student was to have a minimum of fifty feet of floor space and that all were to avoid crowds.[20]

An emergency faculty meeting was called to discuss the turmoil. The dean of the university and his senior staff held an inspection in the hopes of returning the campus to some sort of academic respectability. An article, possibly written by Aley, appeared in the *Bangor Daily News* describing the SATC as seeming "to possess all the ingenuity of the Yankee combined with the devilish cunning of a German on a rampage." The military protested to the governor about the article, but by the time of the protest the war was over and the members of the SATC were discharged. The horrible experience was nearly finished.[21]

Later Aley summed up the wartime events at Maine for SATC directors in Washington. He said that military duty interfered with academic work, the many changes in classes caused problems, the majority of the SATC men were not interested in academic work, supervised study was a failure, the change in commanding officers created difficulties, and that the faculty was at first enthusiastic, but the enthusiasm dampened rapidly. At the end of his report he did say that although the situation was difficult, the university, if needed, "is now as she will be, in the future, ready to respond to any call made by Nation or State."[22]

The readiness of the university to cooperate again was perhaps overly optimistic. In private correspondence Aley and others described the experience as a "hard blow" educationally and financially. One letter described the SATC as "a nightmare." In fact, even when dealing with the potential return of the ROTC, Aley was quite explicit to the War Department.

> At the present time if the morale of the institution is to be recovered, we need a military officer of experience, high character, and a sympathetic attitude toward college work. . . . It is probably unnecessary for me to say so, but I am particularly anxious that no one of the officers . . . [from SATC be part of the U. of M. ROTC][23]

When the war ended, the campus reacted much as did the country; first, a false celebration, then, on November 11, a real celebration. Classes were dismissed, the SATC assembled, drilled, and went to Bangor to participate in a big parade. The marchers were rewarded with passes from 4:30 p.m. to 11:00 p.m. SATC members were all discharged by December 21 in time for the Christmas vacation. When college convened after the vacation, Aley told the students in chapel that the campus must be brought back to a peacetime condition, that spring would have to be a period of restoration of standards. This, he prophesied, would take money and sacrifice, but was imperative.[24]

As part of this process of restoration, those who had gone to Officers Training Camp were given credits toward graduation; three received two full years, while another twenty-seven received from one to three semesters credit for

their wartime officer service. Aley afterward told the trustees that it took three months to rid the campus of unnecessary influences and to catch up academic life. However, he pointed out that inflation and lack of tuition funds caused a financial deficit that would still be very troublesome in the future.[25]

While the SATC was outwardly the most troublesome problem on the campus, there were other difficulties associated with the war period. At the law school a dormant situation was brought to the surface by the wartime hysteria and anxiety.

The law school had been founded in 1898, during Abram Harris's presidency, after initial authorization in 1893. A board of eminent jurists acted as an advisory council to the school, and local lawyers and jurists did much of the lecturing. Louis Southard, for instance, gave an annual series of lectures until at least 1915, and did it for expenses. The school was located in Bangor, not Orono, and the distance between campuses caused friction. The trustees often discussed moving it up the Penobscot; however, faculty were usually engaged in legal practice, and with the court in Bangor it was not practical to move the school, so the friction remained. Still, on the surface it seemed to be an active, promising school, publishing a law review, and having as its dean William A. Walz, a distinguished lawyer with a strong personality. The school even survived the destruction of its building in the great Bangor fire of 1911, soon finding new and better quarters in the beautiful house at the corner of Second and Union streets in Bangor (now known as the Farrar Mansion). Eventually the university purchased the building, and all seemed serene.[26]

There were difficulties, however. One of them was salary. Lawyers made much more money than did professors of law. Walz himself asked for more salary nearly every year. Too, Walz wanted control over appointments, but Aley also wanted a voice. Nonresident tuition was an issue. Aley and Walz apparently did not get on personally so the relationship between the two parts of the campus deteriorated steadily.[27]

The correspondence of the law school before 1912 is missing because of the Bangor fire, but after that time the letters between Aley and Walz are cordial, but stiff. Throughout 1913 and 1914 a number of letters appear concerning the

William E. Walz

Candidly speaking something must be done. I am sure you have a definite idea of the lamentable and much to be regretted opinion in which the Law School is held by the members of the Supreme Court, and the best portion of the bar of Maine. [After urging Aley to call a meeting.] We will then take definite action.[30]

Aley did call a meeting, on March 10, 1916, in the Penobscot Exchange Hotel. At that meeting, stronger entrance regulations were put in force and the school was reorganized, with two part-time professors let go, to be replaced with one full-time person. The law students were unhappy with these alterations and sought and received an interview (a stormy one) with Aley. There is some evidence that Walz urged them to this course. Aley, after receiving many letters from the alumni, wrote to Walz urging him to resign with no recriminations. The two principals held several meetings, and the upshot of the matter was that Walz remained, ostensibly because his wife was ill. However, troubles with the law faculty continued all spring. Eventually one more instructor was fired, while others were told to limit their outside engagements. Walz and Aley also clashed over law enforcement in Penobscot county, especially over the role of the county attorney and liquor traffic.[31]

A growing emphasis on case work and an attempt to increase the size of the student body apparently created a better atmosphere for a time. Unfortunately for Walz and the law school, the war intervened. Walz was of German descent and very proud of it. One of his favorite lectures, one he had given many times locally, dealt with Bismark's legal ability. At other times he was wont to compare famous leaders and their legal acumen. One of his comparisons was Bismark with Lincoln; in the comparison Lincoln was shown to be a very compassionate man, but not a very good lawyer. The law school, in deference to Walz's Germanophilia, had even proclaimed the Kaiser an honorary member of the school. When the war hysteria rose in Bangor, Walz was a perfect target.[32]

At the January 1918 meeting of the law school faculty all seemed calm. However, Looney was active; early in February the letters concerning Walz began to flow. "He too, (Professor Peabody), thinks that something radical should

failure of the school to grow, even though new brochures and special editions of the *Maine Bulletin* were prepared and a special campaign of personal letters was started. Aley discussed the project with an ominous note early in 1914. "I have wondered a great many times why the College of Law is not growing as are the other colleges of the institution."[28] By 1915 enrollment was down, and fees and tuition were raised to compensate for the drop. Sometimes guest lecturers, like university treasurer and judge, Charles J. Dunn, did not meet their advance publicity claims and this caused trouble.[29]

The situation was made worse by the appointment of William Looney as a trustee. Looney wanted a law degree from the school. Walz told him he would have to attend classes to obtain one, which Looney apparently did not like at all. Aley became friendly with Looney, and an investigation of the law school was begun. A letter of this period, from Looney to Aley, is an example of the type of correspondence exchanged.

The University of Maine Law School building, Stewart Hall, Bangor. Originally constructed as a home for a wealthy lumberman, it has also served as headquarters for the Northern Conservatory of Music. The building has recently been restored to its original state. The law school moved here after its original home was destroyed in the Bangor fire of 1911.

be done before the end of the school year. You and I can appreciate the embarrassing delicacy of his position." An investigation committee consisting of trustees with Looney as chairman was named, and on March 9 a six-hour meeting was held at the Tarratine Club in Bangor. After a general discussion, Walz was sent for and informed that if he would resign, without pay, in the best interests of the state and the university, all would be well, but if he would not, he would be fired anyway. "From that moment" the law school was moved to Orono. Some trustees were very unhappy at the kangaroo court atmosphere and the vigilante tactics of Looney and Aley, but no one spoke out except in let-

ters. Walz later petitioned for readmission to the deanship and for some pension rights, but the trustees did not accede to his demands and instructed the president to write him an "official history of his dismissal."[33]

The dismissal was a nine-days wonder in the state. Walz was popular; thus, some newspapers used this event to attack the university. Others, unfortunately, had fallen victim to the hysteria. The *Bangor Commercial*, for instance, had written in February:

The Commercial believes that this [Walz's address on Lincoln and Bismark] is a matter that should be taken in hand by the trustees of the University of Maine. They should determine whether such constant references to Germany are in line with correct teaching in a law school for young Americans at a time when the entire resources of the country are being mustered in the effort to crush German savagery and brutality . . . .

The *Portland Evening Express* and the *Lewiston Journal* were others that called for and welcomed Walz's dismissal, applauding the university for firing German-lovers. Only the *Bangor Daily News* urged restraint and printed correspondence from former students attesting to his patriotism. Walz, however, went — along with the law school and the study of German, all victims of hysteria exaggerated in part by the activities of the president of the university himself.[34]

The demise of the law school, at least in its Bangor setting, is another case in which the historian is at a loss to explain precisely why it occurred in the way it did. Some of the problem undoubtedly lay in the differences between Walz and Aley. Walz was an expansive Victorian type with a very sophisticated background, having lived in Germany and Japan, and with a wide circle of acquaintances. Aley was much more formal and apparently harried by his desires for a great university but with not enough money to support his visions. Walz was a Republican, Aley a Democrat. They were on opposite sides in the preparedness campaign of 1915-16. Walz was very active in the Republican organization, the League to Enforce the Peace. This group was founded by William Howard Taft, who spoke at both the law school and the university campus in 1913 only because Walz was able to obtain his services. Although Aley had spoken for the league in 1915-16, he was not later the enthusiast that Walz was for the organization which opposed Wilson. Walz's position was certainly antithetical to Aley's rather strongly belligerent pro-England stance, and a sample of his correspondence reinforces that impression. Walz said in one letter, "It is to be hoped that this war will not last till England has borrowed her last dollar, or Germany put her last man in the field."[35]

Walz's relationship with Looney is more obscure, in part because several letters are no longer in the files. Looney finally was unable to take his work at Maine, in part because the degree via examination only was eliminated, and he went to a New Hampshire school. He

was apparently an enemy of both the law school and Walz from an early date.[36]

The geographical separation of the law school from the main campus was a problem, as must have been the different styles of the schools. Academic life with its slow pace and piling up of evidence is somewhat in opposition to law schools, which tend to live from issue to issue and use evidence to buttress an adversary point without weighing the relative merits of evidence as carefully, or at least until the final judgement. All of these factors must have played a part. The law school was weak, especially after the fire. Aley and Walz did not get on well, and in the crucial issue of World War One they were on very different sides. Walz, in a letter, remarked on the difference between Bangor and Orono, and made the following comment, ostensibly about the weather, but perhaps about other matters. After saying that the temperature was -32 in Bangor and -24 in Orono: "Orono may not be colder than Bangor but it feels colder."[37]

The German language was not restored as a course at Maine for a number of years. The president, in response to one query, remarked, "I think the demand for the German language will be slight for some time to come. My own feeling is that you do better to major in some other subject." Even appeals to anti-Bowdoin feeling did not turn Aley's mind. One of his correspondents remarked when indicating that Bowdoin still taught German, "As much as we would like to get away from the fact, Bowdoin is associated in the minds . . . as the sacred head of pure education or culture in this state . . . . If we intend to increase the strength of the College of Arts and Sciences, we cannot leave out of consideration the subjects which Bowdoin teaches." Eventually German was reinstated, and in 1927 even the Duetscher Verein was reinstituted, but German has not yet (1977) attracted the numbers of students it did at its pre-World War I peak.[38]

More important from the point of view of the whole university was the fact that the war had brought severe financial difficulties. The 1919 legislature, as has been noted, approved appropriations of $180,000 a year, only enough to hold the line. It was felt at the time that this reduced amount would be sufficient until the postwar situation was clearer. Three buildings authorized by the legislature had not been built

Dances

11. WALTZ—Lilac Domino

12. ONE STEP—When You Wore a Tulip

13. WALTZ—Love's Melody

14. TWO STEP—It's a Long Way to Tipperary

15. WALTZ—Destiny

16. FIVE STEP—Meadowbrook

17. ONE STEP—I'm Glad My Wife's in Europe

18. WALTZ—Where My Caravan Has Rested

19. ONE STEP—Same Sort of Girl

20. WALTZ—Cecile

Engagements

11. .... X ....

12. Littlefield (Sawyer)

13. Tabachnick

Thayer

Military Ball

University of Maine

April the thirtieth
Nineteen hundred and fifteen

A dance card and program from the 1915 military ball. The song titles evoke the era very well. Soon those dancing might be in France.

because of the war: an administration building, a dairy building, and an armory (the latter vetoed by the governor). In the fall of 1919 a special hearing was held in Orono on the university's future and needs, and a second followed in Augusta. Testimony was heard concerning the merits of a mill tax, state ownership and management as a state administrative division, the need for higher salaries and new buildings or, as an alternative, the turning away of students. In the event, no more funds came, and the university was in serious difficulty.[39]

In fact the school found itself cutting back in many quarters. First to go was a steer-feeding contract with the Maine State Fair. At about the same time a genetic experiment on blooded cattle that had dated from well before the war was severely curtailed. Scholarships were cut back. The School of Pharmacy, begun in 1893, was discontinued, as was the law school. Work for the State Highway Commission was reduced, and expenditures on buildings and grounds were as limited as possible. The department of Greek civilization was abolished,

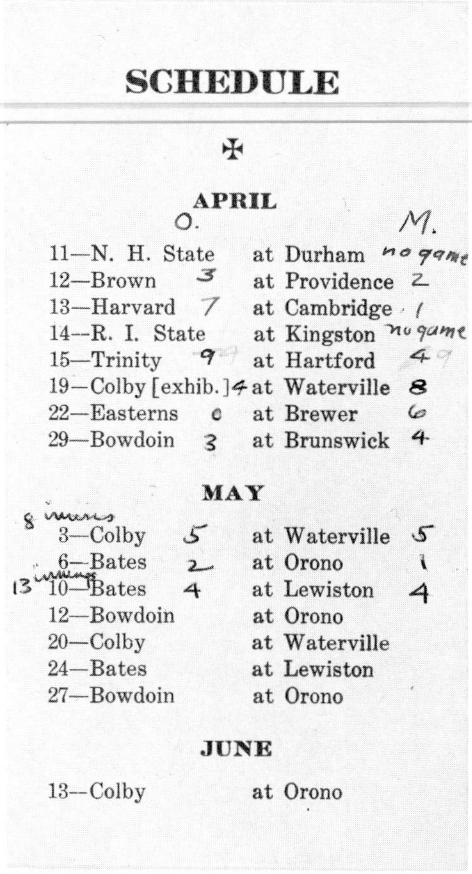

SCHEDULE

✠

APRIL

O.   M.

11—N. H. State   at Durham   *no game*
12—Brown   *3*   at Providence *2*
13—Harvard *7*   at Cambridge *1*
14—R. I. State   at Kingston   *no game*
15—Trinity *9*   at Hartford   *4*
19—Colby [exhib.] *4* at Waterville *8*
22—Easterns *0*   at Brewer   *6*
29—Bowdoin *3*   at Brunswick *4*

MAY

8 innings
3—Colby *5*   at Waterville *5*
6—Bates *2*   at Orono   *1*
13 10—Bates *4*   at Lewiston   *4* *innings*
12—Bowdoin   at Orono
20—Colby   at Waterville
24—Bates   at Lewiston
27—Bowdoin   at Orono

JUNE

13—Colby   at Orono

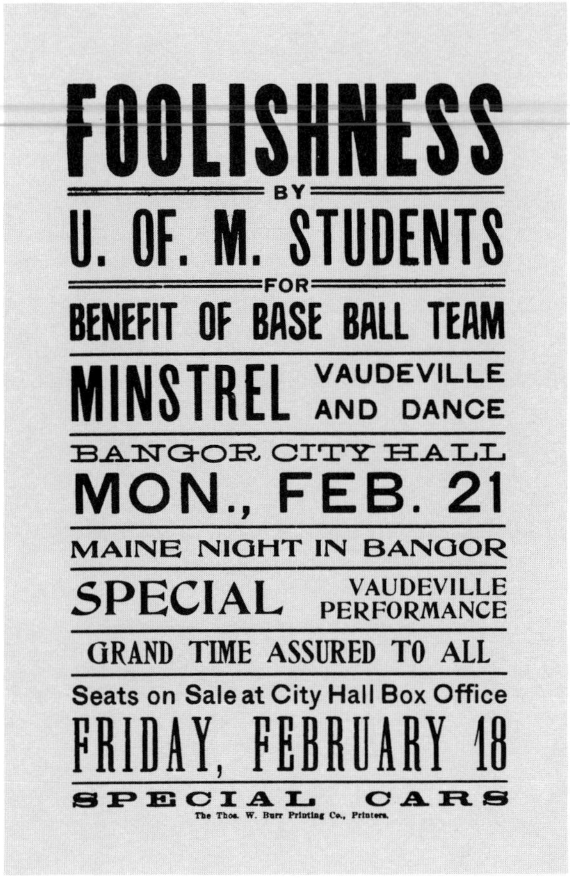

FOOLISHNESS
BY
U. OF. M. STUDENTS
FOR
BENEFIT OF BASE BALL TEAM
MINSTREL VAUDEVILLE AND DANCE
BANGOR CITY HALL
MON., FEB. 21
MAINE NIGHT IN BANGOR
SPECIAL VAUDEVILLE PERFORMANCE
GRAND TIME ASSURED TO ALL
Seats on Sale at City Hall Box Office
FRIDAY, FEBRUARY 18
SPECIAL CARS

The Thos. W. Burr Printing Co., Printers.

The baseball schedule shows 1916 games. Maine had won 4, lost 3, tied 2 (the Bates game went 13 innings), when this student stopped indicating the results. The handbill advertised a special Maine night program to benefit the baseball team. Sports were a central activity to the students of this period, but funds often came from such special performances.

although after several months of alumni and faculty protest, Professor Huddilston was rehired, but in the new department of ancient history and art. (Huddilston was also informed when rehired that he must divest himself of his dairy farm, which was a bone of contention to many on the campus.) Aley set the tone of the future in a departmental memo that called for the "most rigid economy to be carried out." No over-expenditures at all would be countenanced. A new faculty salary scale was introduced. In an inflationary time, faculty paid quite a price for retaining their jobs at Maine; that new scale listed the president at $6,000, deans at $3,450, registrar at $2,150, professors at $2,400 to $2,700, associate professors at $1,750 to $2,050, assistant professors at $1,400 to $1,800, and instructors at $1,000 to $1,200 per year.[40]

The post-war period opened with one of the largest registrations in the university's history: 1,187 students, of which 956 were males and 231 females. The freshman class numbered 451.

One of the faculty's difficulties concerned what to do about returning servicemen. After much discussion, students who had spent substantial time in the military were given a year's credit if they did satisfactorily in their first term. They had to have completed one semester before re-entering and have been on active duty. If they were in service from three to nine months they received one semester's credit on the same terms.

The trustees authorized a committee of faculty to meet with them to discuss the poor salary situation and other conditions "necessary for high standards" on the campus. The faculty, for their part, after endorsing the idea of a League of Nations at their first meeting in the fall, began to teach their peace-time classes. One supporter of the school remarked in a letter to Aley,

> If rash people can be kept from creating unnecessary difficulties, I believe that you will soon have the machinery of the University running smoothly again, and it's with hearty relief that I read your words of confidence as to the future.[41]

This letter was overly coy; earlier letters from the same source more closely mirrored the difficulties in Orono. There was great dissatisfaction everywhere. Salaries were low, conditions in the English department deplorable, and the various deans were disgruntled and discouraged. The alumni at the Boston meeting were very critical of Aley. Although a vote of nonconfidence was beaten down, another meeting was held and it was obvious that dissatisfaction was high.[42]

As is often the case, discontent from a number of sources centered on one place. The focus was the president, Robert J. Aley. If the college was to weather this storm and restore itself even partially to the pleasant and serene conditions of before the war, a new person was needed. Aley apparently realized this and began looking for another position. Louis Southard told Aley plainly what the difficulties were in a blunt letter of May 1919. Southard was and had been close to Walz, but he also was a strong supporter of the entire university. His letter merits long quotation.

> Speaking from such criticisms as I have heard, I should think that lack of discipline, which was complained of before these last outbreaks, and which it was said was evidenced by the lack of orderly conduct on the part of the students at Chapel; the destruction of the Law School, and the consequent loss of interest of Bangor's people in the University, and the loss of influence through Law School students and graduates; the imprudent contracting of debts, the weight of which is impairing and will impair the efficiency of the Institution; the lack of cordial relations between the President, Faculty and student body; and the failure to maintain its high standards of the past were among the most serious criticisms.[43]

Aley was not to blame for all of this, certainly, as the war and inflation due to the war, had hamstrung him and many institutions. On the other hand he had acquiesced in the law school's destruction and he had subordinated academic standards and tolerance to military and patriotic expediency. The good days of the past might be dead, but they died in part because he would not fight to retain them. The World War I period was not a pleasant one for the university. Outside forces had entered the campus, and it had suffered.

1. Trustees, June 9, 1914. There is an $800 discrepancy in the salary amounts in the original.

2. Trustees, November 17, 1914; June 12, November 10, 1916; June 14, 1917 (Bangor), *Legislative Documents*, 1915, H.D. 611, 748; *1917*, 256, 578; *1919*, Sen. Doc., 121; *Laws of Maine, 1917*, Resolves, Ch. 68. *1919*, Ch. 49.

3. J.S. Hart to Guy H. Albright (Colorado Springs), November 14, 1916, in Hart Corr., 1915-1916, Folder #1, (A-B). In 1921 the legislature would mandate a University treasurer and auditor. *Laws of Maine, 1921*, Ch. 151.

4. RJA to J.M. Callahan, West Virginia University, April 30, 1918.

5. Trustees, April 15, 1915; *Campus*. February 29, March 7, 14, 21, April 4, 1916.

6. Faculty, November 9, 1916; Wm. H. Taft to R.J. Aley, December 19, and return December 21, 1916. While this was going on students were reading anti-militarism articles by Yee Tin Hugh, '17. See *Campus*, November 28, December 5, 12, 1916.

7. Joe W. Gerrity, '09, to Aley March 27, and return March 28, 1917; C.G. Cushman, '89, to Aley, March 23, and return March 26, 1917.

8. Aley to Wilson, March 7, telegram April 4; J. Tumulty to Aley, April 5, 1917; Aley to faculty members, March 31, F.H. Parkhurst to Aley, April 5, Aley to Parkhurst, April 5, *Campus*, March 13, 20, 1917. Yee Tin Hugh was still saying stay out of the war in this issue.

9. Broadside, Bangor Chamber of Commerce; for atmosphere in state, see Rita J. Breton, unpublished M.A., 1972; Faculty, April 3, 1917 (special); *Campus*, April 3, 10, 1917.

10. The student note is Walter Niles to mother, April 10, 1917.

11. Hart Corr. 1917-1919, Folder #3, letter to W.F. Sewall, April 20, 1917. R.J. Alex to E.J. Haskell, May 3, 1917.

12. Faculty, April 3, May 14, June 9, 14, 1917; January 14, 1918. Aley to Trustees June 11-12, 1917 discusses his activities (trips to Washington) and his recommendations.

13. Trustees, April 18, June 11, 1917. Aley to Trustees, June 11-12, 1917.

14. Trustees, June 11, August 14, 1917.

15. *Campus*, October 16, 23, November 6, 1917; Alumni letters, especially George Adams, to Gannett, January 16, 1918; Hart to W. MacNeile Dixon, (London) November 10, 1917. In this letter Hart said that $5,000 had been raised locally for a YMCA friendship fund. Dixon had sent him books and pamphlets from England. On Aley's trip see R.J. Aley to R.L. Wilbur, August 20, 1917. Aley also spoke on "Why We Are in the War." He was lecturing as a representative of the N.E.A. See Wilbur to Aley, August 15, 1917.

16. R.J. Aley to George W. Norton, May 25, 31; to George E. Simmons, (farm supt. 1911-34) December 6; Aley to Col. Strickland, January 26 (on meeting with Governor); letter to Governor and Council, May 2, June 2, return May 4; Hart to T.H. Hamlin, December 17, Agriculture Faculty Meeting; April 10, 23, Arts and Sciences May 6, June 4, *Campus*, March 20, 1917.

17. *Campus*, January 22, April 9, 16; Faculty May 13, 15, Hart to E.B. Skinner, February 4, Aley to Henry R. Warren, April 8 (on German as language); to John W. Gravlus, January 21; to James J. Storrow November 17, 1917; Storrow to U of M, November 2, Storrow to Aley, February 8, 1919 (telegram) on fuel; Aley to Boston *Sunday Herald*, June 24, on errors in their report of June 14 on U of M's contribution; Aley wrote an article, "The War and the Secondary Schools," *The American School*, December, 1918.

18. Harold Sewall to Committee of Public Safety chairmen, July 30, 1918; Aley to Sewall, August 1, 1918; Trustees, September 14; Faculty April 1; Hart to Eugene Nadeau, September 4, 1918; Memo, Col. R.I Rees to Fraternities, October 2, 1918; Augustus Thomas (State Sup. Schools) to Aley June 17; June 24 and return June 21, 1918. Thomas was an active recruiter for SATC.

19. SATC folder No. 1; Aley to George D. Strayer, September 30; Aley to Capt. S.G. Eaton July 30 (women); Richard McLaurin (Washington, D.C.) to Aley, telegram, September 5, 1918; Memo Tracy Tuthill to Students, October 7, 1918 (quoted).

20. SATC folder No. 1; Telegram, Comm. Educ., Rees to U of M, October 5; Aley to J.H. Ropes and Robert I. Rees, October 29 (rep. to Rees October 29); Hart to Joseph W. Barbeau, October 21; Carl H. Ranger, December 3, 1918.

21. Faculty, October 28, November 4, Bangor *Daily News*, December 12; letter H.M. Halls to Carl Milliken, (N.d.); Milliken ret December 24; Rees to Aley November 27 (SATC folder No. 1).

22. SATC Folder No. 1, Aley report (undated) — to SATC (Collegiate Division).

23. Aley to George C. Chase (Bates Pres.) December 6, return December 8; Hart to Richard Willard, December 6; Aley to War Dept., December 9, copy to Frederick Hale, December 9, 1918, Trustees, May 3, 1928.

24. *Campus,* November 12, 1918; January 7, 1919.

25. Faculty, February 10, 1919; Wallace Craig to Aley, June 26, Aley to Col. Frank S. Clark, April 17; Aley's annual report to Trustees, 1919.

26. Trustees, July 17, 1893; September 14, 1897; October 28, 1898; March 27, 1899, December 12, 1899 (Bangor); November 20, 1900; August 25, 1911; June 10, 1912; *Campus,* April 20, 1909 (on Walz); to Trustees from George E. Goodman, April 7, 1899, curriculum, Andrew P. Wiswell to Harris, April 30, return May 3, 1898; L.W. Southard to Harris, November 17, return November 27, 1898; Southard to Harris, April 25, 1899; Haines to Harris, May 25, 1898; *Maine Law Review,* VI, 309-317, No. 8, (June, 1913). William A. Walz on History of School.

27. Walz to Aley, April 12, 1912 (on salaries).

28. Walz to Aley, July 18, and return, July 21, 1913. Aley to Walz, February 6, 18 (unquoted), 1914.

29. Walz to Aley January 19, and return January 20, 1916.

30. Looney to Aley, several letters. The one quoted is late 1915, early 1916, and undated.

31. Minutes meeting of March 10, 1916; students to Aley, March 16; Aley to Walz, March 10, Aley to F.H. Strickland, May 12, Walz to Aley April 12, Aley to Walz April 17, Bangor *Independent,* March 25, April 1, 8; Walz to Aley June 6, to Freeland Jones, June 8, Walz to Aley, June 10 (six pages of history) Trustees, June 12, 13, July 10, November 10, 1916; Aley to Walz July 11, 1916. All the letters are in the folders, "Law School."

32. Bangor Chamber of Commerce to Aley, January 4, 1917; Bartlett Brooks to Aley, March 5, Aley to Walz March 8, 1917; *Campus,* May 13, 1913, Walz lectured to the Deutscher Verein on "Bismark: A Soul Battling With Fate." Minute Book, Maine Law School Debating Society, September 29, 1916, should suppress peace propaganda; March, 1917, attempted to expel Kaiser, and couldn't as there was no provision in their constitution.

33. There was an informal meeting to determine course of action as early as January 17, and Aley spoke to the Trustees about Walz, the "widespread suspicion that he is strongly pro-German." Trustees,

January 17, 1918. Trustees, May 18, 1918; minutes of Tarratine Club meeting, March 9, 1918; *Campus,* March 12, *Maine Law Review,* Vol. XI, No. 5 (March, 1918), 142-3; Freeland Jones to Aley, March 12, 1918 ". . . the committee let Brother Looney run away with it. . . ." Law College minutes, January 28, May 17, 1918; Looney to Aley, February 19, 21, 1918, quoted; undated memo Aley's corres. late 1917 to Bangor Citizens, remove to Orono.

34. Bangor *Daily Commercial,* February 27, March 4, 9, 13, 1918; Lewiston *Evening Journal,* February 28, March 11, Portland *Evening Express,* March 11, *Kennebec Journal,* March 11, Bangor *Daily News,* March 8, 11, 26, 1918. This last was a reprint of a Walz article, without comment, but next to the editorial column. "The State University Law School and Its Duty to Teach the Law of the Jurisdiction." For an excellent discussion of the hysteria in the state, the reader is again referred to Rita M. Breton, unpublished M.A., 1972. Aley's "official history" does not appear in the Law School files, nor in Aley's correspondence either. Guy A. Thompson file, and many letters, and ironically his anti-German articles in New York *Sun,* July 28, August 4, 1918; Trustees, April 10, 1920 (Bangor). On fees and tuitions and enrollment see L.A. Emery to Walz, August 5, 23, 1915, Walz to Emery, August 3, September 5, 1915. Emery was chief justice of the Maine Supreme Court. On Judge Dunn, see Walz to Dunn, April 2, 1914. The *Maine Law Review* accounts were very sloppily kept, see 1913-1914 correspondence, folder No. 2, "A-H."

35. Walz to Augusta J. Cadwallader, June 11, 1915; to Franklin W. Cram, August 2, 5, 1914. The quoted letter is to E.H. Dwinel, September 17, 1915.

36. Looney to Walz, October 20, 1914, Walz to Looney, October 10, 27, 1914, Looney to Walz November 24, 1914.

37. Walz to R.J. Sprague, March 16, 1914.

38. Max C. Harmon to Aley, April 4, 1919; Aley to Harmon, April 15; R.R. Drummond, to Aley, April 19, 1919; Aley to Drummond, March 30, 1918; *Campus,* March 3, 1927. Drummond, who was a Professor of German taught English for a while, until German was restored in the early 20's.

39. *Campus,* February 25, March 18, 1919; January 13, 1920; Aley to Elbert Hayford, January 13, to ?? (Governor), January 18, 1918, to Gov. Milliken, December 21, 1918; to A.E. Tanner, April 12, 1919; Haines to Aley, December 16, 1918 — better postpone asking for armory, "I think we all better try the arts of peace a while and the war equipment can wait."

40. Trustees, April 11, June 20, 1919; undated memo Robert J. Aley to all departments, possibly 1920 at beginning of fiscal year. On attempts to bring

back the Law School see Trustees, June 4, 1920 (Bangor), July 1 (Bangor) July 28 (Bangor), (August 11 but not in records), 1920; January 6, April 9, 1921; *Campus,* November 19, 1924. Eventually Stewart Hall was sold. See below.

41.   *Campus,* September 23, November 14, 1919; Faculty, February 24, March 10, April 14, June 9, 24, 1919; February 9, 1920; on League, special meeting of March 14, 1919 with petition to Maine's legislative delegation with 78 signatures of every major faculty member and dean, as well as Aley. Trustees, June 20, October 31, 1919; April 10, 1920; Tom Jones Meek to Aley March 26, return April 4, I.P. Hartford to Aley April 8, and return April 10, on a sponsored speaking tour for League; Louis C. Southard to Aley, July 12, 1919.

42.   Southard to Aley, May 1, return May 5, Faculty June 16, Aley to Brautlecht, June 18, return July 20 (on problems); James Stevens to Aley, February 21 (English) Boardman's annual report April 25, 1919.

43.   Louis C. Southard to Robert J. Aley, May 6, 1919, reporting on alumni antagonism to Aley in the Boston area, and elsewhere.

CHAPTER SIX

Which Way the Future?

THROUGHOUT MOST OF THE YEAR 1921 the university trustees searched for a successor to Robert J. Aley. Their eventual choice was Clarence Cook Little, but he did not arrive until the summer of 1922. In the meantime, Percival Baxter had become governor, and his view of the university and its future proved to be at odds with the views of those on the campus and of Little's. For the next several years a rousing battle was fought in the state over the direction and cost of the university's development. Some aspects of Little's proposed programs were to be instituted, but too few and too slowly for his liking, so he resigned to go to Michigan. Much of Little's plan was put into action during the term of his successor, Harold S. Boardman. Unfortunately, just as the program was stably funded with the passage of a mill tax, the depression came and the gains of the previous period appeared in danger of being wiped out in the economic disaster of the country.

As had been forecast, monies appropriated in the first peacetime legislature had not been enough; the appropriation ran out in December 1920. No interim funds were made available from the state treasury, and by the spring of 1921 incomes from other sources also were used up. Salary checks for March 15 were not paid. The prime difficulty was Governor Baxter. Catapulted into the governorship when the incumbent died, Baxter was a maverick who was waging a long and lonesome fight against the paper and power interests to achieve a great park in northern Maine. He felt that the university should be paying for itself completely, without state appropriation, as did his college, Bowdoin. For that reason he wanted the appropriations cut back to a minimum.

Ordinarily the fiscal emergency would have been met by the state until the regular appropriation came in, but with the gulf in understanding, no funds were released. Finally the legislature passed an emergency appropriation of $30,000 to pay the bills (chiefly salaries) because the legislature felt the university was of "great importance to all the people of the state, and necessary for the preservation of the public peace, health and safety, . . ." The university asked for $750,000 for its new appropriation, the appropriations committee recommended $575,000, but Baxter wanted a further cut to $500,000. Even though it was clearly indicated to him that most of the requested increase was due to the rise in the cost of coal ($110,000) and much of the rest was necessary for restoration of the campus after the SATC sojourn, he still recommended the cut and urged the alumni to raise the deficit. Eventually the legislature passed another emergency measure appropriating $125,000 for the six months of January to June 1921, $195,000 for the next year, and $225,000 for the fiscal year 1923. In addition another $45,000 was allotted for payment of debts. The governor vetoed the bill, but it was passed over his veto (with only two negative votes in each house). However, this battle strained relations terribly, and a war, if not already declared, was certainly imminent.[1]

A major effort had been made to save the entire appropriation. The alumni were mobilized, statewide publicity was generated, and faculty hiring was deferred to cut down the amount asked for.[2] For the people of the state, it was difficult not to accept the governor's claims, as this was only part of an attempt to cut taxes substantially in an effort to meet the inflation in the country since the war. As Baxter said in his communication recommending the smaller funding, "Whatever is done, there should be impressed upon the University authorities the need of strict economy and of living within their

The Kennebec Valley Alumni Association at an Augusta banquet, April, 1920. President Aley, at right, headed the table. The alumni association, organized by W. D. "Pep" Towner, '14, now met regularly in many sites throughout the country. Aley was not a popular figure with Alumni groups. Everyone in this photograph seems grim.

income." He apparently believed that the university was a private institution working with state funds, and although the State Supreme Court was to rule against that view in the next year, this belief did temper his judgement. In his veto message, the governor cited the great rise in salaries as a major reason for his veto. He urged the institution to consider restricting admission to Maine students. Calling upon the alumni to meet the deficiency in funds, he said that he had been told that the alumni would not respond even if asked, and went on, in a passage that indicated how strong his feelings were,

> I believe the alumni of the University of Maine are loyal. I believe they are interested in their institution, and their united and earnest efforts to induce the Legislature to make a generous appropriation proves that they are alive to the situation and know how pressing is the need of funds. I do not believe that the alumni of the University of Maine will fail to respond if a proper appeal is made to them. At least I believe they should be put to the test.[3]

At the end of his blast at the school, Baxter stated his conviction that he was looking out for the boys and girls of the state and finished his veto message (after indicating that he thought it would be overridden) by saying that he supported "liberal aid" for the university, but that the alumni should help, that Maine students should come first, that the amounts asked for should be trimmed, and that if all this happened the university "will continue to do good work for the boys and girls of our State of Maine."

President Aley attempted to mend the breach with the governor by saying, "We have won in this matter and as victors can afford to be generous. Nothing can be gained by speaking against anyone who may have opposed us."[4]

Percival Baxter was not beaten easily, and certainly not in this fashion. Many felt the university's "victory" pyrrhic and most felt that as soon as the new president came, sparks might again fly between the governor and the Orono school. On the campus there were quiet efforts to deal with possible reductions in the teaching force. The search for someone who could deal with Baxter had begun. Dean Hart was especially active, as was F.H. Strickland, president of the board of trustees. Hart wrote to one correspondent his views of the seriousness of the choice.

> We who are on the grounds regard the position as a difficult one . . . bad financial condition . . . The president should be a man of good judgement, as well as executive ability, one who will get on well with faculty, students, and the public, and who can go before the legislature and plead the cause of the institution successfully.[5]

Three months later he was even more explicit about the university's needs.

> I do not know what the Trustees will regard as most important qualifications but in my own mind business ability comes first, standing as a scholar second, and ability to deal successfully with men particularly with the Maine Legislature, and the alumni of the University third. It is difficult to place one of these qualifications as more valuable than another. All three are absolutely essential.

Colonel Strickland addressed the students as well with his views as to the type of person needed.

> We are searching for a full blooded American; with ability, spirit, and energy sufficient to mold into solid union all the stable forces needed for the good of the University of Maine.[6]

Governor Baxter also was interested in the new president and the work of the university because he was running for reelection. He came to the university, prior to the choice of the new president, to make his own case. He was met at the trolley waiting room on College Avenue by the band and the ROTC and conducted to the specially decorated chapel where the faculty, deans, and students all waited to hear his views on their institution.[7]

Baxter opened his remarks by describing the school and its students as "splendid" and went on, "I feel that I have the right to say to you here on behalf of the people of the State of Maine that they are going to continue their loyal and generous support, that they are going to stand behind you in whatever you need." He promised to place the institution upon a sound and enduring financial basis. He mentioned the three other colleges in the state, but assured the university people that as titular head of this "splendid University" he would always support them, and that their sacrifice endeared them to him. He also spoke of the amounts spent for education, counseled them to put this money to the best use, urged public speaking as a good field of study for all, told them they ought to remain in the state, and mentioned the ROTC and said he opposed military training except in very limited measure. He then called for observance of the spirit of Armistice Day, again promised to help and to work with the faculty, and finally declared a student holiday. This speech was transcribed by the president's secretary, and later Baxter's remarks, which were published and sent out to the state, were to be of interest in the battle with the new president.[8]

At the university itself the educators were not all of the same mind concerning their own governance. With Aley gone, a Committee on Administration was in charge of the institution, and a small number of faculty wanted more power. A special meeting of all faculty was called to end the "obvious disharmony." The dean apologized for not informing people satisfactorily and appointed a liaison group to deal with faculty relations and to work out lines of authority for the transition period. A monthly report to the faculty was instituted, and the situation ameliorated while the search for a new president continued. As Hart, who was acting president, remarked to the wife of a former president,

> We think that the University is having an excellent year in spite of the fact that there is no President. We have a faculty committee of conferences with the Deans and this committee is having numerous meetings to work out a scheme of cooperation between the Administration and the faculty and is now taking up the matter of University standards.[9]

He also said that the trustee's search was difficult and no one on the faculty (apparently including himself) wanted the job.

Then another candidate for governor used the chapel in order to appeal for votes and urged the state to be more generous, including with scholarship aid, and remarked that the university should not be sacrificed for Katahdin State Park (Baxter's project). It was becoming increasingly obvious that unless a new president was found soon, political pressures might damage the university severely.[10]

The faculty had actually heard its new president during the previous year. Clarence Cook Little, a distinguished geneticist, had spoken at chapel and to the faculty in February 1921. He was then head of the Carnegie Institute's research project on experimental evolution and was publishing a work, "Evidence for Sex-linked Lethal Factors in Man," among others. In March of 1922 he returned and made a tremendous impression speaking at chapel, saying the university must challenge the mind and the body. The *Campus* urged his selection as president, and the trustees announced his nomination a month later.[11]

Clarence Cook Little

Little had been in negotiation with the trustees for some time. He had said to his prospective employers that he would have to have, in addition to the usual fringe benefits, an absolutely free hand, and he asked for $3,000 to support his research, especially for several students he was to bring with him. He said he could get the Carnegie people to match this grant. The trustees agreed to this request, but they wanted to consult with Governor Baxter. Little agreed to that and said, "I feel that the interest and cooperation of Governor Baxter is of the utmost importance . . . . I hope and expect that he would take an active and important part in raising the standard and in otherwise strengthening the University . . . . If his attitude is unfavorable . . . I should wish to know it at the earliest possible moment."[12]

Little, who arrived on the campus in the late spring, realized that the governor might be hostile to him and to the school. In June Baxter, having won renomination in the Republican party primary, wrote to Strickland requesting trustee ideas for the budget and urging a meeting between Little and the state auditor. He said that it was necessary to get a budget with no overdraft as he wanted to help the university so that the next winter, when the legislature convened, he could recommend amounts that would "help you in every proper way," within the state's financial limitations.[13] Little responded to the letter with one that called for sufficient appropriation to put the buildings and heating plant back into proper condition. He said the staff was overworked and the equipment outdated and badly used. However, since Baxter would not meet with his correspondents until the general elections were over, the summer was spent in anxious waiting. Strickland found this refusal to meet ominous. "I have an idea he is a slippery customer and a mighty smooth talking one, and this is not because I am a Democrat."[14]

The meeting was finally held in Augusta on September 26, 1922. Strickland, Little, Baxter, and Earl Bangs, the state treasurer, were in attendance. Little and Strickland made their presentation, and Baxter responded by asking for information on costs at the campus from 1920 to 1922. Little wrote a letter with this information; when he received no reply, he sent another letter saying he had formulated a long-term program, to be financed by a mill tax, probably to be passed by referendum, and he asked for an opportunity to discuss the program with Baxter. Baxter thanked him for the letter, but stalled on a date. No matter how much Little asked for other dates, he could not get an appointment. What he did get was a letter from the governor saying that the university's budget was much too large: "There must be some way to effect economies in your mangement." Baxter told Little to ask for only actual needs, no growth. He did not like the mill tax idea and again urged Little to go to the alumni. Finally he told Little to go back to the board, reviewing every item, because he could not ask the legislature for the requests as they appeared.[15]

Overt hostilites erupted. Baxter opposed observance of Navy Day, October 27, and Little attacked him for this in the public press, as did several newspaper editors. Little went to the Land Grant College meetings in a effort to drum up fraternal support for his plans. At these meetings in Washington, D.C., he gave an interview in which he discussed his proposals and Baxter's opposition. He said that he believed that the state wanted people to be educated and to live in Maine and threw down the gauntlet to the governor with:

> I like a fight. There are only one or two other states in the Union that have such splendid American stock as Maine, and yet Maine spends a miserably small amount of money for education compared with many other states that have less population than Maine. I am not trying to make the University 100 per cent perfect. That is out of the question at the present time. It is too much run down in every way. All I am trying to do is to make it respectable.[16]

This announcement stirred up the proverbial hornet's nest. Augustus Thomas, the State Commissioner of Education and a trustee, ranged himself against Little, calling himself amazed at the statement and saying, "He shows his misconception of conditions and ignorance of the facts." Then Thomas dismissed Little as a young man who had a great deal to learn. The Portland *Press Herald,* which had printed the original interview, attacked Thomas and said that many in the state agreed with Little, especially on the public schools about which Little had also offered trenchant criticism.[17] Baxter, for his part, wrote Little and asked him if he had been quoted correctly as to liking a

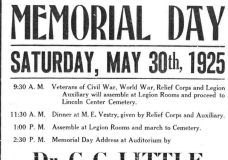

Little was an indefatigable speaker. This broadside poster advertises such an occasion in Lincoln, Maine. The university's contribution during World War I had been well received, and this ceremony, commemorating the war dead, was an appropriate joining of patriotism and education.

fight. Little said he had made no personal attacks, but that he did believe his remarks to represent the case and that the governor was wrong.[18]

The governor did not respond until the legislature met, but Little knew he had made an enemy. During the rest of the year the president toured the state making speeches in an attempt to gather support for his program. Little had some fame as a follower of Margaret Sanger and as a friend to women's rights, and he enlisted one strong group when he spoke before the Federation of Women's Clubs on women's rights. The *Christian Science Monitor* reprinted this speech which was widely circulated in the country. Other groups he addressed included the Economic Club of Portland, the Twentieth Century Club of Bangor, and the assembled county agents. This last meeting brought a favorable letter and editorial from the *Maine*

Farmer. On the campus he built strength with addresses to the various faculties.[19] But the legislature was soon to meet and Baxter would have his chance.

Baxter was a consummate politician who made no moves without building the largest support base he could. In his inaugural he barely mentioned the university, only indicating that state support was necessary, with the implication that it would be strictly dispensed. Little himself organized a lobbying campaign, using as his headquarters outside the legislature the office of Roy Flynt, sales manager of the *Kennebec Journal.* The day of the inaugural, Little remarked to Flynt on the "primitive viewpoint concerning the status of the University," but said that the campaign would proceed. Baxter had hoped to prove the university to be a private institution; however, immediately after the inaugural, the deed transferring the property to the state in 1870 was located. On the campus this was a cause for rejoicing as it seemd to spike Baxter's guns. The campus newspaper was restrained but happy.

> From this it can be seen that the State not only has a moral responsibility but a legal responsibility as well in the proper and adequate maintenance of the University of Maine. As to what effect this discovery will have on the future policy of the State Legislature in its relation to the University is hard to say at present but it may have a great influence not understood at the present time.[20]

Little's main agent inside the legislature was Ellis F. Baker, a Republican from Steuben in Washington County, who agreed to "lead the fight in the House for the University." Baker and Little rode to Boston on the train together and Little outlined his desires, among them a separate women's college, more out-of-state students, and a considerable amount of building repair. Later Baker told Little that he could not have the first item, but that he could get many of the rest.[21] In the Senate there was no specific spokesman, but William Tudor Gardiner, soon to be governor and already a power in state politics, used his influence in support. One of his letters will indicate how he worked.

> Adams [Herman H., Belgrade] is non-communicative. Wadsworth [Herbert E., Winthrop] open-minded. Said to the wife something

about 500,000 a year. Not an economist. Has a little hesitation in giving you all you want until a thing is tried out. Impression of Aley not eradicated yet.[22]

Flynt and the *Kennebec Journal* were the big guns since the newspaper was widely read by the legislators. The newspaper published articles and editorials on the university, some of which were drafted in Orono. Flynt also arranged for editorials to appear in such papers as the Boston *Transcript,* the Portland *Press Herald,* and the Houlton *Times.* And Flynt lobbied, not necessarily for the college, but against Baxter.

Little made a number of speeches and sent copies to all the papers, mobilized the Bangor Chamber of Commerce (he had written their resolution), and worked with alumni and powerful figures outside the state to enlist their support. The women's clubs were persistent supporters, sending delegations to the hearings and writing letters, and the old tried and true advocates, such as the various Pomona Granges, also were mustered behind the school.[23]

The main issue was whether the university would continue to grow or would stabilize at its existing condition. The Little forces hoped for passage of the mill tax to free them from the incessant lobbying, and Baxter was not necessarily completely opposed to that; what he wanted was a standard amount of funding, at a relatively low level. Before the battle was completely underway, the legislature held its hearings. The first occurred February 27, in Augusta, and Little and Strickland attended. They asked for $147,900 for urgent building repairs and a biennial budget of $682,735 for the first year, $705,276 for the second. Little spent considerable time in his statement on the necessity to educate women. Seventy-five had been turned away for lack of facilities, and he wanted to be able to accept 300 over the current registration. He also mentioned the dairy building, authorized in 1917 but not constructed; the heating plant, which was in serious straits; and other repairs which were needed.

Little discussed cost ratios to other state institutions and pointed out that the university fared badly in comparison. He then moved to the crux of his speech. It was time for a ten-year plan. This plan would save time and money and would raise the morale of both students and faculty. It would allow the university to give greater aid and cooperation in teacher training to the State Department of Education. Hiring, promotion, and administrative costs would be rationalized and lessened. The college would be enabled to do long-term bulk buying as an economy measure. The curriculum would be stabilized, with the general object of insuring retention of Maine youngsters in the state after graduation. A mill tax would allow the university to do all this, but if the legislature would not go along, then at a minimum the biennial requests must be funded.

A week later the legislative committee visited the university, inspected the buildings, and attended a chapel where Little opened the campaign for the Memorial Gymnasium and field house. The students oversubscribed their quota almost immediately, and a telegram was sent to Baxter to let him know the extent of campus committment and to ask his.[24]

The college community settled down to wait; Baxter had yet to speak. By the fifteenth of March, Little was anxious to bring a full-fledged lobbying campaign to bear on the legislature, but, fearing he hadn't enough votes to override a veto in the senate, decided to wait for the committee to make its report. He did allow himself to give one interview, to his favorite paper, the *Kennebec Journal.* The piece was a gem in molding public opinion. The reporter allowed himself to be taken to the oldest, most decrepit buildings on campus and after indicating how much Little was loved by his students, to plead the university's case. At the end of the article a key quote indicated where the newspaper and Little stood, and part of it was reprinted in the headline.

For the state to fail to provide the financial support called for in the resolve means a general reversion and falling back to conditions of twenty years ago at the University. . . .[25]

On March 27 Baxter emerged with his view of the situation. In a long (thirteen page) statement rehearsing what he had said before about the school and its place in the scheme of things in the State of Maine, Baxter said that he had hoped that Little and the board would cooperate

Winslow Hall and the stock judging pavilion, sometime in the 1920's. The judging of cattle, along with genetic analysis led to better breeding. Cattle had become an important feature in the state's economy after the decline of wheat and other grain crops.

to eliminate past practices and antagonisms. He had worked in harmony, but they had not always been cordial in return; he described the fall meeting as one example of the university's choosing to dictate to him and indicated that the board had threatened to resign if their demands were not met. After referring to Little's Washington interview, the governor got down to the nub of his problem with Orono.[26]

> The University never has been held in check; it has outgrown itself; it has outgrown the ability of the State to properly provide for it. This is the root of its troubles. Year by year, deliberately and regardless of consequences, those in charge of the University in the past have expanded its activities. *They seem to have been imbued with a desire to make the University the biggest educational institution in the State, while there is but slight evidence that they sought to make it the best.* Their hopes for the University have rested upon false foundations. . . .[26] *(italics added)*

He went on to say that, since funds were and would continue to be limited, the university could educate only some of those deserving an education. He was critical of salary increases and returned to his attack saying, "Today this institution is an overgrown school improperly nourished, with both its teaching force and its student body working under difficulties."

In discussing the colleges in the state, Baxter rated Bowdoin, Bates, and then Colby as all being more efficient and generally superior to the university. He asked, "Is the University Justified?" and, charging the school with being too political, called for a full-time president (i.e., no lobbying). He attacked the school for having poor alumni spirit. He also suggested that Little's own research funds be cut back since the research was on animals. (Baxter was a fervent anti-vivisectionist.) He even referred to the idea that only agriculture and mechanics should be taught, urging a reconstruction of the school, perhaps with elimination of the arts college. In any case, wanting "a halt to all expansion," Baxter was only willing to recommend the maintenance funds requested, repair funds, assumption of the university debt, limiting the student body to one thousand, reducing costs, and making the university the best, not the biggest. Other recommendations included: a new board of trustees, emphasis on agriculture, elimination of politics from the school's at-

mosphere, cultivation of college spirit both on and off campus, reorganization of the university on a sound educational and financial basis, and making it a Maine "institution for Maine boys and girls."

This assault, redolent of the past and of Brunswick, agitated the Orono supporters tremendously. Little offered an attack of his own listing thirteen misstatements and nine errors of judgment that had been committed by the governor. He charged that Baxter had misrepresented his (Little's) stands in Washington and elsewhere and had reported a lower cost of education at Bates and Bowdoin in comparison with Maine than was actually true. Little defended his right to do research, saying that it was a condition of his taking the position. He defended the agriculture college. He was incensed by the slur on the alumni (especially as the Memorial Gymnasium fund raising was well along), and said that a new trustee board would be simply a method for Baxter to buck the legislature to get his own way. Little ended with a well-placed thrust at Baxter.

> To follow his financial suggestions would mean a disaster to the university. To follow his administrative suggestions would mean decrease rather than increase of interest on the part of alumni, and to follow his educational suggestions, including the limitations of the number of students, would make the University of Maine and the State of Maine a laughing stock to anyone who took the trouble to consider the situation.[27]

Newspaper comments were even more brutal on both sides. The Lewiston *Daily Sun* printed an editorial entitled "Stand By the Governor" in which the title was repeated five times. The Portland *Press Herald* was equally vehement about Baxter and his message.

> A more pitiful exhibition of narrow minded, egotistical, obstinate hostility to a worthy State institution, which has turned out some of the first citizens of this state, has never been exhibited by a Governor of Maine.[28]

The legislature passed the university bill fairly quickly. It went through on April 5, providing $600,000 for the biennium, $125,000 for repair and equipment, and $170,000 for a new arts and science building. The university had won this battle, even if it had not received a go-ahead on its ten-year plan or passage of a mill tax, but those might come eventually.[29]

People had watched the exchange with interest. The Boston *Globe* solicited an article from Little on his "conception of the duties and opportunities of a State University and saying what you please about the present policy of Governor Baxter." When the article came the editor thanked Little, commending him for the good he was doing "in this neck of the country where folks are so slow in waking up to the possibilities of state institutions." In the article, Little called for the university to serve the state directly and defined as its duties: to educate the youth of the state, train teachers, reach adults through extension and summer schools, insist on the highest moral standards for its students, foster liberalism and tolerance, and minimize class and group lines while encouraging individual responsibility.[30]

Others also regarded the battle as important, and newspapers out of the state such as the Boston *Transcript* and inside such as the Houlton *Times* all praised Little. Former professors commended him and Little let out a bit of his feelings in his answer to one of them. "At the end of the session I could not help sympathizing with the gentleman who made that time-honored remark that 'the more he saw of men, the better he liked dogs.' "[31] Oddly enough Percival Baxter would have accepted that view of life completely.

Feelings ran very high between the governor and university alumni after this conflict. As an example one could cite a confrontation between Baxter and James M. Eaton and Arthur "Scrapper" Hayes, both of '10. The alumni were dining with family at the Hotel Touraine in Boston when Baxter, who knew one of the women present, introduced himself and made some rather gratuitous remarks about Little's lack of experience. After joshing him a bit, the exchange grew more serious, and Baxter was asked some pointed questions about his lack of experience as governor, at which time the meeting broke up and Baxter left for his room without any farewells. Alumni felt that they had to answer Baxter's attacks wherever he made them.[32]

In retrospect it seems that the differences between the two principals would inevitably lead to conflict. They were exact opposites.

The interior of the library, Carnegie Hall. This photograph, taken about 1910, looked much the same to generations of students from 1903 to the 1940's. The building now houses the university art department and galleries. Other Carnegie libraries, located primarily in small towns, look very similar.

Baxter was a great governor primarily because he was a loner and because he could appeal over the heads of his opponents to the people. For the most part he chose issues that time has endorsed. However, he was idiosyncratic in some of his views, taking as one strong element in his creed opposition to vivisection and support for the rights of animals. As a wealthy, educated man he brought the background of his familial ties and history and ancient culture to his office. Little, on the other hand, was gregarious, a scientist committed to experimentation on animals, and one who believed that an appeal to analytical reason was sufficient cause for people to accept his views. Baxter's Bowdoin ties were strong, his feelings about the university undoubtedly colored by these ties. Little had no time for that ancient history.[33]

The real bone of contention was Little's research, and he and Baxter had one clash in the newspapers after the research had begun to receive nationwide notice. When Baxter retired from the governor's chair he mentioned in his final remarks the need for humane education as to the proper treatment of animals and attacked

Clarence Cook Little in his laboratory with experimental animals.

Dwight B. Demeritt

Little for his experimentation on them: "I cannot refrain from saying that the 1,200 boys and girls at Orono are of vastly more importance to Maine than all the experimental research herein referred to."[34]

The result of the differences in personalities was to give the state some difficult times and incidental entertainment and to outline the problems quite well for other men to solve.

Baxter's term of office lasted only until January 1925, and the legislature did not meet again while he was governor. Little mostly bided his time until a new governor was in the office though he and Baxter continued their sniping at each other. One area of difficulty was in forestry. Although instruction in the subject was given at Orono, the teaching position was only partially funded by the university, and the State Forest Commissioner and the governor had a voice in the appointments, curriculum, and research. Over half the funds came from the forest commissioner's office. In 1923 Samuel F. Dana was the forest commissioner. A new professor was needed at Orono, and Little wanted to appoint Dwight Demeritt to the position. In the past the university's choice for appointment had received automatic acceptance by the other officials involved.

The forest commissioner told Little that Baxter had indicated that he did not want Demeritt and, in fact, that forestry instruction was an unnecessary expense at Orono. Little queried Baxter about his views. Baxter's secretary responded, saying that Dana was resigning and that the only reason for delay was to determine the new commissioner's views. The secretary then went on to say that the governor took the deepest interests in these matters, and although there were differences of opinion, "he never allows himself to be disturbed by them." Finally, Baxter accepted Demeritt but closed his letter with a cryptic remark wishing the school success "and some time when I come to Bangor I shall come out and see you all." Later Little and Baxter had a strange and unproductive correspondence over whether or not Coolidge Clubs should be formed.

In August 1924, Baxter sent the board of trustees a copy of a photograph of him and his Irish setter, Garry, saying, "I thought that the University would like to have this and shall appreciate it if you will have it placed in some appropriate position in one of the University's

Balentine Hall, first dormitory constructed especially for women. This photograph is from the 1930's. The diamond motif set into the brick work makes this one of the most distinctive buildings on the campus, along with the sun porch, not seen here.

buildings." He wished the university well in this letter, also.

In his farewell address Baxter was once again critical of both the university and Little, bringing up the political atmosphere, the need for a full-time president, the animal research, of course, and calling for a long-range plan. Thus, this particular feud ended. A long-range plan was already under discussion when Baxter made this point and he must have known it. The state and the university awaited the new governor.[35]

The first appearance of the long-range program in any form, was in a 1923 letter of Little's stating that his guiding principle was to set estimates of needed funds low, but at the same time sufficient to cover new requests made during the decade the plan would cover. He felt that proper equipment and facilities to instruct the qualified youth of the state were imperative and should include an experiment station, extension service, and forestry program. He hoped for alumni gifts of one million dollars. The funds from one mill taxation, plus the alumni gifts, would provide over the decade $747,300 a year, the equivalent of 1.11 mill of taxation each year. He would utilize the money as follows: $625,000, or .93 mill, to the university itself; $28,500, or .04 mill, applied to the

deficit; $30,000, or .04 mill, to the experiment station; $48,300, or .07 mill, to the extension service; and $15,000, or .02 mill, to forestry. This program, thought Little, would allow for no increase in male students but would allow admittance of all qualified females applying, many of whom were then being turned away. Little's letter closed as follows:

It is, of course, impossible to foresee possible complications that may arise, but if we were given the income from a tax of one mill annually, I think that by rigid economy and the introduction of all the money-saving reforms that we could institute without hampering of instruction, that we could get by without a deficit.

He went on to say that if there was a deficit he would raise the funds outside the state. The above figures were given to his correspondent,

. . . with a feeling that there is a real desire on the part of the present legislature to give the University a new start and a square deal, holding it completely responsible for its methods of expenditure and for the results obtained.[36]

In 1924, in the spring, the steam plant began to leak severely. Little formed a special committee of trustees and alumni to make recommendations for dealing with the plant and to offer suggestions on the long-range plans of the school. After two or three meetings, this committee put together a list of buildings needed, among them a dairy, a greenhouse, two women's dormitories, an engineering building, an addition to the arts building, and an infirmary.[37]

The committee continued to work on a long-range plan, soon to be described as a ten-year program. The work was intensified by an attack on Orono at the 1924 Bowdoin commencement. The ten-year program soon began to include higher education away from campus, especially in regard to teacher training. The early drafts discussed recommendations to absorb the normal schools or perhaps to use the extension service to strengthen their offerings. Gradually certain principles became central, both to the planning and the thinking about the future. They deserve quotation.

    1. Equality of opportunity to sexes.
    2. Personal contact with candidate before admission.
    3. Quality of education as good as endowed universities.
    4. Limitation to those qualified.
    5. Importance of foundation subjects.
    6. Correlation and interrelations of Agriculture, Technology, and Arts and Sciences.

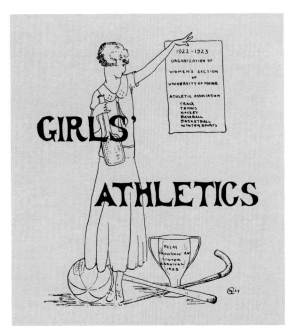

From The Prism, *1924.*

The plan specified raising salaries by ten to fifteen percent by the fifth year. It also contemplated tapping private sources for a large chapel and union, a college store, a gateway, a field house for women, the planting of a Maine Botanical Garden, and the building of a teaching museum of natural history and art. In the sixth year the law school would be opened again. At first 100, and eventually 400, state scholarships would be provided to undergraduates. A teacher training institution would be in operation by 1926, and by 1928 both engineering extension and general extension (similar to the present Continuing Education Division) would be underway. Forestry was to be housed at Orono completely. Little hoped to admit 300 to 400 more women and 100 to 200 more men to the university as well. All this was hammered out in a series of detailed conferences with deans during the summer of 1924.[38]

At the budget hearing in November 1924, Little began to allude to his program, and Ralph O. Brewster, the new governor, asked him to spell it out. Little presented it orally in late November, discussed it, and asked for an opportunity to address the legislature with it. After the trustees accepted Little's drafts in principle at their December 24 meeting, Little began to press Brewster for his acceptance as well. At his inaugural Brewster did indicate sympathy with all but one of Little's goals: equality with other institutions; however, he specifically mentioned the arts college, saying "It is probable that a strong College of Arts and Sciences affords an excellent foundation upon which technical training may be built." Brewster also praised the alumni for their work on the new gymnasium.[39]

Little now held a short alumni school on campus from January 15 to 17; he outlined his ten-year plan to alumni, presented a detailed printed discussion of it, and urged those attending to go out and work for the university. Copies of the plan were also sent to the governor, members of the legislature, and to the press. On February 18, Little made to the education committee of the legislature a presentation that was widely commented on and apparently well received. The State Superintendent of Schools was an advocate of the plan as were various alumni, such as George H. Hamlin, '73, Winthrop H. Jordan, '73, and Austin Jones, '12.

Unfortunately, neither the legislature nor the governor was ready to make the necessary commitment, either to the mill tax to finance it, or to the decade it would take for the plan to work. The legislature did allow $400,000 for each year of the biennium, but the disappointment in Orono was very deep, as it had been felt that Brewster was a proponent and that the incubus of legislative appearances could finally be shaken off.[40]

The failure to get the mill tax and the plan was apparently the last straw for Little. At the farmers' week activities in April he criticized the legislature bitterly. After citing the need for new buildings, he said that the governor wanted economy, but that education and charity were not the places for economy. In June he wrote to the governor himself with a list of questions. Would Brewster support a mill tax in the future? Should the trustees be more political in the future? Should there be alumni trustees? Would Brewster comment on whether the university could have a whole sum appropriated or should the bit by bit method be continued? He then remarked,

> I am particularly anxious to obtain answers to these questions because at the present time a situation has arisen through no seeking of mine which makes it absolutely essential to have a clear understanding of the governor's attitude in these matters.[41]

Apparently the answers were either not forthcoming or were not the right answers, for within a week Little submitted his resignation to the board of trustees, to be effective at the beginning of the next school year. He announced that he was going to Michigan State University where he was being "offered an opportunity to try on a very large scale the educational policies which the State of Maine has not as yet been willing to adopt."

Little's letter of resignation was a powerful indictment of the state, and much of it deserves quotation.

> At the present time the State of Maine is lagging woefully in its support of the State University. It has departed somewhat from an *absolutely inadequate* appropriation in 1922 but it is still far from realizing its objectives and even from adopting as generous attitude as that shown by smaller and poorer states.

The electrical engineering shop in Lord Hall, sometime in the late 1920's. The equipment is of an advanced type from that shown previously.

> It seems entirely probable that the Legislature and the politically active elements of the State will require at least two more years to reach a point where they have recovered from the shock of having given additional support and are ready to progress even further. There is not as yet enough unprejudiced support of higher education in the State to have outgrown criticism of the College of Arts and Sciences at the University — a criticism as primitive and unintelligent in its way as is the legislation against the teaching of the evolution theory.[42]

His original draft then included a paragraph which considered the fact that no governor yet had caught the vision of higher education. He finally excised this paragraph but did say that no representative of the people had been willing to support a vote of the people on these issues.

President Harold S. Boardman, '95, CE, '98, at work in his office, about 1930. "Boardy," as he was affectionately called, moved steadily through the ranks of his alma mater and was an obvious choice to serve as president. His office was still located in Coburn Hall.

He discussed Maine's potential, the desire to keep young people home, and offered a comparison of costs with New Hampshire. In discussing his program he remarked,

> . . . there is a 'ten-year' program which may be attenuated to a 'hundred and fifty' year program but which *is* nevertheless a *program*. The trustees have adopted this as a general guiding policy. There is a plan for campus development already becoming visualized.

Praising the faculty and the alumni at Maine, Little agreed to help select his successor, whom he hoped would be an alumnus and a Maine native.

The trustees, accepting his resignation, indicated that they believed that he had stamped his personality upon the school, had visualized its future needs, and set up a program which would meet those needs. The *Maine Campus* reprinted much of Little's letter, once school had begun again in the fall, and praised Little by saying, "his accomplishments in the University is our heritage which we never relinquish."

Little's career at Maine was unusual in that he did make a major impact in a very short time. However, he did not achieve his goals. In 1929 a mediocre novel entitled *Wings of Wax* appeared. It recounted the problems and failures of a young college president who flew too high and failed on the issues of feminism and equality for women, which the novel said he did not understand. Many thought this a biography of Little. If it was, the title was appropriate with regard to his time at Orono as well. However, like his predecessor from Greek mythology, by trying and failing he set a pattern of behavior and created knowledge so that the future would be more satisfactory.[43]

With the two principal antagonists gone from the scene, both the university and the legislature went about their business with dispatch during the next four years. In 1926 a large contingent of students, faculty, and alumni met with Governor Brewster at the Bangor House. The governor was the main speaker. He discussed university growth and made a strong plea for agriculture, but also praised the college of arts and sciences. The *Campus* termed his remarks "entirely satisfactory."[44]

In September the new president, Harold S. Boardman, '95, longtime dean of the technology college, was inaugurated. In his inaugural he called for growth and the elimination of tensions. He said that if people were to "Boom Maine" (a theme of a statewide publicity campaign then underway) they should boom its education as well. In February the *Campus* thought the attitude in Augusta the best in years. Boardman was well liked. The budget committee which had held its hearing in Bangor in late November was impressed, and the education committee hearings in February went smoothly. Brewster had used phrases like "most promising prospects in its half-century" and described the state as being "fortunate" in having Boardman, though he did ask the state to view the problem of mass education and the costs of college.[45]

The legislative committee recommended providing $420,000 each year for current expenses, and $70,000 each year to be used for a new dairy building, greenhouse, and hydraulic equipment. The bill passed both houses and was enacted with very little difficulty. An additional $35,000 came in each year for various agricultural research and extension projects. By this time the university budget looked as follows:[46]

Income

Source	Amount
Land Grant	5,915
Morrill Act	50,000
State	420,000
Const.	70,000
Highway	3,050
Smith/Hughes	4,000
Tuition	158,300
Diplomas	1,200
Misc.	500
Coburn Fund	4,000
Hill Fund	24,350
Rents	2,000
Interest	3,600
Press	20,000
Ag. Sales	27,000
FW Hill Will	1,400
Total	795,315

Expenditures

Department	Amount
Administration	77,000
Maintenance	98,000
Utilities	55,000
Extension	5,000
Grad. Work	600
Ag. College	129,000
Arts & Sciences	161,000
Tech. College	122,750
Law	650
Library	18,000
Phys. Ed.	26,315
Mil. Sci.	1,000
Summer Session	2,000
Press	20,000
Dorms	2,500
Const.	70,000
Supp. Const.	5,000
Contingent Fund	1,500
Total	795,315

The atmosphere was even more cordial by the beginning of the next legislature in 1929. The governor, William Tudor Gardiner, had been active earlier in the mill tax fight. He thought "the removal of educational matters from active politics is a wise policy," and he called for placing the budget on a "definitely recognized and established" revenue basis. The legislature apparently agreed — it enacted a mill tax.

Although there had been an attempt in the senate to continue the usual method of biennial financing, with an increase, it was withdrawn, and the mill tax bill passed the legislature without a dissenting vote. First year funds from this tax amounted to an increase of $151,500 over the previous year's amounts.[47]

Boardman hailed the bill, as did the *Campus*, which thought the bill brought the university "out of the dark." Little telegraphed his congratulations to the university community and must have thought that his actions had had a great deal to do with the eventual passage of the tax. The trustees increased appropriations to agriculture by $11,200, to arts and sciences by $19,300, and to technology by $10,270. The library received $2,000 extra, and the graduate school $1,500. $55,000 was allocated for buildings and landscaping, while $45,750 was put in reserve. The reserve was fortuitous since by the time the funds were actually available in the state's coffers, other influences, beginning at the corner of Wall and Broad Streets in New York, would be making their appearance.[48]

Although the passage of the mill tax and the effort to place the school on a regular financial footing were central in the affairs of the college from 1921 to 1929, there were changes in the general campus life, especially in governance, curricula, and attitude. Many of these changes could be traced to the influence of Little. Most of the college's business had been run by Dean Hart who was replaced by James Stacey Stevens. The old role of faculty dean who taught a full load disappeared as increased enrollment made the deanship a full-time job important in the governance structure. The general faculty meetings, which had been the dean's responsibility, were limited to two a year while routine business went on in the college faculties.[49]

Not all was sweet and easy. At various times faculty personnel or ideas created problems. The new men in philosophy were philosophers, not psychologists as had been traditional, and this caused comment. It was difficult to meet student demands for courses until the budget stabilized toward the end of the decade. Little had brought in a new head of the biology department who was not very satisfactory and was let go soon after Little himself left. Credit for physical training was a long-range problem, but by 1925 most colleges retained it only for freshmen, if at all.

Photograph taken as classes opened in September, 1928. Visible are the carpenters shop, the observatory, and in the background the college farm buildings and Rogers Hall. The vehicles were probably owned by the faculty.

Important from the point of view of students was the beginning of freshman orientation week. From 1915 to 1917 a few meetings of new students had been held with deans and the president, but were abandoned during the war.[50] When Little came he revived the idea, but with a full week for freshmen before classes began in the fall. The week soon included instruction in the use of the library, note taking, the duties and responsibilities of students, and a good deal on the customs and traditions of the school. Faculty from all areas spoke, and attention was focused on difficult courses and on problems. The evenings featured mixers. By 1927 the *Campus* was hailing this orientation as a major step in making college life good and maximizing its benefits.[51]

The graduate program grew to be more important, was created as a separate school in 1923, and by 1926 had fairly detailed rules laid out for students to follow. The establishment of standard scholarships, especially to Maritime Province students, aided this program. On the undergraduate level, departmental honors programs were established and made a strong impact on some undergraduates.[52] The new dean of technology, Paul Cloke, put a good deal of effort into beefing up that college, with the establishment of required research and the elimination of correspondence courses. Professional societies were promoted, and instruction improved generally. The new areas of emphasis were highway construction, pulp and paper, power, and communication. Little began a program of intensifying instruction in agriculture.

The different research and teaching aspects, i.e., the experiment station, extension, and regular faculty, were regularized to some degree. Through a series of committees now reporting directly to the dean, duplication of effort was cut back substantially. A school of education was instituted in 1930. A medical school was discussed at length, but finally rejected on the grounds of cost and better application of limited funds. Research on the campus was given a strong boost in 1927 when Thomas Upham Coe died and left $100,000 to be used for research purposes. Since then much extracurricular research on the campus has been funneled through the committees set up to administer this fund and its successors. Off campus, a reciprocity system was set up with

Two famous and well known deans in the inter-war period. The top photo is Paul Cloke, Dean of the College of Engineering and the bottom photo is James Stacey Stevens, Dean of the College of Arts and Sciences.

The original arts and science building, Stevens Hall. Wings, connected by arcades, have been added later to give the appearance of today. This photo dates from 1924 or 1925.

Caroline Colvin was a central figure in the University, serving as professor and chairperson in history, and the first dean of women. The building named for her is shown below, some time in the 1930's.

Bangor Theological Seminary in 1925 and a similar one for nurses' training at the Eastern Maine General Hospital in 1926.[53]

Caroline Colvin, professor of history, was appointed Dean of Women in 1923, in a move universally applauded. She immediately began to consolidate and strengthen the position of women on the campus. After the new gymnasium was constructed, women took over the former gymnasium and a new Women's Student Government was formed. As Colvin said, "Our ideal is training in self-direction rather than official control." She began to call for more dormitory facilities, and Little aided this cause. When the first of these new dorms was built, it was named, appropriately, Colvin Hall.[54]

A number of important buildings were constructed in this era. The central structure of Stevens Hall was built by 1924, and the entire building completed and dedicated in 1934. Merrill Hall, designed to house "residential teaching, extension, and experimental work" all in one building devoted to agriculture, was dedicated in 1931. Oliver Crosby, '76, left $400,000 to the school in 1923 which was used to build and house the Crosby Laboratory, although funds for final completion did not come until the governor and the council provided them in 1928. A new greenhouse and horticultural building was also put up in that year. The most famous and the largest building was the Memorial Gymnasium and Armory constructed in honor of the forty-one Maine alumni who lost their lives in World War I. The structure was entirely funded by contributions from faculty, students, administration, and mostly from alumni. With its construction the university's physical plant reached an excellent comparative status with the other colleges of its size.

The University Inn disappeared in this time, or, more precisely, the university did not renew its lease. Faculty housing was now at a premium, and the trustees finally had to allow some faculty to live elsewhere than Orono. The president was given the power to choose "what members of the faculty should be allowed to live in Bangor." In Bangor the university divested itself of the old law school building, first to the YWCA on lease, and eventually to the Bangor Symphony Orchestra. The trustees also sold, for $450,000, some 34,841 acres of land received by will. Both of these transactions were caused by the need for money early in the decade.[55]

It seems ironic that just as the university had surmounted the great difficulties caused by the war, inflation, the SATC, and the abrasively antagonistic personalities of Clarence Cook Little and Percival Baxter the great depression should come and halt its growth. Actually the school was able to meet the depression and face it with relative ease and small financial damage because of the mill tax and the fact that the decade had been spent, albeit grudgingly, in returning the campus to the idyllic days of before the war. Little had been an excellent president, though he had stirred up a turmoil. His successor, Boardman, was something of a calmer personality chosen to smooth down that turmoil, and this he did brilliantly. The gentle pastoral scene over which he presided was soon to pass.

These three photographs illustrate the early stages in the construction of the athletic field house. President Little, and members of the board of trustees, observe the ceremonial ground breaking. Portions of the frame are raised via a steam powered hoist. At the bottom, workmen are preparing the external skin for the frame. The steam engine is still in place. This building was one of the finest of its type in the northeast when complete.

Notes

1. Faculty, March 14, 1921; *Campus*, March 15, April 23, 1921; *Laws of Maine*, 1921, Ch. 151; *Resolves*, Ch. 10; Ch. 173.

2. Aley to J.F. Gerrity, June 5, 1919 (preparing an alumni campaign); Hart Correspondence, Alumni, to Raymond Douglas, January 27, 1921; 1921-2, folder No. 1, to Norman Anning, February 15, 1921; Folder No. 5, to Prof. RGC Richardson, March 23, 1921; personal file, to L.C. Southard, Campaign a success in view of Governor.

3. *Laws of Maine*, 1921, communication, p. 912; veto, 898-902.

4. *Campus*, April 13, 1921.

5. Arts and Science Faculty Minutes, May 2, 1921; R.J. Aley folder, Hart to A.R. Crathorne (Univ. of Illinois), August 13, to Everett O. Fisk, October 3, 1921; Strickland's remarks are in *Campus*, September 21, 1921.

6. *Campus*, September 21, 1921.

7. *Campus*, November 23, 1921.

8. *What the Governor Promised the University of Maine*, n.p., n.d., transcription of Baxter's speech of November 16, 1921.

9. Faculty, December 15, 1921; January 9, 1922; Hart to Lucia Fellows, March 8, 1922.

10. *Campus*, February 15, 1922.

11. Faculty, February 13, 1921; *Campus*, March 8, April 12, 1922; C.C. Little, "Evidence for Sex-Linked Lethal Factors in Man," *Proceedings of Society for Experimental Biology and Medicine*, XVIII (1921). He had been a track athlete at Harvard and was well known to competitors of his time. The University already had a strong genetic research program so he was known there as well. Little was a prominent birth control advocate and eugenicist. See David M. Kennedy, *Birth Control in America*, 1970, pps. 118-9, 121, 198-9, 205.

12. Little to Strickland, March 7, 12, (quote) 1922; Strickland to Little, March 9.

13. Baxter to Strickland, June 30, 1922.

14. Little to Baxter, June 26, 1922 (dates on letters are wrong); Strickland to Little, September 26; Strickland to Louis Southard, (quote), September 8, 1922.

15. Little to Baxter, September 29, October 11, 13, Baxter to Little, October 12, 18, 1922.

16. Boston *Evening Transcript*, October 24, 1922, and Little files, Portland *Press Herald*, November 24, 1922 for the interview.

17. Lewiston *Evening Journal*, November 29, 1922; Portland *Press Herald*, November 30, 1922; James N. Hart to Pres. Frank L. McVey, November 16, 1922, we need help and I hope you will help Little. McVey was president of the University of Kentucky.

18. Baxter to Little, November 24; Little to Baxter, November 27, 1922.

19. Roselle W. Huddilston to Little, October 22, various letters from people requesting reprints, Bangor *Daily News*, September 23, speeches in Pres. file, 1922-23; *Maine Farmer*, December 28, 1922; letters, *Farmer* to Little, December 29, 1922; January 4, 1923 offering further editorial support for university, and Little to Dudley Alleman, January 2, 1923. Little really worked the newspapers. Also see Waterville *Sentinel* December 23, 1922; Arts and Sciences faculty minutes, October 2, November 6, 1922.

20. *Inaugural Address* of Percival P. Baxter, January 4, 1923, esp. 13, 36. Little to Roy H. Flynt, January 3, 1923; *Campus*, January 24, 1923. The deed was recorded January 28, 1870, after the transfer from the people of Orono to the Trustees, March 26, 1868. Vol. 394, p. 430, Penobscot Register of Deeds. For a newspaper opposed see Biddeford *Daily Journal*, February 2, 1923. They wanted the University to return to the 1865 activities.

21. Baker to Little, December 9, 1922; January 6, 23, 1922; Little to Baker, January 3, 8, 1923.

22. Little to W. Tudor Gardiner, March 3; Gardiner to "Pete", March 9, 1923.

23. Flynt to Little, March 16 (2); 28; February 14; Little to Flynt February 18, March 19, 30; Flynt to Charles Fogg, Houlton *Times*, February 10; Little to W.F. Schoppe, Bozeman, Montana, February 28; to P.F. Walker, Lawrence, Kansas, January 28; to W.J. Armstrong, Galveston, Texas, February 28; to Cyrus H.K. Curtis, February 16; Mrs. C.W. Richmond (Bangor Women's Club) to Little February 10, 25; return February 13, 28; Little to W.A. Hennessy (Bangor Chamber) February 16; *Kennebec Journal*, February 14, 16, Portland *Press Herald*, March 16, all 1923.

24. Little's statement is in 1923 folder; *Campus*, March 7, April 11, 1923. Pres. Board to Governor and Council, January 27, 1923.

25. Little to Strickland, March 15; *Kennebec Journal*, March 20, 1923.

26. Baxter's statement "The University of Maine" March 27, 1923, *Laws of Maine, 1923*, 1026-1038. This quotation is from 1028.

27. *Dr. Little's Reply to Governor Baxter's Message of March 27, 1923,* n.p., n.d.

28. Lewiston *Daily Sun,* March 28, 1923; Portland *Press Herald,* March 30, 1923. The Governor's speech to the students in 1921 was probably reprinted at about this time.

29. *Laws of Maine,* Resolves, 1923, Ch. 105.

30. Lawrence L. Winship to Little, April 1 (telegram), letter April 3; Boston *Globe,* April 8, 1923.

31. Little to Editor, Boston *Transcript,* April 2; Houlton *Times,* April ?, 1923, clipping in Little papers, Portland *Sunday Telegram,* June 10, 1923, a 12-page supplement on the University; Letter Little to Ralph McKee, April 29, 1923, in McKee's file.

32. James Eaton to Little, April 25, 1923 describing the encounter.

33. There is no biography of Baxter, although one is badly needed. My appreciation of him in another context appears in my *History of Maine Lumbering 1861-1961,* Orono, 1972. No biography of Little appears, either, except a novel, *Wings of Wax,* for which see below.

34. On research, *Campus,* November 26, 1924; January 14, 1925; February 18, 1925; *Popular Science Monthly,* January, 1925; Minneapolis *Journal,* November 23, 1924, and many others, Bangor *Daily Commercial,* May 9, and *Kennebec Journal,* May 10, 1924.

35. Little to Baxter, July 5, G.R. Chadbourne to Little, July 20; Little to Baxter July 23, Little to Baxter August 6; Baxter to Little August 18, all 1923; on Coolidge, Baxter to Little, August 23; Sepember 12; Waterville *Sentinel,* September 19, 1923; on Garry, Baxter to Strickland, August 30, Strickland to Baxter, September 24 (the photo had disappeared by 1928); Baxter, *My Irish Setter Dogs,* n.p., n.d., and other pamphlets; *Farewell Address,* January 7, 1925, esp. 29-30.

36. Pres. Corr. 1922-23, Little to Harvey D. Granville, February 12, 1923.

37. *Campus,* March 19, 1924; minutes of committee, July 2, 1924; statement presented to Committee by Little?, in "Proposed Ten Year Program" folder.

38. "Proposed Ten-Year Program" folder, with reports of conferences with Deans, draft statements of purpose and desires, etc., Trustees, January 9, 1925, for final acceptance.

39. Arts and Sciences Minutes, November 4, 1924; Brewster to Little November 4; Little to Brewster November 5; December 18; January 12, 1925; Brewster's inaugural, 630-1, of *Laws of Maine, 1925.*

40. *Maine Alumnus,* December, 1924; *Campus,* January 14, 21, February 25, 1925; Bangor *Daily News,* January 19, 1925; Little to John W. Leland, March 5, 1925, report of a conference with Brewster on March 4, and opposition to mill tax; *Proposed Ten-Year Program For the University of Maine,* Orono, 1925; *Laws of Maine, 1925, Resolves,* Ch. 94. (Letters in Ten-Year folder on appearances)

41. *Campus,* April 15, 1925; Little to Brewster, June 26, 1925.

42. Little to Strickland, July 2, 1925, in Trustees Minutes of that date.

43. *Campus,* September 23, 1925. In 1929 he returned and gave a chapel address discussing loyalty to one's university as a first requirement for students, May 9, 1929. The novel in question is by Janet Hoyt, and it was published by J.H. Sears and Co., New York, and it had at least two printings, although its literary value is somewhat limited. The subject matter accounted for the interest, both in Orono and in East Lansing.

44. *Campus,* January 21, 1926.

45. *Campus,* September 23, 1926; February 10, 24, 1927; *Laws of Maine,* 717, on University of Maine.

46. *Laws of Maine, 1927,* Resolves, Ch. 221; House Doc., 624, 1927; Trustees, May 12, 1927.

47. Inaugural Address of Gardiner; House Doc., 87, 1929; Sen. Doc. 18, 1929; *Laws of Maine, 1929,* Ch. 11; Trustees, April 25, 1929; *Maine Alumnus,* April, 1929.

48. Trustees, April 25, 1929; *Campus,* March 8, 1929; Little to Boardman, February 28, 1929.

49. James S. Stevens to Little, November 22, 1924; Little to Stevens, December 15, 1924; Faculty, November 8, December 13, 1926; January 10, October 10, November 21, December 12, 1927; January 9, March 12, 1928; October 14, 1929. In 1928 meetings were limited to appearances by dignitaries, and none were held in 1929 at all.

50. Little to Stevens, April 5, 1923; *Campus,* May 12, 1927; Faculty, February 17, 1930; Arts and Sciences Faculty, May 2, 1927; on phys. ed., agric. October 27, 1924; October 25, 1925; A & S, October 6, November 4, December 7, 1925; Tech, September 28, October 27, 1925; Hart to A.C. Baebenroth, March 21, 1917 (on Freshman week). Regularization of program changes also occurred about this time. Student Affairs and Dean's Committee Minutes, May 3, 1915; J.A. Gannett to J.N. Hart, March 4, 1917.

51. Faculty, May 14, 1923; Freshman Week *Programs,* 1924, 1925; *Campus,* September 30, 1927.

52. Trustees, November 2, 1923, June 5, November 7, 1925; April 15, June 12, 1926; George D. Chase to Little November 2, 1923; *Campus,*

November 26, 1924. Arts and Sciences, January 5, 1926, Superior students report. Little's efforts to end cribbing attracted much attention as well. *Christian Science Monitor,* March 20, 1925.

53. Arts and Sciences Faculty, November 2, December 7, 1925; Trustees, June 18, October 4, 1923; January 7, April 15, 1926; August 6, 1925; February 3, 1927; January 5, April 5, 1928, March 6, 1930; Tech Faculty, October 25, 1926; May 31, June 11, September 26, October 31, 1927; April 28, 1930; Folder, "Medical School Proposed 1925" many, many letters, especially Mark A. Barwise, to A.W. Harris, January 29, 1925; *Campus,* January 14, 1926.

54. Trustees, January 5, 1923; February 6, 1930; Bangor *Daily News,* ?1923; and others, along with her files, esp. memo June ? 1925? on her views, and the quotes. Colvin was an active suffragette. See the article on Maine, probably prepared in part by her in *History of Women's Suffrage,* Vol. VI, 1922.

55. Trustees, May 8, 18, July 27, 1923; Exec. Committee, September 13, November 2, 1923; February 7, 19, 28, November 2, 1924; April 5, 1925; April 24, 1928; Boardman to E.M. Lewis, no date, 1931, quote on Merrill Hall; folder "Oliver Crosby Bequest," See *Maine Alumnus,* February 1923; November 1929; *Eastern Gazette,* Dexter, January 18, 1923; Folder "Memorial Fund — Memorial Union," *Maine Alumnus,* December, 1922; *On The Firing Line For Maine,* Bangor, 1923; a field guide for solicitation; *The Gymnasium Armory,* Orono, 1923; *Maine Bulletin,* XXXVII, no. 3 (October, 1934), "Dedication of Stevens Hall," XXXVIII, no. 5, December, 1935, "Dedication of Merrill Hall". Some gifts were turned down as they seemed to have a catch; see folder, "E.S. Lincoln Correspondence re: offer of a Gift."

CHAPTER SEVEN

Depression and War

THE PASSAGE OF THE MILL TAX to support the university should have solved many of its problems. Unfortunately the worldwide depression intervened, although the mill tax through its more regular source of funds allowed the university to meet the earliest and most difficult years of this depression with minimal damage. Also, federal aid offered by the new administration in Washington was accepted, though somewhat reluctantly, by the new administration on campus. Too, faculty and others helped weather the crisis. During the depression years the university's academic and educational goals were reexamined and overhauled. Soon, however, the European war drew the attention of all, and by 1940 the school had begun to gear up for the war. When it came to the United States, the campus was prepared and served well, without the many problems of the First World War. By 1945 those on campus were weary and involved in the difficulties of postwar adjustments. The calm and pleasant days receded even faster into the past.

Harold S. Boardman served well as a transition president between the stormy regime of Clarence Cook Little and the crisis period of Arthur A. Hauck. Boardman seemed to sense his transitional role when he remarked in his inaugural address,

> I presume at a time like this a new college president is supposed to give a statement of his future policies. If this is what you are expecting you will be disappointed. I have nothing radical to propose nor do I intend to make rash promises of deeds to come, neither do I intend to state any platform except in so far as you may draw your own conclusions.[1]

Boardman did go on to state certain important problems that faced the school. The first was financial, which passage of the mill tax was designed to alleviate. The second concerned the purposes for spending the money. The quality of education was an issue to which Boardman seemed prepared to address attention during his term in office.

As has been suggested, Boardman worked, during the first part of his presidency, on achieving passage of the mill tax and on reestablishing smoother relationships with the state's political leaders. He even accomplished a genial correspondence with Percival Baxter.[2] In an attempt to solidify relations with the alumni, a homecoming day was instituted and a photographic brochure outlining the accomplishments of the university in recent years was published and distributed.[3] The first homecoming day, November 7, 1931, featured a Bowdoin-Maine game and Robert H. Fernald, '92, son of the founder and president, as speaker. Faculty members were in their offices to meet former students, and alumni were encouraged to participate in classroom exercises where they were held. The brochure, which stressed needs of the school, mainly for increased endowments, had mediocre success due to the drop in many incomes after the stock market crash.

While all this went on, a major effort was made to determine precisely what the college should be teaching and to whom, and to rework the various curricula. Outside consultants, associated with Columbia University, spent nearly two years on the project, presenting the first of their reports in 1931. Six areas were discussed in detail: Instructional Activities, Student Personnel Problems, Staff Personnel Problems, Institutional Research, Publicity and Public Relations, and the Library. Substantial mathematical, statistical, and informational research studies were undertaken, and a detailed

(202 pages) report was submitted to Boardman and to the board of trustees in April of 1931. Specific college reports and analyses were to follow.[4]

The Columbia experts felt that the current allocation of funds was approximately proper, although somewhat more money should be provided for instruction. The consultants made many recommendations, among them: attract more students, build more buildings to house them, coordinate student personnel work, coordinate and expand the health program, make available more loans and scholarships, put more emphasis on vocational guidance and placement and study the various curricula with a view to broadening institutional offerings. With regard to the professional staff and faculty, the consultants recommended modest salary increases, a retirement provision, group insurance, regular sabbatical leaves, and the extension of limited health services to faculty and their families. In the area of research the group proposed a move to contractual research, better

publicizing of findings, and better use of money. These plans would necessitate hiring a full-time institutional director of research, with a staff and a budget, to supervise the research mission of the university. The final area involved hiring a full-time publicity and public relations person and staff and was closely tied in with the research idea. The investigators were extremely critical of the library, calling for establishment of a library commensurate with the school's aims, one that would act as a radiating force for the intellectual life of the community. All specifics connected with the library were discussed, for instance, longer hours, a new building, better and larger staff, and a 50 percent increase in purchasing power (at a minimum). Overall, the report was somewhat more critical than it was in its separate parts, with the exception of the section on the library.

In the final summary the consultants said they had "gained the distinct impression that the University of Maine is more an aggregation

A campus panorama from the north about 1926. Center Stevens, without its wings, is in central left. Lord Hall and Aubert are in center right. The cement bleachers at the first athletic field are in right front. Barns and out buildings are in the left rear while Winslow Hall looms over Alumni Hall. Wingate's tower rises on extreme right.

of colleges and schools, perhaps even of departments, than a unified, integrated University . . . . Its major consciousness seems to be group consciousness rather than institutional . . . . The study to date has not clearly revealed such unity of spirit, purpose or activity as a general, pervasive force in the entire staff."[5] They returned later to what they saw as the overriding problems of the university when they again mentioned the problems of coordination and integration of activity, both of which they deemed necessary for the final goal of greater educational effectiveness. In further reports the experts, and some additional personnel, also studied the curricula in the various colleges.

Altogether, this work, which was carried on from 1930 to 1934, was a detailed and serious effort to take one institution, subject it to intellectual thought and analysis, and finally to provide recommendations that would enable it to maximize its services. In a sense the University of Maine familiar to readers of this book was recreated from the summary recommendations. The report is important and is summarized here in this detail because it so clearly marks the development of the modern institution. Some of the problems identified almost a half century ago still are not resolved, but others, for instance, research and publicity activities, stem directly from the report in their foundation and organization.

Most colleges began immediate efforts to meet the recommendations of the report, with the technology and the arts and science colleges completely remodeling their curricula. The technology college adopted essentially two curricula, one in general engineering and one in special training. Guidance, development of aesthetics, and the development of five-year courses were signally important. Paul Cloke, new dean of the college, was very interested in educational training for engineers and the curricula clearly demonstrated his interests.[6] The arts college modified its curriculum quite drastically, with a change in emphasis from department to subject. Establishment of discrete majors, with major advisors and comprehensive examinations followed by 1934.[7]

While all this was going on, the funds from the mill tax allowed the construction of a number of necessary buildings, the wings on Stevens Hall, a modern heating plant, a re-

Crosby laboratory soon after its completion in 1926. It was the gift of an alumnus, Oliver Crosby, '76.

construction of the interior of Alumni Hall, the development of fire protection (in the wake of the fire at Mount Vernon in 1933), and completion of the field house. A new campus plan for roads, trees, parking, grading, lawns, and new buildings was authorized, and approved after development by Olmsted Brothers (descendants of the designer of the first university plan in 1866).[8] A new system of dormitory food production, with the establishment of an organization involving cooks, matrons, janitors and so on, was also begun during this period. It was little wonder that in 1933, although apprehensive about the legislature then in session, Boardman could remark to one correspondent,

> It may sound egotistical for me to say so but I feel that the institution has made decided improvements during the past few years. It has been my aim to develop a strong and better faculty and in spite of adverse conditions I have done so. Our enrollment has kept up . . . our building program . . .has been much as we could expect. If the legislature doesn't soak us too badly we will still be able to function.[9]

The campus did not experience the impact of depression as soon as most other places. In 1931 the technology faculty was told that promotion and salary increases were unlikely after that year. Paul Cloke undertook a campaign, associated with the Hoover "Give a Job" pro-

The new Memorial Gymnasium interior. This scene is from the formal dedication June 19, 1933. The photograph was taken just before the academic convocation and unveiling of the dedication plaques. Although construction showed a rather spartan aestheticism, the building has served the community well.

The gymnasium and field house, June 7, 1941, just prior to graduation exercises. White flannel trousers for men and light dresses for women signal a Maine summer day.

gram, to aid in ending the business depression. After some research in the state, Cloke told the juniors in chapel that most depression cures were "platitudinous bunk." The agriculture faculty was told of the difficulty that graduates would have in obtaining employment and of the "vital importance" of faculty aiding with the problem.[10] Other than these instances little notice was taken on campus of the depression. The president remarked that some economies had been made and no raises were contemplated, but that the university construction plans would help in the local unemployment situation during the summer. There was some adverse newspaper comment as the slump grew outside the campus, but the school's press bureau reacted to that with a discussion of building needs and said, "Splendid business management and a very conservative expansion policy has saved the University of Maine from feeling the full effects of the depression."[11]

Unfortunately the amount of the mill tax began to decrease as the depression made its impact, and, worse, the 1933 legislature began to search for methods of meeting the state's diminished tax revenues; some of the methods might affect the school. The new governor, Louis Brann, was an alumnus, class of 1892, but he was a Democrat, which posed a problem

The scene is the dedication of Stevens Hall in its final form, June 9, 1934. These guests travelled to the campus by auto, as the world was becoming increasingly motorized.

to a board of trustees and president of the other party. Soon after the election letters went back and forth as to his intentions. He did return to the campus for homecoming and called professors by their nicknames, which was thought to be a favorable sign. Boardman and Brann apparently negotiated a gentleman's agreement that the university would come forward with a volunteer contribution if the mill tax idea could be retained: the university returned $50,000 from its mill tax funds immediately, cut its budget by about one-seventh, and began to discuss mandatory pay cuts sponsored by the legislature.[12]

There was an attempt in the special session called in December 1932 to cut the university's funding by $400,000. Brann announced that he would veto this bill, which failed of passage as a result, though the gentleman's agreement superseded it anyway. Faculty volunteered a cut of 5 percent of their salaries (after it was indicated that they really had little choice); the price of board to students was reduced one dollar a week, with a consequent lessening in food quality; a considerable reduction was made in administrative expenditures; building maintenance was cut back. Other items such as the farm and home week were curtailed somewhat as well, although many protested this

This summer scene shows Stevens Hall – the center and south portions. In the left distance the gymnasium may be seen as well. The photo dates from the end of the 30's. The trees were lost when construction of the new library began.

This winter aerial shot is from the middle 1930's. The cement bleachers still persist, but Stevens Hall (upper right) has its wings. Hannibal Hamlin and Oak Halls are the residence dorms in mid-photo. The fraternities are Theta Chi and Beta Theta Pi. Other buildings include the carpenter shop and Crosby Laboratory (upper left) and Aubert Hall (center right).

sort of economy.[13] The trustees reduced salaries, other than faculty, by an eighth, and in all the 1933-34 budget was reduced by $75,000. The university took a slash in the mill tax, by $100,000 for both 1934 and 1935. Although Boardman thought the financial problems fairly difficult, the school was able to make the necessary adjustments. The board was more worried about a possible federal cut in its Morrill funds, so one or two specialists were released and the activities of Four-H Club agents curtailed. But, as Boardman said when queried, the university was still in fairly good shape.

> For your confidential information, and I hesitate even to put it on paper, will say that at the last two meetings of our Board of Trustees it was decided that in building a budget for next year we should carry over both a surplus and an emergency fund. If the Morrill fund is cut it may thus be taken care of.[14]

In fact Boardman and the school had weathered the storm reasonably well. However, the stress

of dealing with the depression had taken its toll and the president wished to resign. He said that great changes were coming to the university because of the close scrutiny due to the depression and it was time for a new person.

> Conditions of the past few years have had their effect upon my vitality and I feel that a change in the presidency will not only be beneficial to the institution but to myself as well.[15]

With this Harold Boardman took his leave, providing as a legacy a university in good financial, physical, and moral shape, but with major international problems to face, and soon.

The new president, Arthur Hauck, was a Minnesotan, educated at Reed College and Columbia, whose field of specialty was international relations. He had taught at Punahoa School in Hawaii, at Vassar, and at Lafayette, and had been active in such organizations as the Institute of Pacific Relations. He promised no new philosophies, although it was obvious that he had high hopes of modifying student attitudes to provide the state with even higher standards of work. He began with this theme at the opening assembly on September 19, 1934, when he discussed his ideas of volunteerism rather than compulsion, telling the students, "When society has assisted in providing educational facilities it is entitled to some volunteer service in return. . . .[16] He urged students and others to take a constructive part in the civic life of community and nation. At his November inaugural he promised to maintain high standards, saying that he was pleased that Maine had not confused bigness with greatness. He also said that the arts college had a special role to provide both a foundation for living in the changing world in which people found themselves and a service for the other units of the school; he urged the university to constantly reappraise its work and to attempt to attract and retain scholars of character and distinction to help it reappraise; he felt that the school must teach all who might profit and must deal with persons as individuals. Returning to his theme of civic duty, he closed with this remark:

> Service to the State, cooperation with all its educational agencies, the maintainence of high standards in everything we undertake, emphasis on those elements in our University life that make for good citizenship and abundant living; these are the goals we see before us. Toward their attainment I pledge my best efforts.[17]

Others at the inaugural offered much the same, with the State Commissioner of Education focussing on student teaching possibilities and the board of trustees urging a more conservative attitude, while pledging no political involvement by faculty, students, or trustees. This last promise of aloofness was not necessarily to be in the university's best interest in time to come.

Hauck's everyday style stressed continuous contact with the students. The tone of the campus changed considerably in his time to a more informal, more pleasant relationship between students and faculty. He was the first president who was not distant from the student body. As one undergraduate noted in a diary,

> . . . Heard about long dresses to Presidents Ironed mine . . . dinner at President's. Very good time — steak. Pete the dog cute. Hauck's informal and nice. Like singing.[18]

The top photograph is President Arthur A. Hauck, as a formal young administrator. The bottom photo is "Prexy", early in his career at Maine, but in one of those informal poses most alumni remember best. These aspects of his personality marked his tenure from the first days.

These photos indicate the path of change. Top is Oak Hall, the earliest dormitory. The building was destroyed by fire in January, 1936 as the bottom scene shows. The building to replace it, with the same name, is pictured opposite. No lives were lost in the fire which moved with speed through the building.

With the depression on and the mill tax diminished, Hauck found himself in essentially the same place as earlier presidents — without enough money to accomplish both his and the university's goals. A three-man trustee committee was formed to consult with the governor with regard to university affairs, but the full mill tax funds simply were not available. Some remodeling, such as furnishing sprinkler systems for several buildings, was undertaken in 1934, and faculty salaries were restored to their original level in February 1935, but basically an austerity budget was in effect. Tuition was raised by a small amount, and out-of-state tuition more, in 1935, and the trustees finally established a guide as to who was an out-of-state student. (The depression had created some movement back to the state, complicating matters.) The 1935, 1936, and 1937 budgets all exceeded income, but, as the trustees said, obligations were so great, especially in the areas of maintenance of buildings, that they could not produce "a balanced budget without seriously impairing necessary and important functions." As long as no emergency arose all would be well.[19]

In January such an emergency did occur when Oak Hall, a men's dormitory, burned at a loss of $400,000. The trustees asked for $110,000 to add to the insurance to rebuild the dormitory. After much discussion, and unfunded authorization of the construction, the governor and council provided $75,000.[20]

The difficulty in obtaining the funds to replace the necessary building apparently made the trustees feel that they needed to go on the offensive for restoration of the mill tax. The board produced a broadside in the fall of 1936 calling for a better effort at providing the funds, saying,[21] "The financial condition of the University of Maine has reached a point where due regard of our obligations and responsibilities requires the Board of Trustees to report to the people of the State concerning the critical situation and the reasons therefore." With the mill tax limitation the construction reserves that had enabled the university to survive the early thirties had disappeared, and the working capital of the school had nearly disappeared as well. Without help the institution would be in a deficit situation by June 1937. The trustees wanted restoration of the full mill tax, and the governor, in his speech to the legislature, echoed their plea. The trustees were blunt, finishing their document with this statement:

> [The Board of Trustees] believes that the time has come when the people of Maine through their representatives . . . should express definitely their intentions with respect to the University . . . . We perceive no advantage to anyone in further postponement or delay.[22]

This plea apparently helped; although the entire cut was not restored, the deductions were limited to a token $5,000 per year, as opposed to $174,000 for 1933, 1934, and 1935 and $110,588 for the years 1936 and 1937. Governor Barrows did not mention the restoration in 1939, but as he told Hauck, "I simply included it in my budget," and, "I sincerely hope that it will be unnecessary for you to make any further concessions."[23] In 1939 the university actually received 11 percent less funds than in 1929, while it served 25 percent more students. The state's share had fallen from 50.5 percent to 38.1 percent of university income.[24]

Altogether the school received nearly $700,000 less during the depression years of the 1930's than it had been entitled to under law. Of course the availability of federal funds made some of this difference quite academic, and in fact the school was able to spend $159,416.71 for remodeling buildings and another $12,442.14 for equipment for these buildings from 1934 to 1938. Major work was done on Wingate, Lord, and the library, as well as lesser amounts on Coburn, Fernald, the infirmary, and some of the buildings of the college farm. In addition, $256,568.31 was spent on new buildings: mechanical shops, $43,589; agriculture shops, $37,420; cabins, $10,303; and dormitories, especially Oak Hall, $133,904, as well as $17,795.77 on equipment for these buildings. Also funds were spent for fences; land; roads, $18,096; tennis courts, $8,347; sidewalks, and steam pipe extensions $24,676. Altogether during this period of stress the university spent $475,860.52 for buildings and $30,237.91 for equipment. What had occurred was a shifting of

monetary sources, and it is surprising how much resistance there was to the change.[25]

By 1939 and 1940 the university income was nearly $2,000,000, with expenditures close to $1,700,000. The table indicates both income and expenditure on the eve of World War II. [26]

INCOME
(Some figures rounded)

	1939	1940
Students	$ 329,964	$ 332,352
Endowment	13,735	13,800
Federal	354,126	352,870
State	656,209	672,089
Depts.	44,734	46,731
Sales	37,800	39,000
Rents	9,450	9,450
Summer School	23,860	21,850
Dorms	205,250	195,000
Press	32,000	32,000
Athletic Association	19,448	16,965
Scholarships	9,303	8,829
Retire	26,264	22,900
Misc.	1,598	1,560
Totals	$1,763,744.86	$1,765,418.14

EXPENDITURE

	1939	1940
Admins.	$ 139,205	$ 141,148
Salaries: Agr.	219,770	216,924
A & S	189,326	198,439
Tech.	151,757	150,382
Educ.	19,732	18,486
Grad.	1,825	1,930
PE (F)	7,714	8,319
PE (M)	13,046	14,968
Misc.	928	971
Research	216,376	222,450
Extension	207,644	203,822
Library	25,921	28,200
Summer School	20,311	21,850
Maint.	145,400	139,035
Dorms	275,935	261,815
Other (non-educ.)	25,355	25,519
Totals	$1,651,241.35	$1,564,243.14

The university took advantage of the surplus of labor to do a good deal of needed maintenance work in the early years of the depression. Most of the funds came from regular sources. By October 1933, some $63,181 had been expended in this way, mostly on the carpenter shop, observatory, and on Crosby, Rogers, Fernald, and Alumni halls. In 1934

further remodeling, totaling some $115,500 (Wingate, Fernald furnishings, Lord, and the sprinkler systems), was authorized in this period of abundant labor and low wages.[27]

It soon became obvious that fairly large amounts of federal funds were also available. Many on the board of trustees did not want to apply for these funds, and some trustees and President Boardman were frustrated by this hesitation. Boardman sought information elsewhere in an effort to win over E.E. Chase, chairman of the board, to use of this money. Chase was a reluctant convert, however, as the quotation shows:

> As you know, I am skeptical regarding the desirability of the University getting mixed up with these Federal government activities, and while it seems to me impossible not to 'co-operate', I feel that every proposition must be analyzed on the possibility that these undertakings, once started, may be dumped in our lap to finance.[28]

This attitude did not help in allowing the university to apply for federal funds, and at least once later on some funds that the Public Works Administration attempted to press upon the school went elsewhere because they simply were not applied for. How many other funds may have been available, but were not sought by the administration, is unknown and rather frustrating even today. Although the president was certainly at fault to some extent, more of the blame should be put on E.E Chase. Ludicrously, this same board was only too willing to take funds under the Morrill Act and other similar legislation. But, perhaps something of the national politics and political parties involved may have colored the response to the new funds.[29]

Even with all this footdragging, a fair number of federal dollars did find their way to the campus. It will be impossible to deal with all, but several areas deserve some brief discussion. The first is the work relief grouping begun by Federal Emergency Relief Administration (FERA), continued by Works Progress Administration (WPA), and carried on still further by Civil Works Administration (CWA). These agencies were all designed to provide work for the unemployed and undertook a vast array of projects throughout the decade. In 1933-34, close to 200 students worked for FERA on the campus, planting trees, working in the greenhouse, and assisting various members of the history department. This agency became the WPA in 1935 and went on with more force under the federal administrator, Harry Hopkins. Paths were made in the botanical plantation, beautification projects were done along the river, and a new athletic field and cross-country track were completed. The tennis courts and many of the campus sidewalks were built by this agency in 1936-37. Associated with this work were projects under the Resettlement Administration which worked with parks along the Stillwater River. The CWA also did a great deal of similar work, though of a more limited nature, for example, repair of buildings; classification and filing; checking and repair of laboratory apparatus; preparation of card catalogs; construction of relief maps; overhauling, cleaning, painting and oiling of equipment; performing soil tests; and preservation of library books.[30]

The National Youth Administration (NYA) was directly concerned with students and provided a substantial amount of funds, either in fellowships, scholarships, or loans. Some $62,439 was expended, of which $56,186.83 went to undergraduates. These funds were earned through research projects and other academic methods. In addition, in 1937 NYA funds were used to help build the University Cabins, residences to aid impecunious students to continue their attendance. The administration was so happy with this program that it joined in an attack on Bernarr McFadden who charged that the program was communistic. Hauck attempted to keep the NYA in business when the war came, even though the Congress wished to close it down, and it did remain in effect until June of 1943. Hauck wrote President Franklin D. Roosevelt in 1942 an enthusiastic endorsement of the NYA.

> The value of the National Youth Administration college aid to students at the University of Maine during recent years has been so considerable that we are deeply concerned over the question of its continuance in the future.[31]

Certainly the agency did its job well, and this federal money, at least, was more than welcome.

The other area in which the federal government made a major impact on the University of Maine was in the construction of the women's

A wing was built on Aubert Hall from available federal funds. Pulp and paper technology and chemical engineering were housed in the new area.

dormitory, Estabrooke Hall, and a wing on Aubert Hall. The trustees still were skeptical, but finally asked for and received permission from the governor and council to borrow the necessary funds for the university's share of the financing. Forty-five percent of the funds came from the federal government. Although the amount of paperwork required was fairly large, the money came quickly and the buildings were soon built and available. Unfortunately the school did not then follow up and receive the additional funds available under the act. Federal funds were all right, but some were bothered because they had to be used for specific projects and were not at the pleasure of the board of trustees and the faculty.[32] Later, the university would not be as chary of such funds when they became available.

These early years of Arthur Hauck's administration were not taken up entirely with meeting the depression and administering the new federal funds. Some updating or modernization was done in the various curricula. As was indicated in his inaugural speech, much effort would be put into the education of teachers. Normal school instructors were offered a year's free tuition, and graduates of the two- or three-year courses were given an opportunity to get their degrees with a one-year

Professor Horace M. Estabrooke, '76, was a force on the campus until his death in 1908. His wife, Kate "Ma" Estabrooke served for many years as house mother in Mount Vernon and is pictured in 1916 in her sitting room. She was awarded an honorary degree in 1926. An early dining hall was named for Horace in 1911, but the building did not survive long. When federal funds made possible a new women's dormitory in 1940, the logical name was Estabrooke Hall, this time honoring Kate and her service. It is pictured at the tope of the page.

tuition scholarship made available to graduates of the normal schools. Many took advantage of the program in the years before World War II. In addition, the education curriculum was overhauled to aid in state certification of teachers. In another area, there were efforts to increase the work in economics in the hope of eventually establishing a college of business administration.[33]

Other programs included the start of a wildlife conservation course in 1936 and the establishment of joint programs with Westbrook Junior College and Portland School of Fine Arts leading to a fourth year and a bachelor's degree from Orono. A plan for cooperation with hospitals and a degree in nurse's education was authorized in 1937. Summer institutes in local government, with resulting consultancies, also began, and the city manager program, later so prominent, could be said to date from these ventures.[34]

The colleges themselves began to revamp their curricula throughout this period, following in many cases the recommendations of the Columbia report of 1932. Engineering physics was established as a choice in technology, advising was reorganized in the arts college, and the agriculture faculty kept up its constant analysis of teaching through student surveys, introduction of new methods, a committee on effective teaching procedures, and a detailed discussion of examinations. New course outlines were developed for most courses in the agriculture college by 1940.[35]

Other items of interest in this era included establishment of a placement service in 1935; development of practice teaching facilities, at first in Orono and later in a wide variety of places; the instituting of the first scholarships (free tuition) for Native Americans who lived in Maine;[36] the discussion held by the trustees in late September 1941, of an agenda dealing with Superior Students and the university's role toward them. There were peculiar episodes as well, as when in 1940 there was a brief and abortive attempt to cut back the teaching of philosophy, by firing one of its most distinguished members. The American Association of University Professors, although quite weak, investigated this attempt and the case was dropped. The trustees meeting of September 1941 was concerned with other matters besides Superior Students: promotion of more im-

aginative thinking by the staff, the urging of more Maine employers to give summer jobs, and the role of final examinations.[37] These discussions were remarkably academic with the war so much talked of and in fact only ten weeks away.

As the university prepared for that war in its general way, it did stop in the spring of 1940 to hold exercises in honor of the seventy-fifth anniversary of its founding. The affair included a founders day dinner, special editions of various newspapers, and a two-day academic convocation with the proceedings broadcast over the state's radio stations. After talks by the trustees and the governor, greetings were given by representatives of the private colleges in the state. The rancor of early years was noticeably absent. Local speakers presented the various colleges and programs of the university and dwelt on the history and accomplishments of their areas. On the second day the alumni had their turn, and a student skit representing the past was given. Others important on the second day included Payson Smith, the Commissioner of Education, who called for the university to live up to its goals of freedom.

> The University of Maine, in common with all schools, faces a changing world. What parts, in such a world, shall the Universities play? Above all, one part, certainly. They must be persistent and constant in their high resolve to be always on the frontiers of truth. Now while the lights of learning are paling before the assaults of totalitarianism . . . recall . . . Washington's . . . *Farewell Address,*
>
> 'Promote, then, as the object of primary importance, institutions for the general diffusion of knowledge.'

As the proceedings closed with the *Stein Song,* many in the room must have looked into the future with some trepidation. Whether the university they had known would survive, and in what form, was a question for which few answers were forthcoming.[38]

The war building in Europe since the signature of the Versailles Treaty did not, at first, make much impact in Orono. In 1934 some effort was made to find places for displaced German scholars, and there was a discussion over compulsory ROTC in the middle of the decade. The *Campus* was active during the thirties in various campaigns, of which more later, but the student body remained calm.

Another view of Stevens Hall at the time of the dedication, June 9, 1934. Apparently the planners did not anticipate attendance very well as in both photos there are large numbers of standees, as well as others lounging on the lawn.

More and more commencement speakers mentioned the approaching conflict; occasionally the messages were stark, and, as the decade wore on, more piercing. In 1939 James Phinney Baxter delivered an address on "The 'Maginot Line' of American Democracy." The convocations to open the college in September 1941, were very blunt, with Bishop Oxnam speaking on "A Date With the World." By that time most people were making preparations for that date.[39] Some alumni opposed entering the war, but Hauck answered with his views in a letter to one in late 1941, saying, "A Hitler victory or a Hitler-dominated negotiated peace would be a calamity."[40]

As time went on the war began to obtrude on the campus in other ways. Assistant Professor Louis A. Vigneron was granted indefinite leave in the fall of 1939 to join his French army regiment. "National defense" began to be heard throughout 1940 and the trustees authorized the executive committee and the president to make necessary decisions to contribute to it. Leaves

of absence were authorized for some of the faculty; retirement annuities were to be paid while they were gone. In May of 1941 the ROTC officers were called up, the professor of home economics was called to Washington for a national nutrition conference, and E.F. Dow, chairman of the history and government department, set up and chaired a conference on the campus to deal with federal-state cooperation and the defense emergency. Discussion centered on what the local communities needed to provide and what services they could provide. Labor, federal funds, public health, public housing, planning, mobilization (mostly through the existing New Deal agencies), costs, highways, and the Bangor Air Base were all topics in the two-day conference.[41] On the campus some thirty-one defense training courses, ranging from elementary drafting to combustion calculations, were offered in the summer, and the fall opened with special defense courses for women in first aid, nutrition, and tinfoil collection.[42]

When the war came in December 1941, it took about a month for the campus to settle to its activities. But when the first semester ended in January 1942, Hauck reported to the trustees that a University Defense Council had been created with subcommittees on air raid precautions, safety, nutrition, first aid, student relations, extramural teaching of defense courses, and a committee to study economies and the administration of the university in the years ahead. Acceleration of courses was discussed and authorized, as was a twelve-week term (four a year). The summer session of 1942 was the first such twelve-week session. ROTC was offered during the summer with a program designed to give entering freshmen a complete first semester's activity. It was planned that entrance in the summer of 1942 would allow graduation in the fall of 1944.

President Hauck opened a student assembly on January 12, 1942, with, "No words of mine are needed to remind you that this is a war for national survival." He urged the students to avoid rumors; official information would be sent out when known and a selective service committee would have information also. After discussing the reasons for acceleration, Hauck said that activities would be as normal as possible, but with an intensification of physical education. Students were asked to volunteer for first aid, nursing and air raid warden duty and counseled to practice "simplicity and moderation" in expenditures. At about the same time he wrote an alumnus, Alton L. "Ding-Dong" Bell, '37, "We are in for a good hard job but it has to be done. We couldn't continue to live in a world of threats and brutality."[43]

When the university opened in September 1942, each faculty held special meetings at which Hauck spoke and plans were laid for dealing with the emergency. In arts and sciences, the math progression was changed, more navigation was offered, and some courses were eliminated and others combined. Classics professors were sent to other areas to teach. The engineering faculty began to prepare for the arrival of the Army in their courses. Physical education was stressed, and a special course in American culture was discussed. In agriculture some courses were merged. In general, a greater stress was placed on immediate ends in agriculture with tightly technical materials elminated from course con-

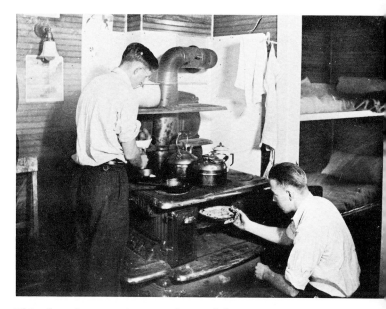

This shot shows an interior of one of the University Cabins. The students, Kendrick Hodgdon, '39 and his brother, Kenneth '41, are shown preparing a meal. The cabins, built with NYA funds, allowed students to cut costs to a minimum.

The Cabins colony had a cooperative store for the residents. Such prices as are seen reflect the nature of the store and the time, as do the products. Students are Norman Hunt, '42, Sterling Cobb, '41, Earl Leavitt, '38, and Ralph Littlefield, who as an Orono resident originated the idea of the cabins.

tent. In education some emphasis was placed on the preservation of values now under the pressure of the war effort. The scarcity of teachers, along with the necessity to provide retooling for those returning to the classroom, had to be dealt with. The entire theme was stated by Hauck at the general faculty meeting that followed these special gatherings: "Long range values, important when college opened a year ago, must now be subordinated to the immediate needs of the Battlefront."[44]

The university would eventually, in 1943, be turned over in great part to the regular military training programs of World War II. However, the experiences of World War I and the difficulty of knowing precisely what sort of training was necessary led to a delay, nationwide, and for a year the training programs begun were without much guidance from the military or the War Manpower Commission, which had eventual authority over such courses. At Orono a beginning had been made in 1939 to 1941 with the training of 129 people in three summer courses in aircraft mechanics.[45] Starting in 1942 the National Defense Program Technology offered courses in drafting in Bangor and Orono. Paul Cloke was primarily responsible for this work, which later blossomed into the Engineering Science and Management Defense Training (ESMDT) program which offered fifty-six courses at nine locations in 1942, and forty-seven courses at ten locations in 1943. Altogether, twelve subjects were taught including two specific programs in ordnance inspection and pre-radar. A total of 429 students graduated by March 1943.[46]

Typical of the courses were mathematics for engineers, construction methods (of roads), aerial bombardment protection, soil mechanics, electric power generation, fundamentals of radio, drafting, internal combustion engines, physics, foreman training, and personnel management. Classes were twelve to sixteen weeks long, held two to three times a week in the evening for two hours, tuition-free. Faculty went where courses were needed and requested by the towns involved. No college credit was given, and only a high school graduation required for admission.[47] Open to both men and women, the courses were designed to provide necessary preliminary training for those about to take war jobs. Special wartime curricula de-

signed for women was provided, especially in the summer session of 1943.[48] Special programs in radio technology, with civilians constituting the enrollment until January 1943, became a pre-radar training course later in 1943. During that year thirteen separate groups attended continuous twelve-week courses in ordnance inspection, a program that received plaudits from the military figures involved.[49]

Although at one time or another there were five reserve groups on the campus (Air Force, Army, V-1, V-7, and U.S. Marine Corps), most students were in the Army Specialized Training Program (ASTP). The university was chosen for the program since it was already involved in Army ROTC; thus, transition to the ASTP was relatively painless. The program, put together by the Army and the American Council on Education, was the equivalent of the better-known Navy V-7 programs. Students attended college year-round for from three to seven semesters, depending on the training necessary. Regular courses were offered, as well as plenty of drill and physical training, along with classes in military courtesy and similar topics. Theoretically possible to obtain a degree from the program, it was difficult to do so because of the lower grade of the courses and the shorter time involved. The Army's need for combat personnel made the ASTP less important as the war went on.[50]

The university was ready for this program with the twelve-week summer session authorized and under way. In 1943, for instance, some 353 students (240 men and 113 women) attended the summer session. Another 345 Signal Corps personnel were on campus as part of the ASTP program which had begun in the spring semester. Initially plans were made for about 1,000 men to be involved in the ASTP program, but the final figures were nearer 750. At first 75 percent of them were in what was essentially a basic training course, but by January 1944, these were withdrawn (because of combat needs in great part) and only the advanced group remained. A Navy V-12 program did take up some of the slack in numbers.

The civilian-soldiers and sailors were basically students in the prewar sense of the word, helping edit the school newspaper, participating in Masque productions, and generally living a college life. Altogether some 1,100 were on the

These two photos capture some flavor of summer session. To the left the serving line at the annual picnic. Boiled lobster is being served to President Hauck and his wife. Watermelon chunks are also on the menu. In the bottom photo a group is conducted in a song session, on the library steps, accompanied by a few musicians. This last photo is from 1944, while the other date is not known.

The top photograph shows University of Maine women entertaining invalid soldiers during World War II. This was an official U.S. Air Force photograph but it does not name the figures unfortunately. In the bottom photo, not official, ASTP men march to class. The men were well drilled, and here all are in cadence.

campus for some time in this program. In the spring of 1944, after the Battle of the Bulge, the program was curtailed even more, and the men transferred to the 26th Infantry (the Yankee Division). The almost inevitable comparisons with the SATC of World War I were nearly all favorable, as the war came slowly to an end.[51]

Campus life itself changed to a small extent at first, and later fairly radically. Blackouts, income taxes, sale of war bonds, collection of scrap and other materials, meatless days, and gasoline rationing were all subjects of much discussion among those on campus. Victory gardens were important as faculty in particular were involved in extension of the nation's food reserves. Hauck, in commenting to homesick former students, remarked on the changes,

> While life here is in many ways 'collegiate', we are, of course, greatly affected by the war. Enrollment dropped by early 1943 from 2,200 to 1,300 and every day more boys are leaving for service . . .[52]

To another correspondent, he was more blunt.

> We miss you and the other fellows who had to leave so hurriedly. Each week sees more boys leave. The comfort in all this is as we build up our forces we get ready to strike the blows at Japan and Germany which will bring the victory.[53]

Fraternities were taken over by the military, and the various houses pooled their activities in the fall of 1943, splitting expenses evenly. Most fraternities survived the war in fair condition thanks to rent paid them by the ASTP and the university for housing freshmen.

Two rather severe fires occurred during the war period, the first in Wingate Hall in 1943. Partially as a result of this fire a university fire department was organized, but the preparations were not sufficient to halt the fire in Hannibal Hamlin Hall in February 1944, in which two soldiers burned to death and others were severely injured. Inquests into the fires determined nothing of suspicious action, simply the circumstances of late nights, cold weather, and probably (although this was not in the report) the extreme tiredness of men engaged in a difficult and emotion-draining effort.[54]

More Maine alumni than ever before were involved in this war, and writing to them took a

Honorary degree recipients at the June, 1945 commencement with President Hauck. They included, from left to right, Rev. H.H. Flagg, Col. R.G. Isker, Edward E. Chase, chairman of the board, Governor Horace A. Hildreth, President Hauck, and James T. Shotwell, the famous educator. The mixture of clergy, military, government, and the famous international scholar along with the educational establishment symbolized the era that ended well.

great deal of time for various faculty and especially President Hauck, who did yeoman work in responding to letters he received from homesick alumni. In addition several letters were sent from the General Alumni Association to all known persons in the service. They told something of the campus and provided a touch of home for those a long way away.[55]

The death toll rose steadily, 9 by December 1942, 18 by a memorial service in May of 1943. The Armistice Day Assembly of 1943 commemorated even more, and by the end of 1944, 69 deaths had been totaled from the 3,225 alumni in service. Nineteen more were missing, and 15 in prisoner of war camps. The final total was 177 dead. (47 had died in World War I and 6 in the Spanish-American War.)[56]

Even with all this grim news the campus rapidly returned to normal in the spring of 1945. Although basketball, winter sports, the Masque and the *Campus* were all operating, Arthur Hauck told one alumnus how astonished he had been to discover that "when a group of seniors came to see me about some activities recently, I realized that no students now on campus have been here during a normal year."[57] When V-E day came in May, Hauck read President Truman's message and speakers from the classes of 1941 and 1946 appeared. Hauck spoke on what was ahead for his listeners. It was a "quiet celebration" with emphasis on those who had sacrificed for all. On V-J day the celebration was more joyous, but "not too riotous. We had a big bonfire and did some shouting and singing. Of course the bell was kept going for hours."[58] Fall registration came back nearly to normal, with 460 freshmen, 263 sophomores, 181 juniors and 139 seniors. Eighty-four others were registered in special or graduate programs.[59]

The campus had come through the war relatively unscathed. Now it was time to prepare for the returning of Ulysses, and Penelope too, as a grateful nation provided a college education for all those who wished it and had served during the great conflict.

Notes

1. *Inaugural Address* of Boardman, June 12, 1926, n.p., n.d., (Orono, 1926?).

2. Baxter to Boardman, March 26, 1931 on board *Albert Baltus*.

3. *Alumni Homecoming Day Program,* November 7, 1931; *The University of Maine, 1930,* Orono, 1930.

4. "The University of Maine: A Study of Six Aspects of Its Work," by F.B. O'Rear. This report followed logically a Maine Survey of Higher Education, asked for by Boardman in his inaugural address. The copy I used was in the President's files.

5. From the report, with the recommendations occurring at pages, 23-4, 64-5, 135-7, 149-152, 179-181, 196-201, and 202-5. On the library see Louis Tappe Ibbotson, "What Price Library?", in *The Maine Alumnus*, January, 1934, 59-60, which represents the criticisms of the report.

6. Technology faculty minutes, November 27, 1933; January 15, 29, 1934; Report of the Technology Committee on the Curricula, October 30, 1933. The trustees were instrumental in establishing a first two years of a general nature in all colleges, see Trustees, (Bangor), June 28, 1933.

7. Arts College minutes, October 3, 1932; January 9, April 10, September 1, 1933; February 5, 1934; Letter James Muilenberg to Boardman, May 13, 1933, enclosing report on proposed changes taken by Arts faculty committees. On superior students, January 13, February 3, March 2, 1936 on Graduation Honors, on pre-med, Arts and Science, January 7, February 4, 1935.

8. Executive Committee, Trustees, November 7, 1931; letter to Boardman October 20, 1931; Boardman to Hosea Buck, November 21, 1931; Trustees, March 3, July 25 (Augusta), October 5, 1932; December 9, 1930, E.E. Chase to Harmon G. Allen, January 10, Olmstead Brothers to E.E. Chase, January 9, 1933; Olmstead Brothers to E.E. Chase, June 5, 1933; Trustees minutes, January 12, (Augusta), June 10, October 5, 1933; on parking, Student Parking Committee to Boardman March 2, 1932; Boardman to John R. Moore (ch. of committee), March 4, 1932; Trustees March 3, 1932; faculty petition of fall, 1931; *Campus*, September 28, 1933 on fire June 14, 1933 at Mount Vernon.

9. Boardman to George H. Jewett, undated, perhaps February 1933, in presidential correspondence 1932-1933.

10. Technology faculty, April 27, 1931; Agriculture faculty, January 25, 1932; *Campus,* October 22, 1931; February 4, May 6, 1932.

11. Boardman to Thomas E. Kane (Univ. No. Dak.) March 16, 1932; Press Release, December 6, 1932, *Campus,* January 19, 1933.

12. B.E. Packard, to Boardman November 14, 1932; Boardman to Packard, November 16, Boardman to Lewis (UNH), April 18, 1933.

13. Trustees, February 4, 1932; February 2, 1933; Faculty, February 8, October 17, 1932; January 30, 1933, February 11, 1935 (return of the pay cut); *Campus,* February 10, 16, 1933; Austin Stearns to Boardman February 27, and return February 28, 1933; A.L. Deering to Boardman, December 6, 1933; B. Packard to Boardman, February 11, 1933; Arts Faculty Minutes, February 6, 1933.

14. Trustees, January 12 (Augusta), April 21, (Bangor), 1933; E.M. Lewis to Boardman, March 17, May 8, 1933; Boardman to Lewis, March 18, and May 9, 1933, the last is quoted. *Maine Alumnus,* January, 1934, 64.

15. Trustees, January 4, 1934; letter Boardman to Board of Trustees, December 7, 1933.

16. *Campus,* September 27, 1934. The campus was changing in many ways as hazing began to diminish. *Campus,* April 13, 20; May 19, 1932.

17. *Campus,* November 8, 1934. *Inauguration of Arthur Andrew Hauck, Maine Bulletin,* Vol. XXVII, no. 6 [December, 1934]. Maine won the football game that afternoon from Colby 20-7 to cap the day.

18. Stewart diary, February 28, 1935.

19. Trustees, January 4, March 20, December 6, 1934; February 7, (Augusta) May 2, 1935.

20. Stewart diary, January 15, 1936; Trustees, February 6, March 4 (Augusta), April 3, May 7, June 6, October 8, 1936; letter Trustees to Governor and Council, March 3, 1936; Hauck to B.E. Packard, April 27, 1936; Harmon Allen to Hauck, April 24, 1936. A Poultry experimentation building also burned on January 20, 1936 with a loss of $2,500 and 520 hens. Insurance replaced it.

21. *Statement of the Board of Trustees of the University of Maine* [Orono], October 8, 1936.

22. Trustees, November 6, 1937; Barrows Inaugural, 1937, *Laws of Maine, 1937,* 701.

23. Secretary [FEJ?] to William S. Cole, August 29, 1938; Cole to Hauck, August 27, 1938; Lewis O. Barrows to Hauck, January 10, 1939.

24. *Board of Trustees to the Members of the Maine Legislature,* February, 1939, [Orono].

25. Trustees, October 29, 1938. Report of Major Building and Campus Improvements, January 1, 1934 to June 30, 1938.

26. Trustees, May 4, 1939; One other change occurred here and that was the pooling of the investment funds. See Trustees, August 30, 1941; *Laws of Maine, 1941,* ch. 21.

27. Executive Committee of Trustees, Report, October 5, 1933; Trustees, March 20, 1934.

28. B.E. Packard to Boardman, October 7, 1933; Trustees, November 10, 1933 (Bangor) with letters, Harry Sutton to Boardman, October 16; Boardman to Edward M. Lewis, October 18, E.M. Lewis to Boardman October 21, 23, 1933 (on Univ. N.H. RFC funds); Chase to Hauck, July 16, 1935.

29. The funds not received were from the PWA in 1939, See Public Works Administration Folder, and especially H.A. Gray to Hauck November 19, Hauck to Chase November 26, and Senator Brewster to Hauck, July 22, 1939.

30. Trustees, September 5, 1935; September 3, October 8, December 1, 1936; March 9 (Augusta), April 8, 1937; USDA Bulletin No. 1, 1936; *Agricultural Conservation Program, Northeast Region;* Bulletin No. 2, 1936, *Soil-Building Practices, Maine,* (May 25, 1936). FERA folder, Maynard Hincks to H.S. Boardman, June 29, 1934; WPA folder, W.R. Crowell to Hauck November 8, return November 11, 1935; Hauck to Crowell November 10, 1936; Crowell to A.L. Cotton November 5, 1936; Exec. Committee, Trustees, March 9, 1937; C.W.A. Work Projects, undated report; *Campus,* March 1, 1934 on FERA.

31. National Youth Administration Folder, project proposal, July 28, 1937 (for Cabins); Hauck to Bernarr McFadden, July 13, 1939; Hauck to FDR, February 5, 1942, as well as letters to Maine's congressional delegation, Paul McNutt, Aubrey Williams, and others. Letter to all institutions, from Leon J. Kowal, July 5, 1943; Trustees, March 9, 1937 (Augusta); The only history of the NYA is still Ernest O. and Betty Lindley, *A New Deal For Youth,* New York, 1938, which has two contemporary photos of the Cabins.

32. Trustees, August 2, (Bangor); September 9, December 28, 1938; February 2, October 11, 1939; February 26, 1940; Exec. Comm. Report, August 2, 1938; Pres. of Board to Governor and Council, September 12, 1938; Council Order, December 21, 1938; Hauck to Barrows, February 3, 1939; Barrows to Chase, February 6, 1939; Type Memo "A Plan for Constructing a Women's Dormitory at the Univeristy of Maine on A Self-Liquidating Basis," July 1, 1938, in PWA folder; also Ray S. Cuddy to Hauck, July 6; Hauck to R.E. Mullaney, June 16; to M.W. Gilmore, September 10, to L.O. Barrows, September 12, Gilmore to Hauck telegram, September 16, R.O. Brewster, to Hauck, telegram, September 20; Hauck to Brewster, September 21; to Gilmore, September 22; to R.E. Mullaney, September 27; Memo, Charles Crossland, Report of Conference in New York, September 29; Mullaney to UMO phone call memo, November 14; News Release, November, all these 1938.

33. Trustees, June 8, November 9, 1935; Education Committee Report, November 7, 1935; Trustees, February 6, 1936; Hauck to Walter· Linscott, November 26; Linscott to Hauck, October 30, November 29, 1935.

34. Trustees, February 6, June 6, March 4, 1936; October 7, 1937; January 6, 1938; Education Faculty, September 28, 1937; April 30, November 12, 1935; January 21, 1936; Letter, Hauck to James Muilenberg, June 9, 1936; Program of Local Government Institute, June 26, 1936.

35. Trustees, December 9, 1937; Arts Faculty, March 1, 1937; Agriculture Faculty, September 26, October 24, 1938; January 2, September 21, October 23, 1939; January 22, May 20, 1940; Paul Cloke "Economic and Social Status of the Engineering Teacher: An Outline of Ideas," *Journal of Engineering Education,* XXVII, no. 10 [June, 1937], 726-8.

36. Trustees, December 7, 1933; January 3 (Bangor), 4, May 3, 1934; March 8 (Augusta), 1935.

37. George D. Chase to A.A. Hauck, June 10, 1940; Committee "L" Report, March 21, 1941; Hauck to D.R. Drummond, March 25; to Milton Ellis, March 25, 1941; Ronald B. Levinson, "Philosophy at the University of Maine 1926-1940," July, 1940, and numerous other documents on this strange case, Trustees, September 27, 1941.

38. *Campus,* February 22, and special supplement, February 24, 1940; Founders Day Dinner Program, February 26, 1940; *Commemorative Exercises for the Seventy-Fifth Anniversary of the Founding of the University,* February 25, 26, 1940, *Maine Bulletin,* XLIII, no. 3 [October, 1940], Smith's quoted remarks appear at 35-6; Bangor *Daily News,* special supplement, February, 1940.

39. Trustees, June 9, 1934; June 6, 1936; Armistice Day Assembly program, November 11, 1936, Moritz J. Bonn, LSE, "Economic Self-Sufficiency," Robert P. Tristam Coffin, "Maine, A State of Grace," Commencement Address, June 14, 1937; Robert Gordon Sproul, "The Task of Your Maturity," Commencement Address, June 13, 1938; James Phinney Baxter, 3rd, "The 'Maginot Line' of American Democracy," Commencement Address, June 12, 1939; Carl Edwin Ladd, "The Land-Grant College in Changing Times," Commencement Address, June 9, 1941 (Various issues of the *Maine Bulletin);* Convocation Program Assembly, September 18, 1941; Sunday evening services, Freshman Week, September 14, 1941 (mimeographed); H.D. 727, 1937 (on compulsory R.O.T.C. being repealed, not passed).

40. James A. Connellan to Hauck, October 10, 1941; Hauck to Connellan, October 13, 1941.

41. Trustees, December 14, 1939; June 8, 1940; February 6, 1941;*Campus,* May 1, 8, 22, 1941. Program, Conference on Federal-State Cooperation and the Defense Emergency, May 9-10, 1941, mimeo.

42. *Campus,* May 1, October 16, 1941.

43. Trustees, January 8, March 24, 1942; *The Maine Bulletin,* XLIV, no. 9, March 9, 1942; Typed Report, "A Review of War Activities at the University of Maine," dated March 17, 1942; Student Assembly speech January 12, 1942, in folder "Defense-

Accelerated Program," Hauck to Alton L. Bell, January 15, 1942.

44. Hauck's notes at these special September meetings, the general faculty meeting was September 21.

45. Folder, "Civil Aeronautics Authority," and esp. Harry B. Watson to Hauck, August 15, 1941.

46. Cloke to Hauck, January 8, 1942; February 5, 13, 28, 1941; December 12, 1940; J.W. Studebaker to college, June 1, Cloke to Hauck, June 4; Hauck to Studebaker, June 5, 1940; Folders, 1942, 1942-3, ESMDT, ESMWT, brochures listing courses, locations, types and descriptions.

47. Brochure, *Engineering, Science and Management War Training,* Orono, fall, 1942?

48. Brochure, *War Training for Women at the University of Maine,* Orono, summer, 1943?

49. Brochure, *War Training for Students at the University of Maine,* October 1, 1942; folders, "Radio Communication Training," John A. Fox to Walter J. Creamer, January 7, 1943, especially; "Junior Inspectors of Ordnance Materials," folder, especially, Major John E. Ratigan to Hauck, January 27, 1943; Major General L.H. Campbell Jr. to Hauck, February 11, 1943.

50. The standard histories of these programs are Henry C. Herge, *et al., Wartime College Training Programs for the Armed Services,* American Council of Education, 1948; and T.R. McConnell, and Malcom M. Willey, *Higher Education and the War, The Annals,* Vol. 231, January, 1944.

51. Trustees, March 24, 1943; August 18, 1943; *Campus,* June 17, July 15, 22, 1943; November 29, 1945; Faculty Minutes, January 9, March 19, May 18, September 21, November 19, 1942; January 4, June 24, December 21, 1943; March 17, October 9, 1944.

52. Trustees, January 8, 1942; *Campus,* February 19, 26, March 12, October 29, November 12, December 10, 1942; June 17, July 15, 1943; Committee on Administration, December 15, 1941; Hauck to Richard A. Pierce, '41, March 20, 1943. Mimeod, "Proposed University Air Raid Precaution Organization." Professor W.S. Evans was chief warden. Stu-dents were registered as to their abilities by this group and the data is summarized in this document dated February 13, 1942. On gasoline rationing see C.C. Crossland to Trustees, September 8, 1944; C.C. Crossland to Hauck and others, July 15, 1942, Memo, Gasoline Rationing, on fuel, Memo by Crossland, Fuel Conservation, October 16, 1942. On Victory Gardens, see Hauck to Robert D. Larsson, August 17, 1944; (the impact of the summer drought), and to Robert B. Deering, March 27, 1943. On faculty reaction, see College of Agriculture, January 26, 1942; Arts and Sciences, January 12, 1942, pledging support, March 2, 1942, on fire extinguishers and air raid wardens; Tech College, January 26, 1942, don't excite students by inordinate amounts of attention to various phases of war.

53. Hauck to Hong G. Yuen, '46, April 12, 1943.

54. On fraternities, folders of Fred C. Loring, Report of May 4, 1943; June 2, 1944; November 12, 1945; Crossland to Trustees, September 8, 1944; Trustees, January 22, March 4, 1943 (Augusta), *Campus,* February 18, September 30, 1943; Bangor *Daily News,* February 17, 1943; on Hamlin fire, *Campus,* February 17, 24, 1944; Faculty, March 17, 1944; "Hearing Re: Hannibal Hamlin Fire," February 11, 15, 16, 1944, a 311 page typed document; Bruce B. Miner to author, Feburary 25, 1974; Hauck to Trustees, February 14, 1944.

55. General Alumni Letters to Service Personnel, August 20, 1942; December 10, 1942; December 14, 1943; December 5, 1944; *Country Gentleman,* April, 1945, "A Message to Pine Tree Staters," 20-22.

56. *Campus,* January 7, 21, May 13, 1943; January 13, April 27, October 12, 1944 (57 faculty were on leave by fall of 1944). Armistice Day Assembly Program, November 11, 1943; Memorial Day Assembly Program, May 31, 1954. *The University of Maine and the War, The Maine Bulletin,* Vol. XX, No. 6, [January, 1918].

57. *Campus,* May 17, 1945; Hauck to Donald W. Bean, '44, January 3, 1945.

58. Hauck to Major George Hargreaves, '31, May 8, 1945; to Robert S. MacDonald, '40, August 16, 1945 (identification of MacDonald tentative).

59. *Campus,* October 4, 1945.

CHAPTER EIGHT

From the End of World War II to the Centennial

BY 1944 a few veterans had already returned to the university and others were making inquiries about what would be available to them upon their return. Thus the first task on the campus in the postwar world was to prepare for and deal with the influx of veterans, a task much intensified by the passage of the G.I. Bill of Rights extending higher educational opportunities to a much wider group than ever before. In addition, the war had caused problems in both curricula and campus needs. During the years of the veterans and immediately thereafter the campus changed rather rapidly. By 1949 the legislature, having expended a tremendous amount of money in meeting the needs of the school, returned to its more parsimonious ways. The university also returned to a more normal atmosphere, with a somewhat smaller student body and plans for more than what available funds would permit. President Hauck remained until 1958, fighting these and other battles. His successor, Lloyd Elliott, was able to capitalize on Hauck's efforts, his own great abilities, and the impact of sputnik on science and other aspects of higher education, to bring into focus a massive building program, culminating in the celebration of the university's centennial in 1965. Although many had thought the postwar era would bring a return to the normality of earlier periods, what happened, in fact, was that the university, with institutions like it, found itself reacting to events over which it had little control.

First came an effort designed to get back the mill tax funds lost in the depression years. Raymond H. Fogler, head of the library fund-raising effort, and Arthur Hauck spearheaded this program. A favorable hearing was held in late 1944, and in 1945 the legislature appropriat-ed $629,176 (the amount of the mill tax loss) to provide two buildings: Deering for plant science and Boardman for engineering.[1]

These buildings and the interior of the library, built as a shell but uncompleted since 1942 because of the war, could not be constructed in time to meet the torrential influx of veterans. The first of them arrived on the campus in the spring semester of 1944, and by the fall the university had had to create a veterans' office. Hauck corresponded with other presidential colleagues as to their plans. He wrote to one of them a piece of understatement he may have later regretted. "It seems to me that the Colleges are going to have a real problem in that area. [advising and credits].[2]

A questionnaire was distributed to those in the service who had attended the university and nearly three-quarters indicated that they wanted to return. A number of one-year and refresher courses were provided to accelerate these undergraduates on their way. A folder was prepared and sent out to prospective veteran students, with the state veterans' office also publishing bulletins and brochures. But none of this was really sufficient because of the great numbers of veterans who wished to take advantage of the G.I. Bill benefits.[3]

The trustees did establish a priority of acceptance to the school: (1) former students in good standing; (2) state residents who met the entrance qualifications; (3) out-of-state veterans; and (4) out-of-state civilians. By early 1946 some admissions officers were apparently telling veterans they needed an alumni parent in order to qualify for admission. It was an effort to stem the flow of applications but it was stopped as soon as Hauck found it out. As he said, in response to a critic. "This problem of selection is a terribly difficult one and you simply can't please everyone.''[4] The first year was not run well because the college simply did not anticipate the numbers enrolling under the G.I. Bill. By 1946-47 the situation improved somewhat, but the report of the first year's activities was fairly dismal.

There was an acute shortage of housing to accommodate returning students, and Hauck appealed to the governor for financial and other help. Large trailers were imported and Dow Air Force Base facilities in Bangor were used, but the arrangements were insufficient and generally unsatisfactory.

The university leased thirty-two trailers (eleven of which were expansible) with kitchen facilities, tables, chairs, and daybeds.[5] However, 400 more veterans came in the spring of 1946, making the total over 700 at the beginning of the semester. The numbers increased every day until, by the end of February, of the 1,848 students on the campus, 928 were veterans (406 of them were former students). Of this number of students, 281 were married, giving a new dimension to the campus. Two hundred of the total were housed at ''WAC Hill'' on the Dow Air Force Base, and special busses were used to carry them to and from the Orono campus. In May the *Campus* predicted 2,000 veterans would soon be enrolled. When classes opened in the fall 120 men were sleeping in the women's gymnasium as the prefabricated housing for them was not complete. A Brunswick campus on the former Naval Air Station was also opened to hold some 800 or so students. The official opening of the university was delayed twice. The North dormitories emergency housing, erected by the federal government, were completed and plumbing problems finally overcome by the end of October so all students were in some sort of decent housing, and the Dow Field students (some called them pariahs) were back in dormitory facilities at Orono. The food was none too good however; in November there were difficulties over both the quantity and quality of food served in the cafeterias. A change in personnel followed an investigation, and William Wells took over the food service. Registration in the spring of 1946 was 3,972, with 764 of this number at Brunswick.[6]

In the fall semester, enrollment, including Brunswick, exceeded 4,000 with three-fourths of these students veterans. During the summer the Federal Public Housing Agency erected

twenty-three two-story buildings to house 196 families. These buildings, called the South Apartments by the administration, and the ''Fertile Crescent'' by the more imaginative, helped somewhat. Forty faculty families were also housed in this complex. In addition to the North dormitories for the veterans, two other barracks were used to house women students. They were placed near Carnegie Hall. A temporary dining room was built in the field house with the gun room providing cold storage for the kitchen goods.[7]

Obviously, with all these problems, and with classes running from 7:45 a.m. to 5:45 p.m. and occasionally into the evening, something else needed to be done. The board of trustees approached the governor and through him the forthcoming special session of the legislature. The first meetings were friendly. Costs were rising, but if the university was to take all who wished to come and who could profit, money needed to be spent. It was estimated, for instance, that the deficit under current conditions would be $600,000 by 1949. The special session was asked for $250,000 to meet current demands, but this involved setting a ceiling of 3,200 enrollment at Orono. In addition it was hoped for authorization to borrow $2,000,000 to build three new dormitories and another $400,000 to meet the rising costs of the plant science and engineering buildings already authorized. The governor, Horace Hildreth, was sympathetic, and in his message to the legislators discussed the trustee ideas plainly. He called for a major committee hearing to discuss all the ramifications of such expenditures. (The same legislature also considered a massive expansion of aid in the fields of primary and secondary education and a $1,000,000 appropriation to support vocational education for the returning veterans.)[8]

It was clear that the mill tax was no longer sufficient to meet these demands. Hildreth asked the legislators to give guidance for future financing and long-range policy. A major hearing was held July 17, 1946, in the chamber of the House of Representatives. E.E. Chase, chairman of the board, and Hauck testified in detail. The special session authorized $250,000 immediately and provided $1 million for the dormitories, with a tacit agreement to allow the borrowing of another million in the next legislature. The trustees then decided to move

The top photograph shows President Hauck speaking at a ceremonial function dealing with the library construction. The building shell was not completed until after the war. The bottom photograph looks south down the mall toward the new library, now named for Raymond H. Fogler, '15. Stevens Hall is to the left. With a recent large addition the library has served the University well for thirty years.

President Hauck inspected the Brunswick Naval Air Station before accepting it for the campus. Here he is shown on that trip with the naval officers. Acceptance came in his letter to the Commanding Officer of July 29, 1946.

ahead and build these dormitories, two on the then athletic field and one across from Estabrooke Hall. Room and board were increased and the lease on the naval air station at Brunswick extended, both at the same trustee meeting.[9]

The present (1976) athletic field was constructed with new grandstands in the summer and was used in the fall for football games, as the dormitories began rising on the former field's location. By October, when the trustees met again with the governor and the budget committee, the costs of the buildings had been stabilized at $1 million more. Other costs were estimated to be some $350,000 over the mill tax. Although the legislature had included $400,000 to finish the two 1945 buildings, plant science and engineering, this money had been defeated in referendum along with a tax and bonus for veterans which were part of the same bill. Now

the trustees asked the 1947 (93rd) legislature for the regular mill tax, $350,000 for each year of the biennium, the $400,000 previously requested, and $150,000 each year for continuation of the Brunswick campus. That legislature granted the right to borrow the million promised before, alloted the $300,000 for Brunswick, with the provisions that enrollment remain between 4,000 and 4,800 and that Brunswick classes be terminated at the end of the biennium, if not before. In addition to the mill tax they provided $175,000 for each year of the biennium. The long-suffering 1945 buildings were funded again, this time without referendum.[10] The body also began to discuss, although it did not pass, legislation limiting the number of students, some according to their place of residence.

The school was able in this period to alleviate its problems somewhat with the erection of a temporary building, East Annex, formerly a

A class at the Brunswick campus annex in 1946 or 1947. These men, many of them veterans, crammed into the room, demonstrate the intent with which they soaked up knowledge. Facilities were not as important as the instruction.

bachelor officers' quarters at Sanford and moved to Orono.[11] During this time the library was completed, dedicated, and made available for use. The former library, donated by Carnegie, was turned over to art and music as a fine arts center.[12] Architects' plans were drawn and a major fund-raising effort was undertaken to construct a new student union as a memorial to the 3,882 Maine alumni and students who served in the second war and to the 175 who lost their lives in that service. This building was finally raised and dedicated in 1952.[13]

The Brunswick campus remained open for three years and made it possible to deal with the flood of students. Bowdoin was of immense help with material and social comforts, at least in the first phase. In the first year some 150 Bowdoin men were domiciled on the naval base as well. Classrooms were the former infirmary and some barracks. Most of the faculty were

hired directly from the armed services and were in transition along with their students. Orono continued to run the campus from afar, but soon the Brunswick campus community's own ideas and traditions were important too. Even in the third year, 40 percent of the students were veterans, although the hope had been to move the veterans to Orono as rapidly as possible. A student newspaper, *The Maine Annex,* was published, the first edition dated January 10, 1947. The campus functioned as an annex, electing its own mayor, promoting an Outing Club, and producing a Maine Masque performance or two. The Brunswick students raised some $54,000 for the new union, even though most of them would never see the building while students. Altogether, some 2,400 students (1,679 veterans) were in attendance at Brunswick in the three years the annex operated. Newspapers in the southern half of the state were impressed, and a reservoir of good will was founded with this venture in widespread administration.[14]

The other emergency housing provisions, the North dormitories, lingered on into the fifties, along with the South Apartments. By the sixties, however, only the East Annex remained of the temporary buildings, at that time, and now, a fixture of the campus. Trustees estimated all veteran costs at $545,928.22; the trustees provided $130,928.22 of this and the legislature the other $415,000 by appropriation. The table gives veteran registration from 1944 to 1952.[15]

VETERAN REGISTRATION — UNIVERSITY OF MAINE

Semester	Orono	Brunswick	Total
Fall, '44	19		19
Winter, '45	21		21
Spring, '45	26		26
Summer, '45	21		21
Fall, '45	203		203
Spring, '46	959		959
Summer, '46	758		758
Fall, '46	1,981	802	2,783
Spring, '47	2,061	770	2,831
Summer, '47	762		762
Fall, '47	2,575	505	3,080
Spring, '48	2,470	447	2,917
Summer, '48	564		564
Fall, '48	2,474	314	2,788
Spring, '49	2,113	224	2,337
Summer, '49	580		580
Fall, '49	2,140		2,140
Spring, '50	1,885		1,885
Summer, '50	458		458
Fall, '50	1,157		1,157
Spring, '51	910		910
Summer, '51	422		422
Fall, '51	573		573
Spring, '52	456		456

The veterans took the university by storm due to the huge numbers that wanted an education. Certainly the school had been apprised that it had to plan for the postwar period, a time quite different from any that faculty, staff, or students had known before. Hauck, himself, had responded to a question put to him by a journalist by specifying problems of international relations, race relations, and rehabilita-

tion for veterans as problems the university and higher education had to face.[16]

Former students also had something to say to the planners. One, in response to a questionnaire addressed to those who had not finished their degrees, indicated that he was planning to return, and he spoke for many when he said, "When this war is over, I'm coming back to your lovely campus; for the months that I spent there were just about the happiest ones of my life."[17] Five other former students sent Hauck a letter that became a factor in planning.

We want to return to the University that was 'Maine' before the war was a reality. We want to return to normal semesters, to Easter vacations, to hard working days in laboratories and shops, to 'cokes' over the 'book store' counter, to all the little and big things that made 'Maine' mean education and home. We've had enough of restricted schedules, of 'high pressure' education, of 'speedup' programs. We've seen them — we've studied under them — we don't like them. We want to take our time. We want to be able to go beyond our classes, to do more research, to have time to understand. We also feel that we can do more for our country and ourselves that way.[18]

Hauck read part of this letter to the deans and the postwar planning committee. He responded to the veterans that the deans agreed about the high-pressure accelerated education and went on, "We are trying to plan for the future as carefully as possible, and you may be sure that we shall hold fast to traditions and policies that have been acceptable in the past."[19]

The student newspaper also called for thoughtful proposals and welcomed the planning committees from the colleges when they were appointed. The paper urged the committees to discuss comprehensive examinations, advising, honors, the twelve-week term, majors, research policy, and the publish-or-perish policy advocated by some. A postwar planning course was offered in the history and government department in the spring of 1944, and a series of town meetings on the campus were also held that year, although attendance was none too good. (One coincided with the Thanksgiving Ball; the small attendance at the town meeting infuriated the editor of the *Campus*.)[20]

The trustees, engaged in the planning process, devoted several meetings in early 1943 to discussion of a reorganization and coordination

The montage of photographs graphically shows South Apartment life. These pictures show one student family during a day as mother gives her oldest son a swing and then he joins a friend in the second snapshot. Their Father, John Benoit '59, is in the next picture with two neighbors after playing catch. Maine classes of '78, '80, '83 are represented by the three Benoit children.

The building at the bottom is a survival of wartime days, a former barracks, the East Annex. Long a center of power at Orono, is still endures as an office building.

Societies for student majors were increasingly important after World War II. This photo shows the student members of the American Chemical Society in 1947.

of the agriculture effort. With the new plan the dean was given supervision over extension, research and teaching, with a common financial budget. The experiment station and the extension service directors were to become his subordinates. The agriculture advisory council was revised to meet these new demands with a better representation of the state's new agricultural interests. Trustees also discussed the size of the university, opposed the proliferation of nonacademic subjects, and urged the establishment of more scholarship aid. They hoped that the first year of studies, and possibly the first two, would be as nearly uniform as possible for all students. Later a postwar building plan was begun. It included the buildings already mentioned and authorized in 1945-46, as well as a new service building, an infirmary, a swimming pool, an inn for guests, wings for Aubert, the refurbishing of campus roads and walks, a better water system, the location of electric lines underground, a better telephone system, and a skating rink, along with renovation of Coburn, Alumni, Fernald, Holmes, and Hamlin halls. A five-year plan to upgrade faculty salaries was discussed and adopted, as was

the establishment of a stronger and better endowment program, with Charles S. Crossland II as director. The existing endowment program, the University of Maine Foundation, had begun in 1934, but had been nearly moribund during the emergency period.[21]

The university postwar planning committee began its work in December 1943, with Weston Evans of Technology, H. Kirshen of arts, and W. Libby of agriculture as members along with the deans. These men supervised planning in their colleges. Results of the planning included more humanistic courses in technology (something Paul Cloke had been promoting since 1932), better advising, establishment of a basic two-year course (with the famous Masterpieces of Literature), along with speech, foreign languages, more U.S. history, and comprehensive examinations in arts and sciences. The board of trustees, especially Chase, were quite interested in these developments, following them closely.[22]

The agricultural college provided a common first year curriculum, a choice of a general agriculture or scientific program in the second year, freshman orientation, courses in rural sociology and United States history, and a possibility of agricultural history. In the streamlining, courses were cut from 182 to 164, and there was a strong effort to upgrade and improve teaching effectiveness. The School of Education also did a revamping of its ideas. Payson Smith addressed the board of trustees on the establishment of a stiffer program with more humanistic content.[23] These curricula changes would remain essentially in place until the beginning of the 1960's when, under the leadership of a new vice-president, Austin Peck, most departments and colleges again began to look more closely at their offerings and to revise them, although not as drastically as in the 1945 changes.[24]

As the university grew larger, individual faculty members found themselves removed from direct access to power, and their part of the decision-making process taken over by administrative personnel with direct responsibility usually only to the president and the board of trustees. For that reason faculty meetings after this time became more and more recitals of minor matters. By 1947 an attempt to create a faculty senate led to a reorganization over the next two years, abolition of the general faculty meeting, and establishment of the Faculty Council. This group, designed to replace the older Committee on Administration as well as meet faculty complaints, was somewhat misnamed, since the president, the academic deans, Director of Students, Director of Public Relations, and the deans of men and women were all ex officio members. Faculty members were elected; the first elections were held in December 1949, and January 1950. Membership extended to physical education and ROTC as well as other, more academic areas.[25]

By 1952 the Faculty Council was creating difficulties. Much discussion of the operation of the group, its original purpose, and its usefulness permeated faculty coffee sessions and more formal gatherings. In late 1952 an effort was made to divide the faculty and administrative groups, and although that became a possibility (through separate meetings on petition), it seldom happened. Both the arts and the agriculture colleges seem to have been most active in their opposition to the Faculty Council, but even their opposition was weak and unsteady. Decision making passed fairly clearly to

These students comprised Professor Boucier's French class in 1935-1936. The broadsides on the wall were there when the author took French in the same room, and in 1977 when he taught history there.

A laboratory class in astronomy in 1938. Although posed, the photograph does show clearly student dress, and the laboratory equipment of the time.

*Professor Edward Brush, later long-time dean of graduate studies in his psychology labora-
tory after World War II. Is this an experiment in telepathy?*

a paid professional administrative staff, with
faculty acquiescence, or at least tolerance.[26]

As the student body grew so rapidly, new
faculty members were added. Some who remained to make a considerable mark on the
campus included Harold Young, forestry;
Lewis Nevin, music; Vincent Hartgen, art; John
Lyman, engineering; Alice Stewart, history;
Robert Thomson, political science and honors;
Claude Westfall, general engineering; Bruce
Poulton, animal husbandry; and George Davis,
education. Others, who were to serve as deans
of their colleges later, included Richard Hill,
technology, and John Nolde, arts and sciences.
By 1951 staff reductions had begun, and
twenty-nine full-time and thirteen part-time instructors of 1951-52 were gone by 1953. The
standard salary scale remained for a time, but
by 1960, "in the best interests of the institution," the board of trustees rescinded its vote
on standard salary scales.[27]

Relatively few difficulties were created by
Korean War veterans. The general standards of
World War II on deferments, blanket credits
(for half or more of a semester for those drafted), and, later on, the G.I. Bill veterans were
accepted again and followed. In retrospect the
Korean War made little impact at the school,

except to lower student morale, especially
among the men. It was not until later that such
wars seemed less than normal.[28]

Occasionally there was desultory discussion
of curriculum changes in the college meetings,
but little was done. Arthur Hauck expressed the
opinion of most when he observed in 1951 while
inaugurating a long-range planning group,
"Adopt a limited program, which we can do
well, and not expect to expand into all fields of
instruction.[29]

The state of Maine had made rather good provision for the influx of veterans and the financial demands for an expanded and increased
university during this period. However, by 1948
and 1949 these demands did not meet with as
much favor with the legislators. A split had
begun in the Republican party between conservative and progressive elements which would
lead to a major reorientation of the state's
politics as the Democrats gained more seats in
the legislature, and to capture several, and later
most, of the statewide offices. This reorientation overrode other issues for several years.
When the trustees and President Hauck met in
the fall of 1948 with the legislative budget committee, they asked for $350,000 annually in ad-
dition to the mill tax. In 1947 the amount had

been cut to $175,000 and tuition had risen in response to needs. Also, costs and salaries had both risen and the number of veterans had dropped. By 1949 costs were even higher because the veterans were now mostly upperclassmen who cost more to educate. Still, the trustees were hopeful, and in January they gave a luncheon for the legislators where Hauck made a speech pointing out these problems and then answered questions from the audience. Following a visit to the campus, the legislators reported the trustees' bill "ought to pass," and the House did pass the funds for a new animal pathology building.[30]

The Senate also authorized the building (because of the impact of an outbreak of Newcastle disease in poultry) and called for the reestablishment of the law school (with no funding), but on the last day of the session killed the extra amount asked for, leaving the school with the mill tax funds only ($762,000). Tuition costs immediately rose again to meet the difference.[31] The university was left back where it was during the depression, and members of the faculty and administration and the alumni began to worry about the future.

The 95th legislature, due to meet in January 1951, was sent a special message from the board along with the president's *Biennial Report*. The trustees told the incoming legislators that they needed an appropriation of $1,350,000 for each of the two years, a figure equal to one and three-fourths mills (roughly what the 1929 dollar was worth in terms of one mill). The report stressed the great rise in tuition (to the highest of any land grant institution at that time). The last paragraph is worth quoting in the context of the Korean War, which was also occupying the minds of Maine's citizens and taxpayers.

> The trustees realize that the members of the Legislature have never been asked to consider the University of Maine's needs and its future at a time more critical or more uncertain. None of us know what will happen tomorrow. But we do know that American youth must be equipped to cope with the heavy responsibilities of the future. There never was a time when the University was more vital to the State of Maine and its people.[32]

The governor echoed these remarks in his annual message, and in his budget message called for passage of amounts in excess of the mill tax.

These serious young men were recipients of major scholarships from the pulp and paper foundation in 1953. This program attracted much external support used in this manner. The foundation continues in a new building named for its long-time secretary, Lyle Jenness, '25G.

These men are registering for their classes in forestry in 1949. The lines in the gymnasium were typical of this period. Forestry, begun in 1903, is celebrating its 75th anniversary as this book goes to press.

Professor G. William Small, teaching his Shakespeare course in Stevens Hall. The photograph, taken in 1938, shows his famous model of the Globe theatre. Nearest the camera in the first row is Jo Profita, '38.

These seven men were the raw initiates in 1957 into Alpha Zeta, an honorary agricultural fraternity. Elements of the initiation persist in the straw – both on the floor and in the hats.

By this time the budget and budget making presented a difficult problem. One trustee said that with costs rising so rapidly, every piece of construction became a "special project." Still, the trustees attempted to meet their needs with their request for one and three-fourths mills.

The budget committee hearing was presented with these points for more funds in October and reminded that the failure to appropriate funds in 1949 had led to a $200,000 emergency appropriation in the special session of 1950. Reserve funds had also been used. The trustees made the same case to the education committee, as they did to the appropriations committee. The state did cut the funds to a degree, but a total restructuring of the state's assessment procedure and tax structure, cutting out the mill tax provision, passed the legislature and gave the school an appropriation of $1,268,596, which equaled the mill tax amount plus $500,000. The monies had been provided, but tempers were short, and legislators, trustees, the administration, and the faculty were all unhappy. The future appeared more bleak after these encounters.[33]

Perhaps the most critical person in the 1948 to 1952 effort was a trustee, Frank W. Hussey, '25. After some trustees held a rump meeting with the alumni members of the legislature,

Hussey reported bad news. He thought the alumni needed organization and a strong presentation of the facts. He was blunt with Hauck.

"Being good boys" and going along in that rough and tumble arena does not bring folks on our side when it comes to appropriations.

Hussey advocated a "hard-boiled fighting program." After the legislature's failure to deal with the university except in the default of the new tax program, Hussey was publicly critical of Hauck and his approach. He wrote to the beleaguered president telling him of his criticism and calling for a "more active, aggressive" program which would mobilize alumni from each county to do the work. He said that the trustees couldn't do it, nor could Hauck, "and frankly, Arthur, until we do so I don't believe that we will ever secure from the Legislature what the University is entitled to." Hussey, who was active in the Farm Bureau, pledged that organization to help if Hauck and the trustees would move.[34]

Hauck was aware that his approach was dated; he told Hussey so in a letter which is quite revealing of university problems and ideas at that time.

I only wish that I were better at the job of getting money out of the Maine Legislature. I have never put in more time working with individual members of the Legislature than I have this year and I am sorry that results haven't been better. We are struggling with next year's budget and as usual we are way short of what we need.[35]

To another friend Hauck was less forthcoming, but probably this letter expressed his ideas more closely than his response to Hussey's criticism. As he said,

Public education seems to be having a hard time in most of the states this year. Our legislature was far from generous with the University of Maine so there are plenty of financial problems.[36]

University finances remained in approximately the same position for the remainder of Arthur Hauck's term as president. In 1952, at a conference held on campus, legislators went to the Bates-Maine football game, were served tea, and listened to speeches by Governor-elect Burton M. Cross and those of the trustees who were present. Hearings were held, with good attendance, but the legislators were too con-

cerned with their own political futures to pay much attention to the needs of the school. A tentative ten-year program was set out, and the legislature was asked specifically for a men's dormitory, $400,000; a pulp and paper wing to the chemical engineering building, $370,000; an animal science building, $330,000; and an apple storage room at Highmoor Farm, $65,000. Only the men's dormitory was authorized, with the legislature providing $400,000 and the university given the authority to borrow $400,000 to repay those funds.[37]

Much the same procedure was followed in 1955, when the legislature allowed funds for the chemical engineering building, established a state committee on educational television, and gave the school authority to borrow $465,000 for a women's dormitory. The legislators did not even attend the biennial Orono gatherings in the numbers expected; they and the university seemed to be marking time.[38]

On the campus, the board of trustees, and especially Edward Allen Whitney, trustee from 1948 to 1956, worked on establishing the service infrastructure of a modern university. Cafeteria style feeding (opposed by some), annual giving

A standard event of the spring each year in the 1950's was the military ball. These young men and their dates are accepting honors at the ball in 1954. The gowns date the period perfectly.

(opposed by Hauck), and systematization of the janitorial and maintenance work (opposed by the staff, especially by F.S. McGuire, superintendent of buildings and grounds) were Whitney's major contributions. He also provided liason with the new Democratic governor, Edmund S. Muskie, who was sympathetic, but had only limited funds in this period. Another trustee remarked, "We are a utility institution, it seems to me, in every way, circumscribed pretty severely by the amount of money which is available . . . ."[39] Whitney responded by saying, "It seems to me that we have got to live with this situation until there is a new birth of ideas by the citizens . . . ."[40]

Whitney also supervised a new master plan for the campus, one that would be the background and focus for the efforts of the next president. When Whitney retired Frank Hussey wrote an appreciation of a man that few even knew existed, but who was very important in the postwar transition period.

> [He] . . . combined good business judgement with an appreciation of ideals and objectives for the University.
> All too often we have the limited thinking of men in finance, with no reflection intended of any individual, or the limited thinking of men in agriculture, like myself, or in engineering.[41]

The ten years that began with the first infusion of veterans had seen rather large changes on the campus and the expenditure of $5,777,475.45, as well as another $783,955.14 from reserve funds.[42] This did not include funds for the Student Union; these were raised by the alumni, initiated through an appeal at a memorial service in May of 1946. Alumni, students, and faculty all contributed, and by the first year $600,000 was raised, by the second, $750,000. After a brief flurry over the location of the building, construction began in the summer of 1951 when the total raised was about $1 million. Steel scarcity during the Korean War delayed the work, but after a new beginning in April 1952, construction went ahead and the building was in partial use by late 1952.[43]

Arthur Hauck remained as president, his public honors continuing to grow during this period, with the presidency of the Association of Land Grant Colleges and Universities and honorary degrees from Kentucky and Florida in 1953. On the occasion of his fifteenth year in office in 1949, students honored him with a tribute.[44]

In 1957 one of Hauck's compatriots in administration wrote to him congratulating him on his career in Maine, saying,

> You must feel sometimes now as if this were where you came in. The recurrent presentation of constantly growing demands from education makes me wonder how to tell the story anew, so that it has freshness and influence. We have had to say so many of the same things every year since World War II.[45]

Hauck himself must have felt much the same way as he surveyed the past two or three legislatures. In any case he tendered his resignation in 1958 after serving for the longest period of any Maine president and acting as a character molder during his time on the Orono campus. Again the students gave a tribute to the "Prexy" who had known so many of them during his twenty-four years in Orono. And although that tribute must have made him feel very proud and warm, he had received a letter on his twentieth anniversary there that, if he remembered it four years later, must have made him feel as good. The letter came from Charles A. Snow, '11 (Law), who took a B.A. in 1920 and returned in 1934 to begin work on a M.A. received in 1937. Snow recalled how at Hauck's first meeting on the campus he had spoken to the summer session and had shown pictures of Hawaii. Snow went on,

> About three weeks ago I was driving between Pittsfield and Newport — picked up boy with 'M' on his luggage. I asked him if he knew you personally and he said that, "Everybody at the University knows Dr. Hauck personally."[46]

Truer words were never spoken. Everyone who was at the university during his twenty-four year tenure knew Dr. Hauck personally, and their lives were better for the knowledge. In the business of creating good citizens and good persons, Hauck had done excellent work. In the area of buildings, grounds, and educational experimentation he was not as strong, but he was good nevertheless, and given the Maine legislature one doubts that he could have done much better. The university was a better place for his tenure. Let that stand as a judgment.

When Arthur Hauck indicated that he wished to retire from the presidency, a long (eight

Winter carnival was always a time of snow sculpture, in the 40's, 50's, and recently in the 70's. These three photos are from 1959. The theme was "favorite professors" and in their frozen glory one sees here, Professor Vincent Hartgen, Art; Nelson B. Jones, First Director of the Union; and Clarence "Squeaky" Bennett, Physics.

The new Student Union, begun after World War II and rebuilt with funds generated from alumni, students, and faculty. This scene shows the building soon after construction with no shrubs and few trees. The snow is an inescapable adjunct to the winter months.

These young people, posing together in February, 1948, were the student volunteer corps who raised much of the money for the new Union building. Groups such as this propelled the University into the modern world.

months) search was begun for his successor. The trustees felt that they needed someone who could pick the university up and propel it ahead rapidly; growth in size and service in the coming years was constantly being discussed. The end product of the search was Lloyd Hartman Elliott, then executive assistant to the president of Cornell University. His opening remarks on the Orono campus stressed the people of the state and their love and affection for their university. He said in an interview:

> "We need more education for more people at all levels of the educational ladder . . . . We need more work and emphasis on English, including reading, and foreign languages, beginning at an early age, as well as science . . . . The University's first obligation is to its students, but it should be able to help the state as a whole, through its research facilities in many fields.

Much construction was underway on the campus when Elliot arrived. Physics and animal science-poultry buildings were begun during the summer of 1958. A men's dining hall would be finished that fall and a new men's dormitory due for completion in 1959. The special session

When Hauck retired, a suitable memorial, a theatre-auditorium, was raised behind and connected to the new Union. Here it is nearly constructed in 1959. Since then, the Masque has performed here on a regular basis along with many other artists.

of the legislature had appropriated $345,000 for additional space and equipment for the heating plant. A campaign had begun to fund and construct a theatre complex, to be named after Arthur Hauck, as part of the Memorial Union.[47]

At Elliott's inauguration in the fall of 1958, early speakers talked of the difficulty and desirability of educational leadership. Elliott focused on the need for funds, especially funds for scholarships for those who could benefit from a university education. He called for a strengthening of the humanities parallel to that of science which was then beginning its tremendous boost from sputnik. He ended his remarks with a further appeal to the liberal, not the vocational, ideal.[48] Later he would elaborate on these remarks with, "to build an ideal university is to unite in a noble purpose since there are few earthly things more beautiful. Of such is the work of the professor."[49]

Considerable changes were taking place on the campus. Some of them involved the National Defense Education Act (Pl 85-864) passed in partial response to Soviet scientific success. This bill provided approximately $880,000 for Maine to use in loan funds, graduate fellowships, counselling, testing, language and area studies, and audiovisual impact on education. Another area of change was in the tentative beginnings of the merger of many of the state's campuses, starting with the conversion of Portland Junior College into a University of Maine branch campus in Portland.

Elliot had to establish his own authority as opposed to his deans. A sample will indicate his style.

> It would seem to me that this record [a report of activity] indicated that we are either working at cross purposes with each other or without a clear understanding of what other divisions of the University are doing.[50]

Elliott began his new job with a presentation of an increased budget to the legislature. He did not ask for many new buildings however, only the authority to borrow $10 million to erect housing for young faculty and graduate students. Most of the increase in the budget, a bit over a million dollars, was designed to raise faculty salaries to a level that was not disgraceful. The president also asked for substan-

Lloyd H. Elliott

That 1959 legislature had looked at a great many bills providing for construction on the Orono campus. They included a women's dormitory, a women's physical education building, an electrical engineering building, an incinerator, remodeling of Wingate Hall, a university press building, remodeling of Aubert Hall, completion of the wings on Boardman Hall, further expansion of the steam plant, construction of service buildings, enlargement of the sewer system, and a college of education building.[53] Some of these buildings were authorized, but it was obvious that a bigger push was needed to achieve them all. In 1961 the many bills the legislators again received included remodeling of Aubert Hall, expansion of Boardman, expansion of the electric lines and of the steam plant, enlargement of men's physical education facilities, expansion of the water lines and of sewer facilities, forestry building, an engineering building, a university press building, service buildings, a women's physical education building, equipment for the education building, further construction on Stevens Hall's north wing, campus roads and parking areas, enlargement of the agricultural engineering building, renovation of Winslow Hall, and in addition regular operating funds of nearly $10 million.[54]

The university administration realized that it was necessary to make its case more strongly, not only to the legislature, but also to the people, since many of these bills were now going to referendum, especially those that involved bonding, as many did. Some felt as did Frank Hussey, who remarked to Elliott in early 1963,

> We are still paying a terrific price not only in Orono, but by youngsters in the State of Maine, for failure to set suitable goals and fight for them preceding your administration.[55]

Whether or not Hussey was correct in his analysis, the university did begin a more sophisticated campaign. The trustees decided they needed to create an atmosphere in which people would want to aid their university. A public relations committee was set up, as was a legislative interpretative program with news, editorial features, and a dinner for the legislature. It snowed hard on December 16, the night of the dinner, but twenty legislators came anyway.

tial funds for the Portland branch, which already had about 350 students, as well as increased funds for the library. Governor Clausen included the funds in his message, and the legislature provided the necessary legislation.[51]

But, it was difficult dealing with the legislature. As some of his correspondence indicated, Elliott received a strong baptism. To one friend he said, "Here at Maine we have no problems that fifty million dollars would not go a long way toward resolving." To another, he remarked, "I do not exactly envy you your job of looking for a new Dean of your graduate school. The way the legislature is running me at the moment, I wouldn't have time to look for a janitor." To Frank Hussey, he ruefully told this story:

> After firing one or two people, demoting a few others, the President of Queens College concluded that the President of a University must have "an unusual capacity to inflict pain." While in Augusta on Friday, I came to the conclusion that the Legislature had taken over that role.[52]

President Elliott giving his inaugural address in the gymnasium, October 24, 1958. Address-ing the faculty, board of trustees, students and alumni, he charted goals emphasizing a growth in the liberal arts to match the other areas of the University. The next six years were hectic as a result.

A public relations bulletin was published for alumni and friends, and a booklet, *A Five-Part Legislative Program,* prepared. In addition radio and television were used, and a group of minutemen, each of whom had responsibilty to contact a single legislator, was mobilized. When the appropriation hearing was held on February 15, former governor Lewis Barrows was pres-ent, was called on, and made an extem-poraneous speech in behalf of the university that did good work. Of course, the main speaker was Elliott who presented the uni-versity's case.[56]

The legislature did not provide all the funds requested but did increase its funding to $4,211,287 or 44.2 percent of the total income. Student fees accounted for $2,509,646 or 26.3 percent. The federal share was 10.5 percent, and gifts and other grants brought in 13.7 per-cent. Other funds were scattered over endow-ment, reimbursement for service, and sales of goods. Total income was $9,532,063 for the fis-cal year ending June 30, 1962.[57] The institution

could face its centennial with the idea that it might be in a growth position by its celebration.

When the 101st Legislature met in January 1963, members found themselves asked not only to raise the amounts of operating expen-ditures considerably, but also to provide financ-ing for $9 million of capital improvements. This $9 million was only part of a six-year program to provide all told $20 million in capital im-provements by the end of the sixties. Of this amount $12,715,000 was scheduled for academic buildings, nearly $4 million for physical educa-tion and athletics, and nearly $3.5 million for services, roads, walks, and utilities. Additional-ly, the school began a ten-year program of private support to provide a number of dis-tinguished professorships, graduate as-sistantships and fellowships, undergraduate scholarships, library support, teaching and re-search equipment, and endowments for con-certs, lectures, and other cultural activities. This program was scheduled to cost $5,200,000. Not all these items were attained, but substan-

These three photos illustrate the breadth of the remarkable construction of the early 1960's. Top is Aroostook Hall, a new dormitory, the first to be named for state counties. The middle one is a new dining facility, East Commons, now Stewart, named for John Stewart, long time Dean of Men. Bottom is Barrows, used for engineering offices and class rooms. All are recently completed here.

Women had used the older gymnasium after the building of Alumni Gymnasium and Field House. In 1963 this new athletic facility for women, named for Helen Lengyel, women's athletic director for many years, was constructed and dedicated. This view is from the playing fields.

tial changes were made on the campus because of this planning and program.[58]

Throughout 1963 and 1964 the trustees heard report after report as the new construction rose on the campus. Aroostook Hall was available for the beginning of the summer session of 1963, the largest such session in the university's history, with a speech and hearing clinic, a summer music theatre, a special Peace Corps unit being trained, several special institutes for teachers, and around 900 visitors studying a major eclipse of the sun. By fall Barrows and Lengyel halls were ready along with Androscoggin and East Commons. During that summer the Hauck Auditorium, renovation of Alumni Hall for Educational Television, and the USDA office building were also worked on and near completion. Passage of referenda that fall provided more funds for buildings including Little Hall, the rebuilding of Lord Hall, the service building, the refurbishing of Boardman, and new construction at Portland.[59]

Helen Lengyel

President Kennedy and President Elliott marching to the special convocation, Fall, 1963. The weather and the speech were superb.

One of the high points of this period was the appearance of John F. Kennedy, President of the United States, who spoke at a special convocation October 19, 1963. He delivered a major address on foreign policy, one of his last addresses before the tragic events in Dallas, Texas. The previous evening the Hauck Auditorium had been opened to a packed house. It was Homecoming weekend, made even more pleasant by Maine's outstanding 35-12 win over Connecticut.[60]

The institution was progressing well despite some minor upsets. The state's Bureau of Public Improvements attempted to take over the capital construction program, but the school was able to defend itself and retain its position free from political interests. Planning went ahead rapidly in other areas, with new dormitories authorized to house the increase in enrollment. Both zoology and forestry were

A major educational public television station was established in the former women's gymnasium, Alumni Hall. Here equipment is moved from the library, January 1964.

Dean Mark Shibles of the College of Education utilizing cameras of the educational television facility to teach a class sometime in 1964 or 1965.

planning for their new buildings, now ready for construction. A fairly widespread reorganization of courses, and especially a strengthening of graduate offerings, began throughout 1964 and 1965, primarily because of the new funds available. Several new department heads in arts and sciences and in agriculture administered these changes and their attendant relocations. As the university went into its centennial year, 1965, planning was underway for the forthcoming takeover of the deactivated portion of the Dow Air Force Base in Bangor.[61]

The centennial year was an important one in many ways for the much changed campus. A committee of 100 prominent citizens was created in an effort to set policy for the future. A number of publications were made available, including a brief history. The *Maine Campus* published special issues, as did the *Alumni* magazine, and Homecoming, in October, was devoted to the theme of "New Frontiers" at the university as alumni and friends were invited to tour the new buildings: seven dormitories, two dining halls, seven classroom buildings (two at Portland), four other buildings refurbished, and such new acquisitions as the Darling Center, Hauck Auditorium, heating plant (Portland), ETV station and transmitters, service building, University Park, and the USDA building.

Enrollment was scheduled for 6,800 in 1965, an increase of 1,300 over 1964 and the largest such increase in the school's history. Faculty salaries were raised about 5 percent, with disability insurance added to fringe benefits. The instructional budget was increased by' 14 percent, with many new professors, and the library was strengthened in a number of areas. B.A. degrees were authorized for Portland. A number of new administrative officers with responsibility for Student Services, Off-Campus Education, and the Darling Center were also added. The budget rose about 20 percent in that last year of Elliott's presidency, 1965. Besides all the buildings, he, as president, had been responsible for the upgrading of the College of Agriculture to one of Life Science and Agriculture; establishment of a College of Business Administration and of a new School of Law; the development of a community campus at Augusta, a computer center at Orono, a two-year technology program, a better honors program, wide growth in Continuing Education

Dean Edward Godfrey of the School of Law. More than any other person, he was responsible for this new area of the University. Located in Portland, within a few years it became a dominant force in the state's bar and judiciary.

with establishment of centers at Lewiston and Auburn, WMEB-FM to supplement the commercial television schedules, a number of Ph.D. programs especially in chemical engineering and history, and a program to honor distinguished undergraduate achievement.[62]

Elliott had operated like a whirlwind in his years at Orono. The campus was literally no longer recognizable to one who had been there in the thirties. A blunt and forthright man, Elliott irritated many by his style, especially faculty, who found themselves essentially employees, with relatively little to say in development. After the centennial the university would have to absorb and develop these changes, but due to Elliott it had a major basis from which to work. To a great extent the university in its second century would be a memorial to Lloyd Elliott and one could apply Christopher Wren's epitaph and be accurate: If you would see his monument, look around.

Notes

1. Mill tax folder, especially R.H. Fogler to Robert Owen, October 13, 1944; Owen to Fogler, October, 17, 1944; KCM Sills to Legislature, October 16, 1944; Waterville *Sentinel,* October 16, 1944; *Statement of the Board of Trustees, October, 1944;* Orono, 1944; *Laws of Maine,* 1945, Resolves, Ch. 30.

2. Faculty, December 21, 1943; March 17, October 9, 1944; Hauck to Samuel P. Capen, April 13, 22; Capen to Hauck, April 17; Hauck to Harold L. Bevis, May 8; Hauck to Samuel T. Arnold (quote) May 24, all these 1944.

3. *Maine Bulletin, XLVII,* No. 5 [December, 1944]; XLVIII, No. 2 [September, 1945], *Veteran's Education,* Maine Council of Veteran's affairs, *The Maine Veteran,* Augusta, 1946?.

4. Trustees, December 27, 1945; Hauck to L.O. Barrows, November 30, 1945; Hauck to George S. Williams, January 12, 1946 (quote).

5. *Campus,* January 10, 1946.

6. *Campus,* January 24, February 21, March 14, May 16, October 3, 10, November 7, 14, 1946; March 6, 13, 20, 1947.

7. *Postwar Developments at the University of Maine, The Maine Bulletin,* Vol. XLIX, No. 4 [November, 1946]. An excellent description with photographs of life in the South Apartments is in *Bangor Daily News,* October 26-27, 1946.

8. Letter Chase to Hildreth, November 13, 1945; Hauck to Raymond Davis, December 4, 1945; Exec. Committee, Trustees, December 4, 1945; Trustees, May 2, June 15, 1946; Hildreth's address, *Laws of Maine, Special Session,* 1946; Ch. 149, 1251-3.

9. *Leg. Docs., 1946, Special Session,* 1196, 1240, 1245, 1199, 1200 (House); Trustees, July 17 (Augusta); August 8, 1946. *Laws of Maine, Special Session,* 1946; Ch. 149.

10. Trustees, November 2, 1946; Maine, *Leg. Docs.,* 1947, L.D. 66, 67, 68, 138, *To The Members of the Ninety-Third Legislature,* Orono, December 24, 1946; *Laws of Maine, 1947, Resolves,* Ch. 147, 182; *Special Session,* 1947, Ch. 135.

11. *Leg. Docs.,* 1947, L.D. 62; Joint Resolution Relating to Policy for the University of Maine, *A Report To Alumni, The Maine Bulletin,* Vol. LI, No. 10 [March 10, 1949], *Campus,* April 24, 1947. Only the temporary endures!

12. Trustees, November 11, 1939; E.E. Chase to Alumni Council, November 11, 1939; *Dedication of the New Library, University of Maine,* Orono, November 8, 1947. *Campus,* November 13, 1947.

13. *A Living Memorial;* Orono, n.d.; *Your University Has Grown,* Orono, 1949? (fund-raising pamphlets).

14. Folder, "Brunswick Campus," Jasper F. Crouse, "The Brunswick Campus 1946-1949; A Report," typed; Letter Hauck to Frederick G. Payne, September 8, 1949, Portland *Press Herald,* June 9, 1949; Lewiston *Evening Journal,* June 8, 1949; Committee on Administration, December 3, 1947; (report December 2, 1947 on Brunswick, found in files); Trustees, March 18, 1949; *University of Maine, Brunswick Campus, 1946,* Orono, n.d.; *The Brunswick Campus Handbook, Class of 1952,* Orono, 1948.

15. Trustees, October 20, 1948 (Augusta), Exec. Committee, report by A.K. Gardiner, fall, 1948; March 12, 1952; *Campus,* October 2, 9, 1947; September 23, 1948; January 13, 1949; Folder, "Students-Veteran's Education." Memorandum, March 28, 1952.

16. Hauck to Edward L. Bernays, December 3, 1943; Bernays to Hauck, November 14, 1943.

17. Gladden F. Evans, '48, undated V-Mail to Hauck; Hauck to Evans, October 19, 1944.

18. Robert W. Merchant, '48; Harland H. Hatch, '48; Clifford S. Patch, '48; Donald C. Meade, Jr., '48; Kent H. York, '48 to Hauck, undated V-Mail letter, early 1944.

19. Hauck to Robert W. Merchant '45, April 21, 1944.

20. *Campus,* October 21, November 4, 18, 1943; November 16, 24, 30, 1944.

21. Trustees, March 4 (Augusta), April 8, December 3-4, 1943; January 13, 1944; January 31, 1946; Report of the Executive Committee, c. 1946 on building. *By-Laws,* University of Maine Foundation, 1935.

22. Agriculture Faculty, December 2, 1943; April 10, 1944; Tech Faculty, February 26, March 26, 1945; January 21, 26, 1948; Report in minutes February 14, 1945; folder, "Post-war Planning — Arts and Sciences," Kirshen to Chase February 6, 1945; Chase to Hauck July 29, 1942; Kirshen to Hauck September 27, 1943; Proposal August 12, 1940; November 20, December 20, 1944; January 18, 27, February 15, 24, May 8, 1945; Cloke to Hauck, June 13, 1945.

23. Trustees, February 10, 1944 (on education); folder, "Post-war Planning, College of Agriculture," memo of March 5, 1945; A.L. Deering to Hauck, October 9, 1945; Frank W. Hussey to Hauck, May 8, 1945; Deering to Hussey, May 12, 1945; Agric. faculty October 4, 1945; Chase to Hauck, May 8, 1945; Hussey wanted even more humanistic content to the courses, as did Chase, but the faculty committee was not convinced.

24. As examples of many see H. Austin Peck, to John W. Beamsderfer, October 3, 1961; and four page report on chemistry dated, October 10, 1961, all in folder "Chemistry".

25. Faculty, March 17, 1947; October 18, 1948; February 21, May 23, 1949; Faculty Council, Minutes 1-6, "Brief Resume of Its Inception," elections, A & S and Agr., December 5; Tech December 21, P. Educ. December 7, R.O.T.C., December 12 (last two added by meeting of faculty November 16, 1949; Education, January 3, 1949.

26. Tech faculty, November 24, 1952; Arts Faculty, January 5, 1953; Faculty Council, November 17, 1952; December 15, 1952; January 12, 1953; March 15, April 19, May 17, 1954 (on democracy in the University).

27. *Campus,* September 23, 1947; Hauck to Whitney, March 9, 1956; Trustees (Augusta), March 14, 1951; September 20-21, 1960.

28. Comm. on Administration, November 27, 1950; January 8, February 19, 1951; Faculty Council, November 20, 1950.

29. Educ. Faculty, January 6, 22, March 9, 16, 22, 23, 30, 1948; Arts, December 6, 1948; Faculty Council, March 12, 1951 for Hauck quotation.

30. Trustees, "Notes on Budget Hearing," October 20, 1948; January 19 (Augusta), March 19, 1949. The trustees reorganized their committee structure, and gave the executive committee and the agenda group much more power. G.S. Williams to Trustees, July 21, 1948.

31. Trustees, Exec. Committee, (Augusta), May 12, 1949; Trustees, May 20, 1949; *Campus,* May 12, 26, 1949; *Maine Leg. Docs.,* L.D. 459, 1949; *Laws of Maine, Resolves, 1949,* Ch. 141. The Governor, Frederick Payne, did ask for the extra amount over the mill tax, but with no real fervor in his message, *Laws of Maine,* budget message, 1434.

32. *To the Members of the Ninety-Fifth Legislature,* Orono, December, 1950; Also see Hauck to George S. Williams, November 7, 1949 on Payne's strong recommitment to the University.

33. Inaugural Message of Payne, 1951; Budget Message of Payne, 1951; *Financial Facts,* February, 1951, *Maine Bulletin,* LIII, No. 8 [February 20, 1951]; Trustees, September 28, October 24, 1950; January 23 (Augusta); February 1, March 28, May 17, 1951; Budget Committee Report, October 25, 1950; Maintenance and Control Committee, November 28, 1951; Leg. Docs., 1951, 146, 216; *Laws of Maine, 1951* Private and Special, Ch. 213, esp. section 11 on mill tax repeal.

34. Frank W. Hussey Folder, Hussey to Hauck, February 14, April 26, 1951.

35. Hussey folder, Hauck to Hussey, May 17, 1951.

36. Hauck to Edith MacDonald, July 16, 1951.

37. *The State of Maine and the University of Maine, 1953,* Orono, 1953; Comm. on Admin., November 24, 1952; February 23, 1953; *Maine Leg. Docs., 1953,* 92, 124, 151, 1175; *Laws of Maine, 1953,* Ch. 146.

38. Hauck to Deering, October 28, 1954; *Maine Leg. Docs., 1955,* 341; *Laws of Maine, Resolves,* Ch. 178; *Acts,* Ch. 204, 207. To the Committee on Appropriations, February 16, 1955.

39. Whitney folder, Davis to Whitney, December 20, 1954; a sheaf of letters between Whitney and McGuire, 1948-49; Whitney to Hauck, January 13, 1949; McGuire to Whitney, April 8, Whitney to McGuire April 13, 1949.

40. Whitney to Davis, December 16, 1954.

41. Hauck to Whitney, August 20, 1956; Hussey to Whitney, July 27, 1956. "Plant Funds July 1, 1944-June 30, 1954."

42. Typed memo, January 10, 1955.

43. Trustees, November 9-10, 1945; November 5, December 1, 1949; Exec. Comm., October 1, 1949; *Campus,* May 23, 1946; January 9, February 20, 27, March 6, 1947; February 19, 1948; *Bangor Daily News,* June 19, 1950.

44. Hauck ceremony program, May 11, 1949; *Bangor Daily News,* May 9, 12, 1949.

45. Harold W. Stoke (grad dean, NYU), to Hauck, April 4, 1957.

46. *Arthur A. Hauck, A Student Tribute,* program, March 27, 1958; Charles A. Snow to Hauck, c. summer 1954; The best accounts of the University at the end of his tenure are in Howard A. Keyo, *Paper Trade Journal,* October 19, 1950, and "As Maine Goes," in *Harvester World,* Vol. 46 No. 12, Vol. 47, No. 1 [December-January 1950?-1?] the magazine itself is undated.

47. University of *Maine Bulletin,* LX, No. 14 [April 20, 1958].

48. Inauguration of Elliott, in *Maine Bulletin,* LXI, No. 9 [December 15, 1958], *Campus,* October 23, 1958.

49. Lloyd H. Elliott, "What is a University? - The University and the Professor," *Maine Bulletin,* LXV, No. 21 [April 20, 1963].

50. *Laws of Maine,* Special Session, 1958, Ch. 218; Comm. on Admin., October 13, 1958; Elliott to Mark R. Shibles, September 11, 1958.

51. Clausen's address, 1959, *Laws of Maine,* 1959, 1095; *Campus,* October 23, 1958; *Laws of Maine,* Private and Special, 1959, Ch. 174. On Portland merger, see *Laws of Maine,* 1953, Ch. 122; Inaugural Address of Edmund S. Muskie, 1957, p. 1076 *Laws of Maine,* 1957, Ch. 176. The movement of Portland into the state and then Orono's orbit can be followed in the *Leg. Docs., 1947,* L.D. 898; *1949,* L.D. 154, 1108; *1951,* 915, 147; *1953;* L.D. 52, 1289, 1341; *1955,* L.D. 885; *1957,* L.D. 1458, 819, 734, 127;

1961, L.D. 401, 407. (The last is the final merger.) *Laws of Maine, 1961,* Ch. 213. The active person here was Arthur Benoit of Portland, soon to be a major factor in the Trustees and the establishment of the super-University. See Trustees, August 10, (Elliott, Fogler and Benoit met with Portland University trustees, July 13, 1960) September 21-1; a joint meeting was held in Portland, October 15, 1960, and then a dinner meeting on October 16; November 15-16, (Portland), 1960; September 20, 1961; Arthur L. Benoit to Elliott, October 18, 1961 for an important letter; William L. Irvine to Lloyd H. Elliott, December 10, 1959. On the University apartments, Elliott went to Cornell for help in construction and planning, see Elliott to Julius Weinhold, October 29, F.S. McGuire to Weinhold, October 13, 1959; For Trustees, November 18, 1959. Another part of the Portland merger was the take-over of the University of Portland, which came to the University at this same period.

52.   Elliott to Thomas A. Bullock, March 16, to Eldon H. Johnson, May 1, to Frank W. Hussey, June 1, 1959.

53.   Maine, *Leg. Docs.,* 1959, L.D. 118, 342, 371, 391, 393, 394, 395, 396, 397, 496, 497, 498, 610, (Total approximately $7,700,000). See *Maine Bulletin,* LXI, Vol. 7 December 5, 1958.

54.   Maine *Leg. Docs.,* 1961, L.D., 241, 242, 243, 275, 276, 277, 278, 337, 338, 339, 340, 387, 399, 400, 438, 439, 868, 769, ($7,510,000). The statement of facts accompanying the main bill for funds, L.D. 765, said, "It may be concluded that the decade of the fifties brought some progress . . . but the rate of that progress has not been sufficient to keep pace . . . . Turn away young men and women [who] . . . should be supplied by their State University in the 1960's."

55.   Hussey to Lloyd Elliott, January 16, 1963.

56.   Trustees, working materials for 1961-63 biennium; January 26-27, 1960; Public Relations Committee January 17, 1961; Governor's Budget Message, 1961, 1303-1305.

57.   *Annual Report,* President, 1962.

58.   *Laws of Maine,* 1963, Private and Special, Ch. 206, p. 1350; Maine *Legislative Documents,* 1963, 619, 734, 860, 1336. Trustees minutes and other materials in folders, September 18, 1963, October 20, 1963, Elliott to Trustees, June 8, 1962; "Capital Improvements Schedule 1963-1969," dated June 8, 1962; Mimeoed "The Development Program for the University of Maine" all in Trustees folder 1961-62.

59.   Trustees, September 18, 1963, October 20, 1963, April 15, June 5, 1964; Exec. Committee, April 14, 1964.

60.   *Bangor Daily News,* October 19, 20, 21, 1963; *Campus,* October 19, 26, 1963.

61.   Trustees, April 15, June 5, 1964; January 20, 1965, September 15, 1965 (Executive Session). This last on Dow A.F.B. On the Bureau of Public Improvements problem, Trustees, November 20, 1963, January 15, 1964, joint minutes of Executive Committee and Maintenance and Control Committee, December 18, 1963.

62.   Trustees, April 15, 1964, June 5, 1964, February 25, 1965; Elliott to Board February 25, 1965. He left Orono on September 30, 1965. Maine *Leg. Docs.* 1965, 175, 346, 402, 594, 595, 596, 597, 953, 1120, 1576; *Laws of Maine,* 1965, Ch. 119, 273, 443; *Private and Special Laws,* 168, 185, 190, 191. The Hearing on the University requests was February 11, 1965 and was covered in all the state dailies.

CHAPTER NINE

Life on Campus Since World War I

THE LONG-RANGE, continuous, and often humorous battle between faculty and students was the overriding feature of student life during the first fifty years of the University of Maine. Few vestiges of this battle remained after World War I as students intensified their interests in academic and cultural affairs. By the mid-thirties controversies over chapel, smoking, hazing, and dances were relatively unimportant as compared to the earlier days of the school. Maine Day replaced the class scraps and even Maine Night, which had fallen into disrepute in the 1920's. Organizations such as the Maine Masque and the Outing Club were more representative of the average student's interests. Athletics remained important, but even when superior teams were fielded, as they often were, sports did not dominate student life as they did at many schools.

The course of the future was a general concern of most students, particularly in the days of the great debate over American foreign policy in the 1930's. Although earlier students were often serious, one has a sense of increasing intensity as the campus became more democratic and open to more and more people. The veterans after World War II typify this changing situation and students in this postwar period eliminated many of the frilly aspects of campus life in favor of concerts, lectures, and films. Demonstrations became important as students found themselves, along with the faculty, concerned with influencing action. Women took important roles in both the faculty and the student body. A student from the 1870's might have recognized some parts of campus life of the 1970's, but not many. Familiar would be the Maine "Hello," the "Stein Song," commencement, Fernald Hall, and a sense of concern for the future that had always been a part of the Orono scene.

The rapid change in world affairs caused many to worry about the curriculum. One trustee, writing to President Hauck soon after the Korean War began voiced this concern:

> The more I think about it, the more it seems to me extremely unlikely that young men and women, now in college, can look forward to anything like a normal existence (at least what we used to mean by that phrase) in the foreseeable future.[1]

The trustee hoped that the faculty would be teaching to the future and felt that it would do students a real disservice if normality were taught. He did not like the business-as-usual idea that he felt some faculty members were still promoting.

Earlier there had been efforts to encourage members of the student body along serious lines of thought by instituting some Bible study courses, especially to be combined with other religious and sociological subjects for those contemplating either the ministry or social work. The Bible study courses were indefinitely postponed by the faculty.[2] Instead, stricter working habits in regular courses were urged and public lectures offered for which students could obtain credit. For instance, in 1923 the chemistry department sponsored fifteen lectures to be held on Wednesday evenings, all for credit. Other lectures included Greek and Latin, English, education and philosophy, German and romance languages, biology, history and government, and physics and mathematics. The entire lecture series took four years to complete so that all students could attend and get supplementary education on the application and usefulness of their subjects during the regular four-year career.[3]

More important in this intellectual activity was the work of graduate fellowships and scholarships and the hope and cachet of being members of the honor fraternities, either Phi Kappa Phi (1897), Phi Beta Kappa (1916), or Sigma Xi[4]. As J.F. "Paddy" Huddilston expressed it in 1927,

> Let us not be ashamed to dream dreams, dreams of achievement, dreams of conquest, dreams of victory. Let us anchor up close to that splendid truth *Philosophia* where all sciences and all studies are the windows through which the soul looks out upon the world and feels what it may mean.[5]

Grades and grading were always a problem, although not as bad a one as might be thought. In 1916, one parent complained of his daughter's grade in Home Economics — a D. The faculty response to the complaint was dignified and indicated some progress in attitude.

> I am wondering if some of the comments that have been made concerning the grading in Home Economics courses do not come from the fact that we are altogether too likely to assume that a girl, *because she is a girl,* ought to have no difficulty at all in passing courses in sewing and cookery.[6]

The professor went on to wonder if we were sure that sewing and cooking came naturally to women, and concluded, ". . . if so we are on the wrong side of the question."

The arts faculty spent a good deal of time in the early twenties debating what an A grade represented. As a result of the discussion, A was given a wider range. This discussion broadened into an attempt to set a system of making grades of 90 to 100 equal A, 80 to 90 equal B, and so on. Both the arts and the tech colleges discussed but postponed any decision on this method of grading.[7] More conclusive was the discussion in the early thirties on departmental comprehensives, which most faculty wanted and which eventually became standard, at least in technology and in arts and sciences. The arts college continued to worry about the problem, however, spending much time in 1934 on discussion of examinations in general, their types, purposes, and standards. No real changes occurred.[8]

Veterans of World War II did very well in grades, leading to worries that standards had been lowered. Finally, in 1950, a committee was formed to discuss grading. It provided an analysis that is worth reprinting in tabular form.[9]

ALL COURSES IN THE UNIVERSITY
(Percentage)

	1939	1949	1949 (with no basic courses)
A	11.1	13.0	14.0
B	30.4	35.5	38.4
C	42.4	37.8	37.3
D	12.1	10.3	8.0
E	4.0	3.4	2.2
Point Average	2.33	2.44	2.54

The committee report went on to say that basic courses got the lowest grades and B was the average in many upperclass courses. "Grades represent what is accomplished with the aims of the courses. They are not rewards or penalties for interest or the lack of it, boredom, courtesy, neatness, etc." A majority of the faculty felt B was the expected grade for major students in advanced courses and C represented poor work.[10]

A growing number of incoming students were graduates of public high schools: 161 of 283 in 1900-1901, 250 of 487 in 1910-1911, and 752 of 1,186 in 1922-1923. By 1940 only fifty percent of entrants in agriculture were from rural backgrounds and seventy-eight percent of those in home economics, while ninety-two percent of forestry entrants were nonfarm in origin. Those nonfarm figures had risen by a third from the previous accounting in 1925. Most of these students generally came from schools of 100 to 300 students, although the numbers who had gone to larger schools increased rapidly as school consolidation continued.[11]

Of those who graduated in agricultural subjects only 15.2 percent were in farming ten years later according to one survey taken in 1940. However, the percentage of those in fields related to agriculture was higher. Another survey discussed alumni professional careers in 1934.[12]

OCCUPATIONAL SURVEY OF ALUMNI
MAJOR PROFESSIONS
1900-1934

AGRICULTURE (out of a total of 410)

Farming	100
Commercial Agriculture	36
Government	22
Education	93
Business	68

Forestry (out of a total of 90)

Commercial Forestry	23
Education	12
Government	19
Business (not forestry)	26

HOME ECONOMICS (out of a total of 106)

Home	61
Education	21
Hospital (dietician)	10
Other	6

ARTS AND SCIENCES (out of a total of 805)

Education	226
Government	31
Law	24
Medicine	183
Business	13
Banks	177

TECHNOLOGY (out of a total of 1,280)

Engineering Executives	103
Practicing Engineering	528
Education	80
Sales	27
Chemistry	55
Pharmacy	60
Other	131

LAW (out of a total of 284)

Law	203
Business	20

(2,975 responded, 450 were unknown by this time)

These studies, designed to aid in remodeling curricula and keeping the institution up-to-date, seem to indicate that only about half of all graduates actually pursued the profession trained for. If that was an invitation to broaden and widen the curriculum, few professors or students accepted it. The survey results simply were not given much attention.

The people who gave these grades, supervised these students, and taught the courses were a varied lot, as one would expect. One supposes that nearly all of them made some impact on their students, even those who were at Orono for only a short time. Persons like Raymond Pearl and Karl Sax, both distinguished geneticists; Norbert Weiner, an extraordinary mathematician; E. Faye Wilson, an excellent teacher and historian; and Wilmarth Starr in foreign languages were all people whose personality and knowledge must have been significant for their students. However, a list of all faculty would be boring, so the list that follows is one that includes many of the more significant in the university scene in this century, although another person might regard the list as individually eccentric.

Among the persons whom I would single out for notice are Arthur L. Deering, '12, with the extension service from 1912 to 1957 and dean of the agriculture college from 1933. He capped his distinguished career with overseas work for the

Arthur L. Deering, '12.

The portrait is Professor Ava H. Chadbourne, '15, early in her career. Chadbourne began her work with Four-H clubs, did graduate work, and later taught a quarter century in the college of education. An excellent historian in her own right, she supervised a large number of published theses on the stae's educational history. After her retirement, a women's dormitory, shown below, was named for her. The winter scene also provides a view of Estabrooke Hall through the trees.

USDA from 1950 to 1957. Leon S. Merrill was associated with the university from 1907 to his death and was dean of the agriculture college from 1911 to 1933. Lucius Herbert Merrill, '83, was on the experiment station staff as a chemist from 1886 to 1908 and served as professor of agricultural chemistry from 1908 to 1930. Adelbert Wells Sprague, '05, served at various times at Maine, but was professor and director of music from 1916 to 1920, 1926-1927, and 1929 to 1948. As noted before he adapted the "Stein Song" from an earlier march, in addition to doing outstanding work with the band and chorus.

Edith Patch, a major figure in entomology from 1904 to 1937, may well have been the most distinguished woman ever to teach at the university. She also taught English in the agriculture college and produced a massive bibliography of fifteen books and seventy-eight major articles, including a world famous three volume work on the aphid. Patch came to Maine to work for nothing, as it was felt by prospective employers that a woman could not do the work; she "could not climb a tree," as one man said. But acrobatics was not her field, so she survived even that notice. Of all her work, perhaps her address as president to the American Entomological Society, "Without

Benefit of Insects," is the one that she would most want read by others.[13]

Richard W. Harley was at Maine in mathematics from 1904 to 1943, as department head during the last twenty years. Edward J. Allen was dean of arts and sciences from 1936 to 1941, an important though controversial figure. Rising Lake Morrow, of the same era, died suddenly but was important as professor of history and assistant dean. Paul Cloke served as professor of electrical engineering and dean of technology from 1926 to 1950, contributing in the area of engineering education. George E. Lord worked in the extension service from 1934 to 1962, and was also employed by the USDA in an overseas position after 1952.

Of the famous women at Maine two besides Edith Patch stand out: Ava Chadbourne and Caroline Colvin. Chadbourne came in 1914, was a teacher in history and education until 1942, supervised many graduate degrees, and wrote widely herself. Colvin served in the history department from 1902 to 1932. She was chairman of the department from 1906 to 1932 and, as noted before, was Dean of Women from 1923 to 1927 during President Little's tenure. One of the first female Ph.D.'s in the country, she also may have been the first woman to be a department chairman in a major university. Her impact on bright students was immense.

Others deserving mention include William A. Walz, dean of the law school from 1899 to 1918, and Charles A. Brautlecht, professor of chemistry from 1919 to 1947, department head from 1919 to 1935, a famous starch chemist and instrumental in the growth of the pulp and paper curriculum. John Briscoe served as head of forestry from 1910 until 1933 when he died suddenly in an accident. He was chiefly responsible for the forestry curriculum and did much work in both white and red pine research. He was a central figure in the controversy with the state forest commissioner when both positions were part of the same office.

Windsor P. Daggett, professor of theatre and dramatics from 1907 to 1918, was the real founder of the Masque. He supervised Masque tours before 1917 and converted the theatre to coeducation with the use of a lone woman in 1917. His successor, Mark Bailey, served from 1920 to 1947 and was director of the Masque un-

Professor Edith Patch at her microscope, busy at work on research that set extremely high standards.

til 1937. Herschel Bricker followed in that work.

Paul D. Bray, '14, was important in pulp and paper technology and served from 1918 to 1948 in chemical engineering. James N. Hart, '85, was a professor from 1887 to 1937 and remained active for consultation until his death in 1957. Others who made their mark on the university are Geddes Simpson, a noted entomologist; Cecil Reynolds and Milford Wence in English; Edward F. Dow, longtime chairman of the history and government departments; Charles S. Crossland, serving in a variety of administrative posts from the First World War until the 1970's; Matthew McNeary, in engineering education from the early thirties to 1975; Ronald Levinson, a truly distinguished philosopher and defender of Plato; his compatriot, Charles

This interior shot is Mount Vernon Hall. The building, one of the original farm buildings, was remodelled and used as a women's dormitory. The hardwood floors, curved balustrade, and paintings on the walls distinguish this interior sharply from most dormitories. Later bachelor faculty lived here. The building was lost in a 1933 fire. The date of the photograph is 1915.

Virtue; Katherine Miles, in home economics; and a multitude of others. Again, this list might be extended almost indefinitely, but it is an idiosyncratic one of the author and must stand as that.

After the Walz dismissal during the First World War and the problems relating to protection of senior faculty in the Huddilston episode soon after, some attempt was made to secure tenure, in order to protect rights of academic freedom. The first of the meetings for this purpose were held in 1921-22. Some standards were set up, but it was not until the 1940's, with the case of W. Franklin Dove, that tenure became a real problem. Although Dove lost his position, a standard of appeal was set up and arbitrary firing was made much more difficult.[14]

The twentieth century brought other types of problems as well. Sewerage did not give as much difficulty as in the 1880's, but at least once it was significant enough to warrant the president's attention, as this note attests.

I understand indirectly from inhabitants of the men's dormitory and directly through the medium of my nose that the swill pails at the back of the dormitory should be cleaned out daily, if possible. If it can't be done, let me know.[15]

The automobile made its claims. In 1922, for instance, the trustees authorized payment of $302.75 for injuries suffered by an Oxford County woman whose horsedrawn carriage had been hit by an extension automobile out of control.[16] Such accidents were to occur again, and policies on auto usage insurance and maintenance had to be adopted. Throughout the last years of the 1920's, a number of students were

This delightful group is taking tea in the Mount Vernon dining room in 1915. They are faculty wives, perhaps the predecessor of the Thursday Club of the 1940's and 1950's. From left to right one sees Bertha B. Stevens (Wife of J.S.), Laura Hamlin, Kate Estabrooke (the hostess), Annie Woods (wife of the director of the Experiment Station, Charles), Roselle Huddilston (wife of "Paddy"), Mrs. George Hamlin, wife of head of Civil Engineering, Marian Estabrooke, Kate's daughter. Although the time was apt, given their different views, one suspects they were not discussing women's suffrage.

injured and killed in automobile and even the odd airplane accident. By 1931 students were being arrested by both Bangor and Orono police for hitchhiking. Parking was also a problem by this time and remains so, as the wealth of paper in the files indicates.[17]

Occasionally students wandered away and search parties were mounted, as when Winthrop Libby, '34, his sister, Ruth, and two others became lost at Chemo Pond in the early thirties. They were located, drenched but unharmed, by a full-scale search effort.

Later, fuel was scarce during the Korean War and a cold snap caused some doubling up in rooms in an effort to beat the weather. One student assured his parents that all was well, however, in a letter.

We are making out o.k. now so don't worry. We've gotten so used to studying in different places that the whole situation is becoming a big joke. . . . Finished up my research theme in English yesterday so the two biggest jobs are out of the way now. Have a test in modern society tomorrow so I'd better get busy on that.[19]

The student government began to take over routine administration of the dormitories. By 1922 both men and women had separate governments and when even an organization with high purpose was delinquent, the students ended its life. By the early thirties a university-wide Senate was in operation. Its activities were generally confined to issues such as elections, Maine Day, class parts, freshmen rules, pledging, nominations, and so on, although as the war came closer members discussed such items as fire safety, rubbish disposal, Finnish Relief, and the military use of fraternity houses.[20] Fortunately, the fire discussion was only of possibilities, for except in the disastrous fire in Hamlin Hall, no lives were lost, although bad fires did occur in Oak Hall in 1936 and in Balentine and in the South Apartments in 1952. These last fires caused tightening of the fire regulations again, as they had been after the Hamlin Hall fire.[21]

Chapel continued to be an area of controversy. In 1916 the faculty ruled that a warning would be posted after fifteen unauthorized chapel cuts, and with two more absences students would be censured. The increase of females on campus, and thus at chapel, challenged the more rowdy elements at the meetings. However, chapel remained compulsory. The faculty wished the daily chapel abolished. They hoped for three days per week, one program to come from the faculty and two from the students. Trustees were skeptical, although the president promised to meet with the student organizations "with a view to improving the dignity and order of the chapel service." After six months the hour of the meeting was put off until 11:35 A.M. in the hopes of stimulating attendance.[22]

Following World War I a new chapel plan was put into effect. Monday was the president's day, Tuesday was for special music, Wednesday was a religious service, Thursday was students' day, and Friday belonged to the faculty. In 1920 attendance was made optional, but this plan stirred up both alumni and faculty at the time, both groups feeling chapel attendance was important. Faculty met with the students and worked out a program to "establish a better Maine spirit." Compulsory chapel returned with half of each class attending twice a week. A schedule was made: three to five minutes for devotions, ten to fifteen minutes for music or other matters, to be followed by either the "Stein Song" or the "University Hymn." The faculty, attired in caps and gowns, were to lead

A room (104) in Balentine Hall in 1928. The decor is "collegiate," precise, and ordered. The surprise is the amount of space available, without stereos, TVs, and the paraphernalia of todays dormitory rooms.

the exercises. Students were required to attend regardless of their religious affiliations. As a fillip the first week's music was provided by H.P. (Rudy) Vallee, '25.[23]

The next year chapel was reduced to twice a week and attendance was again made voluntary. By 1924 most students wanted no chapel, while the faculty apparently wanted one of a religious nature. President Little abolished the compulsory chapel, requested those not attending "not to congregate near or at Alumni Hall," and prohibited "freakish" clothing for those attending. By 1925 even weekly chapel had ended.[24]

In 1927 a weekly student assembly was re-instituted for a short time along with monthly vesper services. By the thirties, though, chapel had deteriorated to a sometime assembly of all students, usually to hear an important speaker or to honor scholarship, as in an annual assembly each spring. So many of these various meetings occurred, however, that by the early fifties the faculty was complaining that they cut badly into the time for laboratories, particularly in the multiple section classes. Eventually, shortened periods were instituted on chapel exercise days, but the dissatisfaction continued, and finally the calendar committee began to take over the job of assemblies, which merged gradually into the distinguished lecture series of a later period. Assemblies were, of course, frequently significant with well-known personages appearing, and daytime was often the only time they could appear. Some of those who performed were John A. Lomax, who sang his cowboy songs in 1914, and Sherwood Eddy and Raymond Robins, both of whom were exponents of the liberal Christian spirit. Hubert Prior (Rudy) Vallee gave a saxophone recital featuring classical music in 1923, just prior to his departure from the university. Later, in 1933, he returned and spoke of the major influence that Maine had had on his life. Others included Mary Ellen Chase, Alec Templeton, Eddie Cantor, Norman Thomas, Alexander Kerensky, Trygvie Lie, Paul Blanshard, and more recently, Country Joe and the Fish, who put on a major concert in the late 1960's.[25]

High jinks and hazing continued to be part, but a lessening part, of campus life. Students continued to plague entertainers at local theatres, but with the advent of films these outbreaks were not very significant. A serious fracas, perhaps the last of that sort, did occur at the Strand Theatre in Orono in 1926.[26]

Freshman-sophomore banquets and their attendant difficulties continued, but most now took place on campus. A bad interracial incident occurred at one of these events in 1909, but faculty had most of the affairs under control and when there was another outbreak between classes in 1921, suspensions ended the episode.[27] In the late twenties a Rising Day ceremony, instituted for students to pass from one year to the other, was the scene of some ugly battles between freshmen and sophomores. With women part of the classes now, the rough play of before was potentially even more damaging. In 1926 a small fight resulted in one women being dunked in ice water; in 1927 two small riots broke out near Stevens and Wingate Halls; in 1928 there was a series of kidnappings, but the festivities were more good humored than before. Three women painted their class numerals on public property but were caught and given social probation for a year. Some student displeasure boiled up over this, and the probation was removed after three weeks and a talk by the dean.

South Hall, in Orono, opened as a cooperative self-help dormitory for women in 1935. It remained in use as a counterpart to the Cabins until after World War II.

Fernald Hall exterior, after its conversion to the college book store. This photograph, taken just after World War I, shows the Wingate tower just behind Fernald. Students painted grafitti (here concerning the traditional enemy Bowdoin) on the building. The different tinted bricks are no longer as distinct.

In 1929 Rising Night was very tame, but in 1930 an infusion of tear gas from sophomore chemists caused a fairly bad melee. Students were diverted by a fire downtown and the firemen improved the situation by soaking not only the buildings but the students as well. The bag scrap and pajama parade continued, but with limited participation. In 1933 a severe thunderstorm enlivened the pajama parade. Freshmen generally did not like this kind of atavistic remnant, however, and during Hauck's presidency the customs were all abolished and replaced with Maine Day in 1935.[28]

Hazing still remained, but was confined to fraternities, which were themselves a minor but recurring problem. In 1925 and 1927 a series of "raucous" house parties and difficulties with young women in those houses led Presidents Little and Boardman to try and bring some order, morals, and ethics to the houses by appealing to their alumni. The house parties did not happen often, but the initiation did, and from time to time attempts were made to curb the worst excesses. In 1933 the arts faculty tried to curtail initiation rites, as did the *Campus* soon after the war and again in 1948 with a major campaign against "Hell Week." Some fraternities did move to abolish, and an agreement was struck as to the extent of the rites by the early fifties. Excesses still occasionally occurred, as in 1959 when one house involved itself with an exotic dancer. But apologies were tendered; the incident simply seemed an aberration. By the sixties fraternities were still an important part of the school, though they no longer dominated campus and class politics as

The bookstore interior, taken sometime in the 1920's. The banners appeared on dormitory room walls. Prominent features are the candy counter, and the soda fountain, where students went for "cokes" and conversation until the middle 1950's. The site is now a lunch room and cafeteria (still with plenty of conversation.)

much. As fraternity and sorority members became more and more a declining minority, some predicted the organizations' demise. But their role in housing (fraternities in particular), along with alumni memberships, would probably keep them alive. One thing the houses, along with the rest of the campus, did until sewerage was improved in the early fifties was to give rise to cases of "Oronitis" in summer and fall from the bad drinking water. In 1948, as an example, eighty-four people reported to the infirmary with this disorder, a statistic that helped in the campaign for the new sewer system.[29]

Other issues which troubled both students and faculty were rules about dances, smoking, drinking, and of course the relations between young men and women, especially after the col-

lege moved strongly to a coeducational undergraduate body. Sometimes the responses to these issues were simply amusing, as when the *Campus* editorialized in 1915, "Ragtime is too prominent here at Maine." Occasionally parents wrote about the "indecent dances" that were supposedly held at Orono, but they were always reassured. President Aley remarked to one such distraught mother, "It has not been the policy of the University to attempt to regulate the dress of the young women." This more or less remained the school's policy. Faculty were worried about admission dances, some feeling that they were a "real menace to the genuine tone and true spirit of social functions at a University." Debate continued, not about the dances per se, but about their length. Still, as the faculty debated, the students danced, and by 1925

Junior Week

This typical and lovely drawing of the period is from the 1924 Prism, *where it appears along with a score of others. Was the artist Frederick G. Hills, '24?*

James Gannett could write back to President Little:

> Dr. Norlin (University of Colorado) gave an address at our annual dinner and believe me, Maine is not the only institution having financial difficulties or being bothered with jazz.[30]

Whether or not the two were bound to one another can be doubted, but the dances continued.

Smoking was forbidden in the classrooms, but some of the faculty broke this rule, as some still do, and to this day the matter is discussed among deans. More difficult was whether to allow women to smoke on the street, or

anywhere. Many felt smoking was the sign of a loose woman, so it was forbidden. But women continued to smoke and to petition to have the rules changed. By 1930, after a series of petitions, the women were polled as to their preference. Of those responding, 138 smoked, 64 did not. One hundred seventy-seven wanted the rules removed, 35 were indifferent or voted no. Parents, also polled, were more harsh, but split about evenly. A campaign was begun to get letters opposing change, and the trustees obliged by retaining the rule. But petitions continued, and late in 1934 the trustees ruled that this was an administrative matter and ended the prohibition.[31]

Technically the campus was dry, but there was drinking. In 1919, to rid themselves of trouble, university officials purchased an Orono house which had been a bootlegger's center. Still, bootleggers and their product were evident in 1923. With repeal, however, the university was more concerned about who held the liquor licenses, and conferred from time to time with local authorities. Later, when drinking became troublesome in the dormitories the president and deans attempted to control it, but with little success. The following committee notation tells much.

> President Hauck reported that he and Deans Wilson and Wieman had held a conference with [the proprietor of a local restaurant] regarding the sale and consumption of liquor in his restaurant. He was given to understand that the University would expect the restaurant to observe the law in every detail.

Gradually ideas changed. Drinking became less of a problem and drunkenness, never heavy, gradually disappeared from the campus. By the early sixties, the chief agency concerned with drinking disbanded because of lack of work.[32]

Relations between the young men and women also caused anxiety for the faculty and trustees. By 1918 women were allowed to use the library at night, and in later 1918 young women were allowed to entertain men not "oftener than once in two weeks." This was the nose of the camel into the tent. Soon the women were petitioning for more freedom. Complaints about food broadened to comments on the rules about men callers, dances, and chaperones. Even the president was moved to write to one matron, "Can we conscientiously recommend a University whose rules and regulations for women are narrow, and unjust?'' By 1923, the rules for Balentine Hall for summer session indicated the extent of reform. Students were to be in by 10:00 P.M., and if out after 8:00 P.M. had to sign out for a stated place and time. One could enter an automobile after 8:00 P.M. only with the permission of the matron. No musical instruments were allowed except from 12:00 to 2:00 P.M., Monday through Thursday. Callers could come Friday, Saturday, and Sunday until 10:00 P.M. Women simply could not drink anywhere. In addition, the famous university rule of 1923 was printed and distributed broadside throughout the campus.

IMPORTANT NOTICE

Attention is called to the following vote of the Board of Trustees dated October 4th, 1923.

'Any student found with any portion of his body in contact with any part of a fire escape, except in case of an alarm of fire or fire drill, shall immediately be suspended from the University.'

By Order of the Board of Trustees
University of Maine.

Occasionally the rules were broken; in 1927 a young woman or two used the fire escapes to dodge the matrons; in 1953 one young man would not restrain himself and was captured in the act of rapping on a window. He received censure, reprimands, and counseling "to aid him in getting the best possible results from his college course." Most students did not have to rely on such methods, or so one believes. Occasionally mass meetings were arranged such as the giant panty raid of 1952 which was thwarted by the immense thunderstorm and terrific lightning that came just as success seemed imminent.[33]

As may be remembered, one of the university-wide events was Maine Night. Typically it was the night before the Bowdoin game, when alumni returned to sing songs, listen to addresses, and dance to the music of the university orchestra. By 1912 the theme had shifted somewhat from football, especially as Governor-elect Haines was the main speaker. By 1925 the affair had declined into a drunken scene, about which the faculty began to complain and refused to attend. The *Campus* decried the event, calling it a ''night for artificial spirits and liquid indulgence,'' and

The class of 1917, austere and haughty in their sophomore role, issued these instructions to incoming Freshmen. This set went home on a postcard to mother, but without comment.

hoped it would disappear. Maine Night hung on into the thirties as part of Homecoming, but in fact much of the reason for it had disappeared with the development of alternative recognition assemblies such as Scholarship Recognition Day, an annual occurrence after 1924, though one not always well attended.[34]

Other occasions of similar provenance were the annual Maine Day when students and faculty policed the grounds and in the evening participated in skits lampooning the faculty and President Hauck, who loved these efforts. In 1961 the faculty skits disappeared and by the end of the decade Maine Day too, as campus cleanup had become the province of the regular

MAINE DAY—1935

Evening Program: 7:00 to 11:30 P.M.

Part I: 7:00 to 9:00 P.M. Five Big Stunts.

Part II: 9:30 to 11:30 P.M. DANCING. All students are guests of
the Faculty

Stunt 1. Freshman Class: A Medley Extraordinary.

2. Sophomore Class: Big Time Vaudeville.

3. Junior Class: An Original Play:
   "The True Story of the Rescue of Pale Face Penelope" or
   "The Boy Scouts in the Ozarks."

4. Senior Class: A Playette:
   "One-Star Finale." Scene: Staff Meeting of Small-Town
   Newspaper."

5. Grand Opera: "Julius Caesar" (Apologies to Shakespeare)

Conductor: Reeve Hitchner   Director: Geo. Wm. Small

Properties and Cat's MIAOW: Carl Otto
Lightning and Darkness: Warren Bliss
Prompter (Very important): Geo. Dow

ORCHESTRA

| Karl Larsen | Adelbert Sprague | Harry Smith |
| Franklin Dove | Wm. Sweetser | Robert Drummond |

Reeve Hitchner, Conductor

DRAMATIS PERSONAE

Caesar: Arthur Hauck   *Portia*: Benjamin Kent
Brutus: Lamert Corbett   *Pindarus*: James Gannett
The Three Conspirators: *Cato*: Charles Weston
  Cassius: James Moreland   *Soothsayer*: Olin Lutes
  Casca: Paul Cloke   *Ballet Comique* (Special Release
  Trebonius: Cecil Fielder   from Metropolitan)
The Triumvirate: Irving Pierce   John Klein
  Octavius: Theron Sparrow   James Waring   Delyte Morris
  Antony: James Moreland   William Small   Roger Allen
  Lepidus: Charles Crossland   Edward Brush
Calpurnia: Harley Willard

PROLOGUE: Maine Day Song, by the Ballet

Act I: Scene 1: A Street in Rome (They plot)
    Scene 2: Evening in Same Street (They plot some more)
Act II: Scene 1: Brutus' Garden (Plot thickens)
    Scene 2: Caesar's House (Very sentimental)
Act III: Before the Capitol. (Caesar gets it good and proper)
Act IV: Room in Antony's House. They vow REVENGE
Act V: Battle of Philippi. (All piled up)
EPILOGUE: Stein Song.

DANCING until 11:30
(Lou Kyer's Rhythm Boys)

*Program for the first Maine day. These events were
presented at the end of a day of donated work. Each
class and the faculty presented skits with the president,
deans, and well-known faculty featured. These events
remain as high points of memory to observers.*

maintenance crew. In recent years spring fairs of one sort or another, along with outdoor concerts, have replaced these days. The campus mayoralty campaign related to Maine Day also disappeared sometime in the sixties, since few wanted to run and even more were offended by the increasingly vulgar nature of the campaigns. It was easier to go to Bar Harbor for the day and avoid the crush, and many did. These events fulfilled a real need in their heyday though, providing an alternative to the brutality of earlier times.

Students were polled off and on, so it is possible to ascertain something of their feelings on politics, world affairs, and other concerns. In 1924 most of the faculty favored Coolidge for the presidency, although there was support for both Davis and LaFollette. Of the students, 313 men and 81 women supported Coolidge, while 126 men and 28 women wanted LaFollette. Fifty-seven men and 17 women voted for Davis, while one man voted for William Z. Foster. In 1928 no vote was taken, or at least printed, while in 1932, 656 were for Hoover, 200 for Roosevelt, 129 for Norman Thomas, 2 for Foster, and one for Reynolds, the prohibition candidate. In 1936 the student newspaper supported Landon, as did the student body. He received 520 student votes and 41 faculty votes, while Roosevelt received 253 student and 22 faculty. Lemke received 24 and 2, Thomas 29 and one, and others received 43 student and 2 faculty votes. In 1940 Willkie had 750, Roosevelt 281, Browder 37, and Thomas 5. Faculty supported Roosevelt 32 to 30. FDR could not even win in 1944 among the student body when Dewey received 466 to his 327. Thomas got 14 votes, and the Socialist Labor Party candidate got one. Later elections also tended to support the GOP candidate, until 1964.[35]

The student body was polled regularly on foreign affairs in the thirties, but it was also polled on non-international events. In 1917, the first of the latter polls was taken when students were asked to comment on religious matters. The school split 171 to 163 over whether religious training was a province of the college; 195 found value in chapel, but 155 did not. One hundred eighty-four felt chapel helped in their general religious feeling; 117 did not. Only 14 wanted it abolished, while 297 were for retain-

Julius Caesar, or the ancient world, often played a role in the faculty skit on Maine Day. This photo shows Professor Eileen Cassidy and President Hauck demonstrating their version of an ancient dance, while the faculty chorus hails them – togas, diadems, sandals, and all. This skit was given in 1951.

ing it. One wonders how the poll was conducted.[36]

At the end of 1919 and the beginning of 1920, classes were shortened and special discussions held in regard to the League of Nations. Many faculty members were very concerned with this issue, and a petition went forward supporting the League. Professors Bancroft, Colvin, and Huddilston, and various students all addressed the assembled college community prior to a straw poll being taken. When the results were totaled, 94 students and 28 faculty favored ratification of the Versailles Treaty and the League without change, and 128 students and 1 faculty opposed the treaty in any form. Three hundred one students and 26 faculty favored the treaty with the Lodge reservations; 334 students and 66 faculty favored a compromise between

the Lodge and Democratic reservations. Maine's vote results were nearly the same in percentage as those of other colleges.[37] When other votes were taken in the thirties, a countrywide student organization produced questions on the national issues for the vote and Maine seemed to echo the overall voting patterns.

When polls were taken, local campus issues were also sometimes discussed. For instance, in late 1939, eighty-seven percent of students wanted a one-day reading period before finals. Of those voting, 421 to 260 wanted plus and minus grades, and 439 to 174 wanted the school to hire name orchestras for dances. On socialized medicine, 422 supported and 172 did not; 515 wanted the college bear present at games to 76 who did not; 307 supported a date bureau while 267 were opposed. Eighty-six percent wanted a campus variety show. Only nineteen percent thought there were too many extracurricular activities in 1939. Later, forty percent thought liberal arts education should be subsidized, and sixty-three percent favored a G.I. Bill.[38]

These polls do not prove very much, but are interesting as indicating that students had fairly strong opinions and were willing to express them, although the expression was done through a series of polling boxes in the library, book store, and Stevens Hall.

Interests in the polls may have varied, but a large number of students were concerned, especially about the forthcoming war. The military had always been a source of some disturbance on campus. In 1897, a "good majority" of the debate society ruled that the R.O.T.C. or military department was "not of material worth." In 1913 an Intercollegiate Peace Association was formed on the campus, but the president was a supporter of Wilson so the campus went to war, although some went unwillingly. One or two students attempted to avoid R.O.T.C. in this period, but word always came down to participate. It was not until after the First World War that these matters became a real issue.[39]

At first the campus attitude was evidenced at Armistice Day celebrations and exhibits by the military of their work. An effort was made to enlist the president in achieving better faculty attendance at these affairs. Students occasionally protested about inspections during this period. By the early thirties, with the campus peace movement beginning to show strength in the country, more and more attention was paid, with editorials, polls, and debates. As the *Campus* expressed it for the pacifist group in 1931:

> They [the American Expeditionary Force] fought because of the blind, unquestioning obedience which is taught by the militarists, and pointed to as one of the glorious achievements of militarism. They fought to make the world safe for democracy — and Al Capone![40]

One of the reasons for the furor in the newspaper was that students occasionally refused R.O.T.C., then mandatory for graduation. Now, whenever Armistice Day rolled around it became an occasion for debates and polls on whether the U.S. should go to war, and why or

under what circumstances. Bills were brought up in the legislature to make R.O.T.C. optional; they failed, however, to get out of committee, in part because the trustees opposed them. Confrontations, or near confrontations, occurred over the American Student Union, the Oxford Peace Pledge, as well as peace assemblies and demonstrations in 1937 and 1938. Public debates were held over R.O.T.C., over militarism, and, after Munich, over the war itself. Professors, most notably E. Faye Wilson and Rising Lake Morrow, attacked the Munich settlement as an aid to Hitler. In 1938 James T. Shotwell spoke at a peace assembly. During the three preceding summers, institutes of world affairs were held on the campus to discuss foreign affairs and the U.S. role in them. In 1939 another peace assembly was held, and in 1940 C.C. Little spoke at the Armistice Day gathering urging students to uphold their principles and in this way kill war. It was now time to prepare for the after-war period, said Little, in order to avoid other wars in the future.[41]

The *Campus,* whose editors were often leaders in the antimilitaristic movement, supported the Republican cause in Spain, ran a column throughout 1939 entitled "Foreign Affairs," sponsored speakers on Jews in Germany, attacked the Dies Committee, and sponsored polls as to what the country should do in foreign affairs.[42] When the war came to Europe the *Campus* remained fiercely opposed, although the editors did support repeal of the arms embargo.

Interest on the campus in courses related to the war took a sharp upturn in 1939-1940. The polls continued, with students opposing action generally, but support for England, France, or Finland grew. Two university coeds were at the Sorbonne when war broke out and their story received strong play. By November of 1939 the *Campus* could ridicule the efforts to observe Armistice Days before and call for days for the future, a future which the paper predicted would be riddled with depression if dependence on war appropriations continued. Of students polled, seventy-nine percent wanted war profits taxed, in the event of war, but most did not want to go to war as the year 1940 approached.[43]

A drive in behalf of Finland netted some funds in early 1940, but *Gone With the Wind,*

These three photographs illustrate several aspects of World War II on the campus. At top soldier-students drill in the stadium. To the left university women are engaged in some sort of laboratory work. This may be an ordnance inspection class. The bottom photo shows the men listening intently in a large classroom. The professor may be Charles Weston who was prominent in the pre-radar course at the beginning of the war.

then opening in Bangor, received more interest. There was debate over war aims in the fall of 1940, and in early 1941 the *Campus* supported Lend-Lease and began to reprint letters from Canadian scholars who had left to join the British side. In the spring, funds were raised for British relief. At a special meeting of the Women's Student Government, Maine women were adjured to aid in the crisis.[44]

In the fall of 1941 the campus began to realize how deep the crisis was, and a tinfoil drive was begun. On October 9 Hauck spoke to the International Relations Club and showed slides on "Hawaii and National Defense." When Pearl Harbor came Maine students must have known at least where it was. The campus had been busy in the days just prior to the war's coming on December 7. The previous Friday night, December 5, the military ball was held with Hal McIntyre's band. Campus women had given a party for men at the Bangor Air Force Base on the twenty-eighth of November. Other events of interest in that week included the news that Maine had three members of the allstate football first team and the Masque opening on December 8 of *Outward Bound*, a play associated with Leslie Howard.

The next week the *Campus* called for "Brevity Plus Action." The editors said they wished they knew what to say, and after discussing the "ivory tower," plaintively asked, "In two years, where will we all be?" The songs of that week on the campus Hit Parade were "Blues in the Night," "Rose O'Day," "I Said No," "White Cliffs of Dover," "Chattanooga Choo Choo," "String of Pearls," "Shrine of St. Cecilia," and "Deep in the Heart of Texas." By the time the campus would be normal again, or even remotely so, many of the readers of the newspaper would have visited some or all of the sights named in these songs. The war had come, and for students, faculty, administration, trustees, and above all, the campus as an institution, life would never be the same again.[45] Oddly enough, Maine had, through its continued discussions in both the newspaper and the classroom, done as good a job in preparation for this new world as it was possible to do. If the students thought of it, they might have been very happy they had gone to Maine.

Organized athletics continued to play a considerable role on the Orono campus. Apparently, the last of the bad riot situations occurred in 1915 when the special train going from Orono to Bowdoin had the misfortune to stop at Waterville for water and coal. The band played a few selections and a cheer was given for both Colby and Maine, but Colby students began to tear banners off the cars. A student hit the emergency brake, two or three were kidnapped,

This photograph shows a women's athletic match from the mid-1920's. The large white building, later moved, was occupied by several different administrators as a home. The game appears to be some variant of soccer. Women played primarily intramural sports and this may be a physical education class.

and a small riot began. One yardsman was hit with a brick and another broke an ankle, but the train pulled out leaving some persons in Waterville. The two college presidents intervened in time to prevent a nasty incident. On the way back to Orono, after a 23-15 win, the train sped right through and the replay was confined to shouts.[46]

By the twenties attempts were underway to organize athletics better and to provide guidance both on the campus and in the state. C.C. Little, a prominent athlete in his own day, was instrumental in this move. As J.N. Hart said to a correspondent,

I hope that you did not infer from my letter we have any objection to athletics, or are prejudiced against them. We have to be on our guard, however, against certain men of a different type than Mr. Farrington, who are interested in athletics rather than their studies.[47]

Little called for an emphasis on physical training and the end of the "tramp" athlete so prominent in college sports up to that time. Little hoped to end professional coaching, which he thought was the real enemy. He defined athletic necessities to his coaching staff in 1923 as sympathy with high scholastic standards, rigid and absolute standards of training, regular meetings of athletes with the graduate manager of athletics, participation of all men in physical training, willingness to assist one another, and a cooperative effort to set standards for other departments.[48]

After an incident with Colby over a poorly officiated track meet in 1924, efforts were made to improve athletic relations. A university athletic association, founded in 1923, was the basis of control, and a state athletic association and a New England one, also founded in 1923, became the guiding forces in intercollegiate athletics.[49]

Baseball continued to be a major sport, although the heights reached during the great years of defeating "Colby" Jack Coombs and playing the New York Giants did not recur. The university fielded a representative team, considering its short season. After World War II, southern trips tended to lengthen and strengthen the season, and in 1965 the baseball team went to the college world series. Occasionally players such as Phil Dugas and Carl Elliot played in the high minors.

The women's field hockey team, from sometime in the late 1920's. Those in the back rows are moving and blinking suggesting that the photographer was an amateur. One impression is that these young women were smaller than today's counterparts.

The male student athletic managers in 1921. These men are H.C. Crandall, '21, basketball, H.W. Fifield, '22, track, W.B. Cobb, '21, football, and R.W. Graffam, '22, baseball. Managers aided in coaching in those days.

An early basketball team, 1921 or 1922. The players include C.S. Woodman, '22, H.C. Crandall, '21, the manager, E.S. Judkins, '23, and I.D. Taylor '23. Other names are obscured on the photo back. The knee guards and heavy uniforms attest to the strong contact of that period. Again the players seem small compared to today.

Prior to World War II basketball was a less successful sport. In fact, the sport was abolished in 1929 for game difficulties, (rough play ruled the sport then), poor facilities, and poor support. A student referendum upheld the ban and basketball did not return until 1937. Following World War II a different approach to the game, marked by a racehorse style and high scoring, led to more student interest, and it became a major sport. Maine was never a regional power; games with Rhode Island in the forties may have been the height of the basketball record.[50]

In the years before 1940 Maine was a track and field stronghold. University teams won the New England Intercollegiate Cross County Championships from 1913 to 1915 and in 1921-1922, 1927-1928, and 1934-1935. In 1915

Maine teams were the national champions, in 1934 they were second, the only college of its size, other than Manhattan, ever to place as well. Maine teams also won the New England Intercollegiate Track championships from 1927 to 1930. These were the years of Chester Jenkin's coaching. During that time E.F. "Rip" Black, '29, placed third at the 1928 Olympics in the 16 lb. hammer. In 1936, Donald Favor, '34, was second in the same event. Other significant athletes in this sport included Donald Firlotte, '55, who was world class in cross-country and long distance running.

Football remained the major sport at Maine, with Fred M. "Foxy Fred" Brice as coach until the World War II period. His successor, Edward "Eck" Allen, was also successful, although forced to retire after a small rebellion

A spring track meet at Orono either in 1921 or 1922. The leader and winner is Seth Pinkham, '22, a noted dash man in his time. The observatory, the college farm, Winslow Hall and Alumni Hall can be seen. Students are perched on every point of vantage.

Francis Lindsay, '30 and Henry L. Richardson, '30, co-captains of cross-country, tieing for first in the 21st annual intercollegiate meet, Van Cortlandt Park, November 25, 1929. The Damon Runyon types at the finish line savor their bets and urge them on. Maine always did well in cross-country events.

The Maine football squad leaving the field at the half of the Bowdoin championship game, November 8, 1919. This championship team had a splendid season capped with this 18-0 victory.

by students. Since that time David Nelson, Harold Westerman, and Walter Abbott have guided the team fortunes. Stanley M. Wallace was trainer and professor of physical education for much of this period and was a significant factor in these teams' successes.

Some of the football teams deserve mention. The 1926 team, utilizing new rules, had five touchdowns scored by interior linemen and two more by the ends. The 1933 entry lost only once, to Holy Cross, and Romaine Romansky ran eighty yards for a touchdown against the Cross. The immediate prewar teams did well, losing only a few games, but playing Columbia for three-fourths of the game even, before losing 15-0, in 1941. After the war the university dominated the state, but sometimes found itself out of its class when playing larger schools. Among the players one would mention are Roger Stearns, '41, (thought by many to be the best football player ever fielded at Orono), Roger Ellis, Thurlow Cooper, and John Huard, as well as Dick DeVarney. Ellis, Cooper, and Huard all played professionally after their days at Maine.

Fred "Foxy Fred" Brice — long time football coach at the University.

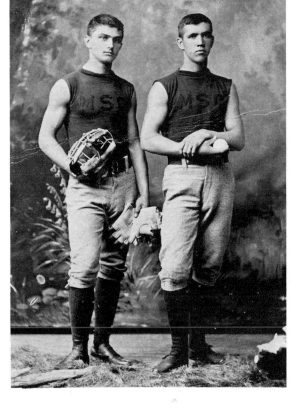

Right: Seymour E. Roberts, left and Frank L. Small, both '88, starting battery on the baseball team. Note the flimsy glove carried by Roberts.

Below: An early action photograph at a track meet. From the clothing one would date this pole vault prior to or in World War I era.

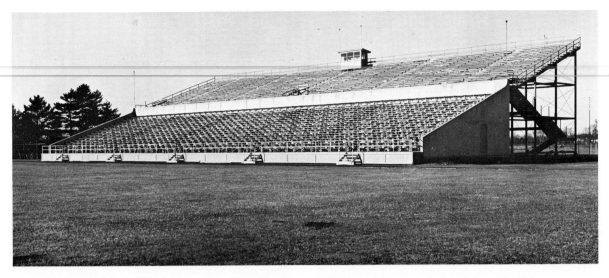

The new stadium seats, constructed after the athletic fields were moved behind the field house.

Harold Westerman, coach, and co-captains Walter Hirst, '66, and Alan Riley, '66 of the 1965 Tangerine Bowl team. This was taken at a skull session prior to leaving for the south.

Sports remained relatively minor in the total scheme of things at Maine. Occasionally the *Campus* would discuss overemphasis,[51] but most were happy. Off-campus press specialists always wanted more, but the balance was regarded by most as within the Maine tradition. Sometimes major attention was focused on sports, as when a student died in a boxing match in 1932 or when a Maine team became a national power as in rifle, but on the whole they were used to train the mind and the body and did not dominate the school. An example is the year 1965 when Maine went to a bowl in football and was of national prominence in baseball, yet the campus took these events in stride — with pleasure, but in stride.

Commencement continued to be the biggest event for most students, although the number and length of the various ceremonies diminished through time. In 1913 Junior Week was still considered the "greatest event of the college year," featuring debates, speeches, the Masque, fraternity open houses, the Junior Promenade (in this year it was Japanese style with "cold tea" served in the booths), and on Saturday a major military drill and baseball with Bowdoin in the afternoon for the state championship. Saturday night the junior exhibition speakers performed and the next day a major vespers service capped the week. The school then got down to finals and graduation.[52]

These two illustrations demonstrate clearly the difference in commencements over time. The top photo shows the academic procession at the June, 1952 commencement. Heading the procession is John H. Reed, '42, later governor of the state. Symbolic of the process of learning is the library with the line of graduates between whom the dignitaries pass. The other illustration is the menu at the commencement dinner June 24, 1885. A deluxe dinner, beginning with ham, beef, chicken and turkey, followed by entrees of salmon, plain lobster, and lobster salad, was served to the graduates of 1885 and their guests.

After the war the ceremonies were less grand, and graduation became more important. In 1924, for instance, Thursday, June 5, was the occasion of the honor societies' initiation, banquet, and scholarship recognition day. On Friday came class day exercises, Senior Skull initiation, and the president's reception. Alumni appeared on Saturday for their day of banquets and dances. Sunday opened with baccalaureate, followed by a band concert, and a ground breaking for the Memorial Gymnasium. On Monday commencement was out-of-doors in the morning, followed by the commencement ball that evening. The other classes no longer took as much part as they had in the nineteenth century.[53]

In 1941, the last prewar commencement, Junior Day was May 2 and the Skull initiation was moved to that day. All events were held then at an assembly with a speaker. Commencement week was June 5 through 9; the commencement ball was on Thursday, June 5. Friday featured a pageant by the All-Maine women and an informal student dance. On Saturday alumni day was held. After the obligatory band concert came the featured event, ground breaking for the new library, followed by banquets, dances, and other social occasions. Baccalaureate was preached on Sunday, and on Monday the commencement exercises were held in the gymnasium.[54]

This sort of program was continued, with a compression of time. After the war the only change was the eagerly awaited charge to the graduates by Registrar George Crosby on Class Day. This day became more and more a personal day for graduates, sometimes with outside speakers discussing world affairs by the late sixties. Graduation exercises were often held out-of-doors (and as often interrupted or

MAINE STATE COLLEGE, COMMENCEMENT DINNER,
WEDNESDAY, JUNE 24, 1885.
BILL OF FARE.

BOILED.

| Ham, | Tongue, | Corned Beef. |

ROAST.

| Turkey, | | Chicken. |

ENTREES.

| Salmon, | Lobster Salad, | Plain Lobster. |

VEGETABLES,

Mashed Potatoes,   Green Peas.
Cucumbers,   Radishes,   Lettuce.

RELISHES.

Currant Jelly, Cheese, Spanish Olives,
Horse Radish, Cucumber Pickles, Tomato Catchup,
French Mustard, Halford and Worcestershire Sauces.

PASTRY.

| Strawberry Pie, | Lemon Pie, | Custard Pie. |

DESSERT.

Lemon and Vanilla Ice Cream, Mixed Cake, Pineapples,
Oranges, Apples, Raisins, Almonds, English Walnuts and Pecans, Strawberries and Cream.

| Tea, | | Coffee. |

FLOWERS.

YOUNG & DeROCHER, Caterers.

The cover of the sheet music to **The Stein Song.** *H.P. "Rudy" Vallee, ex-'25, made the song famous.*

shortened by rain) because facilities simply were not large enough to accommodate all those wishing to view or participate. As an extra touch, the university recognized the different sort of students with special certificates for wives for a time after 1949.[55]

Again one should make the point that this is a history of the college and not its alumni. However, some of them merit particular attention. Perhaps the most famous is Rudy Vallee, ex-'25, who was a student for several years before his music claimed him. He remained interested in Maine and was a considerable benefactor to his alma mater, even though he did not graduate. After his successful recordings of the "Stein Song," some of the royalties came back to Orono. Faculty in his time were very proud of his record.[56]

Other students who represent the Maine spirit, but who were perhaps not so famous as Vallee, included Mary Ellen Chase, '09, a noted educator and author; Kingdon Harvey, '30, a Maine journalist of note; Lee Vrooman and his wife, Helen, both '18, who founded and nursed Maine-in-Turkey throughout the 1920's; Lore

Rogers, '96, a truly distinguished researcher in dairy husbandry; and Louise Bates Ames, '30, the famous child psychologist. Others include Styles Bridges, '18, Percy Leddy, '21; Errol Dearborn, '23; Beatrice Johnson Little, '24; Mildred "Brownie" Schrumpf, '25; John S. Andrews, '26; David Stevens, '29; and many others. To continue the list would be invidious as well as idiosyncratic. The point is made that the university helped to mold persons who used their minds to good advantage after graduation.

Life at Maine was interesting and it was fun, but it was also work which demanded a high intensity, increasingly so as time went on. The following selections from the diary of one student indicate what daily life was for her in the 1930's. Life was not much different for other students at other times, at least for those with a thirst for knowledge.

July 6, 1933 — Have been making out college lists, an appalling number.

Sept. 12, '33 — Found rooms in Balentine, no roommate yet.

Sept. 14, '33 — After assembly we attended a lecture by Dean Muilenberg. Had Campus inspection and a test in English comp. In the afternoon we had an awful math test. Reception at night.

Sept. 16, '33 — Registered early, money mix-up.

Sept. 18, '33 — Went to Int. Rel. Class. Looks like piles of work. First half of a French placement exam. Got pretty lost.

Sept. 19, '33 — . . . Got my textbooks (expensive)

Sept. 26, '33 — '37 boys tore down flagpole of '36.

Sept. 27, '33 — Interesting discussion in English . . . . The pyjama parade and fight was today. What a fight! Most of the girls got trophies. So did I.

October 11, '33 — Berneice and I and the girls went to Prexy's reception. Nice but dull.

November 17, '33 — Had a package . . . Did the reproductive system of the earthworm in Zo lab, and I certainly made a mess of mine . . . .

April 11, '34 — Sunny and warm . . . More excitement Freshman-Sophomore scrap . . . great gangs going up and down cutting hair. Lots of boys cut . . . Boys in trolley to Bangor.

April 12, '34 — What a day! I was quietly talking . . . Sophs raided house. Was the attic a sight! Gang of Frosh girls down to cabin and 'egged' and 'lipsticked' sophs. I fought out in front. Sophs called time . . . .

The cheerleaders in 1935. The head cheerleader, Leo Murphy, '36, is the man in front with the megaphones. The male-female ratio was usual for those days.

May 1, 1935 — Cold and blowy. Maine day. Worked hard all morning raking. Saw competition in afternoon . . . . Entertainment splendid. Skits funny and faculty play marvellous. [Later] Maine day evening one of the best if not the best since I have been here . . . . Hauck did a good job as the corpse with the lily . . . mayor, led the cheers and Stein Song at the end.

October 14, '35 — Very busy. Got an A in Ed and a B in German. Y Cabinet meeting.

November 7, '35 — Studied German . . . Read in libe. Went over to Peace demonstration at 4 . . . . Speaker ranted too much . . . Studied for prelims.

January 28, '36 — . . . Took Ed Exam. Just like last years.

Feb. 20, '36 — Went to L.I.D. meeting at night. A waste of time, I think. Back and did a fair amount of work.

May 21, '36 — Over to Libe and Stevens. There was a tea here for faculty and we cashed in on food. . . . Fire-drill. BR-r-r.

Sept. 28, '36 — Did practice teaching for first time. Large class, very unruly.

October 22, '36 — Practice teaching dull. Back and taught section for an hour. Not so bad at it, talked too much.

November 19, '36 — Went at night to Phi Kappa Phi initiation, then to hear Coffin read poetry. Very well done.

June 14, '37 — Showery, but very nice before graduation. Very nice, impressive ceremony. Coffin's address good.[57]

These excerpts are from a very complete diary kept by a 1937 graduate. Although she was a member of All-Maine women and the usual honor societies, she was an ordinary Maine native who came to the university for an education. The school provided that in a serious businesslike manner as it had since 1865, and as it still does. There was plenty of time for play, nearly all of which was good-natured and harmless, but education remained the central focus for the overwhelming majority of those, both faculty and students, who found themselves in Orono.

Notes

1. A.E. Whitney to Hauck, December 7, 1950.

2. Faculty, February 17, March 12, 1917; October 14, November 10, 1919; October 9, November 19, December 10, 1923; *Accreditment of Bible Study for Students of Secondary Schools*, Augusta, 1922.

3. Arts and Sciences faculty, November 5, 1917; *Announcement of Lectures*, Spring Semester, 1923.

4. Trustees, June 11, 1917; Faculty, November 19, 1923; June 4, 9, 1925; Phi Kappa Phi, *Initiation and Banquet*, 1922; *Information Relating to the College of Arts and Sciences, University of Maine,* Orono, 1916?; J.S. Stevens, to R.J. Aley, March 17, 1916; Percie Turner, *A History of Delta Gamma Chapter; Phi Beta Kappa,* 1973.

5. J.F. Huddilston, "Taking Account of Stock," *Phi Kappa Phi Journal,* 1928, 47-50, quote from p. 50. I am using a separate reprint of the speech given at Honor Societies' Banquet at Orono, June 9, 1927.

6. Hart Corr., 1915-1916 Folder 2 [C-R], E.A. Little to Hart, February 21, 1916; Hart to Little February 23, 1916; Little on S. Merrill to J.N. Hart, February 28, 1916, quote. Home Economics had recently been established as a major field of study at Maine.

7. Arts Faculty, March 1, December 3, 1920; January 3, 1921; Tech Faculty, September 26, 1921.

8. Arts Faculty, May 7, 1934; Tech November 28, 1932; April 4, 24, 1933.

9. Faculty Council, April 17, 1950; May 15, October 16, 1950 (results of questionnaire of that date).

10. Faculty Council, October 16, 1950, quote; March 12, May 14, 21, 1951; April 9, 14, 1952. Veteran's grades are discussed in the *Campus,* March 20, 1947. Of the men on the Deans List, an overwhelming amount, 297 to 85, were veterans. For more on grades, in 1914 of 1,298 grades by entering freshmen, 11.6 failed, and 27.7 received honor [A-B] grades. Some interested mathematician should follow grades (and they are available) from 1865 to date and determine whether any change has in fact taken place. The 1914 grades occur in Hart to C. Parker Crow II, March 29, 1915, Hart Corr. 1915-16, Folder #2 [C-R].

11. Pres. Corr., 1922-23 (undated, unsigned memo); College of Agriculture, entering freshmen, 1940.

12. College of Agriculture, February 24, 1941; October 28, 1940, "Report of Committee on Student Background." Pres. Corr., 1934-35, "Occupational Survey" October 17, 1934.

13. See Portland *Sunday Telegram,* December 27, 1936 for a biography.

14. Faculty, May 8, 1921; Agr. Faculty, May 10, Arts Faculty, June 2, December 16, Technology Faculty, October 31, 1921; Griffee to W. Franklin Dove, January 6, 1942; Griffee to Hauck, January 21, 1943; Transcript of hearing, August 18, 1943; Griffee to R.F. Ludlum, February 20, 1945; most of these are in folder, "Dove's Dismissal File," in Experiment Station files. Trustees, June 23, August 18, 1943. Some are duplicated in President's files. Dove was a good researcher who served Maine from 1925, but failure to fill out the proper reports after much effort to get him to do so caused his dismissal. Tangential but important were his unauthorized experiments to create a unicorn, which caused some at the University much pain, and others much laughter. Interviews with Elizabeth Murphy, Geddes Simpson, and others.

15. C.C. Little to Tom Morton, October 18, 1932, in T.S. Morton file.

16. Trustees, Executive Committee, August 11, 1922.

17. *Campus,* October 1, 22, November 5, 1931; Faculty October 20, 1931; October 13, 1941.

18. *Campus,* November 23, 1932.

19. David A. Chute '53 to Mom and Dad, January 13, 1950, in president's files.

20. *Campus,* December 13, 1922; October 7, 1925 (end of Junior Mask); *Constitution and Bylaws of Women's Student Government,* Orono, 1923? *Constitution and By-laws of the Men's Student Senate,* Orono, April 1, 1924; I have read the student Senate Notebook, with correspondence from 1934-1947; meetings cited occur on May 21, January 2, 1940; January 6, 1943.

21. *Campus,* January 16, 1936; Stewart Diary, January, 1936; Trustees materials 1952-53; report of Henry Doten, December 24, 1952.

22. Faculty, June 15, November 13, December 11, 1916; March 13, June 14, 1917.

23. Trustees, June 4, 1920; Faculty, June 16, 19, 1919; May 10, June 3, 8, 1920; April 11, September 19, October 10, 17, 14, December 12, 1921; R.P. Gray to Aley, c '17.

24. Little Notice, November 25, 1924; Western Maine Alumni to Trustees, April 18, 1921. Trustees, February 12, (Bangor), June 3, September 24, 1921; Faculty, March 10, June 10, November 10, 1924; November 12, 1925; *Campus,* November 26, 1924.

25. Faculty, December 12, 1927; Faculty Council, January 16, February 20, March 20, 1950; November 29, December 6, 1954; January 10, February 21, March 14, 1955; *Campus,* January 12, 1914; November 16, 1923; May 25, 1933.

26. *Campus,* May 15, 1905; January 28, 1926.

27. *Campus*, May 1, 1905; May 6, 1909; October 12, 1921; Hart. Corr., 1921-22 (Folder #1), Hart to J.S. Behringer, February 23, 1922; Faculty, March 18, 30, 1920; April 4, 11, 1921; Aley to George A. Potter, June 19, 1919.

28. *Campus*, April 22, May 27, 1926; April 21, May 26, 1927; April 11, 19, 26, May 3, 1928; April 4, 1929; March 20, October 9, 16, 1930; April 13 (Editorial), 20; May 19, September 29, 1932; September 28, 1933; April 19, May 3, 17, 24, September 27, October 4, 1934; Stewart Diary, September, 1934.

29. *Campus*, April 15, 22, October 28, 1926; October 11, 18, 1945; October 14, 1948, November 18, 1948; Faculty, March 9, 13, 1925; March 14, 1927; Arts faculty, November 11, 1933; Committee on Administration, November 24, 1952; March 9, 1959. The 1926 notes refer to a typhoid epidemic in the fraternities in which three people died.

30. *Campus*, May 14, 1915; Aley to Myra E. Sullivan, September 26, 1917; (her letter to him is September 10); Faculty, June 6, 1919 (quoted motion); throughout the years 1921-23; Letter, Jim to Pete, April 16, 1925.

31. Folder "Tobacco — Use of (Smoking)", "The Smoking Report," 1930, Trustees, December 4, 1930; June 1, 1932; November 2, 1934; Faculty, March 12, 1923; October 4, 1934.

32. Wm. T. Haines to Fellows, May 18; Fellows to Haines, May 17, 1909; more letters in 1923, 1956, see Augusta K. Christie to Hauck June 8, 1956; *Campus* May 17, 1956; Trustees, June 8, 1935, letter to Orono selectmen; Committee on Administration, November 17, 1947 (quote); April 26, 1961.

33. Arts faculty, October 7, 1918; Aley to J.M. Harrington, January 25, 1919; to K.C. Estabrooke, October 28, 1918; to Miss Kellogg, April 4, 1918 (quoted), undated petitions, 1918, 1919; Typed memo, "Regulations for Balentine Hall, Summer Session, 1923," Trustees, October 4, 1923, and a number of the broadsides, Committee on Administration, November 28, 1927; March 5, 27, 1953; and the panty raid on May 22, 1952. This occasioned an assembly with an address by President Hauck the next afternoon.

34. Various scholarship day programs, Maine Day programs, *Campus*, November 15, 1904; November 11, 1925; November 5, 1931, March 7, 1935; Faculty October 12, 1925; Tech September 28, 1931; Haines to Aley October 16, November 4, Aley to Haines October 17, 1912; Committee on Administration, February 9; May 29, 1959; Faculty Council, May 15, 1950; Bangor *Commercial*, March 7, 1925 lauding the move toward scholarship recognition, and reprinting Little's speech.

35. *Campus*, October 8, 15, 1924; October 27, 1932; October 15, 22, 29, 1936; October 31, 1940 (urges backing of FDR at inaugural February 20, 1941); November 9, 1944; on FDR's death, the paper remarked, "F.D.R. was a great man," April 19, 1945.

36. W.E. Barrows to Aley, January 6, 1917.

37. *Campus*, March 18, December 16, 1919; January 13, 20, 1920. Faculty October 14, 1919; Fred K. Hale to Aley, March 29, 1919; Aley to Hale March 18 with petition from faculty.

38. *Campus*, March 9, 23, September 28, October 5, November 2, 16, 23, December 7, 1939; January 11, October 3, 1940; August 12, 1943.

39. *Cadet*, December, 1897; *Campus*, October 31, 1913; Hart Corr. 1915-16 (Folder #2) C-R, Max D. Davis to Hart July 16, 1916; Hart to Davis, July 18, 1916.

40. Faculty, November 8, 1920; L.R. James to Little November 13, 1922, with program of Military Demonstration November 22, 1922; Harold W. Ross to Little, August 9, 1923, *American Legion Weekly,* August 10, 17, 1923, is Little opposed to further aircraft proliferation? they were, and he was. *Campus*, November 19, 26, 1925; December 10, 1931; January 14, 21, 28, February 4, 11, 18, March 17 (quoted), 1932. Apparently, from internal evidence, the administration dampened the exchange, and forebade a poll on pacifism.

41. Lengthy folder "Carl G. Garland, class of 1929"; Arts College, June 10, 1932; Trustees, March 2, 1933; March 9 (Augusta), 1937; many letters in re Richard Howard, from October 7, 1935 to January 8, 1936; Hugh Ross Newcomb to Hauck, April 29, 1937; April 22, 1937; Maine Institute of World Affairs, Programs, July 9-10, 1935; July 22-23, 1936; July 21-22, 1937; *Campus*, November 16, 23, 1933; November 15, 1934; February 7, 15, 1935; March 25, April 15, 22, 1937; December 9, 16, 1937; January 20, April 11, October 27, November 10, 1938; April 27, 1939; November 14, December 5, 1940. Compulsory R.O.T.C. hung on until the sixties, although some exemptions took place, Comm. on Admin., October 3, November 7, 1949. Perhaps the most famous of those who refused to serve in R.O.T.C. was Charles E. O'Connor, '31. He received his degree long after his refusal, when he took a few tests during an Easter vacation and received his degree late in 1936. He was assistant dean of men in 1931-32, and Boardman felt his refusal deeply. As he said to him, come and take the tests, go through the motions, as "military work given at the Institution is not for the purpose of teaching our young men to make war. I consider its first aim is to prevent war." O'Connor later served as secretary of the Maine Christian Association from 1942-1950, Acting Dean of Men in 1950, and director of student Religious Association from 1950-53. See his folder, letter Boardman to W.B. O'Connor (his father) November 22, 1930; Hauck to O'Connor, June 2; O'Connor to Hauck May 30, 1936. On the local scene, and formation of Bangor League for Peace and Freedom, see Arts and Science, January 13, May 4, 1935. Dean Muilenberg presided at the meetings.

42.   *Campus,* November 12, 1936; January 19, February 9, March 9, 23, April 20, May 4, 11, 18, 1939.

43.   *Campus,* September 15, 28, October 5, 12, 19, 26, November 2, 9, 16, 23, December 7, 1939.

44.   *Campus,* January 11, February 15, September 26, October 3, 1940; February 6, (letter), 27, (Women's Student Govt.), March 6, April 10, May 15, October 2, (all letters), March 6, April 24, 1941.

45.   *Campus,* September 25, October 9, December 4, 11, 1941.

46.   *Campus,* November 9, 1915.

47.   Hart to W.G. Colby, September 15, 1922, Hart Corr., 1921-22 (Folder #2).

48.   Little to Alumni, October, 1923; to Kanaly, et al., June 12, 1923.

49.   Pres. Corr., 1924 on Colby problems; Constitution and By-Laws, Maine 1923; New England, 1923; Orono, 1923?

50.   *Campus,* October 31, November 7, 14, 1929; February 18, 25, 1937; Boardman to W.C. Cornish, January 28, 1930.

51.   *Campus,* November 11, 1948; for boxing death, see March 3, 1932.

52.   *Campus,* May 6, 1913; for a similar one see Faculty, March 12, 1918 for the program for that year.

53.   Commencement Program, 1924.

54.   Junior Day Assembly, 1941, May 2, 1941; Commencement Program, June 5-9, 1941.

55.   *Campus,* May 26, 1949.

56.   Vallee's entrance correspondence is in Hart Corr. 1921-22 (Folder #6), Vallee to Univ., March 8; Hart to Vallee, March 10; Hart to N.W. Boston, July 19; to Vallee, July 19, 27; Boston to Hart, July 21; Hart to Boston, July 27; to Martha B. Hopkins, August 23, 1921. Rudy Vallee, "I Always Wanted to Be Just As Busy As I Am Now," *Maine Alumnus,* February, 1930; Hart to Boston, December 15, 1921; F.S. Youngs to C.E. Crossland, May 2, 1931; Trustees, May 7, 1931; *Campus,* May 15, 22, 1930. The W.C.T.U. was unhappy with the spirit of the song and this also occasioned many letters. *Maine Bulletin,* LXIII, No. 16, May 10, 1961. See his two memoirs as well.

57.   Stewart diary, in my possession at this writing.

CHAPTER TEN

Beyond the Campus

ALTHOUGH THIS HAS BEEN primarily a history of the University of Maine at its Orono campus and has dealt to a great extent with campus relationships with the legislature and other official bodies, the real constituency of the institution lay beyond its Marsh Island boundaries in the citizens and taxpayers of the state. For them the Orono campus was a place to find out whether a camp water supply was polluted, whether the strange animal was coyote or dog, and the answers to questions on Maine historical facts, legal opinions on road widths, and English grammar.

From the earliest days the administration in Orono found itself organizing a service designed not only to answer knotty problems, but to anticipate them. An extension of the university was in order. This outreach program manifested itself in many ways, ranging from Farm and Home Weeks to educational television, from Four-H clubs to conferences on game warden training. Serious scholarly and scientific research also was a province of the campus from the earliest days. A book would be needed to deal with these programs adequately; this chapter is but an attempt to indicate the breadth of the undertaking as well as its depth. Perhaps another will someday flesh out the description of this program and render a fuller report on activities, with a deeper analysis of amount of success.

Maine's citizens did indeed look to Orono for answers to their problems. Some of them were importunate and short-tempered. This letter serves as a scene setter.

Dear Sir:
I want a Principle for Clinton High School this fall. What I want is a teacher that is a good explainer and can keep good order. It has got

beyond controll; and what I want is a teacher that can and will streighten it out. No other nead not apply. Please write me at once.[1]

The university has always supplied teachers. In the earliest days of the college, students taught in district schools throughout the state during the eleven-week winter vacation. Later, summer schools were an important source of teachers for school superintendents, supplying both newly certified instructors and teachers more highly educated in the changing methods and principles of pedagogy. Summer sessions have run, with one or two exceptions, since 1895, and although other types of courses have been offered, the sessions have been designed primarily for teachers. In that first year, three-week courses were offered in chemistry, physics, natural history, domestic economy (the beginnings of home economics on the campus?), pedagogy, child study, and civics. Some of the pupils came from fair distances away, and the public lectures, social meetings, concerts, and a picnic supper around a campfire arranged for them began established traditions still for the most part upheld by the summer session. By 1902 the meeting was five weeks long and eighteen courses were offered. More recently a twelve-week session has been available.

The university has also provided programs such as teacher cadet (or student teacher) training, nursery schools for local children, and a rather extraordinary project by Lee and Helen Vrooman, both '18, and Ruth Crockett, '25, called Maine-in-Turkey. Begun in 1922 and lasting until the depression, this was a part missionary, quasi-Peace Corps effort in the Near East. Student donations supported the work, and it was the recipient of the major portion of campus charitable contributions during the decade.[2]

Whitman H. Jordan, '75, M.S., '82, Sc.D., '96, Professor of Agriculture and Director of the Maine Agricultural Experiment Station, 1887-1896.

W. M. Munson, Professor of Agriculture (Horticulture). He laid out the campus paths and planted many shrubs, trees and flowers.

Extension of the university's educational effort beyond the campus began almost as soon as the school began. Professors were always available for lecturing which, for the struggling school, was a method of obtaining favorable publicity. By the early 1880's faculty participation in Farmers Institutes was extremely important. For example, Walter Balentine and G.M. Gowell held such an institute in Canton on November 7, 1883, in which they discussed the experiments going on at the college farm in manuring, feeding values of hay, cream testing, and other farming matters. Throughout the 1880's these institutes continued to be very popular. Some of the professors were blunt with their audiences: Gowell told an Orrington audience in 1885 that he had been there before with his message and they had not heeded it, "but I am expected to come here and make this talk, simply because I am not accredited with knowing anything that is *practical."* The feeling that college professors really hadn't much to offer other than entertainment was always a bone of contention.[3]

By the 1890's the institutes and lectures were held mainly on creameries and dairying, as the state attempted to deal with the revolution that farm machinery and readily available western lands had created in Maine farm life. Some of the meetings were held at Orono, as well as in the field, and the secretary of the Board of Agriculture reported to his constituents: "The professors at the College have all been ready to help in the work as far as their duties would permit . . . ."[4]

Sometimes the professors combined in a sort of traveling road show. In 1894 W.H. Jordan, W. M. Munson, and G.W. Gowell went to Norway, South Paris, and on to East Sumner offering a series of three lectures on "Practical Principles of Agricultural Science," "Small Fruits, Orchards, and Spraying," and "Cattle Breeding and Feeding." These meetings were all-day affairs, with the women of the Grange providing dinners. A local newspaper reported that "the meetings have been well attended by the best class of farmers, and the speakers were able and instructive throughout the whole course of lectures."[5]

The success of such meetings led the college to establish short courses for farmers; the first, in dairying, was begun in 1892. Tuition was free until 1900, and the costs of room and board

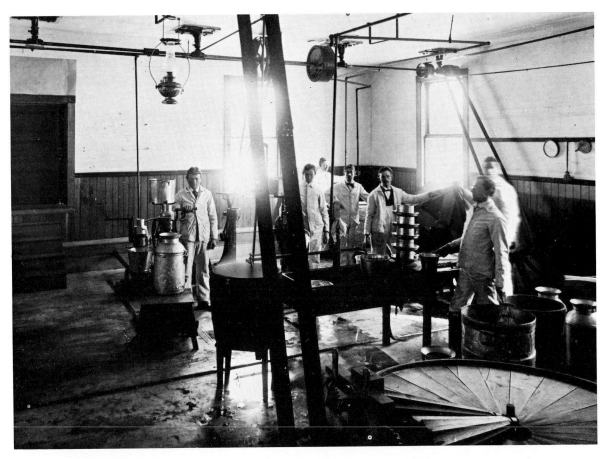

Interest in dairy farming created a need for a facility in Orono. This is the dairy room in the old poultry building sometime in the 1890's. Cream separators and churns may be seen. Note the method of illumination hanging from the ceiling.

were minimal. The courses were generally held in the winter, although other times were tried. General agriculture was added in 1893, horticulture in 1894, and poultry management in 1901. The best attendance in these courses seemed to be from 1909 to 1913, when their content was stepped up substantially.[6] The college newspaper favored the short courses as an aid to the state's farmers, remarking in a 1903 editorial.

> We are glad to note the beginning of the short course in agriculture . . . These courses are designed to meet the needs of young men and women who intend to follow agriculture as a business and cannot take the longer courses. The usefulness of such a course is apparent to every intellectual agriculturist and the fact that more students are availing themselves of the opportunities offered is a testimonial of their growing popularity.[7]

Shorter extension and demonstration schools remained significant and popular throughout the state, especially in dairying. In 1907, for instance, sixty-two such schools were held, averaging sixty-five persons in attendance at each, to "provide new agriculture" for the state's farmers.[8]

After 1914 and the passage of the Smith-Lever Act mandating federally funded extension activities in agriculture and home economics, such short courses were fairly routine. Twenty-seven farmers did demonstration work in Kennebec County alone in 1914. The next year 430 persons registered for a two-day extension school on poultry in Caribou, and Leon S. Merrill, the extension director, reported that he had, in one week, given talks in Bethel, Cherryfield, Greely Institute, East Hebron, Kennebunk, and the Penobscot Pomona Grange. Others were also busy. In that year twenty-four schools held 133 sessions for 4,392 attendees. In 1916 attendance rose to 5,485, with the addition of demonstrations in home economics. New work was started in soil fertility with a soil survey begun in the state. To press this work more quickly, the automobile was used. Schools in soil testing were taught at Cumberland Center, China, South China, Standish, Exeter Mills, and Bridgton. The soil specialist said there was some resistance but 258 persons had registered. However he described his work at that time primarily as "conducting a manure campaign" for he had to proceed slowly.[9]

Later such short schools were even more common; poultry was important in the 1930's, and during the Second World War schools on dealing with the future, the return of veterans, and an effort to understand philosophical positions were offered and were popular.[10]

The longest running and, in many respects, the most successful short school associated with agriculture was the Farmer's Field Day begun in 1891 and continued to the present, although with a name change to Farm and Home Week in 1927. Special trains came to Orono from all over the state bringing farmers and their wives (1,700 by 1894) to a baked bean

dinner, tours and inspections of buildings, drill by the Coburn Cadets, and speeches by members of the State Board of Agriculture, state Grange, the state Pomological Society secretary, and various agricultural editors. Those attending were asked to bring forks and mugs, and it was announced in 1897 that both the major railroads offered half-fare tickets. In 1900 the program was not held, but a series of farmer's institutes was provided on the campus during that summer.[11]

In 1907 a farmer's week was held from March 11 to 15. Visitors were presented with lectures on milk production, tuberculosis in cows, grass and clover cultivation, rural schools, taxation, ensilage, storage of fruit, and a dozen other topics. Thirteen counties were represented, mostly by Grange members. All told, 114 registered. By 1909 a women's section providing information on cost of living, milk usages, household labor, and preservation of food had been added, as had a major analysis of rural communities, town affairs, and other similar topics.[12] Much of this interest was a reflection of the country life movement promoted by Theodore Roosevelt and Liberty Hyde Bailey.

Attendance rose steadily as the program grew wider in content: 402 attended in 1916, 604 in

A very early field day, perhaps the first, in 1891. A buggy parking lot!

1927, 1,282 in 1930 and 1,628 in 1935. By 1941 the printed program ran to twenty-eight pages and something was provided for everyone. In the late forties and early fifties, attendance ranged from 4,300 to 4,500. However, changing conditions meant some other directions were needed. After study the program was continued in 1964 on a three-year trial, and when it was renewed, the emphasis had moved to a series of short schools or demonstrations for special groups. However, the program had fulfilled its purpose during its long run.

Faculty did not always welcome the yearly event, particularly as it usually came during the spring recess. A letter from Dean Joseph Murray to a friend is illustrative of faculty reaction.

> The predictable Farm and Home rain storm is in full sway. However, the visitors seem to pay as little attention to the weather as they do to the parking regulations.[13]

When the farmers could not come to the university it would sometimes go to them; in 1906, 1910, and 1911 special trains were sent out — University of Maine Farming Specials. These trains, a project of the Bangor and Aroostook Railroad and President Fellows, were a smashing success. F.W. Cram, of the railroad,

Another field day photo in the middle nineties. The photographer is either on a building or in a tree!! President Harris supervises the food service at bottom left. The man in the center of the shot is the Commissioner of Agriculture, B. Walker McKeen. The variety of headgear and facial hair is wide.

was enthusiastic when approached. He responded to Fellows immediately; "I am averse to much 'talking it over' where a needed course of action is plain. 'Get there' is best. 'Talk it Over' is the sweeter after getting there." He offered four cars at no cost, to go where the college liked and when it liked.[14]

Response to the idea was generally favorable, although the Maine Central Railroad was not as receptive as the Bangor and Aroostook. Edward Mayo, a Waterville editor, wanted to send a reporter along and later wrote Fellows offering thanks and congratulations "on the gift of that 'gospel train' " going to Aroostook County. After the first trip was over the Bangor and Aroostook remained enthusiastic, the Maine

Central agreed to support the project, and the train went to other parts of the state in June. The state Board of Agriculture defrayed some of the costs for the second trip.

The four car train had special exhibits from the College of Agriculture and the experiment station. Poultry, injurious insects, weed seeds, soil testing, milk testing, and other items were covered in the exhibits. Crowds of people greeted the train when it arrived, and at the larger stops the professors aboard gave lectures. Large crowds appeared at Masardis, Fort Kent, Ashland, Monticello and elsewhere. Island Falls gave a rousing and immense welcome to the touring group. Apparently the planned-for Maine Central train did not run in 1906, but a

The farming special of the Bangor and Aroostook Railroad in 1906. The large crowd has been massed by the photographer to show the impact of the train visit. From the clothing, it is clear that it was a high social occasion when the "Farming Special" arrived and the professors gave their lectures.

The interior of one of the farming special railroad cars. Exhibits were mounted and displayed on both sides of a center aisle and the visitors moved between them.

C.D. Woods giving an address to a crowd at a stop of the farming special. Talks were not long but did stress the virtues of scientifically conducted farming practices.

An early farmers' field day gathering. The building is the first Estabrooke Hall, used as a dining commons, and located between Oak and Aubert Halls. This dates the photo about 1913. Tables were set out for the meal that was a highlight of the visit to the farmer's college.

Professor Herschel Bricker and members of the Maine Masque while touring India in 1962. This world tour of the student organization climaxed fifty years of travelling theatre produced at the University, although this trip was certainly the longest by far.

Registrar George Crosby and Professor Vincent Hartgen inspect a portion of a travelling art exhibit in 1963. The art, from the University collection, went to schools. As many as fifteen a year were provided and were booked solid. This experience in aesthetics was often one of the first for Maine school children, at least in a formal way.

second train did in 1910, and a third returned to Aroostook in 1911. These efforts may not have taught much scientific agriculture, but they did bring the university to the people, which in the long run was their major purpose.[15]

Somewhat similar in purpose were the extensive trips taken by the glee clubs, orchestras, and especially the Maine Masque. These trips were taken throughout Maine, although occasionally the Masque went into Massachusetts. In 1914, for instance the Masque offered Moliere's *The Learned Ladies* to audiences in Brownville, Houlton, Presque Isle, Millinocket, Deering, Gorham, and then to audiences in northern Massachusetts. At Presque Isle in late February 800 people attended a performance. The play was later produced on campus. The musical clubs usually went on their tour during spring vacation, playing to packed houses, particularly at the annual Portland concert.[16] Later similar programs were held on the campus to train such organizations as the state's high school debating teams, and in 1941 the Masque held a two-day theatre festival with sessions on costuming, radio drama, and one-act plays. The festival closed with a major production of *Hamlet,* one of the first uncut versions given in the United States at any level.[17]

Of course these ventures helped to educate the students as well as people outside the school. For a number of years the technology faculty sponsored trips to various firms for the graduating seniors. In 1913 the group inspected the roads and shops of the local railroads (while agricultural seniors visited a local creamery and greenhouses in Bar Habor.) In 1914, forty mechanical and electrical engineering students spent a week in Boston, traveling on the Bangor boat and visiting a number of firms in the area. The 1916 trip extended to New York and New Jersey. The *Campus* ended a story on the 1906 trip with "the week may be said to have been one of the most profitable of the whole college year."[18]

One of the most interesting ways in which extension in the truest sense of that word operated was in the Boys and Girls Clubs, to be called Four-H clubs after the passage of the Smith-Lever Act. These clubs had been begun in New York as early as 1898 for the purpose of growing crops, raising animals, and, specifically for girls, preparation and preservation of food. Early in 1914 a state YMCA conference was held in Maine to discuss organizing such groups. By the end of that year nineteen local leaders had begun thirty-four clubs, with twenty-six groups of boys raising potatoes, five mixed groups raising poultry, and three groups of girls canning produce. The first of these girls groups was Ava Chadbourne's club at Macwahoc which met initially on January 23, 1914. Marie W. Gurdy, the first girls' leader, went to Tennessee to study with another successful leader, who in turn came to Cherryfield to organize a canning group that first year. In 1915 Gurdy spent two weeks going along the Maine Coast among the islands, holding thirteen "missionary" meetings for the movement.[19]

The groups increased steadily and extension bulletins were written to describe how to organize and run such clubs in the state. A state contest and various county contests were held to award donated prizes to the youngsters who had done the best job with their projects. At the state contests, held in Orono, dignitaries spoke to the assembled groups on the virtues of farming and on other topics. Following a major meeting held at Belfast, Waldo County became an especial leader in this field. The Grange, the YMCA, and business organizations such as the Maine Canners Association and several banks sponsored clubs over the state.[20]

One hundred fifty-six persons attended the third annual state contest in 1916. Some winners of state scholarships and prizes then went on to the Eastern States Exposition, although only one first prize, in potato judging, was granted there to Maine entrants. During the wartime period it was "easy to enroll members." In 1918, with strong support from teachers and school superintendents, the numbers enrolled reached 9,065 members in 514 clubs. A school garden project helped immensely. Six county field days were held. Prize money totaled nearly eight thousand dollars. Projects included potatoes, pigs, poultry, sweet corn, and garden vegetables. One young woman engaged in the work while home from college on sick leave wrote to the university leaders with her comments.

I am enjoying the work immensely and I hope it won't get too much for me, as I haven't fully recovered from my illness of this winter. If only the children will profit from my work to such an extent that the parents will want it as a permanent thing in the schools of Wiscasset, I shall be happy. It is a lot to wish for, I know.[21]

These serious young people were winners in the statewide poultry competition sponsored by Boys and Girls Clubs in 1915. For most this was the first trip to the University, but for many, the return would be to register as Freshmen. The young women were substantially larger than their male counterparts and somewhat more self-assured as well.

Two examples of work at Highmoor Farm, Monmouth, a department of the Agricultural Experiment Station. The top photo shows experimental spraying of apple trees around World War I. These experiments had a great impact on Maine farming and have been continued since the 1890's. The bottom photo, from the late 1920's, is a pollenization experiment.

In the 1920's a major public relations campaign was undertaken to broaden the program. Printed articles, a club bulletin, and new handbooks were produced. During that winter 283 community planning meetings were held to support the movement. The Eastern State Exposition trips began to be anticipated by members and Maine won more prizes. By 1924 Maine clubs numbered 237 with 4,128 children. Some of the members were very enthusiastic: one boy reported, "I set two hens; one on fifteen eggs and the other on the 26th of April."[22]

Through the rest of the twenties the club sizes remained about the same with from 280 to 340 clubs working on from 4,300 to 5,700 projects. Beans, canning, chick raising, cooking, housekeeping, sweet corn, dairy, garden, pig, potato, poultry, room improvement, sewing and apiculture were the most usual projects. Some of the clubs were topical in this period; one was even named "Lucky Lindy." In the early thirties the numbers of youngsters increased, and over 7,000 projects were listed at five different times. Once in 1933, 8,482 were begun. Through the decade a state Four-H camp was conducted every August.

When the Second World War came, emphasis was placed on Four-H club work as an opportunity to join in the war effort and to increase the family and nation's food supply. The number of projects rose from 12,833 in 1942 to over 19,000 in both 1943 and 1944. Even 1945 showed 15,685 projects with over twelve thousand Maine youngsters part of the Four-H club movement.[23] Club members, under the leadership of Kenneth C. Lovejoy and Pauline Budge, did excellent work in the wartime period, particularly in canning, preserving, and the 5,477 victory gardens tended. Nearly seven thousand members raised livestock. The value of the food raised and preserved by Four-H club members was estimated to be in excess of $1,750,000 in 1945 dollars, and their contribution was celebrated in an extension bulletin. Other activities included scrap drives, milkweed collection (used in life jackets), sale of war bonds, Red Cross work and tree planting.[24]

After the war the number of clubs and projects decreased, finally leveling at about four hundred clubs with around five thousand members pursuing some seventy-five hundred projects, although the figures in the mid-fifties are somewhat higher. The same types of projects endured, although a few more sheep were involved and some members began to work on tractor maintenance. The state Four-H camp continued to be held for prize winners, most of whom were farm children, of course. Many were introduced to the University of Maine through Four-H and became the scholars of later years. In most ways the program was very successful, both in instilling values of thrift and ethical behavior in the participants, and in creating a feeder system for the state university.[25]

Few words in the university's education history have had more uses than the word *extension*. Since the passage of the Smith-Lever Act in 1914, the university has been charged with providing an extension of its services to citizens beyond the campus through farm demonstration, home demonstration, publication, lectures, and other means such as radio and television. Four-H is one such extension activity. In addition the university has conducted other programs, from time to time, using the same word and meaning the same thing but usually not under the Smith-Lever Act.

Citizens who are members of the more structured extension receive many pamphlets and publications in the mail; they may attend style shows, discussions of water safety, or watch demonstrations on tree planting, tree grafting, clothes tailoring, beekeeping, and the canning and freezing of raspberries. The county agent, responsible for providing what was needed for his clientele, was frequently one of the better-known persons in the community.

This photo of the University farm complex, taken in 1905 or 1906 from atop the stand pipe, shows clearly the extent of activities. Fruit trees, gardens, hen houses, chicken runs, two large barns and other outbuildings are clearly seen. Several wagons are closely placed. The only item usually seen on a Maine farm but not here is a stone drag. These buildings burned coal and not wood. Gardens are present but after harvest in the fall.

Leon S. Merrill, first head of extension. He set high standards for work under the Smith-Lever Act.

what counted, and when it came to determining which tractor or other high-priced machinery to purchase, the word of an extension agent outweighed any salesman's. This work was and remains the day-to-day, face-to-face work of the college, and it was not easy. The following letter, written by an arts college professor working in agricultural production during World War I indicates how difficult it was.

> We must take our coats off and interest Aroostook County in the University. They seem to have very little use for us up here except for agriculture and small appreciation for that . . . . The County is just waking up in reference to colleges and we must be in it in some way.[26]

Extension as described here continued to function and to prosper until well into the 1950's. The university did not, rather surprisingly, use this force as a political weapon either to support its own budgets or to create instant political heroes of the persons well-known through extension. Basic reasons for this failure (as opposed to the practice in several western states) included the constantly diminishing farm population and the increasingly expensive nature of farm production. Maine farmers tended to be isolated by crop and to think in those terms, and so the university never mobilized this force, although such persons as Frank Hussey, university trustee and president of the Farm Bureau Federation (Maine's extension organization, not the mid-western union of farmers), began to agitate, after the beginning of legislative niggardliness in the 1950's, for more political work.[27]

In the early days it was often very difficult to get local farmers and Pomona (county) Grange masters to accept young men from Orono into a field in which they had had previous mastery. Therefore, Leon S. Merrill, who headed the extension service under the Smith-Lever Act, was careful to pick young persons who would not move too quickly to overthrow old dynasties. But when a demonstration of careful, good, new farming techniques was provided, many farmers would accept the agents who then became a conduit for information from the campus experiments and analyses. With this kind of success, soil, entomological, blueberry, potato, dairy, poultry, and other specialists could come into the local area and provide knowledge that easily translated into increased profits. In a state with a constantly dwindling agricultural population this was an opportunity where the result of tax dollars could be seen and appreciated by the taxpayers. "Book-farming" might be a joke to some, but the results were

When George Lord became head of extension he began to remodel the service. Letters went out to all extension personnel asking for advice on program planning, farm and home counseling, the desirability of family life specialists, and the possiblity of using smaller and shorter meetings to achieve results. New bulletins were produced on the meaning of the extension service, but the staff (70) and membership (20,000) was too large and cumbersome and too traditionally oriented to make much inroad. When Winthrop C. Libby replaced Lord in 1963, a series of laboratories was held to discuss the future of the service. A call was sent out for more urban work, a better series of state-wide goals, and improved delegation of authority. This change became a sort of centennial project, but one as honored in the breach as in the observance. Extension still made needed contributions, but to an increasingly smaller group of people, on traditional subjects.[28]

In the seventies, with new state laws on building, environmental impact, and quality of life, the extension service began to work in community planning, land use, and other areas. The problems of adjustment in Maine have been very difficult during the twentieth century, and the extension service has found itself carrying a good deal of that burden, sometimes without much knowledge or training for its job.[29]

As noted above, the university uses the word *extension* to mean other things than the formal federally-sponsored organization under the Smith-Lever Act. Correspondence courses were begun in agriculture in 1900, increased substantially in 1906, and continued as an important part of the program until 1923. In other subjects they lingered on until after World War II.[30]

Extension courses were also offered by areas other than agriculture. Philosophy and education gave a series of lectures in 1915. By 1924 a full-fledged extension division had begun with courses offered in Bangor, Brewer, Old Town, and Orono. Lectures in specific subjects were given on the campus and more general work elsewhere. The program did not work well, with only ninety-six registrants in 1929, so it was discontinued.[31]

The technology college operated an extension division from about 1915 to 1925. For a small fee, evening classes were provided to "carry on practical work on engineering projects and to make investigations for state boards and municipal authorities, furnish scientific information to industries of the state, and distribute accurate scientific knowledge to the people of the state."[32] Although this was a difficult assignment, the work was almost immediately successful under H. Walter Leavitt. The first response was overwhelming, and the college found itself offering courses at Bangor, Orono (English to Italian immigrants!), Bath, Brownville (railroad engineering), and Great Works (papermaking), as well as testing highway materials. The Bangor course, the most successful, dealt with basic electricity. During World War I the program dropped off radically with only the English for foreigners being important as part of the country's and the

Clarence A. Day. Day was an important extension editor and a historian of Maine agriculture. He began his work as county agent in Aroostook County before World War I.

university's Americanization program. When the technology experiment station was reorganized in 1922, an effort was made to restore the extension courses as well, but not much happened until World War II, when courses similar to the previous ones were taught all over the state. Eventually the technology experiment station proved to be of relatively little importance, and after the war a department of industrial cooperation was founded to deal with specific problems. Interest in certain subjects was always intense, but a concentrated program simply did not work too well.[33]

In the 1950's, although some courses date from an earlier period, a general extension division under the education college provided a wide variety of night and Saturday courses for teacher recertification and other purposes. It grew in size and was soon christened the Continuing Education Division (CED), with a multitude of courses leading to the bachelor's degree. By the middle sixties the division offered courses at Bangor, Augusta, Lewiston, Presque Isle, and Loring A.F.B., where teachers flew to their classes once a week. Their stories of forced landings, drill precautions, and once being taken for Russian spies enlivened many faculty gatherings. The division did an excellent job providing an education in bits and pieces to those unable to attend on a full-time basis.[34]

If extension, however conceived, was to be successful, it depended on publicity. For that reason the role of the extension editor, who bore this responsibility, was paramount. A brief look at that role is useful. Publicity was stepped up substantially with the appointment of Frank G. Averill in 1923. A special conference of all extension personnel was held on the campus to

deal with publicity, and regular yearly conferences of all extension personnel were instituted to plan and organize programs. Newspaper contacts were increased; by 1926 both the *Kennebec Journal* and the *Bangor Commercial* were carrying special farm bureau issues and new papers were added nearly every month. Club reports were systematically collected, and agents trained in the use of the press. This new program was made necessary by the demise of the *Maine Farmer* in 1923 and a great decline in weeklies, many of which specialized in farm information. By 1929 the extension editor was using radio to supplement his printed message. By 1931 three stations provided thirty fifteen-minute broadcasts on such items as the fruit show in Portland, woodlot improvement, forest tree planting, and clothing children.[35]

The editor expressed his view when he remarked in a 1931 report,

> The ultimate goal of the services of the Extension Editor is to change farm and home practices. However, contacts are not made directly with farm folks to attain this end . . . . maximum use of the printed word, illustrations, radio and other facilities. . . .[36]

Ernest M. Straight, Maine's first county agent. He began his work in Cumberland County, November 1, 1912. These persons were the leading edge of the University in rural communities.

In the thirties stories shifted to a more local (county) nature and the amount of press space used grew. A weekly home economics column was very successful in this period. The radio talks continued, with a special series, "Increasing Your Income with Poultry," especially successful in 1932 and 1933.[37]

In 1933, at a national exhibition at Champaign-Urbana, Illinois, fourteen classes of publicity materials were judged. Maine entered in nine and won prizes in six: circular letters, photographs, filmstrips, radio, published news stories, and an information contest. The state's entries were ranked fifth in the country, receiving special plaudits from the heads of agricultural journalism departments.[38]

The service provided by 1935 both a daily five-minute summary of agricultural news on radio stations state-wide and special programs. A survey was made of women's listening habits and broadcasting was geared to the results. Women's pages of the state's dailies always needed information to use as space fillers; Some of the pages, especially in the Bangor *Daily News*, were very widely read. The arts

The extension service depended on good publicity. Photographs were key features in that effort. These two photos are the work of the distinguished Maine photographer, Kosti Ruohomaa, both taken in 1956. In the one to the left a specialist demonstrates methods of judging poultry for size and other qualities. In the other, new machinery is being inspected. The clarity of this work distinguished Ruohomaa's work for many international publications.

faculty began to provide materials during this period, and everything except that which qualified as a "controversial subject" (not further identified) was welcomed.[39] The work was primarily the result of the activities of Clarence A. Day, who became extension editor in this time.

Wartime was busy for the publicity forces of the extension service. In 1942 and 1943 nearly twenty separate activities were emphasized through publicity, including the Victory Farm Volunteers (a youth work program), victory gardens, use of fertilizers, gasoline allotments, war bonds, salvage (especially of fats), a health and nutrition project, and fire protection. In 1944 an emergency information specialist worked for three months on publicizing Four-H, farm labor, victory gardens, preservation of foods and nutrition. County agents did outstanding work in radio. A new daily half-hour program was tried and then revamped in 1942. A Portland program geared to that area of the state was broadcast regularly. In 1942-1943 the Cumberland County agent made 143 broadcasts. Special series were very successful; York County had one on machine trading.[40] All in all the war effort was remarkably successful for the service.

After the war the *Maine Farm Bureau News* began publishing, and farmers received detailed information each month from it. The newspaper lasted until into the late sixties, when it was

taken over by *Maine Life*, a private sheet. More and more radio was used, including station CJEM in Edmundston, New Brunswick, and WHEB in Portsmouth, New Hampshire. A three-day workshop was held in Orono to strengthen these media publicity skills even more. As the editor said, "The transition from wartime to peacetime has required very little change in policy . . . . a change in emphasis rather than a change in objectives."[41]

At the end of the Second World War a committee on off-campus activities was created to assess the problems for extension in the postwar period. The group called for widening the approach of the university to include "industry, commerce, education, arts, science and other areas involving human interests." The committee also felt that all activities should be constituted so that the "cultural and/or economic benefits" should outweigh the costs to the state, although it did not indicate how this would be accomplished. In advocating this expansion of activities, with the attendant rise in course offerings, establishment of a radio station, and development of a full-scale adult education effort, the committee stated clearly its view of what extension should be and do. The extension editor's role was central to this view of the world and is worth quoting.

> We believe that all extension services of the institution should be educational in character. They should consist of those activities and projects which will make the greatest contribution to the education of adults in each field attempted. These services should be of such character that the most wholesome and effective public relations will be inherent in, and will grow out of, all contacts made through these activities.[42]

In 1949 a visual aids specialist, Henry W. Briggs, was named. He worked with film, using a plane to provide one-day service anywhere in the state. Aerial photography was a useful aid to farmers and saved a great deal of time. By 1952 radio talks numbered over eight hundred, and the university began a weekly television report over local stations. In 1954 the Maine ETV group was born; at the present time the university program, tied in with the eastern television network of the Public Broadcasting System, provide a service to most of the state through several stations, with the central facilities located at Orono.[43]

The function of extension was, and is, to educate and to educate beyond the campus. Through the medium of publicity, that work was done extremely well. The extension editor was more prominent, and deservingly so, than many other specialists. It was through that office that the citizens learned what their university was doing for them.

Better nutrition in Maine homes was instrumental in the growth of the extension idea. By 1895, following the lead of the Connecticut Experiment Station, the university had begun some research in this area. Experiments in bread making and student nutritional intake were followed by the famous *Studies in the Food of Maine Lumbermen*. Food adulteration, digestibility, wheat flour, Indian corn, and nuts were other items discussed, researched, and the results conveyed either by lecture or publication.[44] A home economics department was formed in 1909. In 1931 a new building strengthened the program, which graduated some 699 students from 1923 to 1948. Its dietary studies and other research were important to the university's general program of nutrition improvement.[45]

The home economics program was especially important in the White House Conference on Child Health and Protection in 1930 and in the war effort during the Second World War. The conference, called by President Hoover, was attended by several representatives from Maine. Following it the state set a special Child Health Day. Finally, in the fall of 1931, a state house conference was called. A.L. Deering helped organize the conference, held in Belfast, on the subjects of medical services, public health, and other matters. The development of the school lunch program in Maine can be dated from this conference.[46] During the war all home demonstration letters were entitled "Victory Begins at Home" and were addressed to "Dear Captain on the Home Front." Conservation of rubber, metals, fats, glycerine, care of stoves, care of garden tools, repair of lighting equipment and maintenance of sheets and pillowcases were all discussed in 1941 and 1942.[47] Later in 1942, as part of the Victory Garden campaign, special canning demonstrations were held throughout the state. Special emergency extension agents carried out this work. Over ten thousand women went to foods/nutrition courses; six thousand completed the courses. Neighborhood

To the left is Merrill Hall, built to house the Home Economics Department in 1931. Today Continuing Education is also located there. In the bottom photo, a class of home economists, are engaged in meal preparation and food service in a Merrill Hall laboratory. About 1950-2, all kitchens are busy with their work.

The cover for the program of a 1936 summer institute.

leaders came from this group to aid the extension service in the much-expanded work.

In 1943 a major conference was held in Orono to beef up the health program, especially with regard to the common cold. Through the winter of 1943-1944 an extension health project was carried out. The state Department of Health and Welfare felt the project was an invasion of its domain and did not help in it, but the university proceeded just the same. County conferences were convened, the Red Cross courses extended, and two special courses on "Sick at Home" (243 meetings, 2,850 people) and "The Common Cold" (276 meetings, 3,493 people) were held. Through the next winter a similar effort was made. The degree of success cannot be determined; however, one suspects that the results were worthwhile. A major bulletin summarizing the results found its way into many homes.[48]

While these special projects were going on, the university researchers continued to do their work and publish the findings. The total of publications in the nutrition, family health, and safety field is quite impressive. Some important topics include electrical cooking, food habits of children, adapting school lunches for teenage appetites, and a pioneer study of food prices.[49]

Another area in which extension was important during wartime was to increase the number of farm laborers available to harvest the greater amounts of crops grown. In 1918 James Stacey Stevens, then dean of the arts and sciences college, organized such a program in Aroostook County, but it had not been too satisfactory. During World War II the governor called a conference to organize and plan for women and youth to substitute for the normal labor force and the migrant force of Canadians. In southern Maine crews of school children helped in harvesting cucumbers, beans, and apples, among other crops. A special one-week course was offered at the university to a more permanent group, the Victory Farm Volunteers. Two hundred twenty attended, along with 95 members of the Women's Land Army, another harvesting group. Others from Kentucky, Newfoundland, and the Caribbean were given shorter training. Eventually 450 boys, averaging forty days of work each, enrolled in the farm volunteer program. The needed wartime food production was achieved in great part through programs like these, and some of the workers remember those days with great fondness.[50]

The organized extension service, the more precise use of the word *extension,* has been extensively investigated in an unpublished work, *Forty Years of Extension Work in Maine, 1910-1950,* written by Clarence A. Day. Items not discussed in the present account that deserve notice include field testing for tuberculosis, the "better bull" campaign of the 1930's, and a later move toward artificial insemination; all were designed to improve both dairy and beef cattle, and to raise profits on Maine farms. Other significant work was done in poultry management and breeding, apple growing, developmental use of machinery on farms, and clothing and foods for the farm wife. More recently small crops, gardens, and blueberries have been subjects of the extension service.[51]

Another way the university reaches out to citizens is by the organization of conferences on campus to use the school's buildings and personnel to accomplish specific aims. Many of these conferences have been held; mention of a few may suffice to demonstrate the breadth of the program. As early as 1914 newspaper institutes were held on campus. From 1935 to 1937 the Maine Institute of World Affairs, with the Carnegie Endowment, sponsored notable conferences on world peace. In 1936 a five-day conference for game wardens was a feature; the next year the cooperative movement held a session in Orono. Others of interest include hotel management in 1941 and the annual series of New England Managers Conferences beginning in 1945, often held in Orono.[52]

Plainly, the University of Maine has had a history of extending out to the broad community, both in the state and beyond. The discussion so far has dealt with the general program and some special efforts put forth in extraordinary situations. However, three special programs should be highlighted as they are out of the ordinary, if not unique, in higher education in the United States. The first of these is the Canadian-American program, culminating in the NEAP-Q (New England-Atlantic Provinces-Quebec) Center and now termed the Canadian-American Center. The others are more specialized and concern the university's work in forestry and pulp and paper.

The university's location made its longtime interest and attention regarding Canada, and particularly the provinces directly to the north and east, a natural matter for faculty and students. Extensive migration from the Maritimes meant that the area was a shatter belt of customs, speech patterns, and economic and social behavior. As early as 1900 the president of the university was a featured guest at the centennial of the University of New Brunswick, and university baseball teams traveled to the provinces on a fairly regular basis after the mid-1880's. By 1925 the Orono board of trustees had authorized graduate tuition scholarships to Maritime graduates, a program that provides a basis for much excellent graduate study and one which continues today.[53]

In 1927 the university began to teach courses in Canadian history. The course schedule was intermittent until 1947, but has been nearly continuous since. Interest in Canadian-American matters increased after Arthur Hauck arrived in 1934. Earlier, the arts college had discussed the "advisability of establishing closer cultural relations with Canadian Universities" and Hauck was committed to exactly that. Since his professional research area was Canadian-American

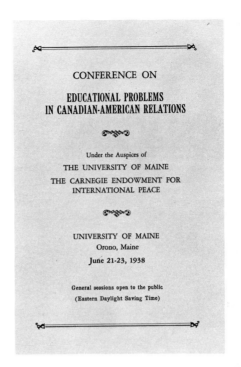

CONFERENCE ON

EDUCATIONAL PROBLEMS IN CANADIAN-AMERICAN RELATIONS

Under the Auspices of
THE UNIVERSITY OF MAINE
THE CARNEGIE ENDOWMENT FOR
INTERNATIONAL PEACE

UNIVERSITY OF MAINE
Orono, Maine
June 21-23, 1938

General sessions open to the public
(Eastern Daylight Saving Time)

The program cover for a major international conference held at the University in 1938.

education, he had already established links with various international groups, not least of which was the Carnegie Endowment. James T. Shotwell, then program director and a friend of Hauck, was personally interested in Canadian-American affairs. At the 1935 summer conference on Causes and Cures of War, sponsored by the Maine Institute of World Affairs, Hauck presided over a session on "Canadian-American Relations" featuring William R. Pattangall, '83, and Herbert L. Stewart of Canada's Dalhousie University. In 1938 the Carnegie fund provided the necessary monies for a major conference on Canadian-American relations, with the emphasis on education. The proceedings of the conference were published, and with three other conferences at St. Lawrence University in 1935, 1937, and 1939 established a firm basis for international academic contact. Unfortunately the war intervened. Although during the war Maine hosted a conference of Maritime university presidents, it was not until later that much more progress occurred.[54]

In 1951 a second conference was held, with interests across the university participating. The

Alice R. Stewart, '37.

Edgar McKay

These two professors were the leaders in the University's Canadian American program.

meeting was successful, but its carry-over was slight. A small faculty group organized on an ad hoc basis to work toward a student-faculty exchange. It provided advice for Congressman Frank Coffin as he developed, with Brooks Hays, the Canadian-American Parliamentary Committee. Other congressmen, especially Stanley Tupper, continued this work. By the end of the 1950's these informal contacts had been broadened in the Pulp and Paper Foundation and also through the Canadian and American historical associations' joint committees and sessions. Professor Alice Stewart was very active in these matters, along with Professor Edgar McKay, both of whose research interests had become cross-border in nature.

Other conferences were held at Maine in 1964, at Dartmouth in 1967, at Hobart in 1968, and at Johns Hopkins in 1970. An international organization, the Donner Foundation, aided some of these meetings. Maine was a significant contributor to these conferences. Through the efforts of Stewart and McKay, with some other help, the NEAP (later NEAP-Q) Center was begun to coordinate local activities. Such diverse activities as membership in APEC (Atlantic Provinces Economic Council), membership in the Atlantic Sea-Run Salmon Group, publication of the NEAP-Q newsletter, sponsorship of conferences and lectures, and considerable graduate scholarship, especially in the history department, enabled the center to obtain a large grant from the Donner Foundation. Maine's had by this writing become one of the most significant university programs in Canadian regional studies, if not the most significant.[55]

Other areas in which it made good geographic and economic sense for the university to focus its efforts were forestry and the pulp and paper industry. This was especially true because of the passage of the Forest Commission Act of 1889 which charged the president of the state college and the Superintendent of Schools to "bring the preservation of forests" to the attention of school children through school books. For the first decade the law was not much observed except for Arbor Day and Ivy Day on the campus and some modest research efforts.[56] In 1903 a regular curriculum was started when the first professor of forestry, Samuel Spring, was appointed. Students began to take annual

Ivy Day, the occasion for planting a vine (usually woodbine) was also an occasion in which classes formally moved to the next year. Here is the class of 1896, taken on Ivy Day, 1894, after participating in the planting exercise. Hats, mostly bowlers, were de rigueur *for this self-conscious group.*

trips into the woods during vacations to observe and to write graduation theses on lumbering practices in the Maine woods. The faculty passed occasional resolutions urging the saving of the big trees of the West, but most of the work consisted of Spring's lecturing through the state. In 1908 a high point occurred when the famous Maine forester, Austin Cary, spoke on his theories of organizing the woods owners and operators in their own best interests. He showed, as was his custom, lantern slides of what could be done through cooperative and scientific efforts. Cary was a missionary whose work instilled a sense of modern forestry practices in his listeners.[57]

In the First World War period a nursery was begun on campus. John Briscoe, then professor of forestry, was instrumental in obtaining the land. Two and one-half acres were plowed, seeded to buckwheat, then plowed under and planted the following spring to white pine. In 1915 a summer camp for foresters was held under Briscoe for the third year and made a permanent feature of the program. Some sophisticated research began to appear. Most foresters had gone to France during the war, but after the war instruction returned to a more normal basis. The Forest Commissioner began to provide funds and men to aid in the teaching, and forestry in the 1920's became a joint effort with Augusta. The appointment of Samuel Dana as Forest Commissioner in 1922 enhanced prospects as he was a strong advocate of forestry education.[58] By 1924 registration had increased by a third, to 128. Dwight Demeritt began working in 1923 in the forestry depart-

This group of Maine forestry professors are on Indian Township observing experimental work in 1957. Those facing the camera are Griffin, Plummer, Pearson and Baker. From left to right, those with their backs to the camera are Randall, Nutting, Young, Frost and Demeritt.

The forestry students and faculty at summer camp in 1952. Here they are perched on a large drum barker owned by the St. Croix Paper Company while on an inspection tour. The sign at the right indicates the cooperative nature of the program.

ment, and a forestry specialist was appointed in the extension service.

New bulletins on forest planting and usage of farm woodlots were prepared and widely distributed. The state nursery produced more than a million and a half trees, and capacity was increased to quarter-million plants each year. These were made available to farmers and others at cost. Much was accomplished in the area of white pine blister rust, especially in destroying its host, the genus *ribes*. Fred Gilbert and Garrett Schenck of the Great Northern Paper Company were courted by C.C. Little. Although they were unable to muster enough support to increase appropriations, the firm did provide a free summer camp near Caucomgomoc Lake during the twenties. A publication, *The Maine Forester,* begun in 1923, was filled mostly with news of the summer camps, but included much information on research and alumni doings also. Increasingly, though, the university ties to the state forestry department irritated many. Finally in 1929 the two were severed, and Orono was able to move out on its own, a position it had had in fact since President Little and Governor Baxter crossed paths. Even where the state and the university were aiming for the same end, the effort could not be coordinated.[59]

The forestry nursery was overused and began to peter out even though greatly increased work was done there from 1928 to 1930. A permanent forest camp was built at Indian Township in the thirties with a matching grant from C.M. Hutchins. An international foresters' survey in 1935 called for overhauling of the forestry course and its equipment, however, and as a partial result and through funding of the Bankhead-Jones Act, the university forest of 2,100 acres was created in 1939. When the war began, 325 acres of this land had to be given up for an airport, but the research results from the forest started to appear as soon as the war was over. Some research continued to be published during the wartime period of semi-austerity and national danger, but the department focused most of its efforts on maintaining itself, improving the wood production of the state, and using the best techniques possible. One of its jobs was to supervise some of the prisoner of war camps where pulpwood was cut. After the war a new push in research was sparked by the world-renowned work of Harold Young, '39.

Culmination of the forestry program was the new (all wooden) building dedicated in 1970. Governor Kenneth M. Curtis presides at the ceremony.

The new building, Nutting Hall, named for Albert Nutting, long-time head of forestry, remains an adornment of the campus. Barns and outbuilding are behind with the garage in the deep background.

Pulp and Paper Open House Day, 1957. President Hauck is at the left, then John G. Strange of the Institute of Paper Chemistry. J. Larcom Ober, President of the University of Maine Foundation, and Professor Lyle C. Jenness, head of the program in pulp and paper at that time. Below, the lovely winter scene shows Jenness Hall, home of the Chemical Engineering Department and the Pulp and Paper Foundation.

Widening of the concepts of year-round recreation and timberland management also became very important. Finally in 1970 a new handsome building was constructed to house the department. On balance good progress had been made, but growth had been inhibited by limited sponsorship from outside the college.[60]

One area of the university that has enjoyed widespread industry support is pulp and paper technology. The support has led to a remarkable partnership on the campus itself. A number of industry spokesmen had been advocating the establishment of serious education for papermakers and paper chemists since the 1890's. The first successful program in the United States began at Maine in 1913 under the sponsorship of Ralph McKee. There were two courses, one on pulp and one on paper. Other courses were added until a full four-year program was set up. Features included a miniature paper machine, regular visits to local mills for detailed observation, and a considerable publicity campaign engineered by McKee. By the end of World War I as many as 160 students were enrolled in the program, by then under the guidance of Charles A. Brautlecht, who was to remain chairman until 1935.[61]

In 1928 the first scholarships were sponsored by the industry and more came in each year. By 1937 the trustees were ready to solicit

Left: Professor Edward F. Dow, history and government chair from 1932 to 1967. He founded the city manager program. Right: Six graduates of 1949 are shown here. Vance Dearborn, third from the left, is now on the faculty. Others went to Madawaska, Portland, Farmington, Ashland, Old Town, Brunswick, and Auburn as municipal managers in that year.

large amounts of private funds to build and equip a new laboratory for the pulp and paper course. Open houses were held in the immediate prewar years, culminating in 1941 in a joint meeting of the Maine section of the American Chemical Society and the Maine-New Hampshire T.A.P.P.I. (Technical Association of the Pulp and Paper Industry). At that meeting a new building for the program was dedicated.[62]

This partnership led to the establishment in 1950 of a pulp and paper foundation, with industry membership supplying most of the funds for research. Faculty members at the university are paid from both sources and the director is of faculty rank, but a wholly independent person nominated by the industry representatives. Research has been geared, in great part, to industry needs, while students have many opportunities to be involved in the research programs of the companies directly interested in the foundation and its work. Recently a new building, Jenness Hall, has been erected on the campus to house the activities of chemical engineering and the pulp and paper foundation. Among those who have contributed considerably to this program, in addition to McKee and Brautlecht, are Lyle Jenness, longtime faculty member and later secretary of the foundation, and Irwin Douglass, who did outstanding research in sulphite chemistry after 1935. More recently Edward Bobalek and Lowell Zabel have received wide recognition. The department of chemical engineering has staffed the program from the beginning, but has also done other work, especially in potato starch under the guidance of Brautlecht.[63]

Two other programs that must be mentioned, if not fully described, are the Bureau of Public Administration and the Bureau of Labor Education. Both are, like the pulp and paper foundation, semi-independent organizations on the campus itself. The first provides research and hosts conferences, among other services, for municipal and public employees. It received its start from the excellent city manager program begun in the 1930's by Professor Edward F. Dow. The logical counterpart to this bureau, labor education, is substantially younger, but it does research and hosts conferences, and generally is involved in the education and training of labor groups. Both of these organizations provide a form of extension teaching in the broad sense that ties the university closer to its natural constituency, the taxpaying public.

Extension activities have been defined broadly in this work. The founders of the university envisaged a university for all the state's people and this meant extending influence beyond the campus. In that respect one must give high marks to the result — these extensions of the campus to the state.

Notes

1. Lee Stewart (Clinton, Maine) to President, June 3, 1907.

2. *Cadet,* June, 1895; *Campus,* May 15, 1902; Summer Session catalogues; Trustees, November 11, 1933; January 3 (Orono), 21, 1934; on nursery school beginnings, Charles A. Dickenson and others to Hauck, June 7, 1938; Hauck to E.J. Allen, June 16, 1938; on Italians, *Campus,* March 17, April 14, 1914; Tech. faculty meetings, February 24, May 25, 1914; Trustees, May 13, 1927 on Maine-in-Turkey, also Charles Crossland to Boardman February 26, 1927; Boardman to Lee Vrooman, Feb. 22, 1927; Vrooman to Boardman January 2, 1927, and *Campus* for the fund drives for the work.

3. *Agriculture of Maine, 1883,* 47-60, 430-441; *1885,* 230-238.

4. *Board of Agriculture, 1891,* "Report of the Proceedings of the Dairyman's Meeting," 120-158; *Agriculture of Maine, 1893-94,* 12 for quote.

5. Oxford *Democrat,* December 4, 11, 25, 1894.

6. *Agriculture of Maine, 1890,* 18-22; *1896,* dairyman's meeting, 92-100, 138-159; Harris to Herbert Myrick, (New England *Homestead),* July 13, 30, 1897, as well as many letters and advertisements for *Youth's Companion,* in Harris Correspondence, "Sundry"; *Cadet,* December, 1890, March, April, 1891; October, 1892; Clarence Day, "A Brief History of Agricultural Education of Less Than College Grade at the University of Maine," c. 1940, typed manuscript.

7. *Campus,* February 2, 1903.

8. A.W. Gilman (Comm. of Agriculture) to Fellows, October 23, 1902; October 29, 1902; William D. Hurd to George E. Fellows, October 29, 1907; Trustees June 9, 1908.

9. *Campus,* April 23, 1914; March 25, April 16, December 7, 1915; February 1, 1916; Cooperative Extension Manuscripts, Box 10, "Annual Report of Extension Work in Soil Fertility . . . Sept. 1, 1915 to June 30, 1916." In 1915 the Extension Division gave 61 farm demonstrations, taught 28 schools to 5,467 people and provided 436 lectures to an audience numbering 43,150. See Howard C. Townsend, "The Extension Division, College of Agriculture, University of Maine," *Practical Husbandry of Maine,* Vol. V, No. VIII [December, 1915].

10. Cooperative Extension, mss, Box 10, Report of the Extension Editor 1931-32, on Second Annual Poultry School, August 15-16; Extension Editors Report, 1940-41, appendix on futurism; Report 1943-44, appendix on veterans.

11. *Cadet,* June, 1895; Oxford *Democrat,* June 8, 1897; Faculty, April 2, 1900.

12. *Campus,* February 26, March 19, 1907; March 17, 1908; *Programme and Information of Farmer's Week,* Extension Circular No. 4, February, 1907; *Timely Helps for Farmers,* Vol. 2, No. 7 (February, 1909), program for Farmer's Week.

13. Box 10, Cooperative Extension Manuscripts, Ext. Editors Report, 1914-1931, especially 1927-28, 1930-31, 1934-35, 1948-49; *The Maine Bulletin,* XLIII, No. 10, (March 10, 1941), program for 35th Farm and Home Week; Trustees (Portland), September 17, 1964; letter Joseph Murray to Robert F. Chandler, April 2, 1952, in Hauck Correspondence, 1951-52.

14. F.W. Cram to George E. Fellows, March 3, 1906.

15. Edward P. Mayo to Fellows, March 8, 1906, quoted; Z.A. Gilbert to Fellows, March 13, F.W. Cram to Fellows, May 11, A.W. Fulton to Fellows, May 4, A.W. Gilman to Fellows, May 7, 26, June 4, July 14, 1906; *Campus,* March 13. April 10, May 1, 8, 1906; May 3, 1910; April 18, 1911.

16. *Campus,* March 10, 17, 24, May 12, 1914; April, 1906 (on musical tour).

17. Theatre Festival program, March 14-15, 1941.

18. *Campus,* May 8, 1906; May 6, 1913; April 14, 1914; Feburary 17, March 7, 1916; Program for Annual Inspection Trip March 15-22, 1916; By the late 1950's a congressional internship program with Maine congressional delegation or most of them, fulfilled this purpose for another group at the college.

19. *Campus,* May 19, 1914; Box 1, Cooperative Extension Manuscripts, Annual Report January 1 to August 17, 1914; Annual Report August 1 to December 1, 1914; December 4, to July 1, 1915.

20. Cooperative Extension Manuscripts, Box 1, Annual Report 1916; Ext. Bulletin 107, 1916, "Garden and Canning Clubs," Bulletin 106, "Boys and Girls Agricultural Clubs," *Timely Helps for Farmers,* Vol. 8, No. 7 (April, 1915); Extension Bulletin No. 103, 1916 "Home Work for Club Girls of Maine," Broadside of Waldo County Contest November 5-6, 1915, in Annual Report Boys Club, 1915, Box 1, Second Annual Meeting, Program, December 22-24, 1915.

21. Box 1, Cooperative Extension Manuscripts, Third Annual Meeting Program, annual reports, 1916-1920, quote 1918-1919, "Memorandum Report . . . School Superintendents and Teachers . . ." 1918.

22. Box 10, Ext. Editors Report, 1919, 1920, 1922, 1951-52; Special Report Assistant State Club Leader, August 5, 1922, Box 1; Report of Eastern States Trip September 19-25, 1920, Springfield, Massachusetts, *Daily News* September 22, 1920; Cooperative Extension Bulletin, 125 (June, 1920), *Manual for Agricultural and Home Making Club Leaders,* 124, *Handbooks* for same; Annual Report County Extension Workers, 1924; quote from Report of Clubwork, January 1, 1920 to May 21, 1920.

23. Annual Report, State Four-H Club leader, 1928-29; 1933-34; 1941-42; 1944-45; all in Box 10, Cooperative Extension Manuscripts.

24. Clarence A. Day, "Wartime Accomplishments of 4-H Clubs in Maine," Extension Bulletin, No. 330, April, 1945.

25. Annual Report, State Club Agent, 1949-1950, p. 53-55; 1951-52, 53-56; Twenty-Second State 4-H Club Camp, August 22-26, 1955 (Program).

26. Cooperative Extension Manuscripts, in general, but especially in the 1920's; Leon S. Merrill, *The Smith-Lever Act and Agricultural Extension Work in Maine,* n.p., n.d. (1914?); "Gramps", by Joseph H. Bodwell, especially Sections VI, VII, (memoirs of an early county agent), *Maine Life,* May, June, 1970; J.S. Stevens to R.J. Aley, July 17, 1918 (from Fort Fairfield), C.C. Little to William L. Bonney, November 16, 1922; publicity was important (see below) but also, Box 10, Report Extension Entomologist, 1918; Agriculture Extension, 1918-1924.

27. Trustees, October 4, 1952, joint meeting with Farm Bureau Federation.

28. A.L. Deering to Hauck, July 6, 1955; Elliott to George Lord, August 4, 1959; Bulletin 477 (December, 1959); Winthrop C. Libby to Elliott July 30, 1964, Elliott to Libby August 5, 1964; Lord's file, (Deering to Hauck, September 13, 1954).

29. Clarence Day, "Forty Years of Extension," typed manuscript, c. 1954.

30. Day, "A Brief History of Agricultural Education of Less Than College Grade . . . ." typed manuscript, c. 1940; Faculty, April 23, 1900; G.M. Twitchell to Fellows, March 20, 1902 (pledging help of Maine *Farmer)*; Trustees, June 12, 1900.

31. Announcement of lectures, 1915, 1922, 1923, 1924, 1925 (three folders of correspondence with details of lecture content) Trustees February 7, 1929 (Augusta), March 8, 1929 (Augusta).

32. Trustees, June 9, 1914, June 8, 1915 quote.

33. *Bangor Daily News,* September 3, 1914; *Extension Courses in Engineering and Industrial Subjects,* Orono, January, 1917; *Campus,* December 4, 1914; March 17, April 14, 1914; Tech faculty, February 24, May 25, 1914; Trustees, December 6, 1945; Boardman to Little, October 19, 1922.

34. University of Maine Bulletin, General Extension Division, February 1, 1953, Vol. LV, No. 8, and personal experience.

35. Box 10, Cooperative Extension Manuscripts, Ext. Editors report, 1923, 1924, 1927, 1928, 1929, 1930. Conference Programs of Extension Agents, January 27-30, 1925.

36. Extension Editors Report, July 1 - August 30, 1931.

37. Extension Editor, 1931-32; 1932-33.

38. Extension Editors Report, July 25-27, 1933, p. 35-36.

39. Extension Editors Report, 1934-35; 1937-38; Trustees, November 2, 1934; Arts Faculty, December 3, 1934; Agriculture Faculty, October 22, 1934.

40. Extension Editors Report, 1941-42; 1943-44 and especially appendices, pps. 43-80.

41. Extension Editors Report, 1945-46; minutes of editors of Farm Bureau News, March 8, 1946; Portland, letter, John Manchester to agents, March 29, 1946, and the various workshops available.

42. "Report of Committee on Off-Campus activities in the Post-War Program," n.p., n.d., mimeoed, c. 1944-45. In another place the committee defined extension work to include correspondence courses, off-campus classes, off-campus short courses, institutes, conferences, interviews, letters of information, bulletins, radio, films, slides, recordings, maps, charts, demonstrations, and lectures.

43. Extension Editors Report, 1947-48; 1948-49; Faculty Council Minutes, November 1, 1954.

44. W.O. Atwater to Harris, September 27, 1895; *Agriculture of Maine,* 1898, (Experiment Station Report, 164-238); *Agriculture of Maine,* 1899, 35-46; Experiment Station *Bulletins,* 37 (Dietary Studies); 97 (Flours); 103 (Entire Wheat Flour); 131 (Indian Corn); 158 (Food of Man); Washington published the Maine lumberman study as part of a greater series, in 1904.

45. Pearl S. Greene, "Twenty Five Years of Home Economics at Maine," typed manuscript, dated December 1, 1948.

46. "White House Conference on Child Health . . . ." in Extension Manuscripts, Box 10. *White House Conference, 1930: Addresses and Abstracts,* The Century Co. 1931.

47. Extension Editors Report, 1941-42, Appendix.

48. Extension Editors Report, 1941-42 (with letters to agents; Deering to Hauck December 18, 1943; June 21, 1944; This was organized under the Maine State Nutrition Committee which issued a mimeoed history July 1, 1945; Extension Bulletin No. 327, December, 1944, "Better Nutrition for Maine Children."

49. Bulletins No. 371, 375, 376 (1934); 386 (1936); 401 (1940); (Also Annual Report Experiment Station 1940-41, p. 431-58); 430 (1944); 475 (1949); 495 (1951); 641 (1966).

50. Stevens to Aley, June 12, 1918 in particular, although others in his file deal with his experiences; Deering to Hauck, February 22, 1944; Extension Editors Annual Report, 1943-44, appendix 72-74, special mimeod report on Farm Labor to Marvin Jones, War Food Administrator, dated May, 1944; "Your Job in This War," Maine Extension Circular No. 214, April 1945.

51. The standard history is Clarence A. Day, "Forty Years of Extension Work in Maine, 1910-1950," typed manuscript, December, 1957, 455 pps. plus index. This work, with considerable revision and with new information, could be published

some day. Other materials from this same era, which was one of transition in the extension service, include, "Information on Maine Agricultural Extension Service," a mimeod folder put together for Lloyd Elliot, June, 1958; Annual Report, Maine Extension Service, December, 1959; *Extension Serves in These Changing Times,* December, 1960; *The Business of Agriculture in the Sixties,* December, 1961; *The Cooperative Extension Service Today; What Farm Folks Say About Extension Work,* mimeoed publication, c. 1940; *Fiftieth Anniversary, 1968,* Aroostook County Extension Association, n.d., 1968?, n.p.; By-laws of the Maine Extension Association, October 1, 1968; Clarence Day, *50 Years With the Cooperative Extension Service in Maine,* Orono, 1962.

52. *Campus,* March 20, 1917; Programs, Maine Institute of World Affairs, July 9-10, 1935; July 22-23, 1936; July 21-22, 1937; Program, (Mimeod), Game Wardens' Short Course, December 28-31, 1936; Program 10th Annual New England Institute of Cooperation, June 16, 17, 18, 1937; Hotel Management Conference Program, March 28-29, 1941; Program, Eighteenth New England Managers' Institute, August 19, 20, 21, 1963; For Impact of Conferences on faculty see Faculty Council, October 8, 1951; January 22, 1952, February 16, 1953 (reports by Alice Stewart, Robert York, and International Relations Committee on conferences dealing with world affairs).

53. Trustees, March 2, 1900.

54. Program, Maine Institute of World Affairs, July 9, 10, 1935; Arts Faculty, February 6, 1933; Graduate Faculty, October 15, 1953; General Faculty Meeting, March 21, 1938; Hauck to Frederick P. Keppel, November 11, 1935 (talk in NYC with he and Shotwell, offers campus for conference); Program, Conference on Education Problems in Canadian-American Relations, June 21-23, 1938; a large box of correspondence setting it up; Rising Lake Morrow, ed., *Conference on Educational Problems in Candian-American Relations,* Orono, 1939 (248 pps.); for newspaper comment at the time, St. John *Telegraph Journal,* June 29, St. Croix *Courier,* June 30, Bangor *Daily News,* June 17, 18, 22, 23, 24, 1938; Presidential Correspondence 1940-41; T.A. Stone to Hauck April 14, 19, 1941; Norman MacKenzie to Hauck, November 4, 1940; Hauck to MacKenzie, November 6, Assembly, Conference of Presidents, March 7, 1941; Schuyler B. Terry to Hauck, May 27, 1942.

55. From a typed manuscript by Alice Stewart, September, 1974, personal participation, and many conversations with Edgar McKay and others.

56. Daniel F. Davis to M.C. Fernald, June 24, 1891; on Arbor Day, *State Pomological Report,* 1887, 59-74; 140-150; C.H. Fernald did research on "Grasses of Maine," *Agriculture of Maine,* 1885; and preliminary work on spruce insect infestations. See my *History of Maine Lumbering 1860-1960* for more detail.

57. Faculty, November 6, 1905; December 15, 1903; *Campus,* March 1, 1905; January 14, 1908; Amos L. Allen to Fellows, December 23, 1907; on Cary see my Maine Lumbering for an extensive comment, also my article on Cary in *Leaders of Conservation,* New York, 1971.

58. Briscoe to Aley, April 24, 1913; *Campus,* May 9, October 24, 1913; April 30, 1915; Experiment Station Bulletin 210, 1913; O.A. Johannsen, "Spruce Bud Worm and Spruce Lead Miners". Aley to Samuel T. Dana, July 29, Aley to Forest H. Colby, January 13, June 6, 16, Colby to Aley, June 13, Dana to Aley, July 16, 26, Aley to Dana, July 19, all 1919.

59. *Campus,* November 25, 1923; January 9, 1924; Trustees, (Augusta), March 8, 1929; Box 10, Cooperative Extension Manuscripts, "Report on the Cooperative Blister Rust Work . . . January 1 to October 31, 1922," for 1923, during 1928, during 1930, meeting minutes Baxter, Dana, etc., Feburary 21, 1922; F.A. Gilbert to Little, February 15, April 11, Little to Gilbert, February 19, April 13, April 16, June 19, 1923; Report of the Forest Department of the Univeristy of Maine, typed, 1923-1924. *Maine Forester* 1923 to date, intermittent.

60. Trustees, November 6, 1930; October 3, 1935; May 4, 1939; agreement E.E. Chase and Henry Wallace, June 13, 1939; April 3, 1941; Presidential Correspondence, John M. Briscoe to L.S. Merrill, January 29, 1931 (detailed report on state nursery); D.B. Demeritt to Deering, May 30, 1944; Deering to Hauck, May 31, Hauck to Dermeritt, undated (use of UMO's campus for POW's); A.D. Nutting to Clifford N. Carver, June 19, 1944; Experiment Station Bulletin, 448, Gregory Baker, *Primary Wood-Using Industries of Maine:* 554 (December 1956), Baker and Frank K. Beyer, *Marketing Forest Products . . .;* 616, (1963-64), Robert Greenleaf, *The Integration of Year Round Recreation and Timberland Management . . .;* Dwight Demeritt, Bulletin 696, Feburary, 1972, *Background and History of the University of Maine Forest; Maine Times,* March 12, 1971.

61. *Paper Trade Journal,* six stories in 1913, five in 1914, two by McKee and various others from 1915-1950; Department of Industry and Labor of Maine, *Second Biennial Report,* 1913, Ralph McKee, "The Training of Men for Positions in Pulp and Paper Mills," *Campus,* October 17, 21, 1913; November 23, 1921; letter with reminiscences, Brautlecht to Robert M. York, November 19, 1954.

62. Trustees, September 13, 1928; November 6, 1937; Brautlecht to A.P.P.A., October 10, 1929, in Presidential Correspondence, 1929-1930; Open House Programs, 1936-1939; Joint Meeting Program, September 26-27, 1941; File T.A.P.P.I., Maine-N.H. Meeting, with much correspondence.

63. Trustees, January 18, 1950; *Maine Alumnus,* December, 1952; Lloyd E. Elliott, *Unique Partners in Progress,* Newcomen Address, 1964; *Paper Trade Journal,* May 4, 1970. For a general picture of the industry and education in the U.S. see my *History of Papermaking,* Chapter 16, especially 613-619.

CHAPTER ELEVEN

Research and Publication

MOST CITIZENS of the state of Maine and even many members of the university community think of the school solely in terms of teaching students. Some may also include extension activities as important. However, there has been since the beginning a third facet of the university's work that has had considerable impact on the lives of Maine citizens: organized research and subsequent publication. Research began in a small way before there were even any students on the campus, expanded in the 1880's to the establishment of a state experiment station, and grew into the federal experiment station authorized by the Hatch Act of 1887. Since then the experiment station has organized and controlled much of the research associated with the university, especially where it dealt with farm and home life.

This growth led to the establishment also of other agencies devoted to research: Highmoor Farm in Monmouth, Aroostook Farm in Presque Isle, Blueberry Farm in Washington County, a technology experiment station, and a marine facility at Lamoine. Not all of these installations have survived, but all have provided substantial research contributions to the state.

Among the research areas which have been of particular importance are genetics and breeding, entomology, forestry, foods, potatoes, and a variety of Maine-related subjects. Much money, from both federal and state sources, has been expended and generally the returns have been very good.[1]

After the school's founding, the superintendents of the college farm began immediate experimentation, focusing on the effects of certain fertilizers. The earliest proponents of the college had all assumed that an experimental or model farm would be set up as an adjunct to the school. Soon they began to press for a full-scale experiment station to coordinate the farm experiments and to undertake research beyond the needs of the state's farmers. In 1877 Lyndon Oak wrote a long letter to M.C. Fernald that outlined clearly some of the hopes and expectations with regard to the experiment station.

> There appears to be a growing sentiment in favor of the establishment of an experiment station somewhere. If this idea is to be realized Orono should furnish the site.
>
> Would the person placed in charge of the station find time to give instruction in Agriculture other than that incidental to the prosecution of experiments? If the management of the station should be kept within the strictest limits of economy compatible with usefulness, what would be the annual cost, including the salary of the person in charge? Would not an effective management of the station, with the incidental instruction, be of as much value to the college as any equal expenditure for agricultural instruction? And would it not be of greater immediate value to the Farmers of the state and thus have the effect to increase the popularity of the college?
>
> Could a person, not himself an expert chemist, avail himself of such aid from the Professor of Chemistry as to enable him to manage the station successfully?
>
> As the question of the establishment of a station is liable to confront us at any time, it is well to give it some consideration in advance. . . .[2]

Fernald replied that some aid to the professor of agriculture would be possible, but limited. He also felt that the experiment station should be headed by a chemist, that it should extend but not supplant the offerings of the college, and that it would increase popularity for the college. He estimated the cost of a station to be from three to six thousand dollars per year. Finally he said, "It [the station] and the college would be mutually advantageous to each other."[3]

As one can see from this exchange, the experiment station under consideration was still a fairly elementary one, with the primary emphasis likely to be placed on soil chemistry and fertilizer experiments. Discussion of this sort of station continued, and the college began to publish some of the results of its experimentation. By 1882 experiments in potato-rot fungus, fertilizers, and early work in animal husbandry were being discussed in the state. The annual meeting of the Maine Board of Agriculture passed a resolution calling for the establishment of an experiment station at Orono "for the analysis of fertilizers and of stock feeds, and the testing of the purity and vitality of seeds. . . ." The board appointed a three-man committee to carry this message to the people and then to lobby at the legislature just going into session.[4] At this time nationwide debate was going on in behalf of experiment stations and several bills were introduced in 1883 in the Congress. Problems of adulteration of stock feed, guano, and other items widely used by farmers prompted the discussion and created the atmosphere in which experiment stations could be funded.

Whitman H. Jordan, '75

In 1885 the Maine legislature, tired of waiting for Congress, enacted a bill setting up its own "Maine Fertilizer Control and Agricultural Experiment Station." With its funds of $5,000 each year, the new body was to publish bulletins and an annual report. In addition, it was to conduct experiments and investigations, particularly of labeling and chemical analysis of fertilizers. Finally, it was authorized to issue licenses, publish the results of its analyses, and to recommend penalties for fraud. The act went into effect by March 3 and the station became active early in April under the guidance of Walter Balentine, acting director. Its quarters were part of the college laboratory, partitioned off, and "a large and pleasant room" in White Hall was used as an office. Whitman H. Jordan, '75, agreed to return on July 1 as the first full-time director.[5]

The first work was not of great significance; however, the report based on the work set the tone for the station itself: "The Station desires . . . to enter into as close contact and sympathy with the agriculture of the State as is possible . . . feel free to correspond with the Station . . . . It is especially requested that farmers bring to the notice of the Station anything new that demands investigation. . . ." By the next year the dairy room had been arranged for experimentation and an acre of the college farm was given over to varietal seed testing. Most of the work consisted of testing of products. Some experimentation was done and published on the composition of wood ashes and harbor mud, both being touted as fertilizers. The first few bulletins were published in the Bangor *Whig and Courier.* In the spring of 1888 bulletins were being published separately; the results of the varietal seed testing was Bulletin No. 24, published in May of 1888. Other experiments on oat seeding, the college farm expenses, and beef production were also published.[6]

In 1887 Congress enacted the Hatch Act establishing experiment stations at colleges, and Maine accepted the act immediately. It coincided with the destruction of the college herd from tuberculosis, so the trustees took the opportunity to reestablish the herd, with the provision that different breeds be used and with the implicit provision that the station would conduct experimentation with them. Other matters considered were the possible formation of a station council to oversee experimentation (as

Holmes Hall as it appeared in 1888 and 1889. Wings were added in 1890 and 1904. Over the door appeared the words Experiment Station. The building was constructed with funds from the Hatch Act of 1887. Experiments have been conducted here to this day.

Cornell had done), building of a new building (Holmes Hall), the role of the university farm (at first to be maintained separately), and the need for a separate library and apparatus. Throughout 1888, as the new building was erected, a slow, deliberate establishment of the station procedures began. The eight major areas of work were to be: cattle foods, cattle feeding, and animal products; fertilizer and crop production; varieties of farm crops, agricultural botany, and entomology; animal diseases; horticulture; agricultural meteorology and physics; fertilizer inspection; and chemical analysis.[7]

In the same year the station was organized, major experimental reports were issued on cattle foods, feeding experiments (hay for both cattle and swine), and the beginnings of a long list of entomological work with papers on "injurious insects," the forest tent caterpillar, the codling moth, and the apple maggot.

Establishing the station was one thing; getting its word to farmers was another. The annual report for 1889 took cognizance of this problem.

The value to practical agriculture of the results so far secured will be in part determined by the nature of these results, and in part by the manner in which they are received by the intelligent farming public. The Experiment Station fulfills its duty when it spreads broadcast over the state the results of its works, but its labor will be fruitless to that great industry for whose benefit the Station was established unless the facts revealed by experiment and investigation are properly studied and assimilated.[8]

Over the next decade the station saw much in the way of construction and other types of improvements. A barn was erected in 1889 for experimental feeding, and a forcing house constructed in 1890, along with a wing for Holmes Hall. The final wing on Holmes was added in 1904 with a formal dedication of the building at commencement that spring. Swine feeding pens were built in 1891, and a new forcing house in 1893. In that year the law relating to control of sale and the inspection of fertilizer was strengthened. In 1897 the college farm was turned over to the new experiment station director, Charles D. Woods, who had replaced Jordan, recently gone to the New York State Experiment Station at Geneva. During this period the trustees took a strong interest in the station's work, mandating certain tests and observing results. In 1891 the horticultural work of the station was reorganized and W.M. Munson began his long and distinguished duties on the campus. Spraying of insects was monitored beginning in 1891. The first of a series of human nutritional experiments began in 1895 with a study of milk intake by students at the college dining room.

Bulletins began to appear frequently on such subjects as fruit culture (No. 6), spraying experiments (No. 8), tomatoes (No. 9), cauliflower (No. 10), and one on the Babcock butterfat test (No. 15) appearing in 1894. In that year the station received, at the Columbian Exhibition, an

Floor plan of the famous Maine State College barn as it appeared in the Report of the State Board of Agriculture in 1874. An item like this would help farmers plan new construction. Modern barns with milking parlors and more loose feeding are much different. Up above in this barn were haylofts.

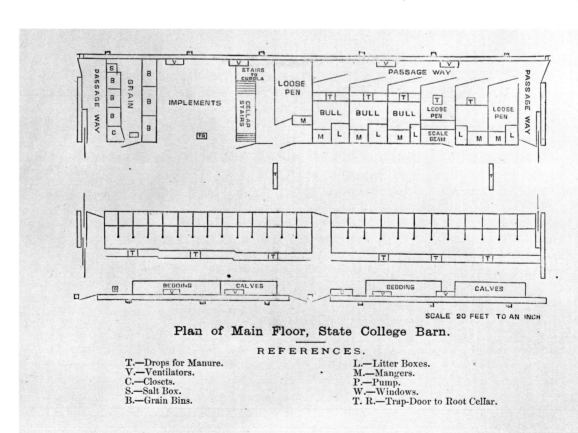

Plan of Main Floor, State College Barn.

REFERENCES.

T.—Drops for Manure.
V.—Ventilators.
C.—Closets.
S.—Salt Box.
B.—Grain Bins.

L.—Litter Boxes.
M.—Mangers.
P.—Pump.
W.—Windows.
T. R.—Trap-Door to Root Cellar.

The top photo is Experiment Station Director C.D. Woods in his office in Holmes Hall. Woods began his work with Atwater in Connecticut and aided in the original nitrogen fixation experiments. At Maine he did distinguished work in human nutrition. He set the tone for high quality intellectual endeavor and scientific work while director and was well-known. However he was deposed by the Board of Trustees after 24 years and 5 months of service as a scapegoat for World War I inflation. This period, 1896-1921, was a bench mark in scientific experimentation at Maine. At left is W.M. Munson, June, 1891, as he arrived on the faculty. He, too, was a significant researcher.

award for excellence of publication of experiment reports. President Harris, an active promoter of the station and its work, discussed in 1894 the work of the future and predicted that it would be primarily concerned with dairy, potatoes, poultry, and testing, with efforts to diminish rural isolation through libraries. His speech engendered a discussion at the annual meeting of the Board of Agriculture where many spokesmen pinpointed discontent among farmers, especially in Cumberland County, a problem that many felt was associated with the Bowdoin opposition.

One of the things that was done to increase popularity was to simplify the bulletins and enlarge the mailing list. The budget went to $15,000, up substantially to increase results of the station's work. Jordan also went on the road to promote the station's interests which he described as one part police work (especially with regard to testing and exposure of frauds relating to fertilizer and to creameries) and one part experimentation, of which he described animal nutrition as the most important, with horticulture (especially pomology) next, followed by the job of the veterinarian (in control of tuberculosis), and finally human nutrition, experimentation on which was then just beginning. The impact of the great campaign to make the college into a university had benefited the station, because the publicity tended to widen the audience for the station's results. With the transfer of the college farm in 1897 it was possible to conduct whatever experiments seemed to be needed. By the turn of the century the station played an important role in the lives of Maine's farmers.[9]

The experiment station continued to grow, both in buildings and in the amount of work performed. In 1905 a new incubator house was constructed. In 1906 Congress passed the Adams Act increasing the amounts of funds available to $15,000 more per year after 1907-1908. These funds were to be used for investigation into human nutrition, orchard problems, plant diseases, and breeding studies. A department of plant pathology was started to deal with the new research. New greenhouses and poultry buildings were erected through the rest of the decade, and in 1909 Highmoor Farm was purchased with a $10,000 state appropriation.

Some scattered attacks were made on the station, chiefly by the *Maine Farmer* in the period from 1903 to 1905, but these were aspects of the problems that culminated in the great 1906 hearing at Portland over the continuation of the arts college. As soon as that was settled, the attacks diminished. In fact, much of the agricultural interests' discussion toward the end of the decade was over the way in which groups like the Maine Dairyman's Association could aid in lobbying for a bigger and better barn. In 1913 Aroostook Farm was purchased to provide close specialized work for the northern outpost of the state. From 1910 to 1918 the students at the college published a monthly journal called *Practical Husbandry of Maine*. Just as was true across the country, the period before the First World War seemed to be the golden age of Maine agriculture, with the university, the college farm, and the experiment station cooperating to provide a better environment for Maine farmers and more profit for their pocketbooks.[10]

The station's duties expanded as it became responsible for inspection of opened shellfish in 1912, and, as they began to sell widely, for the inspection of carbonated beverages and ice cream. In 1914 some of this work passed to the commissioner of agriculture, much to the delight of the station crew. In this period Raymond Pearl began genetics study at the station. Also, substantial time was spent testing for butterfat content in dairy products. This testing caused some conflict in the state because the station's standards were evidently too strict.[11]

After war was declared, work continued without interruption for the first few weeks, but soon Pearl went to Washington to work with Herbert Hoover and was followed by two others, along with their secretaries. Pearl later resigned with his staff to go to Johns Hopkins, where a fire deprived the university of some of his unpublished research on poultry. In 1920 Woods' term as director was terminated abruptly, due in great part to the cost of construction of a barn at Highmoor to house the cattle breeding experiment. Woods himself was impeccably honest, but somewhat sloppy in his administration, and this added to his difficulties. The animal breeding experiment that had been the pride of the station was cut back for lack of money, and the station fell on poorer times.[12]

These three photos show the campus during the period of C.D. Woods administration. At top is part of the campus about 1903. Coburn, Fernald, the Wingate tower, Holmes Hall (with one wing) and Alumni Hall are visible. The middle photo, taken at about the same time, shows the University Farm, with men raking hay in the fields. The Wingate tower and Holmes Hall are to the left, and the creamery and stand pipe to the right. The bottom photo show the creamery building, built in 1891, in a closer shot.

A view of the first University green houses. This photo is from the end of the last century. Experimentation in Orono increasingly was clustered in these facilities. The central wooden house appears to have an early experimental solar heating arrangement in the roof.

Throughout the 1920's the station received little funding from sources other than federal. A department of agricultural economics was begun in 1925, one in home economics in 1927, some new construction took place in the poultry department and as replacement for buildings at Aroostook Farm, but basically little was changed. With the passage of the national Purnell Act in 1925, a few more funds were available, mostly for personnel. Edith Patch, the distinguished entomologist, finally had her salary raised in 1921 to the level of her male counterparts. The board attempted to define activities better, but many on the board felt the research tail wagged the dog, especially where expenses were concerned. The *Maine Farmer* editorialized in 1923, "Let the Good Work Go On!" but more felt like director Morse, who when faced with the reality of the mill tax passage wrote to President Boardman, "My business is to hold things down and cut our garment to suit our cloth." When the depression came, the station, like the rest of the establishment, was in good shape, its work well received, but closely scrutinized, and its

personnel generally well liked, as long as their work did not get beyond what was thought significant and useful at that time.[13] The days of purely scientific experiment had given way under these stresses to more work done on a short-term need, or even crash basis.

Most of the physical changes in the experiment station after World War I involved purchasing new land and increasing specialized farm work away from Orono. On the campus itself the farm acreage diminished steadily as much of the business of the station in Orono became administrative in nature. Experimentation continued, but it was of a type done in a smaller area, in the poultry houses, greenhouses, or in the laboratories. When Maurice D. Jones took over administration of the college farm in 1920 the Orono farm had fallen to 160 acres, 116 on the home farm and 44 in Stillwater. Ten years later the home farm was down to 74 acres, although the total had risen to 172 with the acquisition of 54 acres nearby. Further acreage was added in Stillwater and Old Town, so that by 1950 the total was 223 acres, but the home farm had only 34 of those acres.

A University barn, silos, and the poultry plant. This picture is from the period in which Raymond Pearl and his associates did definitive scientific work on poultry breeding and genetics. Plymouth Rock hens were bred for high laying records in these buildings from 1907 to 1916.

During the period after World War I the farm experimented steadily with crops. From 1921 to 1940 much corn for silage was produced, sometimes up to 300 tons a year. Sunflowers were tried from 1928 to 1935 and millet from 1921 to 1928, with the high production nearing 200 tons. Mixed peas and oats were produced from 1921 on, 100 to 200 tons each year because the crop formed a transition in the potato cycle. As long as draft animals were used hay was a major crop. The college purchased its first tractor in 1926; as late as 1942 five horses were still used, the last one disposed of in 1948. Some years the hay crop reached 400 tons, but experiments in the thirties with alfalfa were not very successful. Increasingly, however, the college farm work was located elsewhere than in Orono.[14]

In 1930 a large, modern poultry house was built and quarters were provided in Merrill Hall for the home economics department. The station director, Warner J. Morse, died in 1931 and was followed by Fred Griffee, who remained director until after World War II. During the thirties a series of fellowships were endowed to encourage special research; the first in 1932 was for poultry and egg production, others later on were for sweet corn and potato research. Potato ring-rot research was successfully concentrated on from 1946 to 1952. Blueberry culture experiments were begun on a broad scale. Soil testing also took a major place in the tasks of the station especially after more funds were freed for it by the passage of the Bankhead-Jones Act in 1935.

Potato diseases and forestry were both important subjects during World War II since both these products seemed essential to the war effort. During this time the station and the extension service were placed under the direct supervision of the dean of the College of Agriculture in order to coordinate all services more closely. George F. Dow, '27, became assistant director in 1947, with marketing problems his primary responsibility. The next year a new plant science building was dedicated (Deering Hall) and plant pathology, entomology, and horticulture had new laboratories. In 1951 Griffee died and Dow was elevated to associate director with Dean Deering assuming the director's position. Departments continued to proliferate as new specializations became important. Agricultural engineering, animal pathology, and food processing were some of the new departments in the early fifties. In 1955-1956 the previous federal acts were amended to gather them all under one blanket act, still named the Hatch Act (P.L. 352). In 1959 extension specialists were assigned to their regular departments to facilitate the total effort in agriculture. By the centennial year the lines between College of Agriculture, extension service, and experiment station were very blurred, except for budgetary purposes, as the emphasis had moved from teaching to research, both long and short-term.[15]

The special farms were purchased to answer the demand for scientific experimentation near the actual locale of the crops in the state. Ultimately three of these farms were bought. Highmoor Farm in Monmouth was the first, authorized in 1909 and voted for by the citizens in referendum in the summer of that year. A farm of about 225 acres, with 200 acres in orchards, fields, and pasture, it was designed for work in fruit, corn, and other smaller crops. About four thousand apple trees were already on the property when it was bought.

In 1914 a laboratory was installed for biology, entomology, and plant pathology. Oats, beans, corn, and apples were the primary crops of experimentation at that time. Some building was

A early photo of Highmoor Farm in Monmouth. Later the lawn became an area for small field crop experimentations. Elsewhere on this farm were many apple trees where most of the scientific work took place.

necessary, including an apple packing building in 1912, new fences, and sheep shelters. Inquiry into the profitability of sheep was begun in the World War I period. In 1920 a new barn was built to house the crossbred herd transferred from Orono. Monies were provided by the state legislature throughout the 1920's, prior to the mill tax act, to build cottages for the summer staff and to add to the land. In 1932 cold storage facilities were erected, along with a new water system. In the 1950's a farm pond was constructed and the housing facilities were completely renovated. By the time the farm celebrated its 50th anniversary in 1960 it had conducted strong research, especially in fungicide usage, plant breeding, and entomology.[16]

Once the Monmouth farm was authorized and purchased, Aroostook farmers, led by members of the Pomona Grange and Clarence A. Day, then working in Aroostook County, began to lobby for a farm in that county for potato research. In 1912 and 1913 various university specialists spoke in that region about the possibilities of such a farm. A farm choice committee was selected, and a bill presented to the legislature to allocate the necessary funds. The bill passed, but with substantial cuts in the funding. A great rivalry rose among local towns wanting to be the location, but eventually a farm was purchased in Presque Isle. Local parties provided half the money and loans for refurbishing the new property; the Bangor and Aroostook Railroad supplied funds for research. Finally in 1915 the legislature appropriated the amount necessary to reimburse the local backers.

Research at Aroostook Farm was conducted in plant breeding, especially grasses, and in potato diseases. Much of this was done in cooperation with scientists from the United States Department of Agriculture. In 1919 the station was forced to divert some of its funds to replace a roof that had blown off. Again, as in the case of Highmoor, the legislature throughout the twenties allocated special funds to maintain research and facilities at Presque Isle. In 1924 a new farm house was built to replace the older one, damaged by fire. In 1926 another fire destroyed the farm boarding house and it was replaced. Toward the end of the thirties two other farms located adjacent to Aroostook Farm were purchased for more de-

A scene in the parking lot at an Extension Field Day at Aroostook Farm in the late 1920's. County farmers, now more mobile, flocked to these affairs to hear the new scientific advice from the University.

At the field days (this one is in 1932) the visitors toured the grounds and buildings, ate a country picnic, and listened to lectures by professors. The stage advertises the Northern Maine State Fair in September, another source for information. Children attended along with parents.

An example of research in Orono. These seed beds were utilized for white pine seedlings, transplanted later into the University nursery. The photo shows several members of the staff broadcasting seed. The man in the long dark coat, fourth from the left, is Professor John Briscoe, a pioneer in this work.

tailed potato experimentation. New buildings, particularly greenhouses, were erected during World War II for the study of potato disease; money for the buildings was raised through a special potato tax. New experimental storage facilities were built after the war when the experiment station began to broaden its attack on farm problems. In the early sixties some research was done on sugar beets, but the farm itself was primarily concerned with potatoes, potato diseases, and the relationship of aphids to disease and disease control. The potato industry had become predominant in the state, in part through the study conducted by the station at Presque Isle.[17]

The last of the outlying farms was Blueberry Farm, purchased in 1946. Located in Jonesboro, it specialized in research on the Maine fruit. Funds for the purchase and erection of the farm buildings were raised through a special tax on blueberries. This farm was a logical extension of the somewhat desultory research that had been carried on in blueberries, especially in diseases, since around 1910. From about 1946 the farm has been increased in size by thirty acres, more land has been cleared, a deer fence erected around the experimental plots, and a plastic greenhouse built. In recent years substantial results have been published from the research at the site, much of which is geared to marketing as well as disease control.[18]

Two other aspects of organized research also deserve mention. The first is the technology ex-

periment station, organized in 1915. President Harris had conducted, in conjunction with the Navy Department, a long, though unsuccessful, lobbying campaign in the 1890's to have such a station authorized. Eventually it was provided for, primarily to conduct research on road beds, metal culverts, and other subjects associated with the growing use of automobiles. The station carried on a halfhearted existence until it was reorganized completely in 1927 with a new board of control covering the entire technology college. Since then it has published a number of widely used studies, some on roadbuilding, others on the career of engineering, as well as significant ones on Maine peat, balsam needle oil, Mount Katahdin, climatic divisions of Maine, and an excellent little study of human geography in Grafton, Maine. Since 1945 the Division of Industrial Cooperation has administered most of the grants and scholarships available to this and related programs. The station itself, now the official laboratory for the State Highway Commission, has continued strong work in highway testing.[19]

Another interesting outlying research facility was the University of Maine Marine Laboratory at Lamoine begun in 1926 with summer research done at Bar Harbor under the auspices of C.C. Little. In 1928 and 1929 the Bar Harbor facilities, leased for the summers, were not adequate and the private funds that Little had solicited dried up. Eventually the research was moved to the former U.S. Navy coaling depot

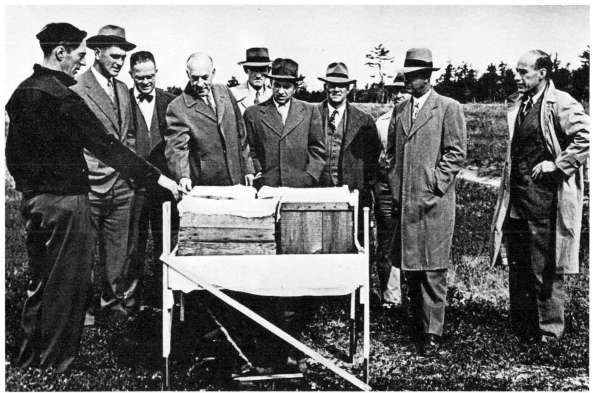

*These two photographs illustrate Blueberry Hill Farm. Top shows the farm research build-
ings after construction in 1946. The bottom photo shows the advisory committee examining a
blueberry fruit fly trap in 1947. The demonstrator is G.W. Wilson, farm superintendent.
George Lord and Fred Griffee are second and third from the left. George Dow observes from
the right.*

Dean Joseph Murray at work in his office. His secretary, Pauline Willett, has served the college nearly 47 years and is contemplating retirement as this book goes to press. Below is Murray Hall, named for the Dean, where zoology is now housed. The building, erected in the post-war building boom, is an excellent scientific facility. Murray, a member of the class of 1925, served as Dean of the College of Arts and Sciences from 1941 to 1966.

at Lamoine beach, near Ellsworth. When Joseph Murray established the summer session there in 1935 it began to fulfill its real purpose. By 1939 a five-year plan for rehabilitation of the Maine fishing industry was in discussion and Lamoine was to be the headquarters for the effort. The budget that year was increased to $2,570 with student fees providing the remainder of the costs. The central work was in marine invertebrate zoology. Laboratory facilities were good, residential facilities adequate, and course credit (six hours) given to those who participated. Collecting was done in small motor boats maintained by the laboratory.

Park pressures for recreational use of the beach emerged at about the same time the session was reorganized. During the war some of the buildings were demolished for scrap and the facility was maintained only in a caretaker status. After the war the recreation pressures built up again, and in 1949 the land was transferred back to the state for use as a park. The Lamoine center, besides providing the basic data for research polished in Orono, has evolved into a new marine and offshore research facility at the Darling Center in Walpole.

The Lamoine marine facility and the University of Maine navy in the mid-1930's. The location is now a state park.

The Darling Center in Walpole is much more attractive. Here student scuba divers and researchers are obtaining crabs for research. This photo was taken in 1968 at the time the marine research work was revived so strongly.

The Darling Center has recently received substantial federal funding under the Sea Grant program. The Lamoine idea was a good one, but in an era of reduced funds was not feasible, so pleasant summers on Frenchman's Bay soon were only a memory.[20]

Just as the research efforts at Lamoine were too little and too early, another somewhat similar project turned out to be costly and provided less benefit than had been predicted. This was the crossbreeding and genetic experiment conducted at Orono from 1913 until 1921. In the era just before World War I the university experiment station and agricultural faculty attracted a number of distinguished and later-to-be distinguished geneticists. Among them were Raymond Pearl and Karl Sax. These people began to produce a number of papers on genetics in a time when few people appreciated the significance of the Mendelian laws of inheritance, and when many people were beginning to discuss the relationship between heredity and environmental factors in human beings.[21]

As a natural result of this interest, great success in an egg production experiment, and these persons, the trustees were presented, late in

This photo, taken in 1939, symbolizes the land grant college in general and Maine in particular. The cows, part of the University herd, are grazing in front of Carnegie Hall, then the library. The mixture of the practical and the learned is precisely what Justin Morrill and the Maine founders hoped for.

1912, with a plan for "Experiments in Breeding." The agricultural college and the experiment station proposed a series of experiments to increase milk production to be financed partially by the Maine Dairymen's Association. Library materials and chemical supplies were also to be provided. Pearl himself was very aware of the time factors; in 1913 he cautioned Director Woods when he said in a letter outlining the breeding experiment, "No definite conclusion . . . can possibly be reached . . . inside of 6 to 8 years." Not everyone on the campus liked the idea, and although funding continued, by 1918 President Aley remarked to Woods upon receipt of a progress report, "I must take exception to the tone of the report. I am very glad to get a report, but I do not care to get a lecture along with it." The lecture was on the scientific value of the experiments, and though the contract was to be kept up, many queries on the work were made that year in the "interests of saving money."[22]

Within a few months the project was attacked from another quarter when the dean of the agriculture college asked whether it should be continued, since the college needed more purebred cows for teaching purposes. The breeding experiment now called for sixty more cows than the regular holdings, so barn space was a problem. A battle seemed imminent over whether the experiments should have been conducted on pure or crossbred animals. Of course, by this time Pearl had gone to Washington, not to return, so defense of the experiments lay largely in the hands of C.D. Woods, already under attack for some personality difficulties. By the end of the spring semester in 1919, President Aley, under great financial pressure, made his move. Just prior to the annual meeting of the trustees, he wrote to Woods, "It is very evident that the expense to the college of handling the breeding experiments has come to the breaking point . . . . I hope you will think out some plan that may be recommended." At that trustees' meeting there was much discussion of the experiment along with talk of breeds, grades of cattle, bulls in use, and milk sales. The trustees, in addition to informing Woods that his children could no longer be employed by the station in any capacity, did allow the continuation of the experiments, but only under certain conditions. They were not to interfere with management of the college herd, their housing was not to be a problem in the dairy barns, and their milk was not to interfere with sales from the college herd, regardless of surplus.[23]

In November of 1919 the trustees' farm committee recommended discontinuance of the experiment. They also decided that both herds, the crossbred one and one of Aberdeen-Angus cattle, be disposed of "as rapidly as is consistent with good business principles." In January the station leaders and professors appeared before an executive session of the trustees and discussed the problem in light of the 1912 agreement. As a result the experiment continued, but at Highmoor Farm.[24]

In May of 1920 the board met with the governor and council and discussed the breeding experiment. No action resulted; state leadership apparently was not prepared to help finance the cost of continuation. Woods appeared at the annual meeting a month later and was queried about the new barn at Highmoor housing the animals. The next week the farm committee viewed the barn, voted that the experiments be continued, and applied to the governor and council for aid. Woods was in the midst of his difficulties at this time and at the November meeting he was fired, but the board continued its discussion of the experiments.

At its next meeting, however, the board, after agreeing to issue no statement in the Woods case, did offer to meet with the experiment station council with regard to the experiment and to write letters to the station outlining "the general attitude of the Board of Trustees towards matters pertaining to the Station." Later the board instructed the president of the college to find out from the federal government if other experiments of a similar nature were being conducted and to ask whether the government could help in subsidizing. Eventually early in 1922, funds for a short continuance were received from the Rockefeller Institute, and they continued in a small way to 1930.

Most of the results of the breeding experiment have been forgotten; some were never published. The experiment had damaged the relationship of the station with the university, had probably caused one person to be fired, and had expended much money for little visible return. Perhaps it had kept salaries lower also. At least, it was a reason given for the failure to advance Edith Patch's salary to the equivalent male counterpart level. One person thought that a

James M. Bartlett, '80, M.S., '83, ScD, '27, served the Experiment Station and the University as a research chemist for fifty years.

Lucius H. Merrill '83, ScD, '08, served on the Station staff and in the College of Agriculture for many years as well. Here he is in a Holmes Hall laboratory in 1905.

Governor E.S. Muskie, with an aide, Dean Winthrop Libby, Director of the Experiment Station, George Dow, President Hauck, and Professor Matthew Highlands all view a new addition to the food processing plant in 1956. The facility was used in sardine research.

lack of knowledge and a lack of publicity created the difficulties. That, coupled with Pearl's resignation, may have been responsible. Too, this was a case of being out of phase with the society around the state. Lack of immediate and visible results also likely hastened the death of the crossbreeding experiment.[25]

The area of publication is probably the least known of any of the endeavors associated with the university. Publicity seldom deals with this side of academic and student life, but publication does spring, in part at least, from the expenditure of taxpayers' money. It seems useful to discuss briefly several areas of continued distinguished work and to set out some miscellaneous publications of significance in the recent years of the university.

The one department that has done the most distinguished work for the longest time, it seems clear from the record, is entomology. One of the reasons for success is that one of the earliest faculty was C.H. Fernald, who began his publishing career almost immediately upon arriving. As early as 1875 he published "Destructive Insects," including life histories. He followed this with another labor on nomenclature, "The Sphingidae of New

England," in 1886, and with these two a tradition of publication was founded. Others in this area were Clarence Ritchie Phipps, who wrote 22 articles mostly on fruit flies; Frank H. Lathrop who produced 50 papers from 1912 to 1950 on a variety of subjects, and Charles O. Dirks who wrote 44 papers on the apple maggot, bees, spruce sawflies, and spruce budworm. Work begun by Dirks is still being carried on by others. Geddes Simpson published some 170 papers between 1929 and 1974, most on aphids, but on a number of other aspects of entomology as well. Edith Patch was the star of the department, however, producing some 78 separate papers in her tenure at Orono and about 15 books on nature study. Her great publication, *Food Plant Catalogue of the Aphids of the World,* (Bulletin 383, 3 vols., 1938) is still in print and remains one of the most outstanding scientific contributions made by any Orono-associated person.[26]

Other writings in this area include the *Entomological Publicity Letters* issued from February 1912 to August 1919. Nearly 400 were published, perhaps the most important being No. 14, "Wire Worms;" No. 57, "Give the Parasites a Chance;" No. 189 "Economic

A University of Maine group displays a Maine pennant deep in Antarctica. They include two students, Richard Dodge '69, Stephan Brown '69, Professor Bradford Hall, '55, and Professor Harold Borns, of the Geology Department.

Moths of Maine;'' and No. 317, ''Are There Weevils in Your Bean Seeds?'' Other works are Albert C. Morse's *Othoptera of Maine,* (Bulletin No. 296, 1921) and more recently Auburn E. Brower's *A List of the Lepidoptera of Maine (Part One; The Macrolepidoptera)* (Technical Bulletin No. 66, January 1974). As one can see, the great strength of the department has been in the area of nomenclature, classification, and ecological relationships. In this last, perhaps led by Patch, the entomology department has been a leader in the country.

Another area that stands out is the recent work in forestry and forest products. Immediately after World War II the most published person in this subject, and probably still the most widely known in the world, was Harold Young. His research, especially in utilization of the whole tree, has received much praise. Another who has been significant is Fay Hyland, a distinguished botanist. Research and publication on methods of using wood, economic studies of the users, and related entomological work with tree related insects have made much progress. The field of forest history has also produced a number of good scholars in other colleges, most notably E.D. Ives, who has

done superior work in oral history, especially of woodsmen, and who has set up a related organization, Archives of Northeast Folklore and Oral History, which produces an annual, *Northeast Folklore* (1956-). Richard Sprague in English has also done notable work in this area, and the author is engaged in these studies as well.[27]

Since 1960, important and distinguished work has been accomplished in the general field of polar studies. In biology, work has been led by John W. Dearborn and others; in geology by Harold Borns, George Denton and their colleagues. The Quaternary Institute was founded to administer research grants and to coordinate research efforts. The results of these efforts are internationally known.

The university faculty has published books and articles on many other subjects including foods, nutrition, potato farming, marketing, and dairying. Some that have been especially important are *Instructions for Canning and Preserving* (Extension Bulletin No. 112, revised 1918), which was widely used with Four-H clubs; W. Franklin Dove, *A Study of the Causes of Nutritional Deficiency Diseases in the Livestock and Inhabitants of Maine With Possible Corrective*

Hadley Robbins, left, retired as Superintendent of the Printing Office in 1975 after fifty years service. His predecessor, Roy Libby, is at right. The white frame building served from the end of World War I to 1968 as the Print Shop. The lower photo shows the new establishment built in that year. In the twentieth century a University Press and Print Shop are central to efficient work. Books, journals, pamphlets, catalogs, flyers, broadsides, and other work all pour from the Press.

Methods Secured From the Utilization of Maine Fishery Products and the Production of Superior Foods (Bulletin No. 375, November 1934); and Kathryn E. Briwa and Gordon M. Cairns, *Meat Preservation For Home Use* (Extension Bulletin No. 318, October 1943), extensively used during World War II. On potatoes one might cite William D. Hurd, *Potato Growing for Maine Farmers* (Maine Department of Agriculture, Quarterly Bulletin, Vol. VIII, No. 2, June 1909); Bulletin No. 334 (1926) on potato spraying and dusting experiments; Bulletins No. 378-380 (1935) on economic studies of Maine and especially potato farming; Joseph A. Chucka, Arthur Hawkins, and Bailey E. Brown, *Potato-Fertilizer-Rotation Studies on Aroostook Farm, 1927-1941* (Bulletin No. 414, 1943); William E. Schrumpf, *Effect of Potato Acreage Reductions on Aroostook County Farm Economics* (Bulletin No. 518, June 1953); and Reginald K. Harlan, *Costs, Returns and Efficiency of Potato*

Production in Maine (Bulletin No. 701, June 1973). Dairying also received recent treatment by Raymond N. Krofta and Richard J. Higby, *Cash Flow Analysis . . . of Maine Dairy Farmers, Research in the Life Sciences,* Vol. 20, No. 14, April 1973, and Howard C. Dickey, *Selection for Type and Milk Production in Dairy Cattle* (Technical Bulletin No. 72, June 1974).

Other works of use to Maine's citizens are early publications on nomenclature, especially those from the Laboratory of Natural History from 1888 to 1898. These catalogued minerals and rocks, various plants, birds, fungi, and dragonflies, and were important in laying a scientific foundation for future work.[28]

Some, among many, significant publications about land use and road building include G.H. Hamlin's "Best Roadways for Maine," in *Agriculture of Maine, 1892,* pp. 100-116; Charles D. Woods' "Influence of Width of Tire on Draft of Wagons," in *Agriculture of Maine, 1897,* pp. 36-58; Andrew E. Watson's *A Study* of Land Use in Thirty-One Towns in Aroostook County, Maine (Bulletin No. 413, 1942); Orlando E. Delogu and David B. Gregory's *Planning and Law in Maine* (Bulletins No. 643, 654, November 1967); Edward O. Schriver's *Maine Landowners Handbook: A Reference Manual for the Layman,* Portland, 1974; and Charles E. Buck's *The Effect of Road Salt on Aerobic Soil Bacteria Adjacent to a Major Highway,* April 1974.

Materials for a closer study of Maine's agricultural history that have been collected and published by the Orono faculty include Charles H. Merchant's *Maine Agriculture: A Statistical Presentation* (Bulletin No. 338, 1927), *An Economic Survey of the Apple Industry in Maine* (Bulletin No. 339, 1927), *An Economic Study of 93 Apple Farms in Oxford County, Maine* (Bulletin No. 347, 1928), *Prices of Farm Products in Maine* (Bulletin No. 364, 1933), and Wilbert C. Geiss and Reginald K. Harlan's

Costs and Returns on Maine Apple Farms (Bulletin No. 704, June 1973). Other useful items include James Stacey Stevens' *Meteorological Conditions at Orono, Maine* (University of Maine Studies, Old Series No. 7, February 1907), G.R. Cooper and R.E. Lautzenheiser's *Freezes in Maine* (Bulletin No. 679, September 1969), and Eliot Epstein's *Variability of Drought in the Northeast* (Technical Bulletin 69, April 1974). Clarence Day's various publications are very significant here as well.

The special collections area of the library showing several rare books. Muriel Sanford, shown here, is responsible for the University archives, and provided many of the illustrations for this book. A fine reading room and research area adjoin the stacks, where much of this book was researched as well.

This discussion has been limited primarily to agricultural and technical research. Of course much other research and significant publication takes place in other areas, although usually on a less well organized basis. The Coe fund, established in 1928 from a bequest of Thomas U. Coe, has supplied some monies to researchers. In the last fifteen years, the fund's committee, called the Research Funds Committee, has sponsored research of all kinds throughout the campus. In addition, private academic research has also been undertaken, with rather outstanding results. Persons active and deserving mention might well include Ronald Levinson, a noted Plato scholar, best known for his *In Defense of Plato;* William Randel, author of several books on the Ku Klux Klan and other subjects in social and intellectual history; Carroll Terrell, founder and managing editor of the distinguished journal on Ezra Pound, *Paideuma,* published at Orono; and Howard Eves, who has done prominent work in the history of mathematics. In the history department alone some twenty major books and many articles were published between 1965 and 1975. Earlier the university hosted and supplied the editors for the journal of history and letters, the *New England Quarterly.* Recently the university library has had a full-time archivist and a special collections room that has undertaken spirited collection of manuscripts, books, documents, and memorabilia under the guidance of Frances Hartgen. Any more mention becomes simply a list. One can see by the breadth and depth of the published works how this aspect of university life is maintained in a strong way at Orono.

Universities have many obligations. They must educate the citizens of their region to meet the future and they must provide an extension of that education for those who are no longer or who have never been on campus. In addition, faculty members have a responsibility to research in their fields and to publish the results. For most of the citizens of the state their university is the place where the answers are, the place where Maine citizens get their money's worth with regard to their questions about life. Research, teaching, and public service are all part of the same institution and its obligations.

Notes

1. Although I have handled and read nearly all of the publications of the University at Orono, there is no way that one can, in a short chapter, detail all aspects of this work. The following is an effort to summarize. My thanks go to Professor Geddes Simpson who has guided me through much of this work, and who provided me with office space and Edith Patch's desk to work from, while doing this chapter and the previous one. I have a full scholarly history of the Maine Agricultural Experiment Station forthcoming.

2. Oak to Fernald, December 22, 1877.

3. Fernald to Oak, December 25, 1877.

4. *Agriculture of Maine, 26th Annual Report, 1882,* Augusta, 1883, 114-129, Walter Balentine, "Experimental Work in Agriculture," 210-218, C.H. Fernald, "Natural History of the Potato-Rot Fungus, 291-304, G.M. Gowell and Walter Balentine, "Farm Experiments at State College"; S.A. Knapp, undated flyer, c. 1884, *Experiment Stations.*

5. *Public Laws of Maine, 1885,* Ch. 294; *Report of the Maine Fertilizer Control and Agricultural Experiment Station; Analysis of Fertilizers For the Months of April, May and June, 1885,* Orono?, 1885?

6. *Annual Report,* (1885-1886) *The Maine Fertilizer Control and Agricultural Experiment Station,* Augusta, 1886 (1886-1887); Bulletins 1-21, all in *Whig and Courier,* 1886-1888; Bulletin 22 is a short history of this station.

7. Trustees, January 20, 1887; Maine Board of Agriculture, Annual Meeting, January 19, 1888 *(Agriculture of Maine, 1889)* 20-25, M.C. Fernald, "The Experiment Station and Its Work," W.H. Jordan, "Clover in Agriculture,"; *Annual Report,* Maine State College Agriculture Experiment Station, 1888, Augusta, 1889.

8. *Annual Report,* Agricultural Experiment Station, 1889, Augusta, 1890.

9. Trustees, November 6, 1890; April 10, 1891; May 11, 1893; June 19, July 17, 1894; June 18, 1895; February 25, June 16, November 3, 1896; January 1, 1897; *Cadet,* September 10, 1887; May 1891; Woods to Harris, June 13, 1899; John Boyd Thacker to Harris, July 8, 1894; *Report,* Board of Agriculture, 1894, Harris, 23-41; 1896 (good photos); Bulletin No. 62, 1900, history of station; *Report,* State Pomological Society, 1898.

10. Trustees, June 14, 1905; Woods to George E. Fellows, December 21, 1904; *Maine Farmer* June 30, 1904; Bulletin No. 98, *Bug Death* was a problem; Trustees, December 1, 1910, and letters from Maine Dairymen's Association and others; *Practical Husbandry of Maine,* Vol. 1, No. 1 to Vol. 8, No. 5-9 [October, 1910 to March, 1918].

11. *Official Inspections,* August, 1912, shellfish, 155-164; ice creams etc., 182-192; Raymond Pearl, "The Need for Endowed Agricultural Research, *Science,* N. Series, Vol. 37, No. 958, 707-9; Folder, "Advanced Registry Work for Maine," Exp. Sta. Bulletin No. 246, [January, 1916], *Field Experiments in 1915;* Trustees, April 18, 1917.

12. Annual Reports, 1915-1921; Trustees, June 20, November 5, 1919 (Augusta); January 23, 1920; January 6, 1921 (Augusta); February 12, 1921 (Bangor); Morse to Aley, May 28, 1921 (Patch). Folder, "Maine Experiment Station," Trustees August 6, 1925 on relationship of the groups involved, E.W. Allen to W.J. Morse, August 25, 1925. Forty-first Annual Report of the Experiment Station, Orono, 1925, has obituary on Woods, "He set his face against the misuse of public funds to satisfy uninformed public demands."

13. Annual Reports, 1921-1932; W.J. Morse to H.S. Boardman, June 28, 1929 in folder, "Maine Experiment Station." Boardman to Morse, July 1, 1929 in same folder; *Maine Farmer,* April 28, 1923, editorial, "Pure Science."

14. Maurice D. Jones, "Twenty-Five Years with the College Farm," typed manuscript, dated January 30, 1952 in Fogler collection.

15. "Dates of Important Developments," mimeoed document, December 12, 1968; minutes Station Council, April 16, 1942; Trustees, February 4, 1932; June 12, 1937. C.A. Day, G.F. Dow and Fred Griffee, Bulletin 616, [November, 1949], *Thirty Minutes With the Maine Agricultural Station;* Annual Reports, especially 63rd, 1947, 503-5; *Maine Farm Research,* a quarterly from the Station, beginning April, 1953.

16. Trustees, June 8, 1909; Minutes Station Council, April 14-15, 1915; *Campus,* January 14, 1919; Laws of Maine, *1921,* Ch. 97; *1927,* Ch. 45; *1909,* Ch. 15; Sen. Docs., No. 12, 1929; Frank J. McDonald, "Fifty Years of Service to Maine Agriculture," *Maine Farm Research,* Vol. 8, No. 2 [July, 1960], a good short history of the Highmoor operation.

17. Clarence A. Day, "Historical Information Relating to the Establishment of the Aroostook Experimental Farm," typed manuscript dated June 20, 1941, includes copies of many original documents, including the minutes of the committee on selection and purchase; *Campus,* May 27, 1913; Minutes Station Council, April 14-15, 1915; Woods to Aley, May 3, 1919; Laws of Maine, *1913,* Ch. 190; *1921,* Ch. 97; *1927,* Ch. 45; Maine, House Documents, No. 280, 1927; Senate Documents, No. 15, 1929.

18. Legislative Documents, 1945, L.D. 68 (Senate); Clarence A. Day, "A History of the Blueberry Industry in Washington County," typed

manuscript c. 1955; M.F. Trevett, "The Integrated Management of Low Bush Blueberry Fields," Bulletin 699, December, 1972; Charles H. Merchant, *An Economic Study of 239 Blueberry Farms . . .,* Bulletin, 351, (1929); *Research in the Life Sciences,* Vol. 21, No. 11, 12, 13 (all on marketing, and bird damage); *Technical Bulletin* No. 70, [May 1974], *Physical and Chemical Changes . . . .*

19. Harris Correspondence; Station Minutes, September 28, 1915; Trustees, May 12, 1927; Bulletin No. 30, H. Walter Levitt and Edward H. Perkins, *A Survey of Road Materials and Glacial Geology of Maine,* (3 volumes), 1935; Bulletin No. 20, "Shall I Be An Engineer?" by Walter J. Creamer; Paper No. 46, Joseph M. Trefethen and Robert B. Bradford, *Domestic Possibilities of Maine Peat;* Charles B. Fobes, *Grafton, Maine . . .,* Bulletin No. 42.

20. Trustees, November 10, 1933 (Bangor); February 7, 1935 (Augusta); March 2, 1939; Execu. Committee (Augusta), February 15, 1949; April 21, 1965; Much correspondence, Little and Boardman 1926-1929 (especially Little to Boardman, September 17, 1926; Boardman to Little, September 21, 1926; Boardman to Little, March 12, 1927; Little to Boardman, March 15, 1927; Boardman to Little, October 3, 1928; Little to Boardman, January 19, 1929); D.B. Young to Boardman, February 28, 1933; Joseph Murray to James Muilenberg, November 5, 1935, report on 1936-37, dated March 15, 1937; *Annual Announcements,* 1936-1941; Frederick G. Payne to Hauck, February 3, 1949; Ralph W. Farris, (Attorney General) to Hauck, February 3, 1949; Richard W. Morgrage to Hauck, June 10, 1949; Laws of Maine, *1941,* Ch. 81.

21. Bulletin No. 79 [1902], G.M. Gowell, *Feeding Chickens For Growth Breeding for Egg Production;* Bulletin No. 204 [September, 1912], and No. 205 [November, 1912], Raymond Pearl, *A Case of Triplet Calves . . .; Mode of Inheritance of Fecundity in Domestic Fowl;* In that same year Pearl published 5 Nos. [33-37] in *Papers From the Biological Laboratory,* see Experiment Station Annual Report, 1912, *Biological Laboratory,* see Experiment Station Annual Report, 1912, as well as papers in a number of national scholarly articles on genetics; Karl Sax, "A Genetic Interpretation of Ecological Adaptation," *Biological Gazette,* Vol. 82[1927], 223-7. Pearl was responsible for a technical development of importance, a trapnest to ensure proper egg/parent analysis.

22. Trustees, November 7, 1912, memo "Experiments in Breeding,"; letter Pearl to Woods, April 21, 1913; Aley to Woods, October 21, 1918, typed memo, "Proposed Plan for a Comprehensive Investigation of the Inheritance of Milk Production."

23. L.S. Merrill to Aley, February 18, 1919; March 1, 1919; L.S. Corbett to Merrill, February 18, 1919; Woods to Aley, January 23, 1919; February 24, 1919; Aley to Woods, May 26, 1919; Trustees, June 20, 1919.

24. Trustees, November 5, 1919 (Augusta); January 23, 1920.

25. Trustees, May 12 (Augusta), June 4, 10 (Bangor), November 29, 1920; January 6 (Augusta), February 12, (Bangor) September 24, 1921; January 20, 1922; W.J. Morse to F.H. Strickland, December 2, 1921; December 18, 1921 (and a whole sheaf on problems of finance from 1922-24); to R.J. Aley, May 28, 1921 (on Edith Patch and the experiments); Some ideas lingered on, see Maine House Documents, 1927, No. 281; Sen. Doc., 1929, No. 13, both to provide $10,000 for animal husbandry. Neither passed. The science involved here is discussed in detail in my forthcoming book on the Experiment Station.

26. C.H. Fernald, *Report of the State Pomological Society,* 1875, 17-31; Agriculture of Maine, 1886; Patch's obituary appears in *American Entomological Society of America,* vol. 48 [1955], 313-4, personal knowledge, interview with Geddes Simpson, 1973, 1974.

27. As examples see Thomas J. Corcoran, Daniel I. Schroeder, David B. Thompson, *An Evaluation of the Distribution of Trucked Pulpwood in East-Central Maine,* (Bulletin 640 May 1966); Norman P. Kutscha and Raymond R. McOrmond, *The Suitability of Using Fluorescence Microscopy For Studying Lignification in Balsam Fir,* (Technical Bulletin 62, November 1972); John B. Dimond, *Sequential Surveys For the Pine Leaf Chermid, Pineus Pinifoliae,* (Technical Bulletin No. 68, March 1974); Fay Hyland, *Fiber Analysis and Distribution in the Leaves, Juvenile Stems and Roots of Ten Maine Trees and Shrubs,* (Technical Bulletin No. 71, 1974); Harold E. Young, "Challenge of Complete Tree Utilization," *Forest Products Journal,* Vol. 18, No. 4 [1968], 83-6; See David C. Smith, "Forest History Research and Writing at the University of Maine," *Forest History,* Vol. 12, No. 2 [July, 1968], 27-31. Another example is Andrew J. Chase, Fay Hyland, Harold E. Young, *The Commercial Use of Puckerbrush Pulp,* (Technical Bulletin No. 65, December 1973).

28. These are all in the publications of the Laboratory of Natural History, with the exception of fungi and dragonflies which are University of Maine Studies, First Series, No. 3 (April 1902), and No. 4 (August 1902).

CHAPTER TWELVE

Since the Centennial

THIS HISTORY was originally conceived as a centennial history, but was shelved for a number of years because of a scarcity of funds and of persons interested in the work. When it was revived, the centennial idea was still thought valid. However, a decade has elapsed since that anniversary, so a brief discussion of that period seems necessary. What follows is a brief look at the last ten years.

The building flurry of the early sixties dwindled fairly quickly and by 1967-1968 the campus had settled down appreciably. Soon however, a period of faculty and student unrest coinciding with the general unrest in the country and focusing on, but not limited to, the Vietnam War caused a rather major reevaluation of the university and its purpose. The early seventies was such a period of reappraisal, as the Orono campus increasingly found itself debating its place within the state's higher education system. During the last decade three presidents have served: Edwin Young, Winthrop Libby, and Howard Neville. With all of them academic excellence ranked high in priority. Growth has been steady both in numbers of students and faculty and, above all, in the general intellectual excellence of the institution.

Budgetary demands have received increasingly stronger scrutiny by the legislature. In May 1968 the colleges in the state maintained by public funds were joined together by the legislature into a "super-university" and from that time Orono's requests have been part of a package covering the entire state. A referendum in fall of 1968 calling for $6.3 million in bonded funds passed, along with another bond issue of $7.5 million in construction, but this was the last of the easier times. Chancellors have had a difficult job of coordinating priorities since then.[1]

The centennial year marked the high point of agreement on what could be done for funds. Governor Reed recommended nearly all the university trustees' requests. In that year congestion in the dormitories was so great that the trustees authorized a crash program, named the 1-0-1 program, after both Senator Roger Snow (R. Portland) and the Education Committee of the legislature suggested an emergency approach. This program called for some students to attend the complete summer session, take perhaps one or two C.E.D. courses in the fall, and return to the campus in the spring semester as full-time students. Dormitory rooms and classrooms would receive maximum usage under this plan, which was continued during the remainder of the construction program through 1967. In additon, building construction was accelerated after legislative hearings on the needs of the school. The Hilltop Complex and some other buildings resulted. Dow Field in Bangor was available for some housing of students, although after much discussion, classes there have not been part of the Orono offerings, except indirectly, and by the seventies the facility became known as Bangor Community College. Its dormitories still served as a housing overflow for Orono, however, and students continued to commute on the hourly bus run between the two campuses.

President Elliott submitted his resignation in July of 1965 and was replaced in the fall by Edwin Young, who had taught at Orono briefly before going on to Wisconsin as a teacher and administrator. In 1960 Elliott had written the following to a fellow administrator who had completed a quarter century in his position.

Perhaps Elliott felt the same when he left his own job.

> . . . I congratulate you upon survival through a quarter century in a game that is sometimes rougher than football, sometimes more frustrating than maneuvering at the United Nations, but sometimes is more rewarding than cotton candy at circus time.[2]

The crunch of student numbers continued through the next few years. The legislature authorized a budget of over $10 million a year in 1967, an increase of $2.6 million mostly to be used for salaries, and even more funds came during the special session in 1968.[3]

The legislature did put a number of items out for referenda, including money for the Law School, Dow Field alterations, a building at the Augusta campus, funds for the Darling Center, a new chemical engineering building at Orono,

and a new physical education building at Orono. The referenda passed, but the result was close enough that the trustees agreed it would be preferable in future to have a package that would appeal to all citizens. In that year 1,000 students above those planned for came to Orono, and 800 extra were scheduled for 1968-1969. This growth occasioned a visit to the special session of the legislature, which was successful. The special session also began discussion of the new super-university and an enlarged board of trustees and a chancellor to run it. The super-university was defeated then because of a lack of detailed discussion, but the next regular session of the legislature did install the wider system. This last legislature also dealt with the smaller university relatively well. The trustees asked for $23.6 million for the biennium, the governor suggested $20.5, and the legislature provided $21.3. Life was still comparatively peaceful, as President Young summarized it in a letter during this time.

> Life goes on about as usual here at the University — more buildings, more students — more faculty — everything to keep us very busy.[4]

President Edwin Young

Life did go on fairly smoothly during this period. Faculty and students also attempted to adjust to the larger population. There was an increase in interest in the Maritine Provinces, leading to the installation of a student-faculty exchange program with the University of New Brunswick. Graduate credit was something of a problem, especially at the Portland branch. The arts and science college cut its hour requirements to 120 from 128 and instituted some pass-fail options. Earlier, the history and government department split into two distinct forces. Most of these changes were an indication of the larger groups of faculty and students, and it was felt that the changes would help solve some of the administrative difficulties. The school of business administration became a college, and a two-year technology program was instituted. The first of several chaired professorships were funded with grants from citizens. The enlarged student body caused some in the state to press for a "more representative" sports schedule, which was accomplished to some extent. The football team, for instance, visited the Tangerine Bowl in 1965. No football scholarships were offered, however, because

The Hilltop dormitory complex taken soon after completion in 1968. A food service area and a conference area are in the middle surrounded by dormitories.

the board, when faced with requests for more funding, called for an "athletic program for students rather than for the grandstand."[5]

Much of the student population now chose to enter the college of arts and sciences, rather than the older colleges of agriculture and technology. In the fall of 1970, for instance, arts and sciences had 2,976 students, with education second at 1,635. Life sciences and agriculture claimed 1,359 undergraduates and technology had 799. Business administration had 561 students. For the older colleges it was a time to analyze where they were going, and for the arts college it was a time to absorb. As early as 1960 the trustees had listened to a detailed report on the College of Agriculture. The report raised a number of questions, among them whether an irreducible number of agricultural programs must be offered and how money for courses beyond this minimum was to be raised. The standard of student research, the role of re-

search and extension in the college, and the status of the department of forestry were also discussed in the report. All the questions led to a reorganization.

From 1940 to 1959 the number of student majors in the agriculture college had dropped steadily from 31.3 percent to 15.5 percent of the total university. The next ten years were a constant effort to deal with the situation. Farm and Home Week was broadened to include the rest of the university. The new forestry building helped create desires for a change in curricula, with a two-year technology program and two new associate directors (one in forest products and one in wildlife), while the research effort was strengthened. A new soil and water conservation center was authorized by the federal government, and in many ways the research/extension goals were extended in this period. Cooperative extension was withdrawn from the college and placed in the new Division of Public

Services although later returned to the college. Much work in soil and water testing began, and environmental considerations became increasingly important. A national task force on the land-grant colleges attacked the national complex for placing an overemphasis on agribusiness and not enough on the family farm. To some extent the criticism applied to Maine, especially in the horrible example of the sugar beet industry. But the reevaluation at Maine came at precisely the time of the national attack, so the future seemed to be brighter. To judge from recent publications and research results, the emphasis has shifted away from industry alone to deal with more of Maine's citizens, including those not in agriculture.[6] Enrollment figures, too, have reversed earlier trends. As campus population has risen, recent student choices have been more career oriented, and registrations in Life Sciences and Agriculture, Business Administration and Technology are high.

The considerable growth in student and faculty population, especially in the arts college, was coupled with a searching examination into national goals and priorities. This was triggered nationally first by the human rights movement, then by the free speech movement at the University of California and elsewhere, and later by a criticism of values in the country in the aftermath of an uneasy peace and unwanted war in the Far East. It led on many campuses to student and faculty unrest. Maine was no exception, although the unrest was less strong. Indeed it often had a strong opposition backlash among students and faculty, as well as the administration.

This backlash was perhaps caused by a certain rigidification of mentality which had begun to set in by the end of the fifties in a number of places. Student protest and political partisanship that had been a strength of the campus in the 1930's began to be subjected to pressure from these more rigid forces. In 1956, for instance, there was much discussion when the student newspaper supported political candidates. In 1962 students stopped a debate when a United States Communist Party member was one of the participants. This engendered protest from the state's newspapers supporting free speech. In spring of 1966 a band of students and faculty protesting and picketing the R.O.T.C.

parade were attacked and egged by other students, without much protest from the administration or the campus police. Some modification of the police rules was later made, however. The director of student services became a target of attack when he seemed to be unsympathetic with the concepts of free speech and academic inquiry. Aligned with this controversy was the increasing effort by many students to free themselves of what were felt to be outmoded regulations of social behavior. A presidential committee was formed in 1965 to deal with these matters, and ultimately parietal hours (dormitory closings) came under sharp and successful attack. The director of student services found another position, and the free speech area was formally accepted by the trustees as being the whole of the campus rather than a small area isolated and alone. To have a campus without free speech seemed to many to be a contradiction in terms.

Throughout 1968 and 1969 a number of outside speakers came to the campus as interest in foreign affairs grew. In 1968, for instance, Eugene McCarthy, William Hathaway, Barry Goldwater, Mark Hatfield, and Mike Mansfield all spoke on the campus. Students and faculty continued to express interest by participation in a variety of off-campus events: strikes, picketing, leafletting, and so on. On the campus several teach-ins were held, all very respectful of the dimensions of academic inquiry. Students and faculty were involved in picketing and a sit-down strike in opposition to recruiting by Dow Chemical on the campus. This led to a sit-down confrontation in the president's office, where President Young was cordial to the demonstrators.

In the spring of 1969 a serious confrontation was just averted following a rally to oppose the war and the R.O.T.C. In the fall a further giant rally was held on the library steps, with perhaps four thousand attending. In the spring of 1970 difficulties over retention of many well liked young professors in the sociology department quickened student interest in decision making. All these situations were intensified by a potentially rough incident which had taken place in the Union during the last days of the election of 1968.

After the militia confrontations and student deaths elsewhere, sparked by the Cambodian

When the Vietnam War reached one height, the protests also increased. Here President Young is somewhat bemused by students and faculty who have come to visit him and protest recruitment by firms profiting by the war.

The top photograph is President Winthrop Libby, '32, in a typical mood. He served in a number of administrative posts in the agriculture area before being named as president. The bottom photo shows Libby and Vice President Bruce Poulton accepting the transfer of the Dow AFB properties soon to be Bangor Community College. Some of those buildings are in the background. This transfer occurred July 16, 1968.

invasion by U.S. troops, a number of large rallies were held on the campus, classes were cancelled and teach-ins substituted. An extraordinary meeting of the arts and sciences college called by young faculty condemned the war, supported the student protesters, and demanded that faculty use their classes to provide education on these subjects. This motion passed by a two to one majority of those present. The protests died away when classes came to an end that spring.

A referendum scheduled for that June was defeated by the citizens, and some have since blamed the defeat on the action of the students. Although there may have been those who voted negatively on this basis, many of the negative votes were cast by voters who felt the amounts spent in the previous decade to be plenty. This feeling was coupled with opposition to the chancellor, to the super-university system, to a faulty publicity campaign, and to what seemed to many to be a poor choice of alternatives in the referendum, which appeared to be providing something for everybody, but without any real attempt to avoid unnecessary or duplicatory expenditures.

All in all, these years had been a trying time and one, in retrospect, that probably could have been avoided with a less rigid attitude by some administrators. Where difficulties did occur, it was usually when these attitudes were rigid. In some areas trouble erupted because no policy was formed until after the event. It is fashionable now to denigrate these protests, and to call the students apathetic in their wake, but in the long run they did the university and the country good, as the spirit of free discussion was once again returned to the campus. Those students and faculty who participated in the events had a sense of historical participation at the time that has not dimmed for most of them.[7]

While this sort of self-evaluation of the country and the purpose of some of its institutions was going on, the university also did a self-evaluation. In the fall of 1970, a report, now known as the Douglass report for its chairman, Irwin Douglass, was widely circulated. The primary mission of the university was restated "to provide the benefits of higher learning to the people of Maine, the neighboring region, the nation, and the international community through education, research and public service." This

Campus social life became increasingly a time for special occasions after World War II. The Memorial Union rooms shown above were the locations for many such events. In the dormitories, house mothers were often the agents for these celebrations. Here, with a friend are Ruby Ingraham, Ella Smith, and Blanche Henry, '33, three well-known housemothers. The top photo was taken in 1967 while the bottom dates from 1970.

mission was to be achieved through a four-year baccalaureate program, graduate programs, associate programs, continuing education, a library, research and scholarly activity into problems of the day, public services for the citizens of the state, the sponsoring of a wide variety of events, programs, and conferences, and a strengthening of student life through a maximum amount of facilities and services. In addition the university was charged with providing a press for publication, as well as with seeking new approaches and reviewing its goals and priorities at regular, frequent intervals. The report went on to spell out in detail educational goals with primary references to students, the educational process, faculty, graduate study, the administration, and the public service sector. Two deserve quotation as emblematic of the tone of the entire document. They are the goals for the educational environment.

A. To promote an atmosphere at the University pervaded by a respect for scholarly attainment, a stimulating spirit of free inquiry and an appreciation of those forms of endeavour concerned with the aesthetic aspects of our culture,

B. To recognize that the search for truth and the transmission of knowledge are the essential functions of the University and that all facilities and administrative activities exist to serve those ends.[8]

Students walking on the mall in 1971. The mini-skirt is not yet gone, but blue jeans are beginning to appear. This photo, taken in the early fall, indicates some of the bustle of the present campus.

This photograph, and those below, indicate student life today. The top photo shows members of the class of 1972 clearly enjoying the remarks of one of their professors. This book is dedicated to that class who symbolize to the author why he wanted to teach. They came to the campus in the fall of 1968 and when they left they had improved it.

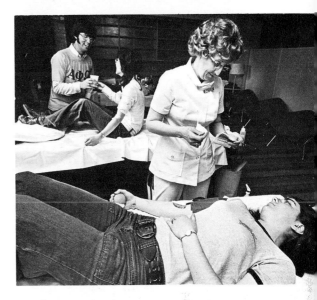

The classes of the middle seventies seemed to have a seriousness of purpose, both about themselves and about the future. The photo, middle left, taken in 1973, shows a dance marathon staged to raise funds for library purchases. The middle right photo, from 1974, is of students donating blood. At the bottom Rudy Valee, ex-'23, returned to entertain a new generation of Maine students but without his megaphone and saxophone properties. They seem to enjoy it in their typically informal way. The photograph is from 1975.

President Winthrop Libby at the annual faculty breakfast, September, 1971.

Chancellor Donald McNeil.

The next year, at the annual faculty breakfast, the president, Withrop Libby, in an apparent reference to the goals, called for continued student contribution into many aspects of the life at Orono, including evaluation of instruction. He also called for better individual evaluation of goals, along with the use of newer methods of instruction where useful. He asked for an improvement in the intellectual climate of the university, as well as better guidance of students in their own goal searches. The chancellor, Donald McNeil, addressed the same breakfast, and he too called for greater attention to students, with greater dedication to the public side of the university work, also. As he said, ''The long term strength of the organization of this University should be in its capacity to guard and foster diversity, innovation, and experimentation, rather than in its ability to spread uniformity, standardization, centralization, and sameness throughout higher education in Maine.''[9] These goals, so clearly expressed by these different orators and writers, remain the goals of the university.

Libby offered his resignation in 1973 and was replaced by Howard Neville, formerly of the University of Nebraska. Neville's inaugural address in January 1974 provided a restatement of some of the priorities in the earlier reports, especially in undergraduate education, and called for the establishment of a fund drive to achieve two major centers for the campus; one a museum and performing arts center, the second, a multipurpose sports arena.[10]

Certainly as one looked about the campus in the mid-part of the decade of the seventies, over 110 years after the first faint glimmerings of the university, one saw a rather massive operation. It utilized computer services widely and had a number of new buildings. its walks were filled with hurrying students and faculty, all seemingly bent in the pursuit of knowledge and excellence. A distinguished professor and researcher were named annually, and a new honors center, so often discussed, was now in use. A library addition had just been finished;

President Howard Neville. He arrived on the campus in the fall of 1973 and completes six years service in the year this book appears. The bottom picture is of his inauguration when he laid out an ambitious program for the next period of time.

Neville's years brought some badly needed construction as the student numbers continued to increase. At top appears an addition to the library designed to provide not only stack areas, but catalog and study space as well. In the center is the complex housing the English and Mathematics departments. They are connected with the new compter center. Both of these photos date from 1976. The most recent addition to the campus is at right, a new skating rink and sports facility, Alfond Arena, named for Harold Alfond, a recent benefactor. Ice hockey has been popularized at Orono with this new building, dedicated in 1977.

Over the years the University of Maine has graduated a large number of persons who have had many family ties to other graduates. The call of Maine to alumni sons and daughters has been strong and their affection to their alma mater great. The photo to the left is Patrick E. McCarthy, '58, now chancellor of the University of Maine system. Below is his grandfather, Patrick E. McCarthy, '02, president of his class.

some funds were available for faculty research. Many of the faculty were nationally known, while some had international reputations. By and large, the Orono campus also held the esteem of the state's citizens. Few would denigrate its work, even fewer if they knew the difficulties of its historic past.

The university was born as the result of much work by dedicated persons who believed that its establishment would aid the cause of making Maine a better place. It lived through early difficult years, always under attack, especially from the private institutions in the state, while it spread its ideas. Occasionally it left the path of academic inquiry, as during both World War I and the cold war periods. Some presidents were flamboyant, others quiet and unassuming. Students came and went, most of them the better for their experience. The university provided wide services for the state. It became a true university for all — democracy's college — to borrow a phrase. More remained to be done, but on the basis of the past, it seemed likely that eventually most would get done. That, in itself, was reason enough to celebrate the past, but always with the future in mind.

Notes

1. *Laws of Maine, 1967,* Ch. 252, 383, *1969,* 114, 164, 190, 229. *Leg. Docs., 1967,* No. 553, 934, 1,160, 1,212, 1,258, 1,362, 1,693, *1969,* No. 234, 235, 406, 407, 1,176.

2. Trustees, January 20, 1965; February 25, 1965; Elliott to the Board, February 25, 1965; Elliott to President and Mrs. Albert N. Jorgenson (U. Conn.) November 12, 1960.

3. Trustees, July 28, 1967.

4. Trustees, July 28, November 21, (Portland), 1967; January 3, 1968 (Executive Session); Edwin Young to Stephen C. Casakis, February 1, 1967.

5. Trustees, Ed. Policy Committee, April 21, 1965; regular meeting, November 4, 1955 (authorized scholarships for Newfoundland students, especially for work in extension, now picked up by Canadian government); April 21, 1965; September 20, November 21, 1967 (Portland); (football quote from here along with A & S 120 hour rule, and exchange with UNB); January 20, 1968; on graduate credit see Earl Brand to Arthur Benoit, May 18; Benoit to Brand, May 23; Benoit to Young, May 20, Young to Arthur Benoit June 22, 1966.

6. Trustees, March 15, April 19-20, 1960; May 31 (Portland); September 20, 1967; January 20, 1968; Bangor *Daily News,* January 22, 1968; Jim Hightower, *Hard Tomatoes, Hard Times,* Task Force on the Land Grant College Complex, Preliminary Report, 1972.

7. From much personal recollection; interviews C. Stewart Doty; James Tierney; Richard Davies; The documentation is still slight, but the following are useful. "Report to the Board of Trustees by the Faculty Committee on Fraternities," January, 1964, mimeoed; Stephen T. Hughes, "The President's Advisory Committee on Student Life," 1967-1969, dated May 1, 1970, mimeoed; Trustees, November 21, 1967; Faculty Council, October 9, 1967, free speech resolution, press release on speakers, February 12, 1968; Robert S. Cobb to Edwin Young, June 12, 1968, on recommendations for protesters; Portland *Press-Herald,* May 10, 12, 1962 on keeping Communists from speaking (paper was unhappy); Petition of May, 1970 on stoppage of classes (in my possession); Winthrop Libby to Kenneth Allen, et al., June 3, 1970, on a committee to redefine roles and responsibilities for faculty, students and administrators (it never met); *Maine Alumnus,* April-May, 1970, an excellent issue on student opinions and the moratorium; *Spark* (Maine SDS paper) various issues; *Marsh Island Bugle* (History Department newspaper) Fall, 1969, a good history of SDS in Orono, 1965-1969. For a different view of many of these same issues, John J. Nolde, *Arts and Sciences in The Sixties,* Orono, July, 1973.

8. *The Mission and Goals of the University of Maine at Orono and Bangor,* Orono, September 10, 1970.

9. Winthrop C. Libby, "The Year Ahead, 1971-72", Orono, September 17, 1971; *Faculty Breakfast at UMO, September 16, 1971,* address by Chancellor Donald R. McNeil; Remarks by Professor William Jeffrey, September 16, 1971. *Higher Education Planning for Maine,* First Operational Report From the Higher Education Planning Commission, April, 1972, also calls for many of the same goals. A salutary exercise, however, for many, would be to read, Peter H. Fitzgerald, "A Survey of Opinion About Resources, Priorities, and the Decision-Making Process at the University of Maine at Orono," mimeoed, 1973, especially 52-6 where the results of an interview technique across the campus are summarized. The goals appear to be fairly well known, but the methods to achieve them are lacking, or perception of them is lacking, which is as bad.

10. *The Maine Alumnus,* Winter, 1974; Howard Neville, *A New Beginning,* Orono, 1974.

A Note on the Sources

It seems unnecessary to provide a formal bibliography. For those who wish to follow my footsteps, most of the materials are located in the Special Collections Room, Fogler Library. When I used them, however, most of them were in a different location and not in any filing order. Now they are easily accessible and freely available. I used the Board of Trustees Minutes from 1865 to 1970, and after 1904 or so, most of the working papers of the trustees were also available. Those prior to that time had been destroyed. Presidential correspondence varies somewhat. For Fernald and Allen it is nearly nonexistent, except for some thirty or forty letters to Trustee Lyndon Oak. One suspects the amount at the beginning must have been tiny, as the school was small. For President Harris, there is more material available, although it was once bowdlerized by Dean Hart. After Harris the amount of correspondence is quite extensive, and I have used the correspondence of the president's office through 1968. Much of it is repetitive and deals with the minutiae of enrollment, graduation, and condolence as well as congratulation. However, I have turned over all sheets of paper in a conscientious way.

Presidential office files are of more use. Some of them go back to the 1890 period, and I have seen everything except the current files of the presidential office. In addition early correspondence with regard to buildings, the college farm, grade reports in the nineteenth century, alumni files, and so on were also used. Faculty minutes exist from 1873 on, first in the form of the general faculty meeting, later in college meetings, and finally in the Faculty Council. I have read all these and found them most useful. In addition the files of such committees as the Discipline Committee, Dean's Executive Committee (from 1921 on), and many other regular and ad hoc committees were also read.

Student newspapers and periodicals cover the history from their point of view monthly from 1874 to 1878, in a yearly form until 1884, and thereafter, first monthly, then weekly, and more recently biweekly. In addition the college annual, the *Prism,* was read. I have also used the files of the Student Senate and a large number of student and faculty organizations. Three student diaries, J.W. Weeks in the 1870's, Clinton Cole's in the 1890's, and Alice Stewart's in the 1930's, were used. Student letters of Merton Lovett from 1904 to 1908 were of much help. I sampled extensively the 34 boxes (then) of the Cooperative Extension Service. Altogether the amounts of material must range to well over 100 boxes of manuscript materials.

In addition there were a number of student letters, memorabilia, and other materials in the class files in Special Collections. More of these came to me personally from those whose grandparents or parents had been students, and I have deposited them in the Fogler Library indifferently with other materials. I have yet to see a piece of the University of Maine china from the 1890's, but most other memorabilia have been examined. I also used Dean Hart's rather good files from 1913 to 1923, most of which dealt with students, although some were of use in other ways. Good photographic records were useful and especially a number of glass-plate negatives from the early era.

I have turned over every piece of paper published by the University since the beginning, so far as I can tell. The materials published by extension, and by the experiment station are remarkable in their catholicity and their high quality. In addition I have read all the publications that appear in this series, many of which are of excellent quality and usefulness. I have also looked at every law passed by the legislature that had anything to do with the university, and all the legislative documents, including those that were not enacted. I have used newspapers where they were particularly relevant; some idea of how much will be obtained from the notes. Individual faculty and staff members were more than kind with their willingness to respond to query or simply to reminisce. Attempts at formal oral interview were less useful, primarily because some of the potential sources either refused comment or feigned ignorance. Fortunately the record is clear, and usually very good.

This history is an attempt to look at a fairly small body of people (before 1895 very small) from a number of points of view; first from the point of view of the trustees, then the faculty and deans, as well as the president, and finally from the vantage point of the student body. Less was done with the staff and work force, in great part because materials were generally unavailable. One can only hope that the University of Maine, and its predecessor, the Maine State College of Agriculture and Mechanic Arts, appear through the text so that readers can recognize it, or at least, their view of it.

Seals of the College and University

| 1868 | 1876 | 1879 | 1885 |

| 1893 | 1897 | 1906 | 1912 |

| 1916 | 1926 | 1958 | 1972 |

Index